British Essays
in American History

*

Edited by

H. C. ALLEN and C. P. HILL

NEW YORK
ST MARTIN'S PRESS INC.
1957

Published on the occasion of the 350th anniversary
of the foundation of Jamestown, Virginia,
the first permanent British settlement in America

PRINTED IN GREAT BRITAIN BY
ROBERT CUNNINGHAM AND SONS LTD.
LONGBANK WORKS, ALVA, SCOTLAND

PREFACE

*

THE original purpose of this book was simple. We thought that a collection of essays on some of the stimulating and significant themes of American history would be of interest and value to British readers. But when we reflected further it seemed to us that such a volume might also find a place on the other side of the Atlantic. Now that it is written we believe that it may fulfil both these purposes.

It is not intended to be in any sense a comprehensive history of the United States; there are many of these. Rather does it embody our belief that the study of American history in Britain has reached a stage at which seventeen British scholars may have a number of things to say which will be interesting, not only to students and general readers but even to professional historians. The essays are not learned articles, nor are they necessarily based upon new documentary work; yet each of them falls within a primary field of interest of its contributor, and many do contain original research. We were not able, nor did we wish, arbitrarily to choose a list of topics, and then to impose them on a team of contributors. Instead we have tried to select subjects upon which our historians were best able to write. We think that these essays will prove of real value to students of American history everywhere; and we hope that they will help to encourage its development in Britain.

The idea of the book was born towards the end of 1955, and it therefore seemed fitting and proper to try and complete it in time for publication during the spring of 1957, on the occasion of the 350th anniversary of the foundation of the first permanent British settlement in America, at Jamestown, Virginia. Through the enthusiastic co-operation of contributors, publishers, and printers this has now proved possible.

H. C. A.
C. P. H.

Bristol, October 1956.

v

CONTENTS

*

vii

*The Front Endcover Map illustrates the main physical features of the United
States and the States of the Union.*

*The Back Endcover Map illustrates the territorial growth of the continental
United States.*

ACKNOWLEDGEMENTS

*

O N behalf of all contributors we wish to acknowledge our debt to, and most warmly to thank, all the many historians of the United States whose works make any such volume as this possible. We are especially grateful to those authorities who are quoted in the essays.

In particular we wish to acknowledge with thanks permission to publish the following: the lines of Langston Hughes in "Reconstruction and the Colour Problem" from *Phylon: the Atlanta University Review of Race and Culture*, and the lines of Stephen Vincent Benét in "F. J. Turner and the Frontier in American History" from *Western Star* and *John Brown's Body*, published in Great Britain by the Oxford University Press.

THE MAKING OF THE CONSTITUTION

By J. R. Pole

*

URING the month of May, 1787, the delegates appointed to represent their states at the Philadelphia Convention began, intermittently, and with an unpunctuality that seemed to betoken a certain scepticism, to arrive and assemble in that city. Many of them had a long way to come. It took some four days to reach Philadelphia by road from Boston; travellers over these rutted and unpaved routes, especially further south, had to await ferries across the numerous tidal rivers; indeed, the best way to make long journeys from state to state was by coastal vessel. The states from which the delegates came were known collectively as the United States, but they formed together a confederation, not a union, and in abbreviation they were known, not as the "U.S." but as the "U. states", the states retaining an emphatic individuality. Between the peoples of the different regions there were differences of society, of religion, of ways of making a living. James Madison himself remarked that of the affairs of Georgia he knew as little as of those of Kamskatska.

Yet these Americans had much in common, more, indeed, than some of them realized. They had in the first place a fund of recent political experience; and related closely to and in large measure derived from that experience, they shared among themselves a stock of political ideas that were often reflected even in the arguments of opposing sides. The Revolutionary War itself had inevitably done much to knit the inhabitants of these several regions into a people with a sense of common nationality; and behind the war lay an experience of colonial government that most of the delegates could remember, and that all knew indirectly from the fact that the new, independent state governments in general were made to resemble the old colonial models.

The characteristic colonial government had at its head a governor appointed by the Crown. The governor was advised by a council, consisting of wealthy men of great social influence, whom he usually nominated himself. But he was also confronted by an assembly that controlled the process of raising all monies by taxation—including the governor's salary. Thus the lower house, in arguments with the governor, held a tactical position analogous to that of the English parliament of the seventeenth century. The governor, by the same token, was a kind of little

1

king, responsible to the authorities in England, but held in check by the representative colonial assembly. These miniature parliaments were very much aware of their ancestry, and made a point of claiming privileges similar to those of the Commons. They were elected on a broad suffrage basis. Though broader in the northern than in the southern regions, it may roughly be called a freehold suffrage, in what was, of course, an overwhelmingly agricultural community. In many places the independent artisan owning his own workshop or smithy would also be able to vote for assemblymen, though he would be unlikely to qualify for election himself. It was a system in which a selective leadership was answerable to a fairly popular electorate. Within this framework, each colony was very largely self-governing. This long schooling in the practice of self-government was reflected in almost every turn of the deliberations at Philadelphia, and made it possible for the delegates to complete a new constitution that owed much in its conception and design to familiar models. They built their new mansion with old and seasoned timber.

In Britain, the Whig conventions of political thought had become a habit that somewhat resembled the Christianity of the Church of England, established but not applied. The Americans on the other hand had tested their inheritance in the fires of revolution, and the patriots were proud to call themselves Whigs. The idea that governments derived their just powers from the consent of the governed was an article of faith. It was supplemented by a strong and almost universal belief in the sanctity of private property, the protection of which was the principal purpose of the rule of law; and if the protection of one's own property was a slightly higher purpose that the protection of other people's, then in this the Americans merely demonstrated that they differed less from the rest of mankind than some of them supposed. Colonial experience had taught them the efficacy of a kind of federal system, in which the acts of individual provinces, though largely self-governing at home, were subject to the veto of a superior authority. This procedure afforded a precedent for the power given by the new constitution to the federal Supreme Court to nullify unconstitutional laws passed by state legislatures.

One of the most pervasive, though most vaguely understood, theories of government was that of the imperative need for some sort of separation of powers. At least three different conceptions seem to have been gathered under this head. One of these was an idea, not altogether consonant with the egalitarian doctrines of the Declaration of Independence, that government represented different estates—in parliament, for example, the Lords and Commons each had their own house, and the Church was specifically represented in the Lords. The separation of powers, seen in this light, was one of the principles governing the system of representation. But under another head it stood for the principle that placemen ought to be kept out of the legislature to avoid corrupting that body with the influence of the executive. This doctrine, drawn from English theory though

decidedly not from English practice, and also from recent colonial experience, played an important part in the debates over the method of
appointing a president. The separation of powers assumed its third, and
most characteristically American, form as a result of the development of
constitutional ideas between the forming of the early state constitutions
and the federal constitution of 1787. It was in this form that the constitution itself was made, each of the three major branches of government
being separately established and defined. Tyranny was believed to consist in the control of all organs of government by the same power; and
the great safeguard of liberty lay in keeping the executive, legislative
and judicial arms separate and distinct. The fundamental importance of
an independent judiciary was, of course, a cardinal lesson of English
constitutional history. The executive office gave especial difficulty because, in a republic, it could not be held by hereditary right; consequently
a mode of appointment had to be found that would not at once render the
office utterly dependent on either the federal legislature or the states.
The early state constitutions, forged in emergency after the deposition
of the legitimate government, were stamped with the simpler principle
of legislative supremacy. The most influential development in constitutional thinking in the first few years of American self-government was
the supplanting of the earlier, simple and practicable system of legislative
supremacy by the more highly articulated and impracticable system in
which all three branches of government, though necessarily in continuous
interaction, were theoretically distinct and autonomous, each the final
authority in its own field.

To all this fund of common experience and ideas was added that simple
factor of such permanent importance, a common language.

When the Americans declared themselves independent, they made
themselves the heirs to a problem that had hitherto been exclusively
British: the responsibility for governing the American continent as a
whole. Governing it as a whole meant seeing it as a whole; the British
had been incapacitated by their inability to sympathize with native colonial
growth, but at least they had been free of colonial provinciality. When
the mainland colonies sent delegates to act for them in a General Congress
in Philadelphia in 1774, there was a short-lived possibility that the new
Congress might become the devolutionary heir to the whole British
sovereignty; but the prospect was soon disappointed by a patriotism that
was rooted in the states and that claimed for each state government,
within its own boundaries, the whole of the authority seized from Great
Britain. It was in the interest of every single state to belong to a confederation that could direct continental affairs and exert more power,
both at home and abroad, than any one state government could hope to
do; but the people who were, on the whole, well satisfied with the place
they had in the governments of their own districts, together with many
of the local politicians who lived by the system, were extremely unwilling

to confide greater powers to a more distant government. If one idea more than another had been instilled into the American peoples by the experiences of recent years, it was the dread of tyranny; and this dread came alive again at the prospect of any government ruling over all the states and greater than any combination of them—a government, in fact, that would inherit the powers of Britain. This fear, associated with various regional and social interests that seemed to be threatened, was the chief obstacle to the adoption of the new federal constitution after the work of the Philadelphia Convention had been done.

The General Congress established in 1774, and representing the several states, exercised the powers of government without any specific authority other than that conferred by the agreement of the states to participate in it, until the Articles of Confederation were finally signed in 1781. The Articles, the first written constitution of the United States, gave the government less domestic authority and less external vigour than that under which any other western nation had grown to be a great power. The Congress was a single chamber in which each state had one vote. A divided or absent delegation failed to register the vote of its state; but abstention frequently had the effect of a negative, because all decisions of any importance required the concurrence of seven states; and decisions as to war and peace, treaties, requisitions of money from the states, the emission of coinage or currency or the raising of loans, required the concurrence of nine states. Alterations to the Articles must have unanimous consent. There was no delegated executive authority other than that of the annually appointed President of Congress; but the Congress developed its own system of committees and eventually established a small number of secretaryships.

The Congress had no power to lay taxes on individuals; the only authority to which the citizens were subject was that of their state governments. To raise money, the Congress had to rely on a system of requisition; the states were required to contribute amounts based on property valuations. These requisitions had the force of law, but the power of Congress reached no further than the issue of its command; it lacked all machinery of enforcement. There was no means of coercing a state. The state governments, showing no inclination to take risks with the strong popular dislike of taxation among their electorates, fell deeply into arrears to Congress, which was enfeebled by lack of money. This was not a problem that could be solved by a mere tightening up of administration. The Confederation was imperilled by a fatal defect in its constitution. Two attempts to remedy these weaknesses by giving the Congress greater power to raise money for itself, the Impost Plan of 1781 and the Finance Plan of 1783, failed for want of unanimous consent.

In face of these deficiencies, the problems of war finance were overcome by different methods. Loans were raised at home and abroad; certificates were rendered by army commissaries in exchange for requisitioned supplies; and, further, the Congress issued its own paper currency. These continental dollars became both the subject and the instrument of a furious money inflation. Thirty-seven emissions were made between 1775 and 1780; the expression "Not worth a continental" became a byword for worthlessness that was current until recent times. Most of the state governments also experimented with paper issues, which circulated freely while suffering various rates of depreciation, so that the country was steeped in the thick falls of numerous currencies that swirled and drifted like autumn leaves.

Paper currency had already long enjoyed the distinction of being an anathema of orthodox finance. In America, the permanent shortage of specie caused it to be viewed by conservatives with more indulgence than would have ordinarily been the case, but the war-time inflation enormously strengthened the power of orthodox opinion. The creation of the new constitution cannot be properly understood without realizing the violence of the shock given to the minds of creditors throughout the country by this experience. In 1780, the Congress called in its old currency, which it replaced at an exchange of forty to one with a new issue redeemable in specie in six years.

The problem of governing the Confederation was made no easier by the fact that much of the power that the Congress lacked was exercised by the state governments. The Congress had no power even to regulate commerce between the states, which, where they could, made profit out of fortuitous geographical advantages. The people of the corridor state of New Jersey were forced to pay duties levied by the ports of New York and Philadelphia. There were quarrels about state boundaries. The end of the war, reducing the incentive to co-operative action, threatened the Confederation with still greater discord.

The war, however, had done more than anything else to foster a new sense of American nationality. There were many soldiers, from Washington downwards, who had learned that their country could never survive as a mere congeries of disjointed provinces. Moreover there were cogent material reasons why both officers and common soldiers wanted a more efficient central government. They were themselves the creditors of Congress. Army pay was deeply and disgracefully in arrears. The men at length were driven to mutiny and Washington himself had to intervene to quiet the officers. There were also many civilian creditors of the government, most of whom were speculative purchasers of the certificates rendered by army quartermasters and of different government bonds. Some of these creditors were of a more, some of a less deserving character, but they all felt a burning interest in the establishment of a government with the authority, the stability and the resources to meet its obligations. Many of the state governments had committed themselves too; and although some of them took steps to discharge their own debts, there existed a substantial body of creditors anxious to see the establishment of a federal government with power to assume the debts of the states, as well as to meet its own. The leadership in the drive for a new constitution was provided in large part by the representatives of those whose hopes for the protection of their rights, or the realization of their prospects, depended on a government that would be firm and solvent. But this leadership was strengthened, perhaps decisively strengthened, by the addition of men such as Washington, Madison and Hamilton, whose services in the war had enabled them to see their country as a whole, and who were freed from the limitations of a provincial outlook.

If the emergencies of war tend to unite people, economic emergency divides them. The Congress, having ceased to issue its own currency, was reduced to dependence upon orders that it had no power to enforce; it had neither resources nor authority to meet the post-war economic crisis. This crisis was largely the result of an adverse balance of payments the effects of which became manifest soon after the war ended and the American market was reopened to British manufactured imports. The shortage of currency reduced six state governments to the old expedient of paper money. In Rhode Island and North Carolina these were the policies of the debtor classes; but in other states, notably Pennsylvania and South Carolina, paper money had the backing of powerful propertied interests whose need, for local but urgent reasons, was as great as that of the mortgage-ridden farmers and indebted artisans. The South Carolina currency proved an outstanding success. But generally speaking the conventional political leadership, especially in states such as Virginia which avoided a new currency issue, regarded these developments with horror. The use of the printing press to solve problems of finance was held to be nothing less than authorized plunder of private property. This judgment, sweepingly applied, even by prudent and experienced men, revealed a certain degree of hysteria, a failure to consider each case on its merits. But it was a feeling that made a decisive contribution to the demand for a new constitutional convention, and it was the direct product of the recent experience of inflation.

Alarm over the debtor policies of state legislatures was redoubled by the threat of rebellion in western Massachusetts. The rigidly orthodox financial policies adopted in that state had made the post-war crisis all the worse; and in the summer and autumn of 1786, the despairing farmers, facing imprisonment for debt, joined in a movement to close the courts that were serving writs of execution. The rising, led by a Revolutionary War captain called Shays, was easily put down, but it sent a convulsive shock through the property-minded people of America. The reaction was out of all proportion to the gravity of the crisis or any threat that it portended; but when armed rebellion in Massachusetts followed on reckless currency laws in Rhode Island and elsewhere, the leaders of the new movement took it as the final signal for action to strengthen the defences of property.

By this time, the movement for a new convention was under way. The delegations of five states, meeting in Annapolis in September, 1786, issued a declaration of the need for a convention to remedy the defects of the Confederation. The Congress agreed, and referred to the state legislatures the responsibility for appointing delegations to assemble in Philadelphia the following May. There were thus two broad strands of interest that interfused to bring the Convention into being and to inspire its debates. The one was essentially constitutional: in order to confront the world, to promote American interests, indeed merely to survive, the government of the Confederation needed much greater power. The other was economic. To meet the demands of large numbers of public creditors, to offer security to property both present and prospective, the Confederation must have sufficient strength to pay its debts and to go on paying them, and to protect and promote territorial expansion. Many of the delegates, indeed, were themselves holders of certificates of public debt; they had, therefore, some personal interest in a government that would accept its financial obligations. But this does not mean that the institutional form of the new government was in any direct sense a result of the special interests of the founders; for, as the debates were to show, men of similar economic interests were to differ profoundly about the form of the new constitution and the powers of the new government.

The earliest delegates to reach Philadelphia were those from Virginia, and they used their spare time to draw up a plan for a new constitution. This plan, for want of any other, became the agenda for debate when the sessions opened. In such ways are matters of procedure inseparable from matters of substance. The Virginia Plan was revolutionary, and to many delegates, entirely unacceptable; but for the fortnight in which it held the floor, its proposals were assumed as the basis for the new government, and by the time a new plan was put forward to challenge it, those assumptions had come to seem more practicable, less controversial, than at first.

The Convention at once agreed to deliberate in secrecy. If this precaution had not been taken, and the various plans had been subjected to concurrent debate outside, while members feared for their political reputations, it is doubtful whether any satisfactory constitution would have been framed.

The Virginia Plan, presented by the Governor of that state, Edmund Randolph, proposed to establish two houses in the new legislature, the first to be elected by the voters, and the second by the members of the first. The suffrage for the lower house would be apportioned among the states on the basis of population of free inhabitants; thus Massachusetts and Virginia, for example, would vote heavily compared with New Hampshire or North Carolina—but it was not conceived that they would be voting as states, merely that their inhabitants would vote as individual electors, for representatives proportional to their numbers. The national legislature would have power to veto state laws that contravened the rights of the Union; and would have power to call out the forces of

B

the Union against any state that failed to comply with its obligations.

The Plan envisaged two other distinct branches of government, in accordance with the now well developed theory of the separation of powers. The executive branch would be aided, however, by a council of revision drawn from the judiciary; by this council the acts of the legislature must be sanctioned before becoming law. The judiciary would now be established as a distinct branch of national government for the first time. There was provision for the admission of new states to the Union, and for the amendment of the constitution.

The Virginia Plan immediately raised a problem of conscience. The delegates were empowered, by the Congress, to suggest amendments to the Articles of Confederation: they were not empowered to abolish those Articles and proceed to an entirely new form of government. But that was precisely what the Virginia Plan proposed to do. On the whole it was with remarkably little hesitation that the members agreed that they had a right to propose whatever seemed to be demanded by the needs of public safety. Opponents of the Plan did indeed object, repeatedly, that it went beyond their instructions; but its defenders replied that they were not forbidden to suggest whatever they thought fit, for their work could be no more than a recommendation until ratified by the people; and if so ratified, it would assume the status of fundamental law.

What the Virginia Plan proposed to do, basically, was to make the United States of America into a nation. The word "nation" had never been used of them before, but the nationalizing principle was insidiously contained in the first clause, for setting up a legislature of two houses. The Americans were used to thinking of bi-cameral legislatures as a feature of independent governments, as in the states (except Georgia and Pennsylvania) and Great Britain. The existing single chamber Congress in its form alone was a sign of the sovereignty of the states, being a place for the meeting of appointed delegations. The new concept was quickly seen and challenged by Charles Pinckney of South Carolina, who asked Randolph to say whether he intended to abolish the states altogether. But this was going too far. Neither the Virginia delegation nor anyone else, with one or two individual exceptions, believed that the states had completely outlived their usefulness. However, it was certainly true that the nationalist group thought that the major characteristics of sovereignty should all be transferred to the new federal government, leaving to the states only the inessential residue: the states were indeed to be little more than convenient organs of regional government. On the third day of debate, Randolph was again challenged on this point, and denied the intention of giving indefinite power to the national legislature; but Madison made the interesting remark that, although he had brought with him into the Convention a strong bias in favour of enumerating and defining the powers of the national legislature, he now had serious doubts. He would shrink from nothing that was found essential to such a form of government as would provide for the liberty, safety and happiness of the community.

It was true that, under the Virginia Plan, the states would no longer be represented as political bodies. They would still act on their citizens in a number of local affairs, but they would have no way of speaking to the general government. The proposal for distributing the suffrage on the basis of free population, that is, for proportional representation, therefore met with fierce resistance. The struggle over representation involved two principal questions: first, whether the states would survive as political sovereignties or become mere wards of local government; and secondly, whether the smaller states would be able to keep any independence or influence in a Union which, they feared, would be dominated by the great ones. "The great difficulty," observed Madison after three weeks of debate, "lies in the affair of Representation; if this could be adjusted, all others would be surmountable." Once it had been allowed that states would continue to exist, but that the people of the Union would be represented in the federal government, not as members of inferior groups but simply as individuals, it became difficult to decide exactly what it was that the small states so greatly feared. Evidently they did not attach undue sentimental importance to the existing state boundaries, for David Brearly of New Jersey made the surprising suggestion that all state boundaries might be wiped out and the states re-formed as from the beginning. This, of course, would have resulted in enlargement for the smaller states; but it would also have cut across much of that local patriotism that meant so much to these early spokesmen of states' rights, as well as raising dire complexities in questions of land titles and law. One fear was expressed by Gunning Bedford of Delaware, who argued that the large states would crush the small whenever they stood in the way of their interests or their ambitions, but the only practical example of how this might happen was that the general government might show favour to the ports of Boston, New York and Philadelphia. Of course, there could never be any doubt in a nation as large and as diverse as America that the different regions would require a measure of responsible local government; but the advocates of the small states seemed to feel, beyond this, that the states, as such, represented interests. John Dickinson of Delaware held that the existence of the states was a source of stability. It was certainly true that the relative political importance of the states was a matter of great consequence to many state politicians. But the problem went deeper than this; for the leaders of the smaller states—or most of them—found it more difficult to take the leap into the new concept of nationhood, leaving behind them the familiar security of old institutions, than those of the larger states. The imagination of the latter may, indeed, have been fired by a greater confidence in their own political survival in the new order.

It was not until well into the third week of debate that the nationalists' conception of a two-house legislature was challenged; William Paterson, of New Jersey, later to be governor of his state and a justice of the federal Supreme Court, then came back to first principles and said that the delegations of the different states were a sufficient check on each other in a single-chamber legislature.

By the end of the first fortnight, however—before Paterson spoke— the nationalists had established a major tactical advantage, although they had not consolidated their gains. They had accustomed many delegates, who had not been in the habit of thinking in national terms, to the idea that a more powerful central authority was both feasible and safe. On June 13th, the Virginia Plan, with amendments made in committee, was reported back to the Convention by the committee of the whole house.

At this point, however, the opponents of the national scheme drew back for breath; and when they returned to the floor they presented a thoroughgoing challenge to the whole concept of the Virginia Plan. The counter-offensive was led by Paterson and the plan he offered is usually called the New Jersey Plan. This Plan proposed to keep within the bounds of the Convention's authorization by attempting nothing more than to amend the Articles of Confederation. It did not state, but, more significantly, it simply assumed, that the legislature would continue as a single house: reference was made to "the United States in Congress assembled", an expression that implied the sovereignty of the several states. Congress would be given increased powers to lay import duties, stamp taxes and postal charges, and to regulate commerce. If the revenues raised by these methods proved insufficient, requisitions might be made on the states in proportion to their population. Three-fifths of the slaves would be counted in calculating that population. Delinquent states might be coerced into payment. The Congress would elect a plural executive, and a federal judiciary. The authority of the Congress would be enforced on a delinquent state by calling forth the military power of the Confederation.

After a debate on the two plans, the committee of the whole voted squarely in favour of that of Virginia. This, however, did not end the question. The small states now fought each clause as it came up, their opposition becoming so determined that the whole Convention seemed in great danger of disruption. The only possible compromise seemed to be that of allowing the states to keep their individual representation in one of the houses of the new legislature, but this the nationalists would not concede. At length, over the strenuous opposition of Madison and James Wilson, it was decided to refer the question of representation to a Grand Committee, of one member from each state. The Committee duly proposed the compromise that had already been advanced and rejected, that the states should be represented in the upper chamber. It was this compromise that was to become the basis of the federal structure of the new Union.

It would be a mistake to suppose that the compromise had only to be proposed in order to be accepted. Madison, whose interventions had repeatedly strengthened the nationalist case with cogent, informed (if not always acutely relevant) argument, now fought so bitterly that he went so far as to say that if the large states confederated they would have no reason to fear the opposition of the small states, which would not be able to remain outside. He declared with a force that can hardly have been concealed by the mildness of his manner, that the states would have nothing to fear from a Union in which they would be mere counties of one entire republic. When the subject was renewed on July 14th he again attacked the whole conception of compromise. Rufus King said that the object was to secure the rights of man and that this substantial good must not be sacrificed to the phantom of state sovereignty. On July 16th the crisis occurred. The small states had gained strength in part by individual conversions, which, for example, split the vote of the delegates of Massachusetts evenly and thus silenced the voice of what was naturally a large state. The small states carried their demand for equal representation in the second branch of the legislature. Randolph then stated that the whole of the Virginia Plan was conceived on the assumption of proportional representation in both houses; he and Rufus King moved for an adjournment to allow the large states to consult. Both sides were adamant; it seemed that complete deadlock had been reached.

On the following morning the delegates of the large states met early, but nothing practical resulted, and the time was frittered away. Nevertheless the adjournment was of vital importance, for it gave these men just enough pause to get used to the idea that compromise was possible, and that even if equal representation were conceded in the upper house, much that was worth keeping had already been gained. On the previous afternoon, in the heat of debate, they were in no mood to admit it. Now, though perhaps unconvinced, they ceased to resist. The foundations of the new federal system were laid. It was now finally agreed that each state, no matter what its population, should be entitled to send two members to the Senate. This point having been gained, the small states' men did not insist upon the rule of the old Congress that each state should vote as a unit. The concession was important; it left the senators free to vote entirely as individuals, although state legislatures sometimes claimed the right to instruct them for specific purposes, and in future years they tended to vote in state units only on very distinctively sectional or state issues.

The most serious defect in the original Virginia Plan was the provision for the coercion of recalcitrant states. It was George Mason who first perceived this weakness and pointed out that the general government must act on individuals, not on states. In the New Jersey Plan, however, this failing was made into a principle; Paterson admitted that the authority of the government could never be enforced without military coercion, to which Mason and Madison replied more than once that such action would closely resemble civil war, and might indeed destroy the whole Union. No answer to this grave objection was ever offered, and the weakness remained endemic in the new federal structure. Only from a legal point of view was it overcome even in the final scheme for the new government. The constitution was declared to be "the supreme law of the land". As law, therefore, it would reach individuals throughout the Union, regardless of the intermediate authority of the states; and as law, it would be enforced by the courts. The machinery for enforcement was provided by the establishment of the new federal judiciary. Legally the system was thus complete; but even so it was not infallible in practice, for the courts could not call out their own battalions, and in the last resort the federal Executive, supported by Congress, was the only authority able to command the power to defend the constitution against disruption. Indeed, when in 1860 and 1861 the seceding states of the South threw down their final challenge to the federal government, the courts hardly entered the picture at all; it was primarily the Executive that they then defied, and it was the president who called out the forces of the Union against them. When this happened, the situation was exactly what Mason and Madison had feared—a civil war between the federal government and some of the state governments.

Until a solution of the problem of state representation had been properly worked out, other issues remained in the background. Yet no sooner had this crisis been settled than a new one arose over representation in the lower house. The problem was not now between states, but between the great geographical and economic regions. Both Madison and King had already observed that the "true dividing line" within the Confederation was marked by the boundaries of slavery. Generally speaking slavery had been abolished, or was being abolished, in the northern states, where it was not required for plantation labour. In Virginia the leading men looked to its eventual extinction, though they were not at all sure how this was to be done or how they would manage to share their society with the freed Negroes. But now it became clear that there were Southern interests, notably in South Carolina and Georgia, that were determined to defend slavery and even to uphold the nefarious African slave trade. What they demanded was special protection, through the enumeration of a proportion of their slaves with the white population, to increase the number of representatives to which they would be entitled in the federal Congress. The proposal was bitterly attacked by King and Gouverneur Morris, who asserted that the Northern states would never assent. They had strong reasons. If the white population of the slave states were to be over-represented by including some of their slaves, and if the slave trade were to continue, then the growth of Southern slavery would threaten an ever-increasing over-representation: the institution of slavery, which as decent men they hoped to see the death of, would be not merely entrenched in the constitution of the nation, but strengthened in its politics.

Morris proposed that only free inhabitants be numbered for purposes of representation in the lower house:

The admission of slaves into the Representation (he said) when fairly explained comes to this: that the inhabitant of Georgia or S.C. who goes to the Coast of Africa, and in defiance of the most sacred laws of humanity tears away his fellow creatures from their dearest connections and damns them to the most cruel bondage, shall have more votes in a government instituted for the protection of the rights of mankind, than the Citizen of Pa. or N. Jersey who views with a laudable horror, so nefarious a practice.

To this, Edward Rutledge of South Carolina replied, with more truth than he knew, that religion and humanity had nothing to do with this question. The debate drew harsh words from the deep South, whose delegates openly threatened that they would refuse to enter the Union unless specially protected.

Northern opinions on the question of representation were divided for reasons very distant from the problem of the South. There were important Northern interests, both commercial and landed, that already felt anxiety about the prospective growth of the West. Gouverneur Morris, indeed, not only expressed his dread that the yet unborn western states would one day outnumber the older eastern settlements, with oppressive consequences for eastern property and commercial interests, but went so far as to suggest that the representation of the West should be subjected to permanent restrictions. He was not alone in his feelings, but fortunately he was in a minority. These westerners, as another delegate pointed out, would for the most part be the children and grandchildren of the existing generation of the East: why fear them? It was Morris who offered a solution to one side of the problem of the basis upon which representation in the federal legislature was to be established; what he proposed to do was to place representation on the same footing as direct federal taxation, so that taxes would be assessed by the federal administration upon the inhabitants of each state, in proportion to the population as enumerated for purposes of allocating members of the House of Representatives. This scheme had some solace for the wealthy men of the East because it meant that the West, which as yet was poor for its numbers, would bear a full burden of taxation. It also went far to settle the difficulties raised by the deep South, whose planters would have been entirely satisfied only if their slaves had been enumerated for purposes of representation but entirely kept out of the count when property was being assessed for purposes of taxation. In this point the planters were prepared to make an exception to their otherwise general rule that slaves were merely one form of property like any other. Morris' proposal was too eminently reasonable to be rejected: the South demanded some form of special privilege for its representation, and it could have it on the basis of a corresponding share of taxation: if it were accused of enjoying over-representation it could in future reply that it was proportionally over-taxed. But the argumentative retort with which the South was furnished by this agreement gave her a slightly specious advantage in debate, for the uses of representation were both real and immediate, but the incidence of federal taxation for many years was very light indeed. The actual proportions used in making up the Southern basis of representation were adopted from a provision in the Articles of Confederation; three-fifths of the slaves were added to the rest of the population. As a portion of the whole compromise, the deep South agreed to a provision permitting the Congress to prohibit the importation of slaves after twenty years.

This issue was perhaps never so dangerous as that of state representation, though for a short time it again looked as though the Convention were in crisis. It was, however, profoundly dangerous to the future of the new Union. There are some moral questions in which compromise is practicable because the convictions on either side, though strongly held, prove impermanent, but this was not one of them. The rise of slavery with the spread of cotton culture in the nineteenth century made the South increasingly fretful under the ban on slave imports; it contained the double sting of a moral rebuke and an economic restraint. The North, watching the expansion of the plantation system into the Southwest, recognized the constant increase in the southern basis of representation as a correspondingly increasing menace to the future freedom of the West. The permanent over-representation of the South gave to slavery a lease of life that seemed, to many in the North, to threaten all that was worth preserving in the Union. Northern discontent over this issue, centred in New England, was stirred to new bitterness under the embargo and the War of 1812, which were seen from the viewpoint of New England's own brand of special interests as being Southern policies; the Hartford Convention (1814-15) adopted a list of demands among which it placed the reform of the so-called "federal ratio" at the head. The same issue played a major part in precipitating Northern opposition to the admission of Missouri as a slave state, and thus had a crucial place in the controversy that foreshadowed the convulsion of the Union.

The debates over representation in the lower house—to be called the House of Representatives—and in the Senate, were so intense that they tended to distract attention from another issue; the Virginia Plan had envisaged the Senate as the special guardian, not of the rights of states, but of the rights of property. There was a widely held belief that government in general acted on two elements, persons and property, and that they should therefore be separately represented. The Senate never entirely lost this purpose, although there was no logical connection between its functions as guardian of the special interests of the states as sovereign entities and its functions as guardian of the special interests of property. The latter intention was secured, as far as possible, by providing that the members of the Senate should be appointed by state legislatures rather than by the electorate. The assemblies would work as a filter of the coarser grain of popular opinion. (This system was altered by constitutional amendment by giving the vote for senators to the electorate in 1913, though popular election was introduced earlier into some states by the method of primary elections, the object of which was to select the candidates from whom the legislature was to choose.) The members of the Senate were also removed from the immediate impulse of popular passion by a six-year term of office, one-third of them retiring every two years. In this way the Convention obviated the danger that any one tide of public opinion might overwhelm the whole legislative body at once; these carefully arranged checks were largely the outcome of the experiences of legislative supremacy in recent state history. The problem for the Convention was not that of safeguarding popular sovereignty, but of securing special interests, which were always likely to be in the numerical minority, from the acquisitive rage of the majority. The Senate was joined to the Executive in certain responsibilities: two-thirds of the members present were required to concur in the making of treaties and in making all appointments under the federal government. These were great powers to be exercised by a small number, and some members, notably George Mason, turned against the new frame of government because they felt that it achieved all too effectively the object of placing decisive weight in an oligarchic body.

The requirement of co-operation between Executive and Senate in certain major tasks cut clean across the doctrine of the separation of powers. That doctrine was entertained in its purity by very few members; for several wanted to join the Judiciary with the Executive in revising the laws. The main principle of separation, however, was firmly embodied in the provision for the three separate branches; but there remained the question of how the Executive was to be elected, and this proved to be one of the most exacting of all. If he were elected by the Congress then he would become its creature and lose all independence; if by the state legislatures, as some wanted, then the principle of state sovereignty would be reinforced in a manner intolerable to the nationalists. It was the nationalist leadership that was most favourable to the idea of a popular election, and it is highly significant that this seemingly democratic plan was opposed by Mason, the opponent of aristocracy. The reason lies deep in the political structure and thinking of the times. The democrats believed earnestly that the safety of the people lay in popular control of local institutions. The representatives of the people, as Mason several times explained, ought to return frequently to mingle with their electors. A great, distant, impersonal government seemed in its very nature to be hostile to this ideal. The people were peculiarly unfit to choose a president—Mason compared the suggestion with that of giving the choice of colours to a blind man. They would not know the candidates, and they could be expected to choose wisely only among men they knew. This was really the crux of his position. Elbridge Gerry, later a democratic governor of Massachusetts, feared that the people would be persuaded to elect a candidate proposed by the Cincinnati, the aristocratically inclined organisation of officers of the revolutionary army. Wilson and Madison, who were nationalists, and Gouverneur Morris, a conservative, wanted election by the freeholders. After much debate and irresolution—for to many this question, too, seemed of fundamental importance—Madison's suggestion of an intermediary body of electors was accepted. The electors were to be appointed, either by the state legislatures or by the voters, for the special purpose of meeting in their respective states—never as a body from all the states together—once only, to elect a President. The electoral college was to be yet another filter in the complicated processes of republican election.

The difficulty of the delegates, after they had agreed on a single executive, lay partly in the fact that they wanted the Union to have a head, but were not sure what they wanted the head to do. The example of the headless Confederation gave them no help; they based their thinking on the colonial models and, in spite of themselves, on the British constitution—which several members admitted to be still the best in the world. Strictly, an Executive had merely to ensure that the laws made by the legislature were faithfully executed; but this modest role allowed no room for the initiating of policy. The Executive was also given the power to veto legislation; the veto could be overridden by a two-thirds majority in each house of Congress. The executive branch was expanded to include the secretaries of departments, to be nominated by the President and approved by the Senate. But the Convention never entertained the idea that this executive branch might sit in the Congress and derive its power from the support of a majority of the representatives. Such a policy would mean legislative supremacy, and it is fair to say that, despite their remarkable wisdom, the nationalist leaders, not the least of them Madison, had wrought themselves into a state of extreme horror of legislative excesses. They deemed it essential to have some check on the legislature, and since their president was not himself to be chosen from among the legislators, they entrusted him with the power of veto, which implied a supervisory control of policy. But they also envisaged him as the chief officer of a day-to-day administration, and finally as the Head of the State. They wanted to give their president some of the attributes of a prime minister, but also some of the attributes of a king.

A more definite responsibility for policy was given him by a provision requiring him to make periodic reports to Congress about the state of the Union with recommendations as to necessary and expedient measures of legislation. It is unlikely that the implications of this decision were fully thought out at the time. Not only did it make short work of the theory of the separation of powers, but of course it meant that the President would need a majority of supporters in Congress to carry the measures he proposed. The provisions of the constitution thus contained the implications of a future development of political parties more distinctly and more logically than seems to have been appreciated. If the measures recommended by the President touched upon questions of serious political import, they must be expected to command some support, and also to meet opposition, in the country, so that even on paper the new system postulated some connection between public opinion, the Congressional majority, and executive policy. It was probably expected, so far as the working of the new system was indeed anticipated, that this type of connection would be formed only to achieve some limited object and would then dissolve to make way for the formation of new groups upon new issues. Madison himself anticipated the growth of political factions representing special interests, and the founders in general feared that in times of crisis the more desperate factions might coalesce into a single party: recent experience had taught them to fear inflationary policies and legislative attacks on credit and property. But what they did not anticipate was that the Executive office would itself be controlled by a party, organized upon a national basis, and armed with a legislative programme. They did not expect the Presidency to become the objective in an electoral struggle between major parties claiming the support of people throughout the Union. It is significant that they thought of the system to be controlled by the Chief Executive, not as a government, but as an administration.

A good deal of uncertainty also surrounded the judicial branch of government. The Congress was to be empowered to establish a supreme court and a full judicial system of inferior courts operating in prescribed circuits throughout the Union. The defenders of the states feared this establishment: they believed that it would cut beneath the authority of the state governments; they fought it both in the Convention and later when the first Judiciary Bill was before the Congress in 1789. It was essential, however, that the federal government should have a judicial branch capable of judging cases in which states were parties, and indeed capable of judging the states. The power of veto over state laws that contravened the federal constitution was taken from the national legislature—to whom it had been confided by the Virginia Plan—and in its place, the federal Supreme Court was given jurisdiction in such cases, which meant that the Court could pronounce state laws to be unconstitutional and of no effect if they came before it; this step was altogether consonant with the conception of the constitution as law—as the supreme law of the land; but it also made certain that its interpretation would depend in no small measure on the accidents of litigation.

If the relations between the executive and legislative branches were carefully defined, and a machinery provided for settling their disputes, the same cannot be said for the relations between the Legislature and the Judiciary. To those members who believed that the courts would, in the ordinary course of their duty, pass upon the constitutionality of the laws —as had once or twice happened in the states—the new constitution was pregnant with the doctrine of judicial review of Congressional legislation (in addition to that of state legislation), as later expounded by Chief Justice Marshall. But few members made their thoughts clear on this point; and Madison was greatly troubled by the logical insolubility of the problem. If all three branches of the government were equal, and if each was the final authority within its own sphere, how could one branch negative the acts of another? The answer was left to the men who would have to make the system work.

The need to protect private property from the depredations of the states led to the adoption of certain specific restraints on the freedom of state legislatures. They might pass no law that impaired the obligation of contracts; they might not issue coin or currency; and they might not lay tariffs or raise troops, or enter into treaties either with other states or with foreign powers. The debts of the Confederation would, of course, be assumed by the new government. But the assumption of state debts was a matter left entirely to future policy.

The question of the mode of ratification, though logically last, had agitated the Convention at intervals. The nationalists saw clearly that it must be done, not by the state legislatures, but by special conventions elected by the peoples of the states. This process would give the constitution the status of fundamental law, and would make it greater than the state governments. All the state legislatures except one existed under constitutions that had not been popularly ratified; if, then, the legislatures ratified the new instrument, it would surely be claimed that the constitution was merely the creature of the states, like the old Confederation. Hence the states' men fought again on this issue, but they were outnumbered. The struggle was even carried over into the question of the wording of the preamble, at first sight a matter merely of style. When the constitution was drawn up, it was first intended to begin the preamble with the words "We, the people of New Hampshire, Massachusetts, etc. . . ." But the constitution would immediately become effective upon ratification by nine states, and the committee on style soon realized that, not knowing which states would make up the first nine, it must find a new formula. The amendment agreed on began with the phrase, "We, the people of the United States . . ." This expression was later bitterly attacked by Patrick Henry, who wanted to know by what warrant the Convention spoke for the people when it was appointed by the legislatures of the states. It was a usurpation. And indeed it is difficult to believe that the framers failed to see the future value of the particular form of words they had chosen.

It had been an exhausting summer. Tempers were sometimes short; and there were crises of principle in which the peril to the future of the American republic was by no means fanciful. At the end, when all was done, Benjamin Franklin, the eldest and next to Washington the most revered of the delegates, gathered a few members about him and remarked upon the image of the sun painted on the back of the president's chair. He had noticed that the artists had never been able to distinguish, in their art, between a rising and a setting sun, and during their long deliberations he had often wondered which of these it was that he saw before him. But now he had the happiness to know. It was a rising and not a setting sun. The delegates had dinner together; and then they left the city for their several homes.

But the ordeal of the constitution was not over. It had still to face the ratifying conventions of all the states, and these conventions, elected by the voters, became the scene of the fierce struggle that had only been hinted at in the final opposition of Mason, Randolph and Gerry.

Today the people of the United States are united above all by their constitution; but in 1787 it divided them. It is true that a full referendum, if one could have been taken, would probably have shown a substantial majority for the constitution, because certain states acceded almost without debate. But in the crucial states of Massachusetts, New York and Virginia, and to a lesser extent in Pennsylvania, whose agreement was essential, the opposition was both widespread and powerfully led. In many areas, however, the supporters of the new instrument—the Federalists—included a majority of the more influential members of society, and their influence exerted the little extra pressure that numbers alone might in certain cases have wanted. They defended the constitution on the ground that it went far to meet all shades of opinion; it was, as Madison said, partly national, and partly federal. It was a genuine combination of principles. Nothing less would give the country the firmness and cohesion that it would need for survival.

The opposition ranged widely from serious principle to parochial prejudice. The absence of a religious qualification for the President was denounced by ardent Protestants as making way for the election of a Catholic, and even, according to one pamphleteer, of the Pope. It was feared that the President would become a king and that the whole system would become overpoweringly aristocratic. The most serious-minded element in the opposition maintained that the new government would serve the interests of the rich and powerful, and that it would take all the essential powers of self-government out of the hands of the common people. A delegate to the Massachusetts ratifying convention argued that "These lawyers, and men of learning, and moneyed men, that talk so finely, and gloss over matters so smoothly", expected to be managers of the constitution, to "get all the power and all the money into their own hands". The Anti-federalists feared that the machinery needed to

control the new political process would be of a sort that could be organized only by the men of great connections throughout the land; they
deeply believed that democracy could be kept pure only in small communities. They did not want to entrust the great new government with
their many local or regional interests. Indeed, this feeling was not
confined to small districts: Patrick Henry made a powerful impression
on the Virginia convention by charging the Confederation Congress with
flagrant disregard for the interests of the whole South-west in its dealings
with Spain.

Many Anti-federalists felt that after fighting the Revolution to free
themselves of an imperial tyranny, they were now handing over their
destinies to a new tyranny, domestic, but continental in scale, utterly
beyond their control, and no less dangerous in its tendencies. In some
of the state conventions they fought for the adoption of amendments, to
be considered by yet another constitutional convention. But the Federalists realized that such a proceeding would throw all their work open to
question once more and would imperil the entire constitution. They
therefore resisted these tactics as strenuously as they defended the constitution itself. In New York, where the Anti-federalists were strong,
the convention was at length persuaded to ratify "in the confident
expectation" that amendments would be adopted under the method of
revision provided in the constitution. This process was in fact initiated
in the first meeting of the new Federal Congress, and the resulting list
of ten amendments, which affirmed the principles that many Americans
felt to have been at stake in the Revolution, became known as the "Bill
of Rights". No small part of the colonial fear for liberty had been aroused
by the threat of an Anglican establishment in the colonies; most of the
state governments, once free to do so, proceeded apace with measures
of disestablishment. That the issue was still alive can be seen from the
very first amendment, which forbade the Congress to make any law
respecting an establishment of religion. The sects might compete freely,
but none was to enjoy political privilege bestowed by the Federal
Government. (The states could do as they chose.) Freedom of the
press, and of assembly and of petition for redress of grievances were also
protected from Congressional encroachment. Persons involved in
criminal cases were not to be compelled to be witnesses against themselves—the fifth amendment that has lately undergone an ordeal by fire.
No one was to be deprived of life, liberty or property without due
process of law. General warrants were forbidden: warrants for searches
and seizures must be based upon probable cause. In brief, the instruments of former British tyranny were outlawed by the constitution; but
the power of the Federal Government was now the cause of fear and the
tenth amendment therefore ordained that all power not delegated to the
United States was reserved to the states, or the people. This declaration
might be considered logically redundant; yet in practice it proved im-

potent to check the assumption of ever larger powers by both executive and legislative agencies of the Federal government by means of subtle but necessary interpretations of the clauses of the constitution. The Bill of Rights was looked on by most of the framers of the original constitution as unnecessary and perhaps as tending to weaken a government already perilously weak. But for the great body of people it was an indispensable declaration of principle—of principle that must become law. These amendments were meant to keep the Federal government in its place, to protect the liberty of the individual and the integrity of the states.

The Bill of Rights was the testament of the Anti-federalists who, if they had had their way in the first place, would have approved a strengthening of the old Confederation, on the lines, no doubt, of the New Jersey Plan; but they were precisely the ones who would have been the first to fly to the defence of any state threatened, even under that Plan, with military coercion by the central government. They were not able to make the imaginative leap from the preoccupations of village politics to an appreciation of the pressing demands upon a great republic among world powers. They would have been happier if history had left them alone.

The new framework of government was adopted, by narrow majorities, after weeks of intense struggle. But it had the good fortune to be launched upon a rising tide of economic recovery. Indeed, the return of prosperity, setting in under the aegis of the old Confederation, would almost certainly have soon diminished the sense of urgency that helped to bring the Convention into being in May, 1787.

The American Constitution is not the only instrument that might have been devised in that period. The New Jersey Plan was certainly no less representative of public opinion. But the New Jersey Plan would not have given the United States a government strong enough to weather the difficulties of international politics after the outbreak of the French revolutionary wars. With state sovereignty constantly holding in check the formulation of a coherent national foreign, or even domestic, policy, no Congress would have been able to hold the sections together.

What the Federalists did was to make a government capable of maintaining American independence through the perils of the immediate future and, in the long run, of making the United States into a great power. They could not know exactly what form the new trials would take, but they could and did realize that the Confederation would not be able to stand up to a long period of strenuous diplomacy, and indeed had hardly enough strength to carry its domestic burden. If they had waited a few years longer, sectional animosity, deepened by conflicting attitudes to the European wars, would have made agreement impossible. The Anti-federalists, meanwhile, reconciling themselves to their defeat, got ready, successfully, to take over the great machinery of government whose creation they had regarded with so much dread.

DIVIDED SOVEREIGNTY

By H. Hale Bellot

★

AN American constitutional historian, speaking to a British audience in 1918, described as the distinctive feature of federalism "that system of political order in which powers of government are separated and distinguished and in which these powers are distributed among governments, each government having its quota of authority and each its distinct sphere of activity". By that McLaughlin referred to something different from what is ordinarily spoken of as the "separation of powers", the distribution of power within a single jurisdiction between executive, legislature, and judiciary. What he had in mind was "an imperial system in which the outlying portions had their own indefeasible share, legal share, of political authority", a system in which "each governmental authority was competent and supreme within its own sphere and had the legal power to enforce its lawful acts on its own citizens". And if, he argued, you eschew abstract logic, and look instead at the facts of eighteenth-century society, you will see that such was then the state of affairs in the British empire.

The inhabitants of the mainland colonies commonly were, and some of them consciously recognized themselves as being, members of two communities. Samuel Johnson, first president of King's College, New York, a Connecticut clergyman, Connecticut born and bred, was quite clearly a colonial. Yet he could think of himself also as an Englishman, and speak of England as "home". His sentiment, moreover, made good law. There was a citizenship of the colony that was distinct from citizenship of the empire, and both could be enjoyed by the same person at the same time. Naturalized foreigners admitted to become citizens of a colony remained aliens in the rest of the king's dominions, including the other American provinces. As such they could not be masters of vessels in the colonial trade. They needed the exercise of the sovereign authority of the crown in parliament to make them citizens of the empire. In certain aspects each person was thus a member of his own local community and as such gave his allegiance to his own colonial government. In other respects he was at the same time a citizen of the empire, and ready to obey imperial fiats in imperial matters. He was even in some respects represented in two legislatures, in two law-making bodies. As a colonist he had his own colonial assembly. As a trader within the imperial system

22

he had his spokesmen in parliament. There were traders in that body who knew what effect any enactment would have upon the mercantile interest and who were competent to give the assent of their estate, being persons who would, among others, feel the consequences. Neither government was omnicompetent—neither the crown in parliament nor the crown in the colonial assembly. To say as Hutchinson did "it is impossible there should be two independent legislatures in one and the same state", was to beg the question. Whatever the measure of progress made within the United Kingdom towards that "unity of jurisdiction and monopoly of power, which, whether vested in a single person, in a popular assembly, or in that composite entity 'the crown in parliament' ", Pollard regarded as "the essence of our ideas of sovereignty and of the modern state", there yet remained beyond its borders numerous communities still conscious of their separate identity and not yet ready to be sunk in the estate of the crown. It was indeed precisely because of the tendency towards an assertion of a unity of jurisdiction when the several estates had not yet lost themselves in what was pre-eminently *the* state, that the revolt occurred.

In these circumstances it was not difficult for the Americans, when they threw off allegiance to the crown and set up in each colony an independent state, to vest in a confederation of their own making a quota of authority in a distinct sphere of activity. In so doing they were not accepting anything that was unfamiliar. They were but putting into effect the doctrine, to each sphere its own authority, which they had sought to maintain in face of the innovations of Westminster. "The Articles of Confederation", McLaughlin argued, "were drawn on the principle of distribution of powers", and while, he added, "it may properly be said that the Articles did not provide for the creation of an imperial state", yet on the whole they provided for "government with distinct spheres of action"; and there is much force in his argument.

Yet, for all this, revolution and war had caused a hardening of the doctrine of sovereignty and a decline in the conception of "an empire that was composite and not simple or centralized"; and this was accompanied by a parallel tendency to neglect the separation of powers within each jurisdiction and to concentrate all authority in a single-chamber legislature. The Confederation under the Articles was charged with the conduct of external relations, and it assumed to itself the execution of tasks for which authority could with difficulty be found in the Articles themselves; and it has been argued that in so doing it exercised a sovereign power. It was entrusted with the sole right of determining on peace or war, and of regulating and using the land and naval forces of the United States, of sending and receiving ambassadors, entering into treaties and alliances, establishing rules for deciding what captures should be legal, granting letters of marque and reprisal in times of peace, and appointing courts for the trial of piracies. It was made the last resort on

c

appeal in boundary disputes between the states and in controversies concerning private right of soil claimed under differing grants from two or more states. It had the sole right to regulate the value of coin, fix the standard of weights and measures, regulate trade, manage all affairs with the Indians, and establish and regulate post offices. Yet it was but a "League of friendship . . . for . . . common defence". It operated only upon states and those, moreover, states that were very jealous of their newly won autonomy. It departed very materially from the imperial pattern.

Each state retained its sovereignty, freedom, and independence. When the Virginia delegates to the Continental Congress wrote to the governor of Virginia in October, 1781, saying that they could not "but view with a suspicious eye the conduct, hitherto observed by Congress towards our country on the subject of western territory", by "our country" they meant Virginia; and William Houston meant the same thing when he wrote to the governor of Georgia from New York in 1785 of his having agreed from "a disinterested Zeal . . . of serving my country . . . to come to a strange land amongst Strangers, under a full confidence that my country whilst I was making every sacrifice in my power to serve her, would not abandon me . . ." When the agent of a land company proposed the submission of a dispute between his company and the state of Virginia "to the arbitration and final Decision of Gentlemen of the first Capacity, Integrity and Experience upon the Continent, to be Chosen by the Hon'ble the Congress", the delegates from Virginia replied, "The Delegates from Virginia Inform Mr Morgan . . . That as the State they represent have finally decided on the Subject to which his proposition relates, it would be manifestly improper for them to attend to it—they think it their Duty to add that if they were less precluded they could not reconcile with the respect due from every State to its own Sovereignty and honor, an appeal from its own decisions, to a foreign tribunal, in a case which involves the Pretensions of Individuals only, and not the Rights or pretensions of any foreign State": and what are here referred to as "foreign" are other states of the Confederation and other Americans who are not citizens of Virginia. Such an attitude, moreover, had the sanction of law. A citizen was a citizen of one of the states. To his state he owed his status and his undivided allegiance. If he went abroad, it was from his state that he received his passport. He was not, as an individual, a member of the Confederation. Madison thought it prudent in 1781 to advise Jefferson, then governor of Virginia, that "they [the state] ought in all their provisions for their future security, importance, and interest to presume that the present Union will but little survive the present war". In 1783, Jonathan Arnold of Rhode Island unhesitatingly put his duty to his state before his duty to the Confederation.

In the mean time, sundry Letters received from Europe, which it was declared necessary should be kept secret, and many transactions, respecting the deputation, wore an aspect which I could not reconcile to my own feelings. Secrecy was enjoined upon Members of Congress, in Matters public in the City, and daily publishing in the Newspapers, until I was obliged to declare, upon the floor, that in matters where the necessity therefor could not be pointed out, and which I deemed Interesting to the State I had the honor to represent to be informed of, I should not hold myself bound by a majority, from making the necessary Communications thereof to my constituents.

This fragmentation, this establishment of thirteen separate sovereignties, this concentration of political authority in the several states and localisation of patriotism, led to obstruction of the operations of Congress and to unfriendly acts by one towards another of the confederates. States having ports for foreign commerce exploited their advantage by taxing their neighbours; in its internal administration one state invaded the contractual rights of citizens of another; and when states themselves were creditor and debtor to one another they varied their mutual obligations by unilateral fiat. There was a want of uniformity in their laws of naturalization and bankruptcy; and since the free inhabitants of each of them were entitled to all the privileges and immunities of free citizens in the others, the more stringent of them suffered invasion by citizens who were accepted by their less stringent neighbours upon easier terms than their own alien immigrants were required to fulfil. They defied federal authority by making wars upon and entering into treaties with Indians, by raising troops and by entering into compacts with one another without federal consent. They violated the treaties which the federal authority had itself entered into, and obstructed the execution of an effective foreign policy. There was even a threat of armed conflict between them. And the sole and ineligible remedy for such behaviour provided by the Articles was the coercion of the offending state: ". . . a negative *in all cases whatsoever* on the legislative acts of the States, as heretofore exercised by the Kingly prerogative", wrote Madison to Washington in 1787, "appears to me to be absolutely necessary, and to be the least possible encroachment on State jurisdictions. Without this defensive power, every positive power that can be given on paper will be evaded & defeated. The States will continue to invade the National jurisdiction, to violate treaties and the law of nations & to harass each other with rival and spiteful measures dictated by mistaken views of interest."

The most striking and the most fundamental of the changes made by the adoption of the Constitution was the direct federal invasion of the jurisdiction of the states and the call upon individual citizens for a share of their allegiance; and this was, as Madison perceived, a reversion to the traditional imperial pattern. The Constitution established a system of federal rights and obligations superior to the system of rights and obligations prevailing within the several states. Section 2 of Article VI runs:

This Constitution, and the Laws of the United States which shall be made in Pursuance thereof; and all Treaties made, or which shall be made, under the Authority of the United States, shall be the supreme Law of the Land; and the Judges in every State shall be bound thereby, any Thing in the Constitution or Laws of any State to the Contrary notwithstanding.

Section 3 of the same Article provided that:

. . . the Members of the several State Legislatures, and all executive and judicial Officers both of the United States and of the several States, shall be bound by Oath or Affirmation to support this Constitution . . .

The Constitution and the laws made in pursuance thereof were thus made binding not merely upon the several states as political societies, but also upon the individuals who composed them. Under the Constitution, every individual, as well as being a citizen of his state, became also a member of a larger community, and his state was not to obstruct him in the performance of the duties, nor to deprive him of enjoyment of the rights, which arose from that fact.

In order to give effect to this, Article III of the Constitution provides that, "The judicial Power of the United States shall be vested in one supreme Court, and such inferior Courts as the Congress may from time to time ordain and establish . . . "; and that that judicial power "shall extend to all Cases, in Law and Equity, under this Constitution, the Laws of the United States, and Treaties made, or which shall be made, under their Authority", together with certain matters of national concern, controversies between states, between states and citizens of another state, and between citizens of different states.

This was not the only way that had been open to the Constitutional Convention. It might have reverted to the imperial model, making the governors of the states officers of the central authority as they had been officers of the crown, and furnishing them with the power to veto the unconstitutional acts of state legislatures. Or it might have set up a council of censors with power to review all legislation, both federal and state, and pass upon its constitutionality, after the manner of a privy council or a *parlement*. Both these devices were proposed and rejected. Preference was given to a method that was both less provocative and more pervasive. The courts, whether federal or state,—and the obligation lay equally upon all—were not, if language be used with precision, to exercise a veto over laws they deemed to be unconstitutional. Their duty, if equally effective, was more restricted and less politically explosive. Constitutionality was not to be challenged until some person thought himself aggrieved and turned to the courts for redress. The courts were then called upon to do no more than, if they saw fit, give as a reason for reaching a particular conclusion in a particular case their opinion that a particular statute was unconstitutional and so void. Yet in so doing, the court in effect gave notice that (unless it reversed itself or, being an inferior court, was over-ruled) this opinion would be equally valid in all other cases, so that the law for all practical purposes was dead.

The implications of these provisions were developed in the Judiciary Act of 1789 and in the judgments of the Supreme Court, particularly those delivered by Marshall as chief justice from 1801 to 1835.

In framing the Judiciary Act Congress found that five points of departure had been fixed by the explicit instructions of the Constitution. That instrument established what was to be the supreme law of the land and bound the judges in every state to obey it. Federal law was thus made of force within each state, whose own courts were required to apply it. By Section 1 of Article III, the judicial power of the United States was to be vested in one Supreme Court and in such inferior courts as Congress might determine. By clause 2 of Section 2 of that Article, the Supreme Court was to exercise original jurisdiction "in all cases affecting Ambassadors, other public Ministers and Consuls, and those in which a State shall be a Party"; and in all the other cases to which the judicial power of the United States extended was to have "appellate Jurisdiction . . . with such Exceptions, and under such Regulations as the Congress shall make". In clause 3 it was laid down that in the trial of crimes "such Trial shall be held in the State where the said Crimes shall have been committed".

It would have been possible in accordance with these provisions to do as had been suggested in the Federal Convention itself and in the ratifying conventions and leave the care of federal law, save in the two specific classes of cases, to the state courts, with the right of appeal to the Supreme Court of the United States. This solution, however, was not adopted. Instead the act set up a system of inferior federal courts consisting of circuit and district courts; while it defined, at the same time, the appellate jurisdiction of the Supreme Court. To meet the requirement of the clause 3 cited above, the establishment of at least one United States District Court in each state was necessary. The United States Circuit Courts enjoyed original jurisdiction in certain cases and were regional courts of appeal. The Supreme Court was allotted no original jurisdiction beyond that with which it was specifically endowed by the Constitution itself; but it became the final court of appeal from the lower federal courts and, as to federal questions only, from the state courts as well. To the federal courts fell the trial of all crimes against the United States, that is to say all crimes created by federal statute; civil actions in enforcement of federal statutes; suits by individuals injured by the violation of federal statutes; and suits by individuals injured by the unconstitutional acts of the federal or a state legislature or the unconstitutional resolution of a state constitutional convention. To the state courts fell a concurrent jurisdiction in controversies "between citizens of different states" or "between citizens of the same state, claiming lands under grants of different states" where the amounts in controversy fell below a specified figure; and even where these figures were exceeded the plaintiff might institute proceedings in a state court, with the option to the defendant in certain circumstances to have the case removed to a federal court. In the state courts there remained vested all jurisdiction in cases arising under state law in which a "federal question" was raised, federal review being available only when proceedings had been through the highest court of the state in which a determination could be had.

What all this meant in terms of sovereignty was spelled out by the Supreme Court in its judgments between 1789 and the death of Marshall in 1835. "The sovereignty of a State", said the Court in *McCulloch v. Maryland* (1819), "extends to everything which exists by its own authority, or is introduced by its permission": but, as James Wilson had put it in *Chisholm v. Georgia* in 1793, "as to the purposes of the Union . . . Georgia is not a sovereign State". "The states", said Story, delivering the opinion of the Court in 1816, "are stripped of some of the highest attributes of sovereignty, and the same are given to the United States; . . . the legislatures of the states, are, in some respects, under the control of congress, and in every case are, under the Constitution, bound by the paramount authority of the United States . . . The courts of the United States can, without question, revise the proceedings of the executive and legislative authorities of the states, and if they are found to be contrary to the Constitution, may declare them to be of no legal validity." "Georgia", Marshall had said in 1816, "cannot be viewed as a simple, unconnected, sovereign power, on whose legislation no other restrictions are imposed than may be found in its own constitution. She is a part of a large empire; she is a member of the American union; and that union has a constitution the supremacy of which all acknowledge, and which imposes limits to the legislatures of the several states, which none claim a right to pass." Moreover, it is not only the executive and legislative acts of the states that are subject to federal control. The state judiciary is likewise subject. The Court in 1816 rejected the argument of Virginia that "the appellate jurisdiction conferred by the Constitution on the Supreme Court is merely authority to revise the decisions of the inferior courts of the United States". The reasoning, said Story, was such as the Court could not accept. "It assumes principles which we cannot admit, and draws conclusions to which we do not yield our assent." The great principle that "entirely pervades the constitution", said Marshall in 1819, is "that the constitution and the laws made in pursuance thereof are supreme; that they control the constitution and laws of the respective States, and cannot be controlled by them".

Federal law, that is to say, must in federal matters prevail over state law. The executive or legislative act of a state, and any resolution of the people of a state assembled in a state constitutional convention, that is in conflict with federal law must be held by the courts to be legally void; and the state courts failing so to rule will be overriden by the Supreme Court of the United States. No state is entitled to obstruct the constitutional action of the federal authority. Any persons, whether private individuals or state officials, committing a breach of federal law or obstructing its execution will be held to account by the courts; no individual, even though he be an officer of the state, can plead the command of his state in defence of a breach of the laws of the union; any person acting in obedience to such law will be protected by the federal authority; any officer of the United States charged with a crime under the laws of a state for an act done under the authority of the United States is entitled to have his case transferred to the national courts; any person deprived of the rights or denied the privileges granted by the constitution and the laws made in pursuance thereof may seek redress in either the state or the federal courts, and failing to obtain it in the state courts may appeal to the Supreme Court of the United States. The authority of the union is thus intruded into the jurisdiction of the states, and to the extent of this intrusion their sovereignty, their claim to the undivided allegiance of their subjects, is impaired. It was precisely in this that the League of Nations fell short. "I spent hours and hours", said Woodrow Wilson, speaking at Bismarck, North Dakota, in September, 1919, "in the presence of the representatives of thirteen other Governments examining every sentence [of the Covenant], up and down and crosswise, and trying to keep out of it anything that interfered with the essential sovereignty of any member of the League." The League knew only nations. It left their control over their subjects untouched. No national threatened with punishment for obedience to its commands could appeal to a court established by the League itself.

"It is of the very essence of supremacy", said Marshall in delivering the judgment of the court in *McCulloch v. Maryland* in 1819, "to remove all obstacles to its action within its own sphere, and so to modify every power vested in subordinate governments, as to exempt its own operations from their influence." "The nation, on those subjects on which it can act, must necessarily bind its component parts." "The Court", he said "has bestowed on this subject its most deliberate consideration. The result is a conviction that the States have no power, by taxation or otherwise, to retard, impede, burden, or in any manner control, the operations of the constitutional laws enacted by Congress to carry into execution the powers vested in the general government. This is, we think, the unavoidable consequence of that supremacy which the constitution has declared. We are unanimously of opinion, that the law passed by the legislature of Maryland, imposing a tax on the Bank of the United States, is unconstitutional and void." The officers of a state, in the event of conflict between federal and state law, must obey the former. When the legislature of Pennsylvania passed an act directing the state executive to resist the execution of a decree of a federal court and recourse was had to the Supreme Court for a writ directing the district judge to enforce his judgment, Marshall said, "If the legislatures of the several States may, at will, annul the judgments of the courts of the United States, and destroy the rights acquired under these judgments, the Constitution itself becomes a solemn mockery; and the Nation is deprived of the means of enforcing its laws by the instrumentality of its own tribunals". And when the writ issued in obedience to the direction of the Court was resisted by the Pennsylvania militia, the federal government procured the indictment and conviction of the offenders. "A void act", said the Court in *Osborn v. Bank of the United States* (1824), "cannot afford any protection to the officers who execute it." In 1855 a marshal arrested for contempt by warrant of the court of common pleas of the state of Ohio was discharged upon appeal to a federal court. "The marshal", the federal judge said, "omitted to do the act ordered to be done . . . , because it would be in express violation of his duty under an act of congress. . . . A sense of duty compels me to say that the proceedings . . . were not only without the authority of law, but against law, and that the proceedings are void, and I am bound to treat them as nullity."

On the other hand, "the Constitution of the United States contains what may be deemed a bill of rights for the people of each state"; and for the defence of these rights from invasion by the states appeal lies to the federal courts. "The Constitution of the United States was designed for the common and equal benefit of all the people of the United States. The judicial power was granted for the same benign and salutary purposes. It was not to be exercised exclusively for the benefit of parties who might be plaintiffs, and would elect the national forum, but also for the protection of defendants who might be entitled to try their rights, or assert their privileges, before the same forum" (*Martin v. Hunter's Lessee*. 1816). "Where . . . a State obtains a judgment against an individual, and the Court, rendering such judgment, overrules a defence set up under the Constitution or laws of the United States . . . the defendant who appeals from a judgment rendered against him . . . asserts a constitutional right to have his defence examined by that tribunal whose province it is to construe the constitution and laws of the Union" (*Cohens v. Virginia*. 1821).

Yet if the sovereignty of the several states was abridged, it was not destroyed. "Every State in the Union in every instance where its sovereignty has not been delegated to the United States, I consider", said Iredell in 1793, "to be as completely sovereign, as the United States are in respect to the powers surrendered. The United States are sovereign as to all the powers of Government actually surrendered: Each State in the Union is sovereign as to all the powers reserved." "In America", said Marshall just over a quarter of a century later, "the powers of sovereignty are divided between the government of the Union, and those of the States. They are each sovereign with respect to the objects committed to it, and neither sovereign, with respect to the objects committed to the other. . . ." Each state continued in the field of criminal justice to be until 1866 the undisputed sovereign. No pardon for any crime other than a crime against the United States could be given by the President of the United States, but must on the contrary come from the governor of the state: and even the United States District Courts tended to follow in each state the peculiarities of state practice in criminal justice. In civil causes practice continued for even longer to vary from state to state; and these variations likewise were followed by the lower federal courts.

At the time of Marshall's death and the succession of Taney to the chief justiceship of the Supreme Court a radical change in the balance of power in the United States was in process. The West, hitherto regarded as a reinforcement, economically, socially and politically of the South, was moving into alliance with the North-East. The South in consequence saw itself faced with the prospect of a steadily increasing exercise of national authority with a diminishing sympathy for its own particular interests and point of view. It was easy in those circumstances to attribute to unfriendly legislation an economic decline that was in fact due to the competition of the virgin soils of the lower Mississippi valley and to the failure of the South Atlantic states to become, like the central and North-Eastern states, the financial and industrial partners of the expanding agrarian economy of the interior. Having lost the power of self-defence in the House of Representatives, where power depended on population; holding but a precarious veto in the Senate; threatened inescapably with the disappearance in the course of time of any hope of controlling the White House; and believing that those into whose hands dominion was passing would show themselves less and less regardful of the limitations set by the Constitution to their authority; the South took refuge in doctrines of state sovereignty and concurrent majority, of which John C. Calhoun became the chief and most systematic exponent.

Calhoun was a nationalist who under the pressure of political events shifted the predication of his nationalism from the union to the individual state. He held, moreover, that, whether in the union or in the several states, it was an error "to confound the numerical majority with the people", and that the will of the people was to be discovered, not in the voice of the numerical majority, but in the concurrent votes of the estates. One way of taking the sense of the community, he wrote, "regards numbers only, and considers the whole community as a unit, having but one common interest throughout; and collects the sense of the greater number of the whole as that of the community. The other, on the contrary, regards interests as well as numbers, considering the community as made up of different and conflicting interests, as far as the action of government is concerned; and takes the sense of each, through its majority or appropriate organ, and the united sense of all, as the sense of the entire community. The former of these I shall call the numerical or absolute majority; and the latter, the concurrent, or constitutional majority."

This provided a political theory that was capable, if with some confusion of principles, of attributing undivided sovereignty to each of the several states and endowing them with authority to veto unacceptable federal legislation or to secede from a union which had ceased to serve their interest. Making a distinction between state and government, Calhoun argued that sovereignty resided, absolute and undivided, with the people of each of the states of the union. The people, so defined, acting in their sovereign capacity, as a state, conferred upon their agent, the government, the duties and powers delimited in the constitution. In this sovereign capacity the people of the several states had chosen to divide these duties and powers between two agencies, one state and the other federal. In either sphere, any act of executive or legislature that was in conflict with the provisions of the constitution thus adopted was illegal and void; and it was the duty of the courts to treat it as such when it came in question in the course of litigation before them. While, however, the courts were thus to restrain the other organs of government within the limits set by the constitution, they themselves were also but agents and had no authority to pass judgment upon the fiat of the people assembled in a constitutional convention. That fiat was a sovereign act beyond their reach.

"The great, original, and primary division", Calhoun wrote, " . . . is that of distinct, independent, sovereign States. It is the basis of the whole system. The next in order is, the division into constitution-making and law-making powers. The next separates the delegated and the reserved powers, by vesting the one in the government of the United States, and the other in the separate governments of the respective States, as co-ordinate governments. . . ." It follows, "if the States still retain their sovereignty as separate and independent communities, the allegiance and obedience of the citizens of each would be due to their respective States; and that the government of the United States and those of the several States would stand as equals and co-ordinates in their respective spheres". "Both governments,—that of the United States and those of the separate States, derive their powers from the same source, and were ordained and established by the same authority": the federal government is "the representative and organ of the States . . . to the extent of the powers delegated to it".

The federal constitution is to the citizens of a state "a law—the supreme law within its sphere. They may be guilty of violating it *as a law*, or of violating the laws and treaties made in pursuance of, or under its authority, regarded as laws or treaties; . . . The constitution was ordained and established *over them* by their respective States, to whom they owed allegiance; and they are under the same obligation to respect and obey its authority, within its proper sphere, as they are to respect and obey their respective State constitutions; and for the same reason, viz.: that the State to which they owe allegiance, commanded it in both cases." Yet, while "they owe *obedience* to both; because their State commanded them to obey; . . . they owe *allegiance* to neither; since sovereignty, by a fundamental principle of our system, resides in the *people*, and not in the *government*. The same authority which commanded *obedience*, has the right, in both cases, to determine, as far as they are concerned, the extent to which they are bound to obey; and this determination remains binding until rescinded by the authority which pronounced and declared it." Had the states "by ratifying the constitution, divested themselves of their individuality and sovereignty, and merged themselves into one great community or nation, it is . . . clear, that the sovereignty would reside in the whole—or what is called the American people; and that allegiance and obedience would be due to them". But "there is, indeed, no such community, *politically* speaking, as the people of the United States, regarded in the light of, and as constituting one people or nation". Sovereignty remains "unsurrendered and unimpaired in the people of the several States". The Union, at bottom, is no different from the Confederation. The states, Calhoun asserted, "are now united, and have been, throughout, simply as confederated States". In consequence, "the [individual] State . . . has the right to decide, in the last resort,—and . . . to determine . . . how far [its citizens] are bound to respect and obey" the federal constitution and the acts made under its authority.

Calhoun had history on his side to the extent that the constitution had been adopted by the concurrence of majorities in the several states, and not by a majority of the American people in the aggregate, as forming one nation. Beyond that, his doctrine could only be sustained by straining not merely the spirit but the letter of the constitution. It was necessary in the first place to re-draft the Tenth Amendment. It runs, "The powers not delegated to the United States by the constitution, nor prohibited by it to the States, are reserved to the States respectively, or to the people." Calhoun, in citing it, wrote consistently "or to the people thereof". It was necessary in the second place to ignore the fact that Section 2 of Article VI provides that the constitution and the laws of the United States shall override, not only the laws of any state, but also the fiat of the people of any state in convention assembled, so that, whereas a legislative act held by the state courts to be incompatible with the provisions of the state constitution can be re-enacted by the people in the form of a constitutional provision, and be made valid in state law, such a provision is itself open to challenge if it is in conflict with the federal constitution or the laws made in pursuance thereof.

The accompanying doctrine of the concurrent majority was offered by Calhoun as a means of defending the rights of minorities. If the South lost its power to block unacceptable legislation in the Senate, as well as all grounds for confidence that the federal courts would protect its interests by a strict construction of the constitution, it must, in his view, if it was to remain in the Union, seek some other line of defence to fall back upon. Within the unitary state, "the interest of each individual may be safely confided to the majority, or voice of his portion, against that of all others, and, of course, the government itself. It is only through an organism which vests each with a negative . . . that those who have like interests in preventing the government from passing beyond its proper sphere, and encroaching on the rights and liberties of individuals, can co-operate peaceably and effectually in resisting the encroachments of power, and thereby preserve their rights and liberty. Individual resistance is too feeble, and the difficulty of concert and co-operation too great, unaided by such an organism, to oppose, successfully, the organized power of government. . . . And hence in no governments, except those that rest on the principle of the concurrent or constitutional majority, can the people guard their liberty against power." This is to be effected "by taking the sense of each interest or portion of the community, which may be unequally and injuriously affected by the action of the government, separately, through its own majority . . . ; and to require the consent of each interest, either to put or to keep the government in action". This "government of the concurrent majority . . . excludes the possibility of oppression, by giving to each interest, or portion, or order,—where there are established classes—the means of protecting itself, by its negative, against all measures calculated to advance the peculiar interests of others at its expense". In a federal state, "the several States, as weaker parties, can protect the portion [of power] not delegated [to the federal authority], only in one of two ways; either by having a concurrent voice in the action of the government of the United States; or a negative on its acts, when they disagree as to the extent of their respective powers".

Thus stated, the doctrine has a metaphysical air. But in practice it is familiar enough. Until the passage of the Parliament Act in 1911, nothing could be done by the crown in parliament without the concurrence of a majority in the house of lords with a majority in the house of commons. But that observation alone is sufficient to suggest that a closer analysis is needed. As early as 1814, John Taylor of Caroline, from whom Calhoun drew so much, noticed that "all sorts of men, make the same sort of lords and commons"; and long before 1911 the house of lords had ceased to be a distinct estate with a separate interest. It is one thing to say that it is a political error to impose legislation, without its concurrence, upon a homogeneous interior group with a peculiar interest, when those enacting that legislation will not themselves be comparably affected: and the theoretical absolutism of the crown in parliament is currently tempered by a careful regard for this principle. It is quite another thing to say either that a right of veto resides in a minority that is substantially homogeneous with the majority, or that an estate that claims the undivided allegiance of its members in all matters without exception can be regarded as an interior group enjoying constitutional rights. No group can be both a "portion of the community" and an absolute sovereign. Estates and the omnicompetent state are incompatibles. The doctrine of the concurrent majority was both incongruous and superfluous once the absolutism of the several states had been asserted. It was but a way station on the road to that conclusion.

When these theories were put to the test in 1861, the answer of the federal government was that, since no state could "upon its own mere motion . . . lawfully get out of the Union", war could not be waged against it; and the acts of violence within any state or states against the authority of the United States were therefore the insurrectionary or revolutionary acts of individuals, operating though they might be in combinations too powerful to be suppressed by the ordinary course of judicial proceedings. Sovereignty was still divided, and what the Constitution called for was, not an attempt to coerce sovereign states, but a reduction to obedience of delinquent individuals who could not divest themselves of their duty under it.

In the event, the war that was begun in order to deny the undivided sovereignty of the several states came near to ending with the assertion of the undivided sovereignty of the union. The federal government found itself faced with an embarrassing dilemma. The Constitution provided that representation in the House of Representatives should be apportioned among the states according to their numbers, which should be calculated "by adding to the whole Number of free Persons, including those bound to Service for a Term of Years, and excluding Indians not taxed, three-fifths of all other Persons". The emancipation of the slaves shifted them from the column of "other persons" to that of "the whole number of free persons", adding two-fifths to the weight of each, and thus increasing the number of representatives to which the state was entitled. At the same time, the Constitution also provided that the electors in each state should be those who had "the Qualifications requisite for Electors of the most numerous Branch of the State Legislature", and that was a matter determined by the state itself. In consequence, if the defeated states so chose, their increased representation could be returned by an unenlarged and unchanged electorate. That the reward of insurrection should be an increase of power in that very legislature whose fiats had been set at defiance was plainly unacceptable; and the answer was constitutional amendment. The Fourteenth Amendment to the Constitution of the United States (1868) declared all persons born or naturalized in the United States, and subject to the jurisdiction thereof, to be citizens of the United States and of the state wherein they reside; and went on—"No State shall make or enforce any law which shall abridge the privileges or immunities of citizens of the United States; nor shall any State deprive any person of life, liberty, or property, without due process of law; nor deny to any person within its jurisdiction the equal protection of the laws." It further provided that when the right to vote was denied or in any way abridged, the basis of representation should be proportionately reduced. The Fifteenth Amendment (1870) requires that "The right of citizens of the United States to vote shall not be denied or abridged by the United States or by any State on account of race, color, or previous condition of servitude". Both amendments specifically vested in Congress the power of enforcement by appropriate legislation.

These amendments, and particularly the Fourteenth, had the most far-reaching results. They formally reversed the priority of the twofold allegiance of citizens, making state citizenship henceforth dependent upon citizenship of the nation; and they afforded to such citizens the protection of the federal authority against any invasion by the states of their constitutional rights. In the event, however, it was not their "privileges and immunities", nor their right to vote, which proved to be the most valuable of the boons conferred upon them. The former were reduced to relative unimportance by the process of interpretation by the Supreme Court; and the latter was successfully denied by the states without a formal breach of the law. But "due process" and "the equal protection of the laws" proved to be instruments of great power. Of the former it has been said by Mayers that "with the incorporation in the Constitution of this seemingly subsidiary restriction on the states was laid the foundation for the development of that supervisory power of the federal courts, and particularly of the Supreme Court, over all the operations of state government, which has revolutionized our federal system". This was doubly unexpected. "Due process" had been guaranteed by the Constitution since 1791, though the court had construed the prohibitions of the first ten Amendments as applying only to the United States; and a similar requirement was to be found in most state constitutions. But the words had been generally regarded as meaning no more than that a criminal prosecution should follow the established legal procedure. They now came to be given a much wider range and to be deemed to require a procedure in criminal cases that was "consistent with the fundamental principles of liberty and justice"; and the subjection of the criminal jurisdiction of the several states to the requirements of the Supreme Court in this respect brought to an end the hitherto undisputed sovereignty of the states in this sphere of their activity. Yet more unforeseen was the use of the doctrine of due process to control the economic and social legislation of the states. Deciding in 1886 that a corporation was a "person" within the meaning of the Fourteenth Amendment, the Court became the refuge of corporations seeking to escape state regulation; and the volume of state legislation that was invalidated increased greatly. The fact that the Court in so acting was for many years dominated by a doctrinaire belief in *laisser faire* and came, as it has been said, to treat as unconstitutional practically all legislation which it deemed unwise, is beside the point. Whatever the motive, its action contributed powerfully to abridge the sovereignty of the states. And in the 1920's it began to extend its protection under the "due process" clause to freedom of speech and religion; and more recently it has used the guarantee of the equal protection of the laws to control state legislation relating to racial segregation.

These tendencies to the more frequent assertion of the paramount authority of the nation were reinforced by the teachings of contemporary political science. The two outstanding American political scientists of the day, J. W. Burgess and W. W. Willoughby, though they differed from one another in other respects, were united in their belief in the indivisibility of sovereignty and the necessity of its location in the nation. J. W. Burgess, a unionist from a border state, trained in Germany, was an uncompromising Austinian. He held that "there is no such thing as a federal state". "The state may constitute two or more governments; it may assign to each a distinct sphere of action; it may *then* require of its citizens or subjects obedience to each government thus constituted; but there cannot be two organizations of the state for the same population within the same territory." Sovereignty is "original, absolute, un-limited, universal power over the individual subject and over all associations of subjects"; and "power cannot be sovereign if it be limited". It resides in the people of the United States: "the people in ultimate sovereign organization are the state"; "democracy" he defines as "the sovereignty of the majority". "The state can do no wrong": "in law and politics it is referred wholly to its own consciousness of justice and expedience". "The individual is . . . defended . . . *against* the government, by the power that makes and maintains and can destroy the government; and by the same power, *through* the government against encroachments from every other quarter." "Against that power itself . . . he [the individual] has no defence." "There never was, and there never can be, any liberty upon this earth and among human beings outside of state organization." It is Calhoun stood on his head.

With such doctrines Willoughby was at bottom in agreement, although he was a better historian than Burgess and criticized the latter's grossly distorted account of the events of the years 1775 to 1789. The state he thought to be "itself above the law"; "to its own citizens and subjects . . . the sole and exclusive source of law". "What the idea of 'value' is to the economist, or 'substance' to the metaphysician", he wrote, "the concept of 'sovereignty' is to the political philosopher. No one has made plainer than Professor Burgess the fact that the first condition of exact political theorizing is the apprehension of the fact that sovereignty means legal omnipotence, and that without this attribute no political unit may properly be termed a State; or that if certain non-sovereign bodies be entitled States, it becomes impossible to distinguish them sharply and logically from other purely administrative units."

Yet for all this the United States have not in fact become a consolidated state, an "aggregate . . . forming one nation", of which the divisions are "mere districts of one great community". In 1911 a justice of the Supreme Court could still employ the language used by Marshall just short of a century before. "The people of the United States constitute one nation under one government, and this government, within the scope of the powers with which it is invested, is supreme. On the other hand, the people of each State compose a State, having its own government, and endowed with all the functions essential to separate and independent existence." If immense economic and social changes have taken place, and are still in process, which steadily increase the interests that are common to all, nevertheless, in a society built upon a continental scale, the peculiar interests of distinct estates are still conspicuous. The government with which the citizen of the United States most frequently has dealings is still the government of his state: and new interior groups are making their appearance. Trade unions have sought to restrict applications to the courts, and business consolidation has resulted in a decline in the volume of civil litigation.

Moreover sovereignty is Janus-faced. That political society which, in dealing with its own subjects, knows no law but its own will, stands by the same principle in a relationship of mere power to its fellows. J. W. Burgess, who occupied a position of great influence in his day, made no bones about it. He regarded the national state as "the significant production of the Teutonic political genuis". This authorized the Teutonic nations "to assume the leadership in the establishment and administration of states". It justified annexations and conquests. "When a state insists upon the union with it of all states occupying the same geographic unity and attains this result in the last resort by force, the morality of its action cannot be doubted in sound practical politics." "Who does not see", he went on, "that the further rounding out of the European states . . . would be in the interest of the advancement of Europe's political civilization and of the preservation of the general peace? . . . it would bring the petty states of Switzerland, Denmark, Holland, Luxembourg, Belgium, and Portugal into connections that would enable their populations to contribute, in a far greater degree, to the political civilization of the world, and receive, in a far greater degree, the benefits of that civilization, than their present conditions permit." Where the political genius of the Teuton is lacking, "the political subjection or attachment of the unpolitical nations to those possessing political endowment appears . . . as truly a part of the course of the world's civilization as is the national organization of states": and beyond the pale of western civilization, "the civilized states themselves are the best organs which have yet appeared in the history of the world for determining the proper time and occasion for intervening in the affairs of unorganized or insufficiently organized populations, for the execution of their great world-duty". In the execution of this duty, moreover, any such power is entitled "to force organization" upon "unpolitical populations", "by any means necessary"; it "may righteously deport" an "ethnically hostile element"; and "if the barbaric populations resist . . . the civilized state may clear the territory of their presence and make it the abode of civilized man".

Since Burgess wrote we have seen these doctrines put into practice upon a grand scale. Today we find them deeply shocking. Sovereignty, absolute and undivided, we come to recognize, is no more sufficient an answer to the problem of the relation of states in an international than in a federal society.

In these circumstances, Woodrow Wilson made the wrong choice from the armoury of American political experience when he proferred to the world of 1918 the doctrines of self-determination and the prevalence of the will of the people. Nationalism, as we have learnt to our bitter cost, is not purified by making it popular. The balance, the limitations, the duties imposed and the rights conferred upon individuals; the elimination of blind obedience and omnicompetent authority; the habitual recourse to the courts as guardians of the rule of law and the balance of rights that arise from divided sovereignty have much more to teach this troubled twentieth century.

THE IDEAS AND INFLUENCE OF
ALEXANDER HAMILTON

By W. R. Brock

*

MORE than a century and a half after his death Alexander Hamilton is still regarded either as the most prescient of American states-men or as the instigator of all that has tarnished American ideals. "Mine is an odd destiny," he wrote in 1802, "perhaps no man in the United States has sacrificed more or done more for the present constitution than myself; and contrary to all my anticipations of its fate . . . I am still labouring to prop the frail and worthless fabric. Yet I have the murmurs of its friends no less than the curses of its foes for my reward. What can I do better than withdraw from the scene? Every day proves to me more and more, that this American world was not made for me." His "odd destiny" had led him from influence enjoyed by no subsequent cabinet minister to the role of an unsuccessful state politician, outwitted by those whom he despised, appealing vainly to leaders who could no longer lead, and meditating upon the future ruin of America. But for the fatal duel with Aaron Burr in 1804, he might have lived on into the Jacksonian era; yet it is hard to imagine any circumstances which would have restored him to influence and authority. Amid the rising tides of a democracy which he feared and misunderstood he was a man of the past lamenting a world which had never existed. Perhaps no one would have been more surprised to find himself placed, by future admirers, among the makers of the nation, to find his view of constitutional power gener-ally accepted, to find the nationalism which he revered fastened upon America by the democracy which he hated.

In 1789 when summoned to the secretaryship of the Treasury no trace was evident of the tragic paradoxes of his later career. Regarded by some as a figure of sinister import, by others as the one man who could save America, he was at thirty-four a young man with the destinies of a nation in his hands. Immersed in public affairs since the age of eighteen, pamphleteer, soldier, lawyer, Congressional delegate, New York politi-cian, and one who had during the war stood closer to Washington than any other man, he was a prodigy among prodigies, a young man in a hurry in an age when men under fifty dominated American life. He came fresh from a rhetorical triumph by which he persuaded a hostile New York convention to ratify the Constitution unconditionally. His anonymous but widely recognized part-authorship of the *Federalist* papers placed him among the first flight of political reasoners.

His thought was distinguished by powerful analysis and decisive conclusions rather than by subtlety. Though professing realism in politics he was far more susceptible to the influence of emotion than was his *Federalist* collaborator, James Madison. Hamilton knew the conclusions which he wished to reach and these conclusions were those which appealed to his emotions; the rational arguments were selected as a lawyer prepares his brief and presented as an appeal to the jury. The cool and intricate mind of Madison was never quite certain of the end to be attained and acutely aware of all the dangers implicit in a clear-cut case. In many respects it was Hamilton who had the radical and Madison the conservative temperament. The differences between them, so skilfully merged during the ratification controversy, were to become of supreme importance when the Federalist tide broke upon Hamilton's *First Report on Public Credit* and divided into two streams, never again to be successfully joined.

There was a basic simplicity about Hamilton's approach to the problems of 1789. The two poles between which his thought moved were a vision of future national greatness and a fear of divisions which would paralyse effort and make the United States the Holy Roman Empire of the New World. He believed that the forces of disunion were stronger than those of union, and that only positive action would make the latter prevail. "We love our families more than our neighbours," he told the New York ratifying convention, "we love our neighbours more than our countrymen in general. The human affections, like the solar heat, lose their intensity as they depart from the centre, and become languid in proportion to the expansion of the circle in which they act. On these principles, the attachment of the individual will be first and forever secured by the state governments; they will be a mutual protection and support." By birth a West Indian, by adoption a son of New York, he never himself experienced the attractions of state loyalty, but he was acutely aware of the passion for local interests which this loyalty might stimulate in others. The United States formed a weak nation, and though "the embryo of a great empire" inactivity at the centre must lead to disruption.

It followed that the new national government must play a decisive role. Throughout his life he believed in the positive contribution of government to human progress and this belief was unencumbered by *laisser faire* inhibitions. When he proposed the encouragement of manufactures as a national policy it was the positive direction given by bounties, rather than the negative protection given by the tariff, which particularly interested him. The concluding sentence of the *Report on Manufactures* asserted that, "In countries where there is great private wealth, much may be effected by the voluntary contribution of patriotic individuals; but in a community situated like that of the United States, the public purse must supply the deficiency of private resource." His proposal of a Government commission to administer a fund to promote immigration, reward inventions, offer premiums, "and afford such other aids to those objects as may be generally designated by law", brings him nearer to the New Deal than to President McKinley. Less specifically he advocated "vigour" in the national administration as the force which might create a nation, and if "vigour" sometimes seemed to be advocated for its own sake it was always the consequences of weakness which provided the real argument.

Hamilton was too clear-headed to believe that men would accept vigorous government unless it was plainly in their interest to do so. The appeal to future greatness might carry men over a crisis, such as the debate on the Constitution, but it could not supply a permanent force supporting government. In 1789 the national government was a government in a vacuum. Though the great majority of Americans, even among the avowed opponents of ratification, were prepared to give the new Constitution a fair trial, acquiescence in government did not mean attachment to it. There must be interests ranged behind the operations of national government just as there were interests grouped around the state governments, and a contest for power between the national and state governments could lead to a favourable result only if enough men had strong material reasons for supporting the government of the Union. Hence came Hamilton's pre-occupation with the problem of "influence". He believed that this problem had been solved with outstanding success in Great Britain; on the one hand the patronage of the Crown was a powerful support for effective action, on the other the landed and monied interests both felt themselves committed to the cause of national stability. In America there existed no such classes with established national interests, and it was therefore the task of statesmanship to create them. The way in which this might be done had been clearly indicated during the struggle over the Constitution: public creditors, thanks to war finance a large and influential group, had the clearest possible interest in maintaining any government which would satisfy their claims; the merchants, gravely embarrassed by state regulation of commerce and currency, formed another interest which might be made to feel the magnetic attraction of strong national authority; property owners in general, alarmed by the debtor revolt in Massachusetts and the behaviour of agrarian majorities in Rhode Island and elsewhere, might be expected to lend general support to the Constitution and to the government which it set up. Injustice is often done to Hamilton in supposing that he intended to use national authority simply to make men who had done well out of the war do even better. Rather, he intended to make their power, which might otherwise be used against the public interest, serve a useful purpose. Concentration of economic power was not an end in itself but an instrument of national well-being; power allied to government, and persuaded to act in the common interest, was more useful to the nation than power diffused throughout the states and pursuing un-co-ordinated ambitions. In the *Report on the National Bank* he wrote that "Public utility is more truly the object of public banks than private profit, and it is the business of government to constitute them on such principles that, while the latter will result in a sufficient degree to afford competent motives to engage in them, the former be not made subservient to it." This remark illuminates his whole attitude towards the capitalists whose interests he appeared to serve so well.

To imagine a system in which economic interest would be allied to beneficent power was one thing; to translate it into practical politics was another. Indeed this argument brings one to the limits of Hamilton's constructive thought; beyond lies a region of dimly realized popular pressures which he never understood. The flaw in his political analysis was that America was not England. No amount of government influence could ever hope to swell, save in the distant future, to the same proportions as the influence of the Crown. No interests could sway the free electorate of America as the landed magnates dominated the tiny electorate of the British Isles. There were no rotten or pocket boroughs and remarkably few white men lived in economic dependence upon other white men. Merchant capitalists are usually comparatively small employers of labour and their direct political influence is correspondingly small. In spite of the deference paid by the yeomanry of the south to the planter gentry, there was never any doubt that the latter's power must be based upon public opinion. Given this situation one must either recognize the predestined failure of his system or be forced to the anomalous conclusion that while a rich man must be swayed by interest a poor man would act upon the dictates of reason. This error was at the root of Hamilton's system and accounts for his failure as a politician. Only at the end of his life did he confess that "the Federalists have . . . erred in relying so much on the rectitude and utility of their measures, as to have neglected the cultivation of popular favor, by fair and justifiable expedients".

Though government was to be supported by influence it must be administered with integrity. Hamilton himself set the highest possible standard, and his share in setting up the national administration is one of the least noticed and most praiseworthy aspects of his career. Professor L. D. White, the closest student of American administrative history, regards Hamilton as one of the greatest administrators of all time. He had to battle against heresies both ancient and modern; against ideas that public office was a species of freehold, that an official superior had no right to dictate to a subordinate his interpretation of the law, that low salaries were a sign of republican virtue, and that efficient government was dangerous to liberty. In the fiscal service he created an instrument which was to be the mainstay of all succeeding governments, and his own enormous industry enabled him to supervise even the details of a system which grew in complexity under his hand without the sacrifice of discipline, clarity, and despatch. Both Hamilton and Washington paid great attention to applications and recommendations for office and sought to appoint only "fit" persons, which meant in practice men of good standing in their communities who were "well affected" towards the government. Before party lines were drawn the net of patronage was spread as widely as possible, though an active opponent of the Constitution was unlikely to qualify as "well affected"; later, party regularity became a requirement for office and some active Republicans were dismissed.

Many of the difficulties encountered in central administration resulted from the obscurities of a constitution which had provided for legislation, for execution of the law, but not for the formulation of policy. The President could urge in his messages to Congress measures which might be implemented or ignored; but the continuous application of principle and the detailed proposals for legislation fell into a kind of no man's land, which could be occupied by the President acting as his own first minister, by Congress (or more probably by a Congressional clique) acting in committee, or by the ministers. If the ministers were to formulate policy and speak through the President it would be necessary for one minister to enforce collective responsibility upon the others. If the Executive captured the initiative in some form or other it would still need the assistance of Congressional spokesmen. Hamilton, like most of his contemporaries in America, showed no understanding of the dual responsibility of English ministers—to King and to Parliament—which formed the keystone of the British system. "See the excellency of the British Executive," he is reported to have told the Federal Convention, "he is placed above temptation. He can have no distinct interests from the public welfare. Nothing short of such an executive can be efficient." This belief in an executive exalted above faction, neutral yet active, the pure principle of public welfare guiding the state, exercised a commanding influence over Hamilton's mind and he never fully considered the problem of an executive elected every four years and of ministers who were responsible only to him.

Far reaching decisions had been taken by the First Session of the First Congress. Two suggestions were made of great constitutional significance: the first that ministers once appointed should be removable only by impeachment, the second that the Senate must concur in the dismissal of those whom it helped to appoint. Both proposals might have led to the rise of conventions whereby ministers resigned when they lost the confidence of Congress, though no one in 1789 envisaged this outcome. Both were rejected and in their place the President was given sole power to dismiss ministers. While insisting on exclusive Presidential responsibility for administration, the House also showed itself very suspicious of executive influence in Congress. The arguments were aired during the debate on the organisation of the Treasury department when the bill, in its original form, instructed the Secretary "to digest and report plans" for the improvement of finances. Page of Virginia believed that this "would create an undue influence within these walls, because members might be led, by the deference commonly paid to men of abilities, who give an opinion in a case they have thoroughly studied, to support the minister's plan even against their own judgment"; while Elbridge Gerry feared "the doctrine of having prime and great ministers of state", soon perhaps to be "distinguished by a green or red ribbon, or other insignia of court favor and patronage". The clause was carried after altering the disputed phrase to read "digest and prepare plans", thus leaving to Congress the right to call for plans when it wished to receive them. Hamilton still hoped that he would have the opportunity of making his reports in person but this was refused in January 1790, and the most persuasive speaker of his generation was deprived of his most effective weapon.

Hamilton stood therefore in that curious position occupied by all subsequent cabinet ministers. No British minister was ever more dependent upon the favour of the King than was he upon that of Washington. The responsibility of every minister to the President meant that none could claim to direct cabinet policy unless specifically authorized to do so by Washington. The exclusion of ministerial spokesmen from Congress meant that the initiative must be exercised, if exercised at all, obliquely and indirectly. The situation was made more difficult by Washington's attempt to act as Hamilton had said the executive should act; that is, to stand above "faction" not as the active head of a government but as the impartial head of a state. Washington was not the man to refuse decision when necessary, but he believed that it was his function to decide rather than to direct. If Washington wished to play the part of President as a constitutional monarch and not as prime minister, there was a good case for making the Secretary of the Treasury the head of the Cabinet, but this Washington refused to do in spite of Hamilton's obvious eagerness to take the responsibility. Politically Washington was quite right—it would have been extremely dangerous to the Union either to omit Jefferson or to subordinate him to Hamilton—but administratively it pointed the way to a paralysis of the executive function. Since Hamilton intended to be an active head of the Treasury, and as financial policy was the key to general policy, it was inevitable that he would try to encroach upon the other departments, even without authority to do so.

Deprived of the direct means of exercising the initiative in Congress, Hamilton was forced to rely more than he might have wished upon those who had a direct personal interest in the success of his policy. Most of Hamilton's leading supporters in the House had investments in the public funds, some had very large interests indeed; for some of them the personal gain to be made from a restoration of credit was a comparatively small matter beside the general benefits which they expected, but for a few the success of his policy meant the difference between affluence and ruin. These active Federalists seized the initiative at the beginning of the Second Session and, with the help of a rank and file mainly representative of Northern, commercial and financial interests, carried through the first stages of Hamilton's policy. Little is known of Federalist organisation at this stage but the solidarity of the vote at roll calls shows that it must have existed and that it must have been efficient. It was a Congressional party, which called into existence a nation-wide opposition. Thus the peculiarities of the American Constitution helped to bring Hamilton into collision with the two men whom he could least afford to offend: with Jefferson, whose departmental responsibilities he attempted to usurp, and with Madison, who had been the leading man in Congress before Hamilton's supporters seized the initiative. It did not need the *First Report on Public Credit* to bring about conflicts which sprang from the nature of the Constitution, but that *Report* determined the character of the struggle and cast a long shadow over the future course of American history. It is therefore necessary to turn next to the *Report* and its impact upon the nation.

It was the great merit of Hamilton to combine long term views with the solution of immediate and urgent problems. The great spectre which haunted the Federalist mind was national bankruptcy, and the narrow view which sees so much history in this period as the outcome of pressure by the public creditors, often does less than justice to the real magnitude of the disaster which threatened the young and insecure country. It is difficult to see how public credit could have been restored without making the fortunes of large holders of public securities, but to Hamilton these few great fortunes were of minor importance. Politically he wished to secure the nation-wide support of all those who depended upon the security of paper assets; economically he saw far beyond the immediate gains of individuals to the invigorating flow of capital which sound credit would stimulate. "Credit, public and private, is of the greatest consequence to every country. Of this, it might be called the invigorating principle." Sound credit meant no more than confidence that debts would be repaid, and the whole network of confidence would be damaged if a single cord were weak. "Credit is an entire thing. Every part of it has the nicest sympathy with every other part; wound one limb, and the whole tree shrinks and decays. The security of each creditor is inseparable from the security of all creditors."

It was therefore certain that Hamilton would insist upon honouring the public debts to the furthest possible limit, though there were ideas abroad, under influential sponsorship, that the debt ought to be scaled down, both to ease the burden of taxation and to make possible its rapid repayment. No one questioned the wisdom of meeting the foreign debt in full, but the domestic debt had been contracted during a period of inflation, the securities had rapidly depreciated, and many of them had been sold by their original holders at low prices. Particular sympathy was attracted to the ex-soldiers who had been paid in certificates, not cash. Advocates of full and of partial repudiation were found, but the most popular proposal was to pay the original holders the full value of their certificates while paying other holders only the depreciated prices at which they had purchased. Madison produced, at a late stage in the controversy, another variant of discrimination between present and original holders, by which all debts should be paid at face value, but that repayment should be divided between present and original holders, giving the former only the price which they had paid and the balance to the latter. This proposal was ingenious because it preserved the principle of paying debts in full while offering something to all original holders, not to those alone who had kept their securities. Against all ideas of repudiation or discrimination Hamilton set his face. "The true definition of public debt is a property subsisting in the faith of the government. Its essence is promise." To compromise the promise in any way would strike a deadly blow at the whole edifice of confidence upon which credit depended.

While Hamilton stood upon the defence in maintaining sound credit against unorthodox proposals to temper financial rectitude with concessions to natural justice, he took an aggressive part in proposing that the national government assume responsibility for the state debts. Probably most Americans believed that something must be done to ease the situation of heavily indebted states such as Massachusetts and South Carolina, but there was a natural reluctance on the part of other states to contribute taxes to help those whom they inevitably suspected of mismanagement or worse. The politic course would have been to await the conclusion of the long and complex process of balancing accounts between the national government and the states and then to propose some sharing of the burdens. Hamilton had a twofold object in acting drastically and without reservations. The existence of thirteen different bodies of state securities, each fluctuating in price with local political and economic changes, would introduce a factor of uncertainty damaging to the whole credit system, while the continued existence of fluctuating state debts would have been an enormous incentive to speculative buying and selling. The second factor in Hamilton's mind was political. The existence of separate state debts would have meant that each state government would remain the focal point of local creditor interests, while their transference to the national government would enormously strengthen its influence. In retrospect Hamilton's arguments seem unassailable, provided that one accepts even in part his nationalist premises; yet even so it was poor tactics to risk a collision with the great state of Virginia,

where the main problem was not the state debt, which had been successfully repaid, but the private debt of planters to British merchants. The
law of diminishing returns on hard-worked tobacco lands meant that the
planter lived on a very small margin of profit; increased national taxes,
added to charges on private debts, might well bring the planter into
serious difficulties. Of course the Virginians made more of their problems
than was justified by the facts, but in ignoring their arguments Hamilton
threw one of the great property interests of the United States definitely
into the hostile camp.

While obligations must be met it was reasonable to spread the burden
over the generations, and Jefferson's belief that all debts should be paid
within the lifetime of those who had contracted them was more plausible
than just. On the other hand an indefinite postponement of repayment
might impair confidence. What Hamilton proposed was a funding
scheme which would include plans for regular redemption, which would
be guaranteed in its interest and principal by the national government,
and which would offer in return for this security a slightly lower rate of
interest than that nominally attached to most of the existing debts. Save
in permitting, in one of the options open to creditors, the transfer of one
third of the holding into claims on public lands, Hamilton did not attempt
to liquidate the debt by selling land or other public assets as had been
suggested by Madison and others. Hamilton disliked the idea of a hasty
dispersal of national resources, he was not anxious to encourage prema-
ture western development, and he was attracted by the purposes which a
funded national debt might serve. Readily negotiable securities could
substitute for a medium of exchange, provide the backing for commercial
loans, and stimulate investment. He did not consider that a national debt
was a national blessing under all circumstances, but he did think that an
indebted nation, which was also short of currency and capital, might make
valuable temporary use of a funded debt, while an unfunded debt lacking
proper guarantees could be used only for speculation.

His enemies believed, and many historians have repeated, that Hamilton deliberately helped the speculators who were grabbing depreciated
securities as soon as a revival of credit appeared probable. Unknown to
Hamilton, who was a singularly bad judge of character, his friend and
assistant secretary, William Duer, was personally involved in the great
speculations which were taking place and undoubtedly parted with
official information to some of his friends. Irving Brant, the biographer
of Madison, has discovered evidence of a gigantic speculation which
involved the purchase of national securities with borrowed Dutch money,
re-investment of the profits from funding in state debts of the Carolinas,
and an enormous gain when these were in turn assumed and rose to par.
Hamilton must have recognised the existence of such possibilities but
there is no evidence that he regarded them as more than a necessary evil.
Contrary to the impression, so often conveyed, all public creditors were

not big speculative operators; even after the speculative activities in late 1789 and early 1790 a great deal of debt remained in the hands of comparatively small men. It was Hamilton's object to serve the nation, not to enrich a clique. Indeed no one who studies his system can fail to see that encouragement of speculative operations was entirely contrary to the general drift of his policy. In 1791 he told Rufus King that "a bubble connected with my operations is of all enemies I have to fear, in my judgment, the most formidable". Though it may be objected that 1791 was not 1790, and that by then the big killings had been made, Hamilton had also told Congress in the *First Report* that delay would increase the opportunities for speculation, and this warning, though specifically directed against foreign operators, could also be applied to those nearer home; indeed in September 1790 Hamilton went anonymously into print with an address to the public creditors urging them not to part with national and state securities at a time when they would certainly rise in value. Everything which Hamilton ever wrote about credit points towards an era of stability and confidence in which productive activity is fostered and speculative activity discouraged. Not only did speculation in the debt throw suspicion upon the motives of financial policy; it also damaged the economy of the country by drawing so much capital away from productive investment. It is noticeable that, in the various options offered to public creditors, by far the most advantageous terms are given to the conservative type of investor who was interested in a guaranteed income, and the least advantageous to the speculative investor buying for a rise.

The heart of the stable economic system which Hamilton envisaged was the National Bank. Among the stockholders of the Bank Hamilton undeniably intended to concentrate those capitalists whose support he considered essential to the government; but the major purpose was to establish a sound and flexible financial system, and, as already noticed, concentration of the monied interest made it easier to ensure that it was serving national objects. Hamilton's opponents charged that he was creating a giant monopoly through which (in Madison's words) "so much public plunder . . . will be engrossed by those already loaded with the spoils of individuals". From dislike of the Bank opponents were led to question its constitutionality and called forth in reply the doctrine of implied powers, which in turn further alienated those who were prepared to believe that Hamilton nourished a design to corrupt the nation and to erect a monarchy upon the ruins of republican virtue.

Hamilton was successful in carrying through his financial programme, but a heavy price was paid. It was nothing less than the rise of an effective opposition, the eventual ruin of the Federalist party, and the sacrifice of whatever further plans Hamilton might have had. Had he been a better political tactician the situation might have been saved; had he understood the American political system it need never have arisen. The real basis for a Federalist party lay in the broad stratum of moderate property owners with moderate views, in the type of men who found in John Adams their pre-eminent representative. In winning extravagant praise from the greater capitalists Hamilton provided little to attract the interest and affections of the lesser men, and while his financial policy caught the big fish, the small businessmen and conservative farmers found less and less in Federalist policy to stir them into activity. Federalist history from 1790 is that of a process of erosion by which its original strength was eaten away. It began with the revolt of Madison in 1790 and an important phase ended when John Quincy Adams accepted office from Jefferson. The Federalists lost not only numbers but also ideas: the organization of the new government was a Federalist achievement which displayed great constructive ability; the implementation of Hamilton's programme was on a lower plane, being the acceptance of one man's ideas rather than a collective effort; after this the creative urge of the party was lost and the ministers whom John Adams inherited from Washington were, perhaps, as unimaginative and sterile a group as have ever commanded the destinies of America. The continued dependence of these ministers upon Hamilton after his retirement from the Treasury in January 1795, and his use of the influence thus acquired, reflects credit upon none of those concerned. It is a hard saying, but true, that Hamilton had sapped the vitality of those whom he had not alienated. Finally Hamilton found himself neatly outmanoeuvred in New York City by Aaron Burr, and could find no better way of spending the months preceding the vital election of 1800 than in intrigue against John Adams, the Federalist candidate. Meanwhile the Republicans had recruited fresh talent, had found in Democratic Republican societies a useful form of local organization, and had made great inroads upon the social groups which ought to have formed the solid basis for a conservative party. Not until 1802 did Hamilton realise the importance of organization in a democratic society, and propose a Christian Constitutional Society which would disseminate information, establish local leadership, and promote fit candidates for office. But by 1802 the Republicans were firmly in power and the Federalists (who ignored Hamilton's advice) were a diminishing band of able but uninspired leaders whose following remained firm only in certain localities.

To understand Hamilton's failure after the brilliance of his initial success it is necessary to know something of the motives and methods of his enemies. In 1787 R. H. Lee, one of the most distinguished opponents of the Constitution, wrote of "two very unprincipled parties in the United States—the two fires between which the honest and substantial people have long found themselves situated. One party is composed of little insurgents, men in debt, who want no law, and who want a share in the property of others; these are called levellers, Shayites etc. The other party is composed of a few, but more dangerous men, with their servile dependents; these avariciously grasp at all power and property; you may discover in all the actions of these men, an evident dislike of free and equal government, and they will go to work systematically to change, essentially, the forms of government in this country; these are called aristocrats, m . . . ites, etc. etc. Between these two parties is the weight of the community; the men of middling property, men not in debt on the one hand, and men, on the other, content with republican governments, and not aiming at immense fortunes, offices, and power." It was fear of the "few but more dangerous men" which was the mainspring of all opposition; economic and sectional interests might supplement the stream of opposition from time to time, but the one consistent aim was to eliminate the nascent aristocracy. Melancthon Smith, an able anti-Federalist, had predicted in the New York convention "that this government will fall into the hands of the few and the great. This will be a government of oppression." It was Hamilton's fate at every turn, to give the impression that he intended to establish a new aristocracy of "the few and the great". The eagerness with which his supporters in Congress pushed forward the funding programme and the Bank inevitably roused suspicions which might otherwise have been lulled. Smith of South Carolina and Wadsworth of Connecticut were reputed to have sent "money ships" south to purchase depreciated securities; Sedgewick of Massachusetts was reputed to be making a fortune out of the funds (though later he energetically denied having done so). Senator Robert Morris had a finger in every major speculation which was going forward. "It pretty clearly appears," wrote Madison in 1791, "in what proportion the public debt lies in the country, what sort of hands hold it, and by whom the people of the United States are to be governed. Of all the shameful circumstances of this business, it is among the greatest to see the members of the legislature who were most active in pushing this job [the Bank] openly grasping at its emoluments." Hamilton's own unguarded remarks about the British constitution, about monarchy, and about "influence" did much to increase these suspicions and create an atmosphere in which political argument was replaced by political invective which was finally directed even at the revered President himself.

For the future history of America one of the profound effects of these fears was to drive into alliance two very different trends of opinion. A principal theme of the Revolution had been the struggle for local autonomy, but it had also released the democratic drive for majority rule. The chief defenders of local autonomy were propertied conservatives; the democrats were lower middle class, artisans and western farmers. It was Hamilton's programme which united the two under a gentleman planter with strong local attachments and a philosophic respect for the small yeoman; the new opposition party was to be both Republican and Democratic. The forces driving the two together are illustrated in the career of James Madison. Unlike Hamilton, who never in his life ran for elective office, the future of Madison depended upon the voters of Orange County, Virginia. By the end of 1789 it was clear that his stock with the electorate was low; he had gained little prestige with Virginians for his labours in the Federal Convention and in Congress, and though he had recovered a little by his sponsorship of the Bill of Rights, he was opposed in the state by the powerful influence of Patrick Henry, and could look forward to certain defeat in the 1790 elections. During the interval between the First and Second Sessions he did what every American politician must do; he cultivated the grass roots. He returned to Congress, announced his opposition to Hamilton's programme, and was for ever afterwards politically unassailable in Virginia. There is no reason to doubt Madison's sincerity. Give and take between the ruling gentry and the electorate were in the best traditions of Virginian politics, and Madison could contrast his own reliance upon the people with the way in which Hamilton's rise to the surface of national life had been buoyed up by Washington's favour, by a fortunate marriage into a family of patrician New Yorkers, and by friendship with men of wealth and influence. One felt himself to be the model of a republican statesman and suspected the other of being a portent of aristocratic government. In Number X of the *Federalist* Madison had laid down the theoretical foundation for his action: "When a majority is included in a faction, the form of popular government . . . enables it to sacrifice to its ruling passion or interest, both the public good and the rights of other citizens." The Hamiltonians might not be a majority in the country but they were dominant in Congress; Madison in 1790 made the deduction that the form of popular government must now be employed not to facilitate but to check the "majority included in a faction" and to save "the public good and private rights" from sacrifice to "the ruling passion or interest".

Madison made the transition from Federalist to anti-Federalist with comparative ease because, as Hamilton once remarked, his attachment to the Union was always a matter of the head rather than the heart. He conceived the national government as a means of balancing the conflicting interests in the nation and not, like Hamilton, as the instrument of a wider nationalism; when the balance was shaken it must be restored by drawing upon reserves of power among the sovereign people; outnumbered in the House of Representatives, the opponents of Hamilton were driven to seek support in the country. Madison's proposal that all the original holders of public securities should receive the face value less the highest market value (which would go to the present holder) had a wide appeal and laid the basis for a nation-wide party among the democrats. The controversy over assumption rallied to the opposition adherents of local autonomy (save those of South Carolina who wished to see their state's large and unmanageable debt assumed). The struggle over the National Bank united both into a combination which just failed to raise Jefferson to the Presidency in 1796.

The significance of the Bank was that it alarmed the defenders of local autonomy as a national institution, the democrats as an instrument of control by the rich and the great, and all those who feared strong government as a demonstration that a power not expressly granted to the national government might nevertheless be exercised by it. Believing that the intention had been to create a strong central government, Hamilton argued that those sovereign rights which had been given to it ought to be limited only by words which admitted of no doubt in their interpretation; Jefferson, believing that the intention had been, or ought to have been, to create a government for limited purposes only, argued that where there might be doubt it ought to be resolved against the exercise of governmental authority. Yet it could also be argued that Hamilton showed a better grasp of the nature of constitutional limitations than Jefferson.

In 1784 he had written that "In the first formation of a government the society may multiply its precautions as much, and annexe as many conditions to the enjoyment of its rights, as it shall judge expedient; but when once it has adopted a Constitution, that Constitution must be the measure of its discretion in providing for its own safety, and in prescribing conditions upon which its privileges are to be enjoyed." He did not believe in 1790, any more than he had done six years previously, that constitutional limitations ought to be explained away by construction, but he did believe that new limitations ought not to be read into the Constitution by the exploitation of verbal refinements more appropriate to the legal defence of an accused person. One objection to Jefferson's strict construction was that it established what could only be an arbitrary distinction between the constitutional and the unconstitutional. The government could not carry on for a day without the exercise of some implied powers; there was for instance no mention in the Constitution of the great departments, of a fiscal service, or of the means by which commerce was to be regulated. A Treasury was clearly "necessary and proper"; where could the line be drawn between this and a National Bank which Jefferson claimed was neither? Hamilton claimed that he observed "a criterion of what is constitutional and of what is not so. This criterion is the end, to which the measure relates as a means." Certain possible means might be expressly forbidden by the Constitution, but Jefferson's attempt to introduce limitations resting merely upon opinion "would beget endless uncertainty and embarrassment". It may or may not have been wise to establish a National Bank, but a conviction of its unwisdom led Jefferson into a realm where even he would have found it difficult to tread; strict construction meant construction by any person or persons who felt themselves qualified to express an opinion; it was certainly not the automatic adjustment of conflicting interests which the eighteenth century expected from a Constitution. Nevertheless Jefferson's argument on the constitutionality of the Bank provided an essential ingredient of constitutional theory to the make-up of the new opposition.

As Republican strength increased in the House executive initiative was more and more limited. It was regained momentarily, and for limited purposes, when French Jacobinism, Citizen Genêt, and the Whisky rebels frightened moderate men back into the Federalist camp. Before the retirement of Washington in 1797 initiative had been lost by the executive branch, and the United States were embarking upon a period of congressional government. The Federalist measures in the last years of the century, particularly the Alien and Sedition Acts and the Judiciary Act, resulted from the initiative of a group in Congress, not from that of the executive. It was not opposition alone which contained the Hamiltonian initiative; the groups through which he attempted to influence Congress were unsuited for the major tasks of national policy which he envisaged. His most imaginative proposals, contained in the *Report on Manufactures*, were ignored by Congress, because the great ship-owners, import merchants and financiers who fought for public credit and the Bank were not prepared to exert themselves for a policy which would benefit immediately artisans and small master manufacturers.

Hamilton's policy might have been able to move forward, despite the opposition of enemies and the apathy of friends, had it not been for the impact of the French Revolution. As in England the Revolution made conservatives into reactionaries and critics into radicals; but the broad American electorate gave the radicals power which they were not to exert in England until late in the nineteenth century. The principles of the French Revolution fed directly into the democratic stream in American politics and provided an emotional stimulus which might have swamped all the checks and balances which conservatives had erected. The real service of Jefferson, Madison, and other Republican leaders, was to ride this storm and guide potential revolution into calmer channels. The Whisky Rebellion was an incident with its farcical elements—not least in the spectacle of Hamilton mobilizing the full military resources of the United States to discipline a handful of ignorant farmers—but it also revealed a dangerous chasm which was opening in American society. Hamilton was not the man to bridge this chasm, for he became convinced that "there are too many proofs that a considerable party among us is deeply infected with those horrid principles of Jacobinism which, proceeding from one excess to another, have made France a theatre of blood". He was incapable of believing that well-to-do sympathizers with the "Democratic-Republican" Societies could be actuated by anything but self-interest, and though not himself its instigator he contributed to that torrent of unmeaning invective which permanently lowered the tone of American political life. Plots, conspiracies, wickedness and atheism seemed to have become the common stuff of American politics and those eminently respectable gentlemen, Jefferson and Madison, were at the head of "a league . . . cemented between the apostles and disciples of irreligion and anarchy". The shadow of the un-American activity was cast upon the land when Hamilton wrote that "the man who . . . shall be the apologist of France, and the calumniator of his own government, is not an American. The choice for him lies between being deemed a fool, a madman, or a traitor."

The pity in this is that Hamilton's concern for peace was genuine and well-founded. America ought not to risk a war, but if war were forced upon her she must choose war with France rather than with England upon whom so much of her economy depended. Anticipating Washington's farewell address, which later he helped to phrase, he wrote that the motto of the United States ought to be "Peace and Trade with all nations; beyond our present arrangements, political connection with none". The economic arguments against war with England were strong, and while he himself was accused of Anglomania he could say that his opponents were dominated by an Anglophobia which had long ago parted company with reason. Jay's Treaty in 1794 was not everything which everyone could wish, but its weaknesses were not those to justify the vicious abuse with which it was received. The truth was that "the great and cardinal sin of the treaty in the eyes of its adversaries is, that it puts an end to controversy with Great Britain". Hamilton was the last person to sacrifice the interests of America, and in 1797 he was justified in saying, "The truth is . . . that we never did tolerate the aggressions of Great Britain; that we have steadily resisted them, and resisted them with success." Later, when France appeared to make a breach with Britain the price of peace, he was prepared for war against France in alliance with America's chief supplier, customer, banker, and the owner of a navy which could ruin the external interests and perhaps break the internal bonds of the Union. But Hamilton's arguments on foreign policy are so clouded with invective, so contemptuous of the motives of honourable men, that the genuine strength of his argument is usually lost from view, and so anxious is he to confute his opponents that one forgets his hopes for the nation.

It remains to ask what kind of nation Hamilton's nationalism envisaged. Accused by his enemies of every heresy in the Republican calendar, he was in fact a Revolution Whig. He believed that the Revolution had defended rights which were antecedently enjoyed, but was often vague as to whether these rights were natural rights or civil rights and was perhaps a little impatient with the distinction which eighteenth-century liberals attempted to draw between the two. In common with most of his contemporaries he believed that the right to acquire and enjoy property was the right which made the exercise of others possible, and that law which existed primarily to safeguard property could not but protect most other rights as well. Men enjoyed liberty when they lived under the equal protection of good laws; liberty was not the exclusive possession of republican governments but popular representation in these govern-

E

ments offered it a special guarantee. In 1784 he wrote that "a share in the sovereignty of the State, which is exercised by the citizens at large, in voting at elections, is one of the most important rights of the subject, and, in a republic, ought to stand foremost in the estimation of the law. It is that right by which we exist as a free people . . . The man that would attack that right, in whatever shape, is an enemy to Whiggism."

Contrary to a belief which is often disseminated Hamilton had no wish to reduce the power of the people, and at the end of his life he suggested that the direct election of Presidential electors should be made mandatory by a constitutional amendment, explaining that "it has ever appeared to me as a sound principle to let the federal government rest, as much as possible, on the shoulders of the people, and as little as possible on those of the state legislatures". On the other hand he was never quite sure how one could enjoy the virtues of popular representation without exposing oneself to the influence of popular vices. All governments had their special dangers and in popular governments they arose from the effects of "passion." "Nothing is more common than for a free people, in times of heat and violence, to gratify momentary passions, by letting into the government, principles and precedents which afterwards prove fatal to themselves." This danger was implicit in the nature of men who were "rather reasoning than reasonable animals, for the most part governed by the impulse of passion". In his time the most dangerous appeal to passion came from the fact that "Religion and government have both been stigmatized as abuses; as unwarrantable restraints upon the freedom of man; as causes of the corruption of his nature, intrinsically good; as sources of an artificial and false morality which tyrannically robs him of the enjoyment for which his passions fit him, and as clogs upon his progress to the perfection for which he was destined." Against this visionary creed the Revolution Whig believed that "Government is frequently and aptly classed under two descriptions—a government of Force and a government of Laws; the first is a definition of despotism— the last of liberty. But how can a government of laws exist when the laws are disrespected and disobeyed? Government supposes control. It is that Power by which individuals in society are kept from doing injury to each other, and are brought to co-operate in a common end. The instruments by which it must act are either the Authority of the laws or Force. If the first be destroyed, the last must be substituted; and where this becomes the ordinary instrument of government, there is an end to liberty."

The written constitution was the principal instrument of a government of laws; it must bind every man, even members of the supreme legislature. "Each house of Congress collectively," he wrote in 1795, "as well as the members of it separately, are under a constitutional obligation to observe the injunctions of a pre-existing law, and to give it effect. If they act otherwise, they infringe the Constitution, the theory of which knows in such a case, no discretion on their part. To resort to first principles for their justification, in assuming such a discretion, is to go out of the Constitution for an authority they cannot find in it; it is to usurp the original character of the people themselves; it is, in principle, to prostrate the government." Or, as he wrote in 1794, "If it were to be asked, What is the most sacred duty, and the greatest source of security in a republic? the answer would be, An inviolable respect for the Constitution and laws —the first growing out of the last. It is by this, in a great degree, that the rich and the powerful are to be restrained from enterprises against the common liberty—operated upon by the influence of a general sentiment, by their interest in the principle, and by the obstacles which the habit it produces erects against innovation and encroachment. It is by this, in a still greater degree, that caballers, intriguers, and demagogues are prevented from climbing on the shoulders of faction to the tempting seats of usurpation and tyranny."

There is nothing in all this which is particularly original. Adams, Madison, and even Jefferson said much the same things. It is indeed a typical expression of the virtues and the dangers which eighteenth-century Americans believed to exist in their republican government. It is, however, necessary to emphasize how close Hamilton does stand to the centre of the main stream of American political ideas; for all his appeals to the English model in constitutional machinery he is thoroughly American in his political creed, and if he did not believe that the American system was all that it ought to be, he still believed it potentially better than all others. There is no need to doubt the sincerity of a passage from Number IX of the *Federalist* in which he rebukes those who believed that republicanism inevitably led to despotism: "Happily for mankind, stupendous fabrics reared on the basis of liberty, which have flourished for ages, have in a few glorious instances refuted their gloomy sophisms. And I trust, America will be the broad and solid foundation of other edifices not less magnificent, which will be equally permanent monuments of their error."

While his political theory is informed largely by the typically Whiggish concept of checks and balances holding conflicting interests for ever in a state of equipoise, Hamilton had a far more vivid apprehension of a dynamic society than most of his contemporaries. The America which he envisaged was moving and growing; out of the almost limitless possibilities of the empty continent he tried to foresee the future of a people who would be free and prosperous. The dynamic element in his nationalism is phrased in economic not political terms; it was from the great wealth of American resources that must spring the future welfare of the people. Hamilton learnt a great deal more from Adam Smith than he rejected. He saw that the real wealth of the nation lay in native resources, native skill and native industry; he had little concern for the exotic and carrying trades in which so much American capital was engaged; he was convinced that the economic future of America lay in cultivation of the domestic rather than the foreign market. He would not, of course, abandon an export trade in agricultural produce, but he did believe that "there appear strong reasons to regard the foreign demand for that surplus as too uncertain a reliance, and to desire a substitute for it in an extensive domestic market". This may be compared with Adam Smith's observation that "The title of Mun's book, *England's Treasure in Foreign Trade*, became a fundamental maxim in the political economy, not of England only, but of all other commercial countries. The inland or home trade, the most important of all, the trade in which an equal capital affords the greatest revenue, and creates the greatest employment to the people of the country, was considered as subsidiary only to foreign trade." Hamilton took most of his basic assumptions about the nature of national wealth from Smith; he differs from him only in advocating different means to develop that wealth in some particular instances. It was the American environment which made Hamilton a protectionist: on the one hand the United States were struggling to free themselves from colonial independence, on the other they already comprised the greatest free trade area in the world; and the development of manufactures made necessary by the first would be made profitable by the second. Aware before most of his contemporaries that an industrial revolution was in the making in England, Hamilton wished to see one commenced in America before the century was out.

While he believed that government must set the course in economic affairs, he relied for the national development upon capitalist enterprise. He hoped that his credit policy and the protection given to manufacturers would provide sufficient inducement for large scale investment. His own Society for the Establishment of Useful Manufactures was intended as a model as well as a profitable pioneer enterprise. It was a gigantic development corporation, under private control but inviting subscriptions from state and national governments who would acquire thereby the right to enquire into its activities. The Charter obtained from New Jersey and drafted by Hamilton exempted from state taxation the property and employees of the society, permitted it to build roads and canals, operate lotteries, and to exercise exclusive municipal authority over an area of thirty-six square miles, as well as to carry out its primary function of establishing factories. The story of the Society and of its failure need not be recounted here; what is interesting is the insight which it gives into Hamilton's plans for development of the economy.

Inevitably Hamilton was accused of wishing to sacrifice agriculture to industry. "This idea of an opposition between these two interests," he wrote in the *Report on Manufactures*, "is the common error of the early periods of every country; but experience gradually dissipates it." He pointed out that "particular encouragements of particular manufactures may be of a nature to sacrifice the interests of landholders to those of manufacturers; but it is nevertheless a maxim, well established by experience, and generally acknowledged, that the aggregate prosperity of manufactures and the aggregate prosperity of agriculture are intimately connected". Though he did not feel that the condition of agriculture in America called for immediate legislative action, as did that of manufactures, he was distressed by its wasteful and primitive methods. In some notes prepared for Washington supporting a proposed Board of Agriculture he stressed the impoverishment of soil by unskilful tillage and the constant temptation to leave exhausted for virgin soils, and he also proposed a counterpart to the Society for the Encouragement of Manufactures which would foster "new inventions, discoveries, and improvements in agriculture". An agrarian revolution would have been as much a part of the Hamiltonian new era as an industrial revolution.

No imaginative statesmen of the period could fail to speculate upon the future of the American West. Hamilton assumed that the main burden of western development would be carried by capitalist enterprise. The men with whom he associated, from the irreproachable Washington to the astute Robert Morris and the disreputable Duer, were all interested in land speculation, and there was no particular reason to regard the interest of the land companies as divorced from that of the nation. At the same time Hamilton was anxious to use national ownership of the public domain as a means of exercising control over western development. The danger as he saw it was that cheap land would drain away men, capital and skill from the east where they were required for urgent tasks of development. "A dislocation of our population" caused by the impoverishment of eastern land "promotes neither the strength, the opulence, nor the happiness of our country." His views on settlement are similar to those which Gibbon Wakefield, the English theorist of colonial development, was to put forward in later years: concentration of population and of effort was to be obtained where it was most needed by creating a stiff but not insuperable obstacle to the acquisition of public lands. There would be time enough to develop the West when strength, opulence and happiness were securely based in the East. His views were written into the Land Act of 1796 which fixed the price at $2.00 an acre and the minimum sale at 640 acres. Unlike some Easterners Hamilton was never, however, in any doubt of the future value of the West to the United States, and in 1803 he parted company with some Federalists to advocate with vigour the acquisition of Louisiana.

Hamilton was acutely aware that American development depended in large measure upon being able to draw off from Europe, and especially from England, manpower, techniques, and capital. He hoped that "as soon as foreign artists shall be made sensible that the state of things here affords a moral certainty of employment and encouragement, competent numbers of European workmen will transplant themselves . . .

How, indeed, can it otherwise happen, considering the various and powerful inducements which the situation of this country offers— addressing themselves to so many strong passions and feelings, to so many general and particular interests." America must borrow from Europe the new industrial techniques such as the cotton mill to which "is to be attributed, essentially, the immense progress which has been so suddenly made in Great Britain, in the various fabrics of cotton". Finally America must offer inducements to foreign capital for it was evident that "in a country situated like the United States, with an infinite fund of resources yet to be unfolded, every farthing of foreign capital which is laid out in internal meliorations, and in industrial establishments, of a permanent nature, is a precious acquisition". It can be seen that Hamilton's nationalism was far removed from the foolish nativism which has sometimes animated latter-day patriots.

The real claim of Hamilton to greatness lies in this comprehensive grasp of the country's future. Not of a future which was inevitable, but of a future which could be directed by a judicious co-operation between government and private enterprise. It is easy to interpret every aspect of Hamilton's policy as part of a grand design to enrich a capitalist class at the expense of the people, but such a simplified view displays neither justice to the man nor an understanding of his problems. Politically the great desideratum was to attach to the national government enough powerful interests to make it effective; this rests upon three sensible assumptions, that the union could not be preserved without strong central government, that government could not be strong unless people wished it to be so, and that a material stake in good government was more valuable than vague well-wishing. Economically the great hope for America was to use her magnificent opportunities as an incitement for enterprise in which all could join. Rich men furnished with ability must lead the way, but the goal is the prosperity of a nation and the welfare of its people, not the enrichment of a class. No statements of this kind are likely to convince those who believe that any policy must serve a class or serve nothing, but they do seem to describe accurately what Hamilton thought he was doing. "It is a truth, as important as it is agreeable, and one to which it is not easy to imagine exceptions, that everything tending to establish substantial and permanent order in the affairs of a country, to increase the total mass of industry and opulence, is ultimately beneficial to every part of it." This sentence from the *Report on Manufactures* may well be taken as an epitome of Hamilton's creed; it is a creed which has carried the United States forward to world power and to a standard of life never before dreamed of in the history of the world.

THOMAS JEFFERSON AND THE
JEFFERSONIAN IDEA

By Esmond Wright

★

Mr Jefferson was a tall strait-bodied man as ever you see, right square-shouldered: nary man in this town walked so straight as my old master: neat a built man as ever was seen in Vaginny, I reckon or any place—a straight-up man: long face, high nose . . .

Old master was never seen to come out before breakfast—about 8 o'clock. If it was warm he wouldn't ride out till evening: studied upstairs till bell rang for dinner. When writing he had a copyin machine: while he was a-writin he would'nt suffer nobody to come in his room: he had a dumb-waiter: When he wanted anything he had nothing to do but turn a crank and the dumb-waiter would bring him water or fruit on a plate or anything he wanted. Old master had abundance of books: sometimes would have twenty of 'em down on the floor at once: read first one, then tother. Isaac has often wondered how old master came to have such a mighty head: read so many of them books: and when they go to him to ax him anything, he go right straight to the book and tell you all about it. He talked French and Italian . . .

Mr Jefferson always singing when ridin or walkin: hardly see him anywhar out doors but what he was a-singin: had a fine clear voice, sung minnits [minuets] and sich: fiddled in the parlor. Old master very kind to servants . . .

SUCH was the portrait left by Isaac, his slave, of Thomas Jefferson, key figure of the first generation of Americans, the man of reason and the man of paradoxes. Even in his own day, he was everything to all men: seen with condescension, by Sir Augustus Foster; with panic, by Timothy Dwight of Yale ["Shall our sons become the disciples of Voltaire, and the dragoons of Marat; or our daughters the concubines of the Illuminati?"]; with a flutter of excitement, by Margaret Bayard Smith ["And is this", said I, "the violent democrat, the vulgar demagogue, the bold atheist and profligate man I have so often heard denounced by the federalists? . . . I felt my cheeks burn and my heart throb, and not a word more could I speak while he remained."]. The coolest-minded of the Revolutionary generation seemed to generate controversy then, as he has done since; the least heroic of leaders has proved the most seminal of minds, the most contradictory of Founding Fathers has been the most invoked.

By birth, Jefferson was both aristocrat and frontiersman. His mother

61

was a Randolph—one of the oldest and most important families in a state where kinship counted. Through her, Jefferson was cousin to the Randolphs of Tuckahoe, one of whom presided over the Revolutionary Congress, another of whom stayed—and died—loyal to his King. His father, Peter Jefferson, less well-born but with literary tastes, was a land surveyor with substantial property in Albemarle County, in the foot-hills of the Blue Ridge—and with greater impact than had the mother on the son. Thomas Jefferson was given a good education: not the best, the education at schools in England that was the preserve of the wealthiest in Virginia, but a good training in philosophy and law at the little College of William and Mary in Williamsburg, the second oldest in the thirteen colonies. Williamsburg, the colonial capital, was a social as well as a political centre, and Jefferson was taught not only by William Small of Aberdeen (in philosophy) and George Wythe (in law) but by the social graces that he learnt from Governor Fauquier. The frontiersman was much at ease, if not with the "fair Belinda" of the Williamsburg dances, at least with the *parties quarrées* of a royal Governor.

The habits he acquired were scholarly. He became a linguist, familiar with French, Italian, Dutch, Spanish and German; he was interested later in Anglo-Saxon and in the vocabulary of the Indians as he came to see in philology an index to the problem of the origin of man. The advice on reading that he gave to his young friend Bernard Moore indicates something of his power of concentration. The student, he argued, should divide his time: from rising until eight in the morning, physical studies; from eight to twelve, read law; from twelve to one, read politics; in the afternoon, read history; from dark to bedtime, belles lettres, criticism, rhetoric and oratory.

Yet even when he was studying and practising law—in the years before the Revolution—his interests were catholic, and in the best sense amateur. When he married the widow Mrs Skelton on New Year's Day 1772, the home to which he took her was one he was building himself, to his own design atop his little mountain in Albemarle. In its grace and proportion, Monticello remains a lovely example of Palladian Georgian. Jefferson's interest in architecture—awakened, apparently, by Dr John Morgan on a visit to Philadelphia in 1766 to secure inoculation against smallpox—remained with him for life. During his Ambassadorship to France (1784-89) he filled his travel notebooks with observations and measurements of houses and public buildings in France, Italy, Germany and Holland—and with designs for home furniture and decoration, with the details of landscape gardening, and even with recipes for macaroni. The great interest of his last years was the building of the University of Virginia, and he could follow the progress of the erection of its serpentine walls and its beautiful pavilions by telescope from his mountain top. He filled his home with books, as Isaac testifies; his library was sold, to become the nucleus of the Library of Congress after the capital was burnt by the British in 1814. Equally impressive were his notebooks, immaculately filed and catalogued. From 1783 until his death forty-three years later he kept an "Epistolary Record" in which he recorded in parallel columns virtually every letter that he wrote or received. It runs to 656 pages. His correspondence is estimated to include more than fifty thousand separate items.

Nor was Jefferson a man of books only: he was an ingenious inventor of gadgets and they still abound at Monticello: a swivel chair, a bed that could be hoisted to the ceiling, a polygraph device for copying his letters; there were designs for a mouldboard plough, for a leather buggy top, for a hemp-beater. The target was not pedantry but useful knowledge. And there was taste too: a taste for music, for colour and texture, and a palate for wine; a cellar that astonished Daniel Webster; and a French chef who persuaded him to feed his guests on something other than his "native victuals", as Patrick Henry called them, of hog, hoe-cake and hominy grits.

This does not exhaust the catalogue: experimental farmer, student of the classics and of the Bible, naturalist, horticulturist and palaeontologist, surveyor and builder, lawyer and administrator, Jefferson in fact was one of the last of the universal men, in the last century that could produce them. There is a Renaissance quality, an emphasis on the complete man, on the need for physical as well as mental development, on the value of literary learning and of the practical wisdom of the classics. His was not only a pre-industrial, but also a pre-specialist age.

The many-sidedness, however impressive, carried political liabilities, as it always does. To his Federalist opponents, especially their editors, he was not a Leonardo but a Devil, Tom the Magician, Tom Conundrum. And they found an even more piquant item against his reputation; her name was Sally Hemings, "mighty near white and very handsome", said Isaac, and one of his own slaves. Historians, as well as contemporaries, have been bewildered by his paradoxes. Henry Adams, who should have been able to sympathize with him, but was in fact a hostile witness, wrote of him as "a martyr to the disease of omniscience". With all his gifts for words and style—and perhaps his most decisive contribution to the beginnings of the Revolution was his "pen-manship"—he was shy in speech. He discontinued the practice of giving his Report to Congress in person; at his Inaugural in 1801 he walked from Conrad's boarding house to the still unfinished Capitol to take the oath (Washington had used a coach-and-six in 1789); he abolished the Presidential levee and the rule of precedence at receptions—to the discomfort of visiting British diplomats, and the greater discomfort of their wives. There was little physical magnetism, little of that surging, almost tangible, vitality that marked Hamilton. There was a sensitiveness that some called womanish, and others feline—the wild despair when his wife died, the timidity as Governor of Virginia during the Revolutionary War.

The cast of mind was speculative—but it was not unambitious. There is preserved in the University of Virginia Library Jefferson's personal scrap-book, indicating a human pre-occupation with his own success. Monticello was remote and on the frontier; in 1801 in the hundred miles between it and Washington eight rivers had to be crossed, and five of them had neither bridges nor boats. Philadelphia was still more distant, a journey of some seven to ten days. Yet Monticello was no ivory tower. The shy man among his books and gadgets was a skilled party organizer, as gifted in intrigue as any more orthodox politician, the friend, for a time, of Genêt, the abettor of editor Freneau, the colleague of Madison; and he was thought of by his Federalist opponents with a certain uneasy fear. He rarely intervened in controversy himself, and when attacked he remained maddeningly aloof—but not unhurt. His main instrument was correspondence, but he could hide his political manoeuvres equally dexterously behind a "botanizing excursion" up the Hudson in 1791, or by doing deals with Hamilton himself, or by acting as adviser to Layafette and his group of would-be liberal reformers in Paris in 1789. The fondness for expediency and at times for the role of the trimmer lay deep in the man's character, the sophistication was rooted in sophistry.

That sophistication was marred by an occasional indiscretion—the reference for instance to "the Samsons in the field and Solomons in the council" who "had had their heads shorn by the harlot England", which he claimed was a reference to the Cincinnati but which Washington took personally; and the sparkling but unfortunate epigrams—"The tree of liberty must be refreshed from time to time with the blood of patriots and tyrants, it is its natural manure." "It does me no injury for my neighbour to say there are twenty gods, or no god. It neither picks my pocket, nor breaks my leg." To use the language of John Adams, who lacked his finesse, Washington's was a character of Convention, but in Jefferson there was something of the Chameleon. The fascination of Jefferson recalls that of Milton and of Michelangelo, of Locke and Burke, of Lamartine and Hugo: the mixture of artist and man of affairs, the tension between political philosopher and political tactician, the search for truth alongside the lie in the cave.

The simple solutions to the puzzle are the explanations offered by orthodox Jeffersonians—that foreign affairs intruded (Jefferson's Presidency co-incided, says Herbert Agar, "with the years from Marengo to Wagram"); or by practical politicians—that once in power an Opposition must accept much of what has gone before as an obligation to ensure continuous and orderly government. Jefferson's was a long life in an age of revolutions, and he learnt to be pliable. "Forty years experience in government" he said, "is worth a century of book-reading." By 1816 he was ready to accept that "moderate imperfections had better be borne with". These explanations certainly go part of the way. Yet in 1800 the die was not cast; a social Revolution was still possible in a society in flux, with a Constitution widely debated and challenged, and with ten amendments added as soon as it was declared fundamental law. Why then the failure to act? Was it timidity, as in 1781, and, as it seemed again, in 1805-6, when he was aware of Burr's intrigues in the West, but was slow to act? Was it that the pre-eminent Revolutionary writer, author of *A Summary View of the Rights of British America* (1774), of the Declaration of Independence of 1776, of the Virginia Statute for Religious Freedom, of the Ordinance of 1784, of the Bill of Rights and of the Kentucky Resolutions, was at ease in his study but ineffective as executive and organizer? Was it his quietness, his faith in peace ("Peace is our passion"), his non-belligerence? Yet he founded West Point, ruled Congress with a firm hand for many of his years as President, went to war with the Barbary corsairs in North Africa, purchased Louisiana without any constitutional "right" to do so, and prepared the way both for the annexation of West Florida and for the War of 1812. Was it, as later with Wilson and F. D. Roosevelt, that the quest for success, and the adulation that followed its attainment, produced not only inconsistency but began a subtle destruction of the original ideals? Or was it that, in fact, by 1800 the Revolution had been accomplished?

The quest for party origins and for continuity in American history, and the effort to associate with one or other political party the hallowed names of the Founding Fathers, have tended to hide the assumptions that were shared by all the native leaders of the Revolutionary generation, and the sharpness of the break that came with their deaths and as a result of the War of 1812. To read Jefferson's First Inaugural (March 4, 1801) is to realize the continuity of his policy with Washington's—and with Adams's. His phrase, "We are all Republicans, we are all Federalists", was more than a form of words. "We have", he said, "called by different names brethren of the same principle." His declaration in the address—expressed, it is true, with an optimism neither Washington's nor Adams's temperament would have allowed them to share—was nevertheless a declaration that Federalists could hardly have challenged:

Let us, then, with courage and confidence pursue our own Federal and Republican principles, our attachment to union and representative government. Kindly separated by nature and a wide ocean from the exterminating havoc of one quarter of the globe; too high-minded to endure the degradations of the others; possessing a chosen country, with room enough for our descendants to the thousandth and thousandth generation; entertaining a due sense of our equal right to the use of our own faculties, to the acquisitions of our own industry, to honor and confidence from our fellow-citizens, resulting not from birth, but from our actions and their sense of them; enlightened by a benign religion, professed, indeed, and practiced in various forms, yet all of them inculcating honesty, truth, temperance, gratitude, and the love of man; acknowledging and adoring an overruling Providence, which by all its dispensations proves that it delights in the happiness of man here and his greater happiness hereafter—with all these blessings, what more is necessary to make us a happy and a prosperous people? Still one thing more, fellow-citizens—a wise and frugal Government, which shall restrain men from injuring one another, shall leave them otherwise free to regulate their own pursuits of industry and improvement, and shall not take from the mouth of labour the bread it has earned. This is the sum of good government, and this is necessary to close the circle of our felicities.

Jeffersonians and Federalists shared a common front against monarchy, against the dangers of an Established Church and against the threat of foreign intervention in American domestic affairs. Jefferson had dropped Genêt seven years before when he found him to be the advocate of a French rather than an American policy. No more than Adams did Jefferson trust financiers, traders or industrialists; when he spoke of the moral worth and the intelligence of "the people", he too meant only the farming element. He did as President abolish the hated excise taxes and he tried hard to discipline the federal judiciary, but the rest of the Federalist structure was left alone. It was Jefferson's own party, to Adams's displeasure and Federalist irony, that re-established the National Bank and passed the first protective tariffs. No attempt was made to curb the abuses consequent on speculation in public lands—the Louisiana Purchase in fact encouraged them further. The critic of Hamilton's loose construction of the Constitution here acted with decision himself, doubling the area of the United States without consulting Congress—but acquiring a vast Empire peaceably, and without taxation. Limitations on the suffrage continued. Four years later, in his Second Inaugural, Jefferson listed, among the obligations resting on a government, the maintenance of "that state of property, equal or unequal, which results to every man from his own industry or that of his fathers".

Jefferson, it is true, offered apologies for the mildness of the changes. "It mortifies me", he wrote to Dupont de Nemours, "to be strengthening principles which I deem radically vicious, but this vice is entailed on us by the first error . . . What is practicable must often control what is pure theory." But what he deplored here was the Hamiltonian rather than the Federalist system—"the contracted, English, half-lettered ideas of Hamilton". To Jefferson, as to many Federalists, it was Hamilton who was exotic, the outsider, as his feud with Adams indicated. The differences between the two camps concerned the extent to which the new national government should take precedence over the state governments, and the extent to which the people could be trusted to govern themselves. As Jefferson put it, again in 1800, "Sometimes it is said that man can not be trusted with the government of himself. Can he then be trusted with the government of others? Or have we found angels in the form of kings to govern him? Let history answer this question."

The difference was less of principle than of mood and emphasis. Where Washington, Hamilton and Adams were gloomy, the Jeffersonians were optimistic—about the American present and future, about its government and its resources. When Adams looked to history, Jefferson deplored "the Gothic idea" of looking backwards rather than forwards "for the improvement of the human mind". "I steer my bark with Hope in the head", he wrote in 1816, "leaving Fear astern."

The first generation in American history, then, was not so much Revolutionary as optimistic; less rationalist than empiricist; concerned rather with problems of moral than of political philosophy; more nationalist and isolationist than internationalist or ideologic; and surprisingly united in the experiment it undertook. To it, as to Franklin, the ground for hope was the chance that opened out in America for a new world to produce "new men". Jefferson has none of the simplicity that is the appealing trait—and symbolic richness—of Washington, little of Hamilton's directness, none of Adams's genial self-importance, none of the Plain Man attributes—so carefully contrived—of Franklin. But of all the "new men" he remains the most significant figure.

The complexity of Jefferson's character stands in the way of any simple statement of his creed. Nor can that creed be understood except in the setting of its own time. Neither a sense of indebtedness to "Jeffersonian liberalism" nor a stress on the historical interpretations of the social contract idea is a serviceable guide. Jefferson makes little use of the word "contract". For Jefferson's primary interest was in Nature, not in History. His empiricism was neither liberalism nor conservatism but practicality. Study of the law had not made Jefferson an admirer of the past, as it had Blackstone and John Adams; he fought against the tyranny of the dead over the living, he denied completely Burke's political view of the social contract, he stood for the sovereignty of the present.

No society can make a perpetual constitution, or even a perpetual law. The earth belongs always to the living generation: they may manage it, then, and what proceeds from it, as they please, during their usufruct. They are masters too of their own persons, and consequently may govern them as they please. But persons and property make the sum of the objects of government. The constitution and the laws of their predecessors are extinguished then, in their natural course, with those whose will gave them being . . . If it be enforced longer, it is an act of force, and not of right.

The past had little to teach. Classicist though he was, Jefferson had small respect for Plato with his "foggy brain" or "the whimsies, the puerilities and unintelligible jargon" of *The Republic*, and little more for Aristotle. "So different was the style of society then, and with those people, from what it is now and with us, that I think little edification can be obtained from their writings on the subject of government." John Adams agreed; all he had ever learned from Plato, he said, was where Franklin had acquired some of his ideas, and how to cure hiccups.

At one point, indeed, Jefferson carefully worked out the length of a political generation and calculated from Buffon's mortality tables that it lasted eighteen years and eight months; and he concluded that laws, since most of their framers would be dead, could not be binding for longer than this. Property and privileges, hereditary offices and, not least, public debts were not binding either. Constitutions were the practical expressions of the idea of consent—but, in this view, they were short-lived indeed. From the revolutionary and anarchic implications of this idea— one infinitely more destructive than the social contract theory—Jefferson was saved by the limited view he took of government and the sharp distinction he drew between it and society.

Government was but an institutional framework, and should be changed *"pari passu* with the progress of science". Though constitutions were "chains to bind rulers", as he described them in the Kentucky Resolutions of 1798, they should not themselves be too well forged, and should not be regarded as eternally binding—or they would become themselves fetters on freedom. Nor, in his view, ought governments to touch the biological core of society; they were not, in fact, primary, and politicians could not do a great deal. The tone of his "Revolution" of 1800 was well expressed in a letter to his friend Walter Jones a few days after the First Inaugural:

When we reflect how difficult it is to move or inflect the great machine of society, how impossible to advance the notions of a whole people suddenly to ideal right, we see the wisdom of Solon's remark, that no more good can be attempted than the nation can bear, and that all will be chiefly to reform the waste of public money, and thus drive away the vultures who prey upon it, and improve some little on old routines. Some new fences for securing Constitutional rights may, with the aid of a good legislature, perhaps be attainable.

We do not seem far away here from Burke's "disposition to preserve and capacity to improve".

This mildness, with its conservative suggestions of administrative rather than legislative or social reform, its suggestions even of a mere tinkering, indicates the highly negative view Jefferson took of the state, and indeed of freedom. His political philosophy is easier to describe by negations than by credos. Man was too varied, natural life too rich, to be reduced to a plan or a pattern, least of all a plan drawn up by governments. Locke had described government as a "fiduciary power to act for certain ends". Certain obstacles to freedom, like aristocratic land laws and human slavery, should be overthrown by positive action by governments. But in essence the state was not itself positive or social or beneficent, and it must be kept in its place, its powers divided among component parts. It was no more than a contrived and controllable piece of mechanics. "That government is best which governs least" is the classic Jeffersonian sentence. Once a strong government was overthrown or curbed, Nature could again be left to herself. Jefferson's real Revolution was accomplished in 1776; the rest was natural growth and fulfilment.

This negative view of freedom was very much the view not only of Jefferson but of the eighteenth century. Jefferson shared to the full the eighteenth-century belief that, in Leslie Stephen's phrase, the Universe was a machine, and God the mechanic—or, to Jefferson, the Supreme Workman. This view has been best expressed perhaps by Addison in his famous Ode:

> The spacious firmament on high
> With all the blue ethereal sky
> And spangled heav'ns, a shining frame,
> Their great original proclaim:
> Th' unwearied sun, from day to day,
> Does his creator's power display,
> And publishes to every land
> The work of an almighty hand . . .
>
> What though, in solemn silence, all
> Move round the dark terrestrial ball?
> What tho' nor real voice nor sound
> Amid their radiant orbs be found?
> In reason's ear they all rejoice,
> And utter forth a glorious voice,
> For ever singing, as they shine,
> "The hand that made us is divine."

The universe was no longer a mystery to be feared, propitiated and worshipped, but a vast machine, obeying certain laws, as falling bodies obeyed the law of gravity.

> All are but parts of one stupendous whole,
> Whose body Nature is, and God the soul.

This view was Newtonian, and it substituted a natural for a supernatural explanation of phenomena. These phenomena could be understood because reason could comprehend their laws, just as it could comprehend the natural laws of human society and of morality. Nature then was materialist, subject to observation and to experiment and, in some measure, to logical analysis; it was Cartesian as well as Newtonian. Christianity itself became "reasonable". Experience and reflection, said Locke, were the only sources of human knowledge; man was a product of education and of his own sense-experience, and of what he made of both; and in all ages and in all climes, he was very much the same. All men were therefore equal, in a state of nature, all were endowed with reason and all were concerned to seek their own happiness. All men had certain rights, of which life, liberty and property were minimal, fundamental and universal. Government protects these rights, but it is not the source of them. "There are also certain fences which experience has proved particularly efficacious against wrong . . . freedom of religion, trial by jury, habeas corpus laws, free presses."

The fascination of Jefferson rests in the interpretation he put upon these postulates in a new and challenging—and delightfully experimental —setting. If there was indeed a laboratory devised by the Supreme Workman for the testing of these assumptions, the New World seemed to be the place. Men everywhere were the same, a single species, and that they were created in a common mould implied equality; the equality was biological, not Christian or "moral". But Man was also diverse and adaptable and in some degree a product of, though not a "creature" of, environment: his power to cope with the natural world around him was the test of his moral value. Man was the best endowed of all animal creation, and responsive to environment. The Jeffersonians made much of Linnaeus' idea, *varians cultura, loco.* Hence the interest in the primitive tribes, the flora and fauna, mammoths and reptiles of the *Notes on Virginia*; hence the long controversy with Buffon, the claim that American wild life was as large as that in the Old World, and not an "inferior" species. And the understanding of this natural world was arrived at by observation and the senses, not by theory or by reason. "When once we quit the basis of sensation", he wrote to John Adams, "all is in the wind. To talk of *immaterial* existences, is to talk of *nothings.*" Hence the notebooks, the experiments, the endless correspondence over the facts of the physical universe, the pervasive interest in the land and its features, an almost pantheistic nationalism. "A patient pursuit of facts, and cautious combination and comparison of them, is the drudgery by which man is subjected to his Maker, if he wishes to attain sure knowledge."

The greatest heresy in the study of Jefferson is to regard him as "utopian" or "moral" or "metaphysical"; Henry Adams is wide of the mark in describing him as "a theorist, prepared to risk the fate of mankind on the chance of reasoning far from certain in its details". As much as Burke, Jefferson deplored "abstractions and universals"; he lived in the world of things, and found them fascinating. What he sought was the opportunity to test his own tentative ideas by the facts, especially the new ones of a New World. Paine's epigram was appropriate, "A fact is superior to reasoning."

This is not to say that man was merely another animal. Among his attributes was a moral sense, but even this was not a matter of reasoning.

The moral sense (he wrote to Peter Carr), is as much a part of man as his leg or arm. It is given to all human beings in a stronger or weaker degree . . . It may be strengthened by exercise, as may any particular limb of the body . . . State a moral case to a ploughman and a professor. The former will decide it as well, and often better than the latter, because he has not been led astray by artificial rules.

The rules Jefferson devised were highly practical, a Franklinian collection of adages rather than guesses at moral absolutes; in morality as in religion his concern was with human behaviour, not with a rounded and consistent "intellectual" system. And since action mattered more than thought, morality, not theology, was the essence of religion. It was the false doctrine that mind and body were separate substances that was responsible for so much religious superstition. "Immaterialism" or "masked atheism", Jefferson called it—"Jesus taught nothing of it."

From the emphasis on Nature, on social justice and on good behaviour emerged what is for us one of the liabilities of the Jeffersonian creed: its emphasis on the rural life. "The general desire of men to live by their heads rather than by their hands, and the strong allurements of great cities to those who have any turn for dissipation, threaten to make them here, as in Europe, the sinks of voluntary misery." Jefferson had not seen a town until he was eighteen; his own thoughts, his system of ideas and his hopes for the new republic were all bound up with land, and the farmers who worked it. "Those who labor in the earth are the chosen people of God, if ever he had a chosen people. Corruption of morals in the mass of cultivators is a phenomenon of which no age nor nation has furnished an example."

This idea was given a political emphasis in the course of the struggle with the Federalists—"farmers . . . are the true representatives of the great American interest, and are alone to be relied on for expressing the proper American sentiments", "Let our workshops remain in Europe." He believed that American governments would "remain virtuous for many centuries, as long as they remain chiefly agricultural; and this will be as long as there shall be vacant lands in any part of America. When they get piled upon one another in large cities, as in Europe, they will become corrupt as in Europe." Like Madison, with a reading drawn from the classics and a percipience about the political pressures that concentrated urban groups can exercise, Jefferson saw in city mobs "the panders of vice and the instruments by which the liberties of a country are generally overturned". Throughout all he wrote and did was his love of the woods and the hills and his own little mountain-top in Virginia— preferable to the mud and bustle of Washington, infinitely preferable to Europe.

Rationalist, naturalist and empiricist, Jefferson saw in a rural America a great testing ground of man's capacity for freedom, where, isolated from the towns, the classes and the conflicts of Europe, a new society could be built.

What then, it might be asked, of man's rights? Surely Jefferson was the great advocate of natural rights? The Declaration of Independence invoked "The Laws of Nature and of Nature's God", and its beginning is an effective if hackneyed summary of the political aspects of the Jeffersonian creed:

We hold these truths to be self-evident, that all men are created equal, that they are endowed by their Creator with certain unalienable rights, that among these are life, liberty and the pursuit of happiness, that to secure

F

these rights governments are instituted among men, deriving their just powers from the consent of the governed, that whenever any form of government becomes destructive of these ends, it is the right of the people to alter or to abolish it . . .

To Jefferson as to Locke there were natural rights obtaining for all men in all societies, quite apart from the civil rights that varied from society to society. But as with the terms "Nature" and "Law" so with "rights", there has come a twist of meaning since Jefferson wrote. While on the one hand the intellectual basis of the legal theory of natural rights has been undermined by historical and philosophical criticism, the distinction between natural rights and positive rights is popularly ignored. Claims are now made as "rights" that include the earning of a livelihood, and compensation for dismissal from it, the provision of food and shelter, medical attention, education, recreation and fourteen days holiday with pay each year. (Cf. Article 24 of the Universal Declaration of Human Rights of 1948.)

To the eighteenth century natural rights were certainly wide—indeed that century would have accepted their universality. But it would not, nor would Jefferson, have elaborated and itemised them in this way, until they trespass on the civil and legal rights—and varied political practices —of different societies. Rights today, apart from being invoked all too loosely and too readily, have become indistinguishable from utopian ideals. But the rights appealed to in the Revolution of 1688 in Britain or of 1776 in America were not ideals and were moral rather than legal: the rebellions began because Americans in 1776, like Englishmen in 1688, believed that the King was depriving them of the minimal conditions of tolerable living. Nor was the protest of 1688 or that of 1776 "democratic", for "democracy" is a word best avoided in discussions of the seventeenth and eighteenth century. The protest against James II by Locke and against George III by Jefferson was a claim for liberty, but not a claim for votes. The absence of a vote was not thought of as a constraint: the will of the majority was, said Jefferson, a natural law, but it was also a practical device to prevent abuses—because the majority, it was thought (naively), was too large to bribe.

"Rights" have been transformed, and understanding of what they meant to the eighteenth century has been hindered, by the modern idea of political power resting in the mass of the people. Until the nineteenth century political power—which mattered less than today, except at moments of crisis, and had much less impact on society—was the monopoly of a few, and against the abuse of that power barriers were erected. There were certain areas in which power could not be exercised arbitrarily or tyrannically, areas protected by "rights". But these areas were few, and the rights, though "universal", were also few. When the majority will itself becomes the wielder of political power, "rights" become totally different claims from those the eighteenth century was making.

Some light is thrown on Jefferson's more precise claims by recalling the words of his original draft for the Declaration:

We hold these truths to be sacred and undeniable; that all men are created equal and independent, that from that equal creation they derive rights inherent and inalienable, among which are the preservation of life, and liberty, and the pursuit of happiness . . .

And even this had been much discussed, and the ambiguous "pursuit of happiness" had replaced "property", a more orthodox eighteenth-century right. There has been much unnecessary discussion of the origins of the Declaration, how far it was derived from Locke, how far from French sources. It is clear that Jefferson intended it "to be an expression of the American mind". Every one of Jefferson's political ideas was formulated before he saw the shores of France in 1784. The ideas were the result of a long evolution, and were certainly more Anglo-Saxon than French in character, but they were designed to meet a current American need. For this reason Jefferson omitted some subtleties, especially the distinction between natural and civil rights. Of the latter, property was the most obvious—since laws for the acquisition and holding of property demand, if they are to be effective, the guarantees of society. But—almost as much as Hamilton, and certainly as much as Locke—Jefferson regarded property as a right, "founded in our natural wants", and confined his wielders of political power to those with some stake in society. He would have found the phrase "a property-owning democracy" highly acceptable, though it would have suggested to him farmers not urban artisans or *rentiers*.

Behind the shelter of these rights, then, men might live in freedom, and freedom was "a thing to use"; Reason again was close to Utility, and utility was "the social test of virtue". In an account of a conversation with Jefferson on his little mountain-top in 1817, the English traveller Lieutenant Francis Hall of the 14th Light Dragoons has some revealing comments:

He seemed to consider much of the freedom and happiness of America to arise from local circumstances: "Our population", he observed, "has an elasticity, by which it would fly off from oppressive taxation" . . . Their ingenuity in mechanical inventions, agricultural improvements, and that mass of general information to be found among Americans of all ranks and conditions, he ascribed to that ease of circumstances, which afforded them leisure to cultivate their minds, after the cultivation of their lands was completed . . . Another cause, Mr Jefferson observed, might be discovered in the many court and county meetings, which brought men frequently together on public business, and thus gave them habits, both of thinking and of expressing their thoughts on subjects, which in other countries are confined to the consideration of the privileged few.

What he sought even more than political freedom was freedom of the mind, and particularly freedom of opinion in religious matters. His

Statute of Virginia for Religious Freedom, of 1786—of which he was as proud as of the Declaration of Independence—was more than usually eloquent:

> Well aware that the opinions and beliefs of men depend not on their own will, but follow involuntarily the evidence proposed to their minds; that Almighty God hath created the mind free, and manifested his will that free it shall remain by making it altogether insusceptible of restraint;
>   —that our civil rights have no dependence on our religious opinions any more than our opinions in physics or geometry . . .
>   —that the opinions of men are not the subject of civil government nor under its jurisdiction; . . .
>   —and finally that truth is great and will prevail if she is left to herself; that she is the proper and sufficient antagonist to error, and has nothing to fear from the conflict unless by human interposition disarmed of her natural weapons, free argument and debate; errors ceasing to be dangerous when it is permitted freely to contradict them . . . ''

All men, the Assembly enacted, were free to profess, "and by argument to maintain" their opinion in religious matters, "and the same shall in no wise diminish, enlarge or affect their civil capacities".

Jefferson saw in the doctrine of natural law and natural rights a re-interpretation—in secular and somatic terms—of the Christian theory of the origin and nature of man. Deist though he was, he admired Jesus *qua* reformer. He took a position close to Unitarianism and in his later years held that Unitarianism would become the predominant religion of the United States. He was opposed to the corruption of Christianity by priests, who had "perverted the purest religion ever preached to man into mystery and jargon, unintelligible to all mankind". "In every country and in every age, the priest has been hostile to liberty." But he described himself as a Christian, "in the only sense" Jesus wished anyone to be—"sincerely attached to his doctrines, in preference to all others; ascribing to Himself every human excellence; and believing that He never claimed any other". God the Father became, in the Jeffersonian view, God the Creator: but He left men to work out their own salvation from study of the Book of Nature, read and interpreted by the light of reason.

If this interpretation of the idea of Nature in American terms has remarkable consistency and unity, it is in its political applications—secondary though they are in Jefferson's mind—that it meets difficulty.

Its radicalism was qualified in practice by the emphasis Jefferson laid on land and property. Although professing himself in favour of universal manhood suffrage, "Still I find some very honest men who, thinking the possession of some property necessary to give due independence of mind, are for restraining the elective franchise to property". His draft of a constitution for Virginia in 1776 conformed to the pre-revolutionary pattern; voters were required to own either a freehold estate of twenty-five acres in the country or one-fourth of an acre in town, or pay taxes within two years of the time of voting. Jefferson never attempted to introduce universal manhood suffrage: he did attempt, however, to widen the property-holding classes.

Indeed, Jefferson's claim to the title of democrat, as distinct from liberal, is most ambiguous. He was an aristocrat converted to democracy by the force of his own reason, but the reluctance—and even a certain condescension—never disappeared. The champion of the common man was never one himself: his humanity was of the head not the heart. He was a member of a landed aristocracy that was not based on inheritance or title but on acquisition; all of its members were in greater or lesser degree self-made men. He recognized that power corrupts—or, in Madison's phrase, that it is "of an encroaching nature". He agreed that "rogues" would always be uppermost in society, and it was of the upper classes, especially in Europe, and most particularly in England, that he had the harshest things to say. But he used words like *"canaille"* and "swinish multitude" for the people—though they were the people of Europe not of the New World. He supported, like all his contemporaries except perhaps Hamilton, the notion of a balanced government; in his draft of a constitution for Virginia in 1776, two of the three branches of government are at one remove from the citizens. He favoured an indirectly elected Senate, with a lengthy tenure. As much as any Founding Father, he could fear the potential tyranny of the people. "It is not by the consolidation, or concentration of powers, but by their distribution that good government is effected." "An elective despotism is not the government we fought for." "One hundred and seventy three despots would surely be as oppressive as one." Or as he put it with some vehemence in the Kentucky Resolutions of 1798, "Free government is founded in jealousy, and not in confidence . . . In questions of power, then, let no more be said of confidence in man, but bind him down from mischief, by the chains of the Constitution." Jeffersonian democracy might be agrarian, but it was not Arcadian; it recognized as well as any Federalist that politics is a study in the exercise of power.

Despite the universality of rights, Jefferson realised that every government had to be adapted to the condition of those to be governed by it. He was sure that Latin American countries would throw off the yoke of Spain and Portugal, but he was highly sceptical about their capacity for self-government. In France in 1789 he acted as a brake on revolution, not as its advocate. His own leisure to think, and to discuss equality and "rights" was made possible by the labour of over one hundred slaves. Sir Augustus Foster was surprised at his emphasis on the inferiority of the Negro race, one "made to carry burthens". "He augured but little good as likely to result from their emancipation, observing that it was an English hobby, and that the English are apt to ride their hobbies to death." And even among free white men, Jefferson recognized as promptly as did Adams or Hamilton or Burke—or Foster—that in practice and as a fact of Nature, there was an aristocracy of talent, that some were born, if not created, to rule.

But, realising all this, he insisted that the defences against the abuse of power be made secure and clear. He sought in politics as in all else to maintain the balance; he opposed whatever appeared to destroy Nature's essential order and harmony. In his day the major threat had come from an over-mighty King. He knew full well, that, in an urbanised society, majority rule would be just as dangerous and that it could be easily perverted, and indeed that it might itself pervert. In his *Notes on Virginia*, his language is not only eloquent but prophetic:

> The public money and public liberty . . . will soon be discovered to be the source of wealth and dominion to those who hold them; distinguished too by this tempting circumstance, that they are the instrument as well as the object of acquisition. With money we will get men, said Caesar, and with men we will get money. Nor should our [governors] be deluded by the integrity of their own purposes and conclude that unlimited powers will never be abused, because they themselves are not disposed to abuse them. They should look forward to a time, and that not a distant one, when corruption . . . will have seized the heads of government and be spread by them through the body of the people; when they will purchase the voices of the people and make the people pay the price.

The impact of Jefferson on the American scene lay not only in what he advocated but in what he did. His practical contributions are in some measure indicated by the words he asked to be inscribed on his tomb: Author of the Declaration of American Independence, of the Statute of Virginia for Religious Freedom, and Father of the University of Virginia. It is striking that he omitted from his claim all reference to his eight years as President, and to the major transformations that his Presidency wrought. He saw himself as pen-man, legislator and educator, and as Virginian.

Little comment is needed on the importance of the Declaration of Independence, or on its accompanying manifestoes, *A Summary View of the Rights of British America*, written in 1774, and *The Necessity of Taking Up Arms*, written in 1775. The first of these is particularly hoary with myths, and is guarded nowadays in a special vault by the United States Marines. It was in some measure the work of Richard Henry Lee—who introduced the Resolution for Independence—rather than of Jefferson; Adams had a hand in the drafting; and it was not signed at all on July 4, 1776, but on August 8. Yet Jefferson and July 4 are irrevocably, and, as to the former, rightly, associated with it. Although the effective break with Britain can be set at least a year earlier, with Washington's appointment as commander, the Declaration was an impressive statement of the rights of man and a robust denunciation of the wrongs of one in particular, George III—also a subject hoary with myths, and not only in

Chicago. It was important both for its claim to a "separate and equal station" for a revolting group of colonies—the first successful colonial protest—and also for its republicanism. War against Britain had been dimly foreseen in 1774 and 1775—with Jefferson still protesting his loyalty to the Throne. By 1776 it was war for a new and revolutionary purpose: and it struck a blow against the divinity of kingship that has not yet ceased to echo. And, at a time when so much is heard of the monarch as head of the Commonwealth, and speculation is occasionally voiced as to what might have been if the British Empire had in 1776 been thought of in Federal terms, it is worth emphasizing that the powers of the King in Parliament then made all such theories unworkable, and hardly conceivable—on either side of the Atlantic. For good or ill, the Declaration marked the complete separation of America from Britain; it marked too the beginning of that revolutionary movement across the world which is still under way one hundred and eighty years later.

Jefferson was legislator as well as draughtsman of revolution. While Washington was leading the armies, Jefferson was setting an example of the changes that Independence might bring to state governments: one hundred and twenty-six bills were devised to rewrite the laws of Virginia, at least half of them drafted by Jefferson himself. A new judiciary was established; the importation of slaves was prohibited (a clause Jefferson had tried and failed to have enacted in the Declaration of Independence); freedom of religion was granted and the Anglican Church disestablished; naturalization and expatriation were provided for; punishments for crime were investigated, and the death penalty confined to murder and treason; a free school system was outlined, though not developed, for the state; primogeniture and entails were abolished; a committee of three, including Jefferson, was appointed to revise the laws and to free them from "their endless tautologies, their involutions of case within case and parenthesis within parenthesis", their "*saids* and *aforesaids*", their "*ors*" and "*ands*", "to make them more plain". In Virginia, for a time at least, men would even have a chance to know what their rights were.

It was not of course, even in Virginia, a total revolution and it was carried through with a lawyer's mildness. Few of Jefferson's provisions were radical. Primogeniture, for instance, had applied only when a landowner died intestate; entail was for many a serious hardship. There were meagre results where schools were concerned. Jefferson contemplated introducing a law for slave emancipation but never did so. The governments, State and Federal, devised in 1776 and 1787 were in fact constitutional and representative, but they were not democratic: slaves, indentured servants, women, and many labourers and small farmers who lacked property qualifications were debarred from voting; in most states there were property qualifications for public office-holding; voting was still open and oral, bribery was rife; and it was still the practice "to go merry to the Court-house". The attitudes of the Founding

Fathers were anti-democratic: the barriers erected were designed to prevent the exercise of government "by the people" as well as by a tyrannical king. Yet there was more democracy in the United States than in Britain: it was easier to acquire land, wages in the towns were higher, property was accumulated more easily and more quickly, and with it came the suffrage.

This was particularly so in the West, and it was in the new states west of the Alleghenies that the earliest genuine political democracy developed, in states like Kentucky and Tennessee, Ohio, Indiana, Illinois and Missouri. Jefferson's interest in the West was less personal than Washington's but just as real: he is honoured almost as much in Missouri and Kentucky as in Virginia. In the West, almost all men held land, but few had vast estates, for labour was scarce. Everyone could meet the property qualification, there was little social distinction, and so political democracy was matched by economic and social democracy. The western states in the Early National period were among the first to abolish property qualifications to vote and hold office. They were also the earliest to elect the state governor and other officials by popular vote. This extension of the suffrage came earlier in America than in Britain, and without the dramatic national struggle that 1832 represented. It preceded the Industrial Revolution and it developed from the small independent freehold of the frontier; it was rooted in land and in the rural values that the Jeffersonians believed essential to effective democracy.

In his brief spell in the Continental Congress in 1784, Jefferson continued his committee activities, and from them emerged his recommendations on a sound coinage system and a draft for the temporary government of the western territories. This foreshadowed the Northwest Ordinance of 1787 in stressing the notion of the equality of the newly-created with the original states—one of the most important non-Imperial features of American development—and in excluding slavery from all the territories after 1800. It was already easier to secure support in the North for anti-slavery measures than it was in the South.

His years as Ambassador in France were more important for his own development than for France, or for America. He had neither Franklin's zest, nor his capacity for winning friends of both sexes. The *affaire* with Maria Cosway has the air of something cultivated deliberately, as if indeed Jefferson were trying to follow, all too completely but without ease, in Franklin's footsteps. He became a friend of Lafayette and of the *salonnières*, and after his return was associated with the French cause, and with the Revolution. But his influence on Lafayette was one of moderation, not of Revolutionary comradeship, and the years abroad made of Jefferson a republican and a nationalist rather than a radical. He disliked the "priestcraft" and the hereditary aristocracy of France, a land where marital fidelity appeared "an ungentlemanly practice"; he deplored equally the dissolute manners, the land monopolies and the poverty he saw in England. He began to draw patriotic conclusions sharply at variance with his theories of the equality of the human species: "The yeomanry of the United States are not the *canaille* of Paris" he told Lafayette; "ours are the only farmers who can read Homer"; "an American, coming to Europe for education, loses in his knowledge, in his morals, in his health, in his habits, and in his happiness".

On his return from France, Jefferson described himself as neither Federalist nor anti-Federalist, "of neither party, nor yet a trimmer between parties". He wanted, he told Francis Hopkinson, to avoid attracting notice: "I find the pain of a little censure, even when it is unfounded, is more acute than the pleasure of much praise". Yet by 1792 he was, with Madison, directing a pamphlet and press war, sponsoring and drafting resolutions and in effect organizing a political party. Concerned as he was with freedom of opinion—he said he would prefer a society without government but with newspapers to one with government but without newspapers—it was a natural step to make of newspapers the instrument of protest and in the end of policy. There was ample material for controversy: the Genêt episode and the "Anglomanny" of the Administration, the excise tax and the Whisky rebels, the Jay and Pinckney Treaties. But it was not until 1798 that the division between High Federalism and Anti-Federalism became clear-cut, with the passing of the Alien and Sedition Acts, which empowered the President to deport dangerous aliens and, in time of war, to imprison or expel enemy aliens, and made it a crime to oppose the government. These measures were pointed at Jeffersonians, and especially at Jeffersonian editors, and suggested a deliberate plan to prevent the development of a two-party system. It was to counter them that, anonymously for reasons of personal safety, Jefferson and Madison drafted the resolutions that the Kentucky and Virginia Legislatures approved and sponsored. The mood of the years 1798-1800 would alone have ensured a change of government in 1800: it was helped by the split between Adams and Hamilton, and by the skill with which for a decade Jefferson had manufactured a national party from a congeries of sectional groups, and given it a liberal and republican character. With Madison's help, he not only made an Opposition, he made it constitutional.

The least striking of Jefferson's practical achievements was his work as President. This was due, in part, as we have already seen, to his character, which, said Hamilton, "warrants the expectation of a temporizing rather than a violent system". It was due still more to difficulties in foreign affairs, which largely limited his achievement to his first term, to the repeal of the whisky excise and to the reduction of taxes, of the civil service and of the armed forces. Louisiana was purchased, doubling American territory—and the national debt—raising serious constitutional issues and temporarily involving the imposition of arbitrary government in the new territory. The liberal could be empire-builder and expansionist.

Into the vast and fertile West he sent the Lewis and Clark expedition, exploring and mapping an area America was "destined to fill with arts, with science, with freedom and happiness". It was "an Empire for liberty"—its extent and variety a safeguard against the evils of "faction". The certainty about western land and American destiny was as striking as Washington's. Jefferson even suggested a design for an American order of architecture: a column fashioned like a bundle of cornstalks, and a capital in the shape of the leaves and flowers of tobacco.

The second term was bedevilled by the problem of Europe. The Embargo Act of 1807 forbade the sailing of any American vessel to Europe, and Federal agents were given the right to search out and seize ships and goods suspected of violating the law. This laudable experiment in peaceful coercion was a failure. Yankee commerce was destroyed, British merchant shipping stimulated; the plantation economy, which perforce honoured the law, was hard hit, the business economy, though less scrupulous, was almost ruined. Meanwhile, the army was increased and curious and unseaworthy gunboats were built for coast defence, each mounting a single gun. These measures provoked anger and contempt, especially in New England. As again in World War I, the effort to preserve both American neutrality and American rights abroad was high-minded but heavy-handed, and became hard to reconcile with liberalism at home. There was significance here: agrarian expansion and even, in Randolph's phrase, "agrarian cupidity" in the West, matching oceanic isolation. A decade later Jefferson was strongly to urge the Monroe Doctrine on his successor. American capital, cut off from investment in overseas commerce, turned to manufacturing, and indirectly therefore Jefferson encouraged the industry he feared. On all sides, the agrarian order was threatened. "We must now place the manufacturer by the side of the agriculturist", said Jefferson.

Madison and Monroe continued a policy which in its nationalism, its preparedness, its protective tariffs, its second Bank and its centralized character was indistinguishable from Federalism itself: the old High Federalists of Essex County found themselves by 1814 in an unnatural alliance of protest with Southern liberals like John Randolph, in opposition to this new and strange Democratic-Republicanism. This pattern too was to recur, as in 1933, when F. D. Roosevelt's Democratic Party showed itself in office more sympathetic to centralized power than it had ever been in opposition.

Jefferson, out of office after 1809, reverted to a more natural, and more consistent, liberalism, to his old interest in education and in local self-government. It was a more appropriate role. He came to stress the importance of native education, to oppose immigration and travel, to set the compass West by South and keep it so. For man's mind, reason was the oracle, he told his nephew Peter Carr, and the uprightness of a decision mattered more than its rightness. But about the future of America there was more assurance. "We shall go on, puzzled and prospering beyond example in the history of man."

Even before Jefferson's death, his views were under challenge: government action was called for to extinguish Indian land claims, to protect infant industries by tariff, to build roads westwards. It was a Westerner, Henry Clay, who expanded the old Hamiltonian programme into the "American system"; it was a Southerner, Calhoun, who, with all his Jeffersonian faith in states' rights and agrarianism, transformed the master's democracy with his contention that slavery was a "positive good . . . the most safe and stable basis for free institutions in the world".

After 1861, in industrial America, Jeffersonian ideas proved singularly adaptable to the changing American context. The *laisser-faire* view of the state that in one age suited a farmers' democracy and permitted agrarian expansion could be used in the next, buttressed by the Fourteenth Amendment and by Mr Justice Field, to defend industrial capitalism and to thwart government regulations. Jefferson was invoked with less subtlety and more emotion to counter the exploitation that in this context his own theories seemed to permit: by Henry George, and by Populists as various as Bryan, Ignatius Donnelly and Tom Watson. Some stayed Jeffersonian, like Benjamin Flower, in the pages of the *Arena*. Most radicals went beyond, into advocacy of nationalization of industry, government ownership of railroads and regulation of trusts.

A world in which increasing economic and technical power was concentrated in fewer hands and in which the majority of men came to live remote from nature could no longer produce a natural harmony simply by advocating the uncurbed pursuit of self-interest, or by urging freedom from government. The right of all to life, liberty and the pursuit of happiness necessitated a positive rather than a negative state, as Herbert Croly emphasized in his *The Promise of American Life*, written in 1909. Government had to discover and impose its own harmony of interests, as Croly urged on Theodore Roosevelt. The power of State and Federal Governments has thus been increased in un-Jeffersonian fashion to secure ends described as Jeffersonian. And Jefferson in all his rich quotability has been appealed to by both the advocates and the enemies of the planned and the welfare state. Jefferson's view of the narrow function of government has become outmoded as surely as his emphasis on its republican and balanced form has become increasingly revered. Similarly, his view of man as rational and of the laws of nature as easily discoverable, his faith in persuasion and in the ultimate triumph of truth in any free encounter of opinion—these certainties would be much less readily accepted to-day. Just as Darwinism undermined the idea of Nature as beneficent, relativism has queried whether it can be said to have a purpose at all. The world of Jefferson is lost indeed.

Yet despite all the sophistication of the twentieth century, the values of the Jeffersonians are hard to question. Jefferson's statements, in private letters as well as in public papers, remain the most durable declarations of the faith of the Revolutionary generation, of the principles that were self-evident to the eighteenth century and on which American government was erected. Jefferson believed in man's capacity for freedom, intellectual, religious, political. "I have sworn upon the altar of God eternal hostility to every form of tyranny over the mind of man." He saw society as in constant flux and recognized fully that the threat to freedom would come in its own fashion to each generation. He was gropingly aware of the dangers implicit in the totalitarian state, in public demagoguery, in racial intolerance, in swarming and congested numbers. He believed in the "illimitable freedom of the human mind to explore and expose every subject susceptible of the contemplation"; his view of society was moral, not economic.

His confidence in America has not been undermined as yet by the recent wave of conservatism that seeks to resurrect strange gods, including that tortured and perverted Jeffersonian, John Randolph of Roanoke. The Jeffersonian values are still a banner to which men of goodwill can rally, even if they cannot share his optimism or his rationalism. As architect and as radical, "temperate, remote and pure of phrase", there remains a sense in which John Adams was right to say, on the day that saw the death of both, July 4, 1826: "Tom Jefferson still survives."

AMERICAN POLITICAL PARTIES

By R. H. Pear

*

POLITICAL parties are institutions of major interest to the political
scientist, for they are the driving power behind the actions of
government. But if they sometimes fail to comply with ideas of
balance and symmetry, order and principle, which the theoreticians would
seek to discover, this does not necessarily detract from their utility or
efficiency. Political parties are the creations of ordinary political prac-
titioners. Theorists may assist them, but have rarely designed them, and
their inadequacies cause less alarm amongst politicians than they do
amongst those who like to see clear and rational distinctions between
those groups of citizens who so fiercely contest for the right to govern
their country.

The average Englishman knows the difference between Socialism and
Conservatism, but at any particular moment since, say, 1951 might find
it difficult to outline clearly and quickly the difference between H.M.
Government and H.M. Opposition on the major questions before the
country. The easy way out for a Socialist—and it is not illegitimate—is
to refer the questioner to the well known programme and achievements of
the Labour Government elected in 1945, or to the inadequacies of Conservative rule in the 1930's. The road back is always clearer than the
way forward. The importance of this consideration, for American politics,
is that the road back stretches, in both imagination and fact, right to the
beginning of the existence of the United States of America. We should
do well to remember that in the field of democratic politics America is a
very old country. Moreover the traditional manner of conducting politics
in the U.S.A. has not produced disaster. It ought to have done, according
to some moralists, but the general opinion of most of the Western World
is that the U.S.A. is a success; let us guard, however, against the naive
belief that this success is due entirely to its peculiar constitutional and
political arrangements.

In both England and the U.S.A. political parties and political habits
have been powerfully and silently moulded by pre-existing constitutional
institutions. Where revolutionary disagreement on political institutions
has been absent, each side has seen its task as the capturing of the
institutions and their utilization for its own particular ends. This agreement about institutions survived even the Civil War in America. It is a

particularly striking tribute to the influence of the Constitution that the South, though bitterly conscious of its military defeat has, subsequently, never suggested a new set of institutional arrangements for the country as a whole. Southerners have learned how to work with the constitution of 1787—and its anti-slavery amendments—just as the Labour Party has learnt how to work with the whole apparatus of the existing bureaucracy, the Army, the Lords and even the Monarchy—the very institution which early Socialists thought would have to be abolished.

This acceptance of, even blind pride and boastfulness about, existing political habits is a trait common to both Americans and ourselves. The uselessness of various parts of our respective systems can be explained and even appreciated as soon as it becomes apparent that they play *some* recognisable part in the totality of public life. Americans often ask why the House of Lords is still with us; why do we not get around to abolishing it now it has no important political functions? They understand and appreciate the answer that people who realise its unimportance are too busy trying to get into it to have time for the question of its abolition. Any freshman can devise a better way of revising Bills or selecting Presidential candidates than the present House of Lords or the American Presidential Convention. But what he cannot do is to devise institutions with the unintentional, unexpected, incidental uses which adhere to these archaic bodies. They serve their main purpose rather inadequately; for purposes for which they were not originally intended, they may do very well. We are all less logical than we ought to be. Some are depressed by this, and others resigned to it, while others again—especially some American political scientists—are elated to find a higher logic in the manifold illogicalities of American politics.

It is an odd fact that many Englishmen appear shocked at not finding in American parties a devotion to theoretical principles which they would be the first to agree does not appear at all times in all British parties. This may be just another case of the Englishman's well-known habit of deploring all foreigners; or it may be simply that he is asking for "principles" because these are so often a convenient abridgment of the complex history of political issues and attitudes. If we leave aside for the moment the distinction between an attitude and a principle, we can get some preliminary clarification of the difference between Republicans and Democrats if we go back into the history of these parties; and this history begins with the inauguration of the Federal Constitution of 1787.

The authors and exponents of the new constitution had to defend their work against their numerous critics in the country. The Founding Fathers were the *élite* of the new Republic; well-educated men, wealthy and successful, who though thoroughly patriotic, were conservative and suspicious of mob sentiment and demagogic utterance. These conservatives provided the first two Presidents of the United States and called themselves Federalists, or supporters of the new constitution. At the

Philadelphia Convention the radical element was hardly represented at all. Jefferson, Sam Adams, Tom Paine—all were absent; but in the country as a whole the spokesmen of the less well-born and successful, the artisans, the indentured servants, the small farmers and the frontier settlers were numerous. Some opposition to the Federalists was inevitable, especially as the Federalist administrations saw to it that only loyal Federalists received the plums of office under the government. The anti-Federalists (the Jeffersonians) took the name "Republicans", because they wished it to be known that they considered the Federalists to be too little devoted to the needs of the Republic and too much devoted to the welfare of the rich and well educated. No doubt the Republicans sought to create the impression that with the pomp and ceremony surrounding President Washington, the Federalists were in truth concealed monarchists who wished to make the President an autocrat. Moreover, the Republicans at first displayed enthusiasm for the French Revolution and its Republic, while at least one prominent Federalist—Alexander Hamilton—was a fervent admirer of the British Constitution. The Federalist party which elected George Washington and John Adams as Presidents of the U.S. never again elected another President. The party, as a party, could not stand up to the greater popular support of President Jefferson and his Republican successors. The Federalists denounced the Republicans as "democrats", and the party became known as the Republican-Democrat party. With the election of Andrew Jackson the term of abuse was worn on a badge of honour, and the Republican-Democrats became thereafter plain Democrats.

By 1815 the Federalist Party had ceased to exist, but support for Federalist principles had not. Furthermore, during this so-called Era of Good Feelings, the Republican-Democrat administrations tended more and more towards conservatism. The outcome was twofold; first, the radical Democratic elements in the Republican party rebelled and, under the leadership of Jackson, seized control of the government in the election of 1828; second, the conservative elements reformed themselves and by 1825 had taken the title of National Republicans—"National" to distinguish themselves from plain Republicans whom they no doubt accused of furthering sectional rather than national interests. The National Republicans became Whigs in 1834 and numbered some of the most brilliant American statesmen in their ranks (notably Webster and Clay), and they sent two Presidents to the White House on the Whig ticket. Until 1854 the Whigs, who were a National party—as were the Democrats—represented very much the attitudes and interests of the old Federalist Party. But the struggle over slavery was beginning, and the Southern gentlemen in the Whig Party began to see that the Whigs were increasingly devoted to the interests of Northern business and decreasingly capable of supporting the interests of Southern cotton growers—in short, the slave-holding interests. The Southerners deserted the Whigs for the

Democrats, and swiftly captured the leadership of the Democratic Party. This Southern domination of the Democratic Party depleted the ranks of the Whigs and increasingly alienated Northern Democrat farmers, whose interests lay not in the extension of slave territory in the United States, but rather in the availability of cheap, or free, land for "free farmers". With the Democrats as spokesmen for the South and slavery, a new alignment of power was necessary to protect the Northern agricultural and commercial interests, and this new formation of anti-Democrats took the name of the Republican Party. We may well ask why the original name of its opponents should have been assumed by the new Northern party. It was a time of increasingly bitter political feelings in which the Northerners felt that the original purposes of the Republic were being debauched by the arrogance of Democratic slave owners. The words of a resolution passed at Jackson, Michigan, in 1854 give us a good indication of these feelings and the reason for the name of the new party: "That, in view of the necessity of battling for the first principles of Republican government, and against the schemes of an aristocracy [the Southern Democratic slave owners], the most revolting and oppressive with which the earth was ever cursed or man debased, we will co-operate and be known as 'Republicans' until the contest be terminated." Those who co-operated to form the new party came from the ranks of Whigs, Free Soilers, the American (or "Know Nothing") Party—a party obsessed with a fear of immigrants and Roman Catholics—Northern Democrats and Abolitionist sympathizers. This new Republican Party of 1854 elected Lincoln as its first President in 1860 and soon became the Grand Old Party, the G.O.P. of McKinley, Theodore Roosevelt, Hoover and Eisenhower. What it then stood for, and against, and what it now represents we shall shortly consider. Meanwhile the Civil War split the Democrats into Northern Democrats who, with notable exceptions, largely supported Lincoln, and the Southern Democrats who ran the government of the Southern Confederacy. Within ten years of the end of the War the "bloody shirt" was all but buried and the Democrats emerged again as a national party. In the South today, however, the Civil War is still not laid to rest, with the consequence that the Republican Party does not yet exist in some Southern States.

This brief exercise on party names may help to fix in mind certain outward signs of party reputation; but names indicate little or nothing of the parties' activities, support and administrative achievements. There is some merit in saying that Eisenhower's party goes back in history only as far as 1854, but that important elements in Republican Party thinking go back through Whigs and National Republicans to the Federalists and Alexander Hamilton; and that the party of Stevenson, Truman and F. D. Roosevelt can trace its history, unbroken except for the Civil War, to Thomas Jefferson. This knowledge is only of use if we now begin to fill in the record of dates and changes in nomenclature with significant facts about political successes and failures, important campaigns and platforms, and great personalities.

In America a party has a name with which the public will associate certain happenings. It has, too, some organizational machinery, but this is more important in the separate states than on a national scale. It has few, if any, important theoreticians; it has few paid-up members, but millions who vote for it; it has a few principles—most of which, but not all, can be forgotten when serious electioneering begins. It has important financial backers, but they do not always call the tune. It has its "regular" loyal supporters in Congress, but its rebels are not expelled from its ranks. It has a thousand discordant voices which are with difficulty persuaded to sing in tune for a brief period every four years when the Presidential campaign is under way. It has a vivid and multiform public life which throws rays of light and obscurity in all directions. It is noisy and boisterous, giving, daily, dozens of examples of its vitality; but it is child's play to demonstrate, on any normal definition of a political party, that it does not exist. It is not a body of men (in the usual phrase) but a rabble. It is not united, let alone united on principles on which it is agreed. Its sole desire is to run the government of the country, or the county, city, or state. To do this it must refrain from attempts to improve the existing Constitution of the U.S. and it must win votes. The party's job is to win elections, not to educate the public so that in 50 years time it may win votes.

It is no good deploring the way in which parties win votes in America, for the constitutional arrangements of the U.S. are stacked against reformist parties hoping for the emergence of a more enlightened public opinion. If there is such opinion in the country it must get inside the existing parties, however distasteful this may be, and influence them from inside. The reason for this is quite simple. It is a President that is the Executive of the United States—not a Cabinet chosen from the leading members of the legislature. A party which fails after a few attempts to win the Presidency will, unless it is very rich and persistent like the present Republican Party, disintegrate. There is a simple reason for this, too. The American political tradition demands that loyal party workers be rewarded, tangibly, for their loyalty. Politics is a business, not an activity for those with leisure, private means and public spirit. If the spoils are not forthcoming the party will find itself without workers, perhaps because the workers have gone off into the next best party that looks like having a chance of victory. Emphasis on the Presidency is important, because the Presidential system excludes the possibility of coalition—the hope of struggling parties in other lands. Had the Founding Fathers decided upon a Cabinet Executive selected from the legislature all might have been different. Parties could have sprung up to support the great variety of sectional, racial, religious, geographical and other interests which are so obvious in the United States, and all governments

G

would have been coalitions—as in France. With the single Executive, however, these different and antagonistic sectional interests have been forced to cohere and to choose between one or other of the great parties. The political prize is the Presidency and often, though not always, the White House is the real seat of governmental power. Thus the parties are James Bryce's famous bottles with labels, but no contents, which must be filled up with a mixture of prominent individuals and public issues and sold to the public at each election; while the President himself, who, in fact, is elected by popular vote, is a striding, or staggering, bundle of compromises and a conscious embodiment of that coalition of interests which cannot be represented by separate parties. The effect of the American system has undoubtedly been to forge a sense of national consciousness and patriotism which might not have appeared under any other system; but one result, that American politics like the subtler plays in American football are enjoyed but not understood by all the spectators, may be a reason for meagre voting figures in many elections. Compromise, bargain, secret or open alliances, these have been the stuff of American politics from the beginning. If American parties score low on attachment to principles and public spirit, on organization and negotiating skills and subtlety they are in a class by themselves.

The important sections and interest groups in the United States can be studied with profit by way of the history of the parties. The Federalists represented the well-born, well-educated and commercially successful men of the Eastern seaboard. They were most strongly represented in New England, and, in the beginning, amongst landowners and land speculators in the South. Their interests lay in the development of a policy which assured the stability of commercial and financial contracts, and which provided for a sound currency and a national bank. Some of them were interested too in the forced growth of manufactures and encouragement, amounting to subsidy, to American shipping—this meant a "deflationary" economy and tariffs on imported manufactures. Politically they were centralizers wishing to put to full use the (limited) powers of the federal government, so that the U.S. could be developed as an area in which it was safe for all with money to trade and manufacture. This made them suspicious of allowing state governments to interfere with contractual obligations or to favour, by state legislation, debtors as against creditors. But already in the Federalist camp there were possible causes of dissension. Those who had speculated in Western lands wanted westward expansion; those who had not, feared that it might alter the value of their own Eastern seaboard real estate. Those who supported them on sound money and contractual obligations did not support them on the tariff. Southern landowners wanted to export their produce and purchase cheap British hardware, not dear American products.

Opposed to the Federalists were the Jeffersonians—small farmers (and some large farmers), small businessmen who wanted easy loans and who might favour inflationary economic policies, town artisans who disliked the wealth and airs and graces of their Federalist employers. This, too, was an uneasy coalition of supporters, but it gave the Jeffersonian Republicans the reputation they needed for political success. It could claim to be the farmers' party because it had no great support from banking and manufacturing, and it could loudly proclaim that it regarded the "national" views of the Federalists as unconstitutional, by asserting that the Constitution strictly construed did not allow for such innovations as the chartering of a national bank while it did allow state governments to interfere by legislation in the field of contract. It asserted that as a general principle the less government men had the better and that all administrations, particularly those of the Federalists, drew around them a host of sycophants and others who worked that government, especially in its fiscal aspects, to support themselves at the expense of the farmers and the public; for, as Jefferson believed, farming was the only really pure way of living. This Jeffersonian agricultural doctrine is a constant and continuing feature of the American political ideology; but what is less easy to explain is why the urban proletarians also supported the Democrats. The simple explanation is that it looked like the underdog's party —and still does—and that natural class feeling led the worker—and still leads him—to identify himself with the party opposed to the banks, the bosses and others of superior status. If it were not for this feeling it would be difficult to explain why, for instance, New York Irish Catholic immigrants can remain in the Democratic party alongside old family Southern Democrats who have loudly proclaimed their dislike of Catholics and immigrants.

As has already been indicated, the National Republicans and Whigs inherited and developed many of the economic and constitutional principles of the Federalists. They were the foremost exponents of the "national" as against the "states' rights" view of the Constitution held by the Democrats, and of an "American system" for the economy, i.e. tariffs and government-sponsored internal improvements to assist trade. The Democrats remained the protectors of farmers and small men and with the raising of the constitutional issue of the extension of slavery into new territories became the exponents of the view that peaceful secession of the Southern States from the Union might be constitutionally permissible. The Southern Whigs entered the Democratic party because their interests as slave owners and agriculturists could be defended by no other party. The next step came when Northern farmers saw that with the Democratic party now entirely slave-minded, their hopes of free land for free farmers in the West were gravely endangered—for President Buchanan, a Democrat, vetoed a Homestead Bill. Allied with Northern Whigs, businessmen, and railroad interests wanting to extend their lines across the continent, these Northern Democrats joined the Republican party. It was not an Abolitionist party. Abolitionism was almost as unpopular in the North as in the South and found little or no support amongst Northern working men. At Chicago in 1860 where Abraham Lincoln (a former Whig member of the U.S. House of Representatives and in 1860 a reasonably successful railroad lawyer) was nominated for President, the platform of the party consisted of a declaration against any further extension of slavery in the territories, and in favour of a Homestead Act and the building of a Transcontinental railroad—and it is reported that the last item aroused the greatest enthusiasm. It would be neat to attribute the birth of the Republican party to a conspiracy on the part of railroad promoters, but, although they benefited handsomely from its victory in the 1860 and subsequent elections, such an explanation would be far too simple.

After the Civil War the Republican party prospered so extravagantly that until the early 1930's a Republican administration was regarded as normal and a Democratic one as accidental. (Since 1932 this assumption has been reversed.) The basis for Republican political success from the Civil War to the Great Depression lay in its identification with economic progress and its alliance with Big Business—an alliance originally based on Republican enthusiasm for railroads, fortunes made out of Civil War contracts for the Union armies, and the open and apparently unashamed corruption of President Grant's administration in the interests of Big Business. The partiality of Republican administrations towards Big Business led to its first defeat in 1884. But the image of the Republican had been created, and there were solid factual grounds for this image. In Republican eyes, the party was the truly American party; it had defeated the Democratic rebels in armed conflict; it had given freedom to Business; it had brought great wealth and prosperity to the country. Americanism is Business plus the Republican Party. As for the Democratic Party, to a Republican not all Democrats were traitors to the country, but indubitably all traitors were Democrats. The Democratic view of the Republican party fastened on to old Jeffersonian ideals. It had neglected and pauperized the farmers; it had crucified them through its extortionate railroad rates, its mortgages, its rigging of the commodity markets, its monopolies in farm implements; it had stolen the government of the people from the people by buying Senators, Cabinet ministers, state legislators; it had corrupted judges and the police; it had beaten down striking workmen. Some of these accusations stuck, for in 1884 enough independent Republicans deserted their candidate, James G. Blaine, to put Grover Cleveland in the White House, the first Democratic victory since 1856. Meanwhile the Democratic Party (but not Cleveland) was moving steadily leftwards and Democratic voters were listening to the propaganda of the various radical "third parties"—the Farmers' Alliances and the Populists. In 1896 the Democratic party, having taken a stand against the "sound money" men (The Gold Democrats) in their own party, gave the nomination to William Jennings Bryan—a Free Silver Democrat who expounded the virtues of an inflationary economy, based on the free coinage of silver, which would remedy the ills of the farmer. The impetus for a new political radicalism came in this election, as in others, from the plight of farmers caught with fixed loan and mortgage payments in a period of falling prices for agricultural produce; but Bryan turned it into a Crusade against Wealth, Corruption and the Trusts, while Mark Hanna, McKinley's political manager, persuaded Big Business that if they lost this election it was tumbrils and the guillotine for Wall Street.

This election probably gave the parties their present reputations. Many other issues have influenced them: tariffs, farm prices, isolationism versus internationalism, civil rights, to mention but a few. But for the convenience of the voter and the reputation of the party, Truman must look more radical than Dewey and Stevenson than Eisenhower. There is a certain strain of consistency in this. The Democrats began as radical opponents of the status quo, the Federalists, Whigs and Republicans as supporters, at least in respect of property. Each party has had its embarrassments and its aberrations, such as the slave-owning leadership of the Democratic party and its continued conservatism on the Negro question; the radical character of the first great Republican, Abraham Lincoln, and the reforming enthusiasm of Theodore Roosevelt; the conservatism of Grover Cleveland's second presidential term. Each party too must live with discordant elements in its make-up. Southern conservatives are allied with urban Northern left-wingers in the Democratic Party; old Southern stock with new immigrants; labour union members with fanatical opponents of unions. In the Republican party in the North-West there are radical elements, too, which the Old Guard finds it difficult to accommodate. The interests of Republicans in the North-West in regard to federal hydro-electric developments are opposed to those private power interests the representation of which brought Wendell Willkie to the fore.

The administrations of Woodrow Wilson and Franklin Roosevelt deepened the colours of the picture of the Democratic party and gave the whole more clearly discernible shape, while those of Harding, Coolidge and Hoover were in character with the régimes of Taft and McKinley. One great change has however occurred in the attitudes of the parties. The Democrats, traditionally the exponents of little government, have now become the enthusiasts for Big Government, increasing and developing the potentialities for federal control and regulation in the administrations of Wilson, Franklin Roosevelt and Harry S. Truman. "States' rights" and strict construction are forgotten. Federal powers and national aims are now proclaimed. As a result, warnings against the evils of federal government expansion and the defence of states rights have become familiar on the lips of Republicans, but the Republicans have in fact done little since 1952 to dismantle the New Deal welfare state.

In all countries many people vote for a party not because of what it promises to do for them, but because of what it has achieved in the past—

on its general reputation in fact. Voters may feel that they know the party even better than its own leaders do. This means that there is always an element of the traditional and the nostalgic in the support which a party receives. The rich Socialist may once have been poor, or his father unemployed, or the flame of undergraduate radicalism may not yet be entirely extinguished in him. Such traditional voting is very common in America; 75% of voters are said to vote the way they do because their families have always been Democrat or Republican. Some groups whose interests may not be more obviously served by one party rather than the other will tend to vote for the party which, in the past, has seemed to appreciate their problems. This traditional support is an important factor in a party's electoral calculations; it will try and keep this support and may modify its platform accordingly. When we know the groups in the country which normally support the Republican or Democratic parties we have advanced some distance towards an understanding of what that party really is, and how it can be expected to behave. For each group supporting the party, adequate grounds of hope, fear, and gratitude for past favours can be discovered, but the more detailed the study of such support, the more difficult it becomes to describe the party with simple political adjectives. "Officially" and traditionally American parties do not rely for their vitality on the strength of class feeling. Sociologically, using the term "class" in the widest sense to include not merely income and position in the productive process but also social status and the expectations and anxieties surrounding it, it is clear that the parties are in many respects class parties. We do not know whether they are becoming more or less class-conscious, for serious study on these questions has only been undertaken in very recent times. But one paradox is of great psychological interest. As prosperity increases for all classes in society and only a small proportion are left near the poverty line, people seem the more willing to consider their class position both subjectively and objectively. In these very broad terms the Democratic party is the party of those of lower social status; the Republican, that of the higher. While a handful of millionaires are regular Democrats, hundreds are Republicans. Most trade unionists vote Democrat (the A.F. of L.—C.I.O. came out for the Democratic candidate in the 1956 contest) but many, since 1948, are Republicans. A further point of importance is the spread of political ideas with the movement of the frontier westward. Migration has been along lines of latitude; New Englanders bearing the torch of enlightenment and politics from North-Eastern States through the Mid-West to North-Western States; and Southerners across the Mississippi to the states of the nearer South-West. Thus in the West and Mid-West, northern states are regarded as traditionally Republican, southern ones as more probably Democratic; while in a centrally placed Mid-Western state such as Illinois, the northern part is less influenced by Southern political attitudes than the area around Cairo.

Against this background it is fairly safe to say that the Democrats' traditional support comes from organized labour, persons of immigrant stock (especially in the great cities), Catholics, Southerners, liquor interests, some business groups more interested in free trade than tariffs, intellectuals, ex-socialists, poor farmers (or farmers temporarily dissatisfied with Republican farm policies) and, of recent years, federal civil servants. Republicans can rely on practically the whole of Wall Street, nearly all industrialists (especially steel manufacturers), Protestants, farmers in the Mid- and North-West (provided they are currently prospering), "old American" stock, almost 100% of newspaper proprietors, money and respectability in general, with fluctuating amounts of support from trade unionists, white collar workers, third generation immigrants who have risen in social status, real estate interests, private power groups, and—a new group—Texas oil millionaires. They are undoubtedly the richer party. In every department of legitimate campaign expenditure they spent noticeably more than the Democrats in 1952: $13.8 millions as against a Democratic and labour union expenditure of $8 millions. (These are the legally limited expenditures reported to the Clerk of the U.S. House of Representatives. In all it is estimated that the total campaign expenditure of both parties topped $100 millions!)

Party organization exists at every level of political activity in the United States, from the 125,000 separate precinct (or polling district) committees up through county, city, and state, to the parties' national conventions. These party organizations are continually at work selecting and voting for candidates for various public offices, for delegates to county and state conventions, for candidates for the two houses of the state legislatures, for Congressmen and Senators, for Governors, Lieutenant-Governors and the chief administrative officials of the state, and for Presidents and Vice-Presidents. When one reflects that the smallest precinct committee is, on paper, geared to the activity of the state and national party in political contests, it becomes obvious why politics are to a large extent in the hands of "professionals"—that is those persons who have an appointment under, or an attachment to, a county, city or state government which allows them, even expects them, to devote a considerable part of their time to politics. It has been estimated that there are over half a million public employees (federal government employees do not come in this category) who are in this manner available for political work. They are the parts of the political machine.

In this essay we can attempt to describe only that part of the party organization which is visible in federal elections; this itself rests on the mass of local party activity which has been indicated.

The Founding Fathers distrusted the concept of party and in the creation of the "Electoral College" for the election of Presidents believed that they had devised a system of selection which could not become the tool of faction. Under this system each state was to appoint, in such manner as it thought fit, a number of electors equal to the representation that State had in the U.S. Congress—i.e. equal to the number of the state's representatives in the lower house plus its two Senators. These Electors were then to cast their state's electoral votes for the men they thought suitable to be President and Vice-President of the United States. It was thought that these electors would be worthy and responsible men who would not be under any pressure from the mass of shallow citizens and that the possible candidates would be obvious to them. When all the electoral votes of the States were counted the candidate with a majority of votes over all others was to be President and the runner-up Vice-President. If no candidate had a majority, Congress was to choose among them, each State having one vote. The Founding Fathers made no provision in the Constitution for the nomination of candidates and as already mentioned left the method of choice of electors to the States.

The democratic impetus soon overwhelmed these cautious arrangements. Presidential electors became themselves elected in a state-wide popular vote—and this meant that before an elector could get support he had to declare himself in favour of one of the contestants for the Presidency. And it rapidly became an all but universal convention in the States that the party name first past the post in the State, by however short a head, was entitled to all that State's electoral votes. This convention is still in force and its consequences have been momentous for the game of presidential politics. A short lead of a few thousand votes in New York gave Grover Cleveland the Presidency, because he thereby obtained all the electoral college votes of the largest state in America. The huge Republican popular vote there was worthless.

Nomination of candidates was in the very earliest days by common consent of the few men concerned. By 1800 the parties' congressional caucuses arranged the nominations for President and Vice-President, with increasing amounts of advice from party enthusiasts outside Congress. From 1824 onwards state legislatures and public meetings took over the job of nominating candidates. In 1832 the first national presidential convention was held—by the Democrats to nominate President Jackson for a second term; and in the following year the Whigs held their first national convention which nominated candidates and presented to the nation a ten-plank platform. From then on, presidential conventions to nominate the candidates and hammer out the platform have taken the traditional form of spread-eagle oratory, noise and heat, impassioned appeals and voting to the order of the party leaders, until we come to the television age, when heightened decorum, wholly artificial stage management, and completely pre-arranged dramatics led the viewers of the 1956 Republican convention to switch off in large numbers.

The convention was thought of as a forum in which the active rank and file could choose their leaders, instead of having to accept those selected for them by the Congressional caucus. But it represented a potential danger both to the professionals and to the amateur rank and file. The rank and file might choose a man quite unacceptable to the party bosses; this was partly true in the case of Wendell Willkie, the Republican choice for 1940. From the point of view of the rank and file, conventions were too obviously packed with state delegations of professionals completely under the control of a powerful state leader. The professionals easily defeated the amateurs when it came to determining the course of balloting. They could make the deals with rival managers; they had the political resources and tactical skill to determine the outcome. The presidential convention became a squalid and degrading exhibition with accusations of bribery, rigging and partiality; and what was sometimes true of national conventions was even more true of certain city and county conventions—notably Chicago in the 1880's where a Democratic delegate who had not served a gaol sentence, or mysteriously avoided one, was something of a rarity. The reformers countered with the device of the primary election, which was to put the choice of the parties' candidates for public office—and of state delegates to the presidential convention— directly in the hands of the ordinary follower of the party. By thus by-passing the professionals it was hoped that eminent non-professionals would offer themselves for public positions and would receive the support due to honourable men. The primary was designed to rectify the abuses of the "convention" method of choosing candidates, for by that method, from precinct meeting to county convention to state and national convention, the professionals of the "machines" had controlled the choice from bottom to top.

A primary election is an election for the choice of candidates for public office, and it is an election in which the electors are members or followers of one party. Various devices are in operation to prevent interlopers from the other party from upsetting the choice of genuine Republican or Democratic voters. Nomination is relatively simple and although the election is a private party affair state law now regulates its procedures and state officials supervise the process. In this way parties are officially recognised and their activity is to some extent regulated by state law— and they may become entangled in it. A voter in a primary is allowed to vote only for the candidates of the party of which he is a follower, and the winner of the primary then contests the final election with his victorious opponent from the other party. Primaries have allowed some public spirited men, not of the "machine", to enter politics, but they have not fulfilled the high hopes of their inventors to any great extent. What the reformers seem to have forgotten is that primary elections like any others cost money—and often huge sums which ordinary men and women cannot find—and that the machine does not retire when a primary is announced; it presents its "slate" of regular approved candidates and works desperately hard to get them elected—and it usually succeeds. Primaries are in general use for the selection of candidates to contest for Congressional seats, U.S. Senatorships and for office as State Governors and Lieutenant-Governors, though there is now a movement back towards selection by state conventions for the most important state offices. In connection with Presidential procedures about a third of the states use the "Presidential primary" to select the state's quota of delegates to attend the national party convention. The rest use the state convention system. The clearest form of Presidential primary is that in which a choice of actual delegates is combined with a vote showing the preference of the whole state (or rather of that party in the state) as between the various candidates. In this type the voter with a primary ballot paper for e.g. Republican delegates representing New Hampshire in 1952 would (if he had been an Eisenhower supporter) have put one cross against delegate "William G. Saltonstall Favorable to the nomination of Dwight D. Eisenhower for President", and another cross by the name of Eisenhower in a part of the ballot paper headed "I hereby declare my preference for candidate for the office of President of the United States to be as follows". Not all Presidential primaries are on the lines of New Hampshire's; but they all achieve the result of testing the preferences of the party's supporters in the state and producing a delegation at the national convention morally pledged to support the state's choice until such time as it is clear that the best interests of the state are no longer served by stubbornly sticking to a loser instead of climbing on the victor's bandwagon.

A national convention consists of 1200 or so voting delegates apportioned amongst the states according to formulae (the Republicans and Democrats differ on these) which give recognition to the size of the state and the number of actual Republican or Democratic voters therein. A simple majority is needed to win the nomination. Balloting begins in alphabetical order of the states—Alabama to Wyoming—and each state casts its vote for the man it prefers. Balloting will continue until one candidate gets a majority of votes. This may be done on the first ballot, with a second to make it unanimous, or it may take many days. Between ballots speeches are made, demonstrations of undying loyalty are undertaken, bands play, singers entertain, delegates sweat and managers make bargains. They are of course selecting a Presidential candidate; yet what they want is not the man most likely to be a good chief executive—and conventions have chosen some very bad men for this high office—but a man who will unite the party for the coming campaign (in which for once the party *must* be united) and one who can win the election. A saintly loser does more harm to the party than a rascally winner—or so tradition has it, and in the context of American politics it is true enough, for no party makes a practice of looking at most more than four years ahead. If a sitting President wishes to run again the convention is, as a place for choosing a candidate, a sheer waste of time (even though for other purposes it is most useful) for a party will not repudiate a sitting President for fear that this open show of no confidence will convince the country that the opposing party is surely right.

If a convention deadlocks and continuous balloting shows no signs of increasing one candidate's votes, the managers of the various candidates must get busy and produce some result. The convention cannot go on for ever. It costs a vast sum of money each day and the delegates, angry, frustrated, and with cash running low, are anxious to get home. Conventions often deadlock because there are strong and worthy candidates who will not give way, and the lesser and uncommitted delegations are waiting to see which way the bandwagon is going to roll before jumping on. In such circumstances lesser men get their chance. A pleasant and innocuous man is suggested about whom nothing much is known, for or against, and in their desperation the delegations will vote for him because it is the quickest way of getting home. This, it is true, does not often happen, but it is always a possibility. The dark horse may be a real outsider, like Senator Harding, waiting for the leaders to collide, or he may, like Mr Willkie, be a most powerful runner, cleverly dressed up to look like an outsider.

Judging the direction in which the bandwagon is going to move is a very important part of the delegation's duties. If you were with the winner from the beginning, by tradition you can expect handsome treatment if your man is elected to the Presidency. If yours was the weight that started the bandwagon rolling the President should remember you. If you got on when it was well under way you are entitled to nothing. What are these favours which the President may bestow? They consist of everything from Cabinet posts, Ambassadorships, other great federal appointments, and consideration of the state's special interests, down to minor federal spoils for the men of your state—or for the men of your particular faction in the state party; and it is these favours which cement together to some extent the cracks in the ever-bursting party structure.

Besides the 1200 or so votes in the convention, the party managers have another figure constantly in mind—266. This is a majority of the total number of votes (531) in the "Electoral College" which elects the President. This figure 531 is made up of 435 (number of Congressmen elected by the states to the lower House) plus 96 (2 Senators for each of the 48 states). A Presidential candidate is assessed by the professionals on the basis of how many electoral votes he can get; that is how many states he can carry—not the total popular vote for him in the nation as a whole. He must be the sort of man who can win an assortment of states large and small. New York has the largest electoral vote (45) followed by California and Pennsylvania (32 each) down to Nevada and Wyoming with 3 each. The calculations that can be made on these figures are infinite in number, but by tradition and experience, the choice is likely to be in the direction of a man who can carry his own state—a largish state

—against a strong opponent. But a large and uncertain state is better than a large safe one. If a state is safe it can be relied upon to vote for the ticket without the added patriotic incentive of sending one of its native sons to the White House. Really safe states can be ignored—be they big or small. Campaigning will be concentrated on the doubtful states and if one of these is of reasonable size and can be carried against its previous vote by a native son, that native son is to be looked on with favour. It is for this reason that New York, Ohio, and Illinois produce so many candidates on both tickets—and California and Texas may soon move into the "large and doubtful" category. All these calculations go by the board when a great non-political national hero like Eisenhower (Kansas, 8 votes) can be persuaded to run. The absence of any past record of political service is often an asset rather than a liability to a candidate provided there is *some* interesting material out of which to manufacture the traditional campaign biography. Prominent Senators such as Taft and Kefauver have been dogged rather than assisted by their records of public service. Public service in a state, however, is a possible advantage, particularly if a man is a governor or ex-governor, not so much because that service has necessarily been good service, but because it can be assumed that such a person has the necessary knowledge and organization to carry that state.

With the Presidential candidate nominated, the Vice-Presidency follows with, usually, little fuss, and the party platform is announced. The platform is supremely unimportant. The Presidential candidate may quite possibly disagree with it. From now on he is in control of the whole campaign—the acknowledged leader of the party on all things— and dissenters will dissent at their peril.

In office the President is leader of his party: the defeated candidate merely one of several possible leaders of the other party. Each party maintains an H.Q. in Washington D.C., but these headquarters organizations have no powers over either policy or candidates. They do some mild public relations work. There is a National Committee for each party composed of equal numbers of persons from each of the 48 states. This Committee, too, is devoid of political power. Its chairman is the President's nominee, but its functions consist largely of raising money and making arrangements for the national convention, and allocating money for the Presidential campaign. In the last year or so President Eisenhower has set his National Committee the task of considering questions of future policy, but in this, as in other things, Eisenhower is an innovator. The effective seats and sources of power remain in the political machines of the great states and cities, in the White House if the President is an active politician, and in the skill and influence of certain Senators and Congressmen. But there is little or no co-ordination of these different powers except when at election time it is necessary to appear as one party; and even then the Senate and House Campaign

Committees are in their activities to a considerable extent independent of the general National Committee campaign. In the legislature itself there are infrequent meetings of all Democrats or all Republicans and they are unimportant. The Congressmen go their own ways on legislation; they are not controlled by a harsh whip; there is no party discipline in the British sense of that term, for it is not the four-yearly party convention, or the President, or the National Committee, or the Congressional party which gives a man his essential party label. It is normally awarded by the party organization in his Congressional district—sometimes not even by them, for as Senator Borah put it in unforgettable terms "any man who can carry a Republican primary is a Republican. He might . . . believe in the communistic state, in the dictatorship of the proletariat, in the abolition of private property, and in the extermination of the bourgeoisie; yet if he carried his Republican primary, he would still be a Republican".

The "locality rule" makes it necessary for a Congressman to be elected from a district in which he is resident. If he satisfies his local party and his constituents he cannot be deprived of his party label. He need fear no whips and can spend his life proclaiming his loyalty to his party and voting against all its measures. He has only one fear—that his constituents will get tired of him or that (should he be a member of the President's party) the President's measures will be preferred to his own and a supporter of the President will defeat him in the primaries.

The President will confer from time to time with the leaders of his party in Congress, but they can offer no guarantees that the legislation he desires will get through unscathed—they may in fact want it defeated. If they can work earnestly for it knowing full well it will be defeated they may get the best of both worlds; they have shown their loyalty to the President, but their constituents have not suffered because the Bill never went through.

Not all are satisfied with this anarchic state of affairs in the American parties. The academic political scientists fear that the irresponsibility of American parties is injuring the health of the democracy; and many of the solidly entrenched Congressional leaders tend to agree, for these veterans have a solicitude for the general reputation of the party. But the average Congressman would most surely oppose any suggestion such as a party council composed of Congressional and State leaders which could deprive him of the party label for acts of indiscipline. And the Congressman would be right, at any rate as far as American political tradition can take him. Government exists to benefit the governed, not spiritually but materially. Congressmen go to Washington to get benefits for their constituents, through private "pork barrel" legislation or by general federal legislation. Congressmen do not exist primarily to support an Administration or to improve the reputation of the party. These are alien concepts.

A last note, even perhaps a sad note, must be appended on the subject of "third parties". The hopes of a "third party" are always present and always dashed. There have been Third Parties in plenty in modern times. Greenbackers, Anti-Monopolists, Farmers' Alliances supporting Independents, Populists, Socialists, Prohibitionists, Progressives (in three varieties: Theodore Roosevelt in 1912, La Follette in 1924 and Henry Wallace in 1948) and Communists. All have put up Presidential candidates and all have failed. Only one such party, the La Follette Progressives, has succeeded in governing a state in the present century, and as has been suggested solid support in the states is a pre-requisite for entrance on the stage of national politics. A national Labour Party is an attractive speculation but in its growing period with whom would it ally itself?— for alone it will face the destiny of all other minor parties. In times of grave depression Farmers may join with Labour. But in normal times farmers' aspirations are those of the capitalist trader—to sell at as high a price as he can get—and if a "beef strike" seems necessary to emphasize this it may be tried. But Labour wants low prices for its urban voters. Farmers will attempt to play off one great party against the other—and have achieved successes by these means. Labour has been less successful with these tactics mainly because the Republicans do not want, or think they can dispense with, Labour support—and this feeling as between Republicans and Labour is often mutual. American unions are now deeply involved in politics, on the Democratic side only, but the United Automobile Workers got a guaranteed annual wage not from Republicans or Democrats but directly from the employers, by the use of aggressive tactics against the automobile manufacturers.

To launch a Presidential campaign of serious proportions even fifty years ago cost far more than any third party ever possessed, and as has been suggested the whole constitutional and political system of the United States works against the gradual growth (or gradual decline) of political parties. If a party breaks up it does so swiftly and dramatically and the broken parts are as swiftly joined to other and different splinters to form a new party, one based to a large extent upon the organization of parts of the old party. This seems to be the lesson of the Whig party's disintegration; and were the Democratic Party to break up tomorrow, its parts—most probably various state machines—would re-join with others to form a new national alignment.

Most Third Parties have fought one or two campaigns and then retired and died. The Socialists are an exception; they have been quietly expiring since the days of the First World War. In one sense the Third Parties have not failed. The great parties live on almost pure politics, not on ideas, and the minor parties have supplied them with the ideas which they were incapable of thinking out for themselves—even the odd idea of Prohibition. Had Bryan lived to see the Democratic New Deal he would probably have been satisfied. Had Debs lived to see the strength of the present C.I.O.—A.F. of L., he too might have been satisfied. Many old Socialists, "Wobblies" and Progressives have lived to see the New Deal and are satisfied—and it is a fair guess that they nearly all vote Democrat.

COMMERCIAL AMERICA

By Frank Thistlethwaite

*

THE news-sheets were quick to report that Lord Cornwallis's veterans had marched to surrender at Yorktown to the tune "The World Turned Upside Down". The seismic repercussions of the American Revolution were registered in the minds of Englishmen, Frenchmen and Americans with shock and heart-searching. For good or evil their world could never be the same again.

But an American merchant, returning to his neglected counting-house, well knew that, though her flag was new, his schooner and her business on the blue water were not. Politically, Americans belonged to a new order; economically, the facts of existence had not basically altered. Back-country farmers, happy to have pushed the "lobsterbacks" into the sea, might be ignorant of it, and Virginia planters, freed from tyranny and tobacco debts, might have forgotten it; but the ex-colonies were still constituent parts of an Atlantic community which had nourished them for a century and would nourish them for as long again.

With the Proclamation Line abolished and royal and tory estates expropriated, there seemed an infinite expanse of fertile land to be had for the taking. Settlers clearing homesteads in the Appalachian wilderness, however, soon found that they were too short-handed to do more than improvise a subsistence; and big speculators like Phelps and Gorham knew that the vast estates in western New York, to which they had acquired title, would be unproductive without credit to sustain settlers before land could be cleared and crops raised, and without investment capital to build roads and the canal which would make it economic to transport crops to markets. In order to break through the conditions which limited them to a sparse and unproductive farming existence on the Atlantic littoral the Americans had to bring capital and labour to the land on a scale far beyond their meagre resources. Such energizing forces could come only from the traditional source: from Europe and, as it turned out, chiefly from the ex-mother country, Britain. Unless it were to remain insulated and stagnant, the American economy had to become re-integrated with the rest of the Atlantic world. This absorbed much of American energies during the quarter of a century after Independence.

The Federalist merchants, ship-owners, jobbers and promoters backed the Constitution of 1789 partly because it provided the minimum conditions of economic progress: courts powerful enough to enforce contracts, a state strong enough to negotiate commercial treaties and financial institutions stable enough to attract foreign traders and capital. They knew that to be truly independent the Republic needed power behind her statecraft; and the naval, military and commercial power effective in international negotiation derived from a thriving economy. Taking as their model the respected ex-enemy, Britain, they saw their destiny as a great commercial nation. Trade must be driven, abroad and at home. Banking institutions must be established to accumulate liquid funds and attract foreign capital which could be used to grow crops, trap furs, cut timber and extract minerals, to build ships and wharves, turnpikes, bridges and canals.

A few, like the Secretary of the Treasury, Alexander Hamilton, went further, and hoped, by raising a protective tariff, to establish in America those modern manufactures which gave Britain the edge on her trading competitors and created fabulous profits for investment in new enterprise. Fortunately for Jefferson's peace of mind such men were ahead of their time. For more than a generation capital and labour were more profitably employed in producing raw, and semi-manufactured, materials and in creating the means of transport than in competing with Britain in "the manufacturing arts". In the Atlantic trading area, North America was still a "colonial" unit, producing raw materials in exchange for the manufactures of a "metropolitan" unit, north-west Europe and predominantly Great Britain. As contemporary writers on political economy recognized, the United States and Great Britain stood in closer relations to each other than the normal definition of "international trade". The opportunities of the younger country, the convenience of the shipping and commercial links, the increasingly liberal commercial policies of the two States and the ethnic affinities between the two peoples encouraged an intimacy which was unprecedented between two sovereign states. Not only were Britain and the United States each other's best customer; British capital and labour often found more attractive employment in the newer country than in the old. The emigration of people and of investable funds westwards along the North Atlantic trade route was on such a scale, especially after 1815, that it is more useful to think in terms of a single, Atlantic economy, directed towards the exploitation of American resources for mutual profit, than of two or more independent, and competitive economies. Until at least 1850 America grew economically under the guidance of an informal partnership between, on the one hand, Liverpool shippers and emigrant brokers, London merchant bankers, British iron, hardware and textile manufacturers, and on the other, the merchants, bankers and transport promoters of Boston, New York and Philadelphia and the cotton planters of the Deep South.

The economic adjustment of the ex-colonies to their changed position in the Atlantic community was not made without friction. A hard-

H

calculating Britain denied American merchants the privileges of the carrying trade within the British Empire, and especially, until 1830, with those British West Indian islands which had been key pieces in their commerce before the Revolution. British merchants, commanding more powerful credit though less economical ships, proved formidable competitors for Yankee masters and supercargoes in the trading ports of three oceans. The ruthless British policy towards neutral traders during the Napoleonic Wars, enforced by her powerful navy, imposed a straight-jacket on American trade with Europe and was the immediate cause of that war between ex-mother country and ex-colonies in 1812 which was from one point of view the last, mishandled, phase in the long struggle for American independence. But after 1815 a more liberal trade policy and a recognition of complementary interests in the Atlantic led to a period of commercially fruitful peace. And even during the worst troubles of Embargo and war the American merchant-shipowners, especially those of New England, who suffered most from the high-handed actions of the Royal Navy, were bitterly hostile to the idea of sanctions against Britain. For the Embargo on exports crippled American trade more than it hurt the British; and war with the dominant naval power in the Atlantic threatened not only to cut off trade with, and credits from, Britain but to sweep the American merchant marine off the seas. From the time of Jay's unpopular commercial treaty with Britain in 1794, which wrested only the most grudging trading rights from the British Empire, to the time when the Hartford Convention met to oppose the War of 1812, the merchants of New England put up with almost any indignity rather than prejudice the overseas trade which they knew, better than the backwoodsmen in Congress, to be essential to national growth.

Until Jefferson put it in jeopardy, American overseas commerce prospered far beyond the hopes of the merchants who had so gloomily contemplated the forest of idle masts in Atlantic ports during the post-war depression of 1783. Established family partnerships with capital and connections from colonial times, and new men with money made in privateering, commissioned ships with crews of Yankee youths and orders to sail for old and new trading grounds in search of profitable cargo. Fishing schooners brought the cod and mackerel of the Grand Banks to Marblehead and Newburyport; whalers supplied the factories of New Bedford from the polar regions; schooners provided the rum distilleries of Rhode Island with West Indian molasses; from Maine forests came timber, and from the farm lands of Pennsylvania, flour, lard, and salted meat; and on the ways of a score of estuaries ships were built, to be sold abroad. With such commodities, merchants in numerous little ports from Baltimore, Maryland to Portland, Maine, loaded their ships for voyages with papers cleared for Charleston, S.C., St. Eustatius in the West Indies or Fayal in the Madeiras, but with the Baltic, the Cape of Good

Hope, Buenos Aires or even Calcutta as the ultimate port of call. Some ports specialized, like Salem with her East Indiamen. Boston, on the other hand, took the lead in another spectacular new market, opened up for the first time by the New York vessel, *Empress of China*, in 1785. Thenceforward China traders habitually sailed from Boston round Cape Horn to the north-west Pacific coast where they loaded furs to be exchanged in Canton for nankeens, tea and china. During these years the Americans were establishing their hold in the most remote ports, returning after a two or three year voyage with a bewildering variety of specie, bills-of-exchange and goods, from Russian sailcloth and Cadiz salt, to wines, silk, pepper, teak and coffee, for home consumption or for re-export.

By skilled shipbuilding and navigation and shrewd bargaining, Americans made themselves masters of world trade and acquired family fortunes which, like that of Elias Derby of Salem or the Perkins's, Crowninshields and Forbes's of Boston, were powerful instruments of enterprise. By the time of the Napoleonic Wars such firms were able to take advantage of the status of neutral trader to sell provisions to Europe and to capture a large proportion of the world's carrying trade. Between 1790 and 1807 American exports rose from $20,000,000 to $108,000,000, of which re-exports jumped from practically nothing to over half the total. Earnings from such voyages provided invisible exports which helped to pay for the manufactures and heavy industrial goods of Europe.

The three decades after the War of 1812, when American-built ships outsailed, and Yankee wits matched, those of their rivals, were the golden age of American foreign commerce and a prosperous high noon for the ports of New England. New London, Newport, Salem, even little Essex and Nantucket, traded independently on the seven seas. Their seamen knew more of the Calcutta roads or Pacific reefs than they did of up-country New England, and the men who owned their counting-houses, ship's chandler's stores and rope walks were prosperous and proud. Boston was in a real sense a world capital: and with her powerful merchant princes, inter-related by family and in commerce, her graceful town houses and her intellectual eminence, she was, indeed, for those brought up there, "the hub of the universe".

But by the 1840's the day of the lesser New England ports was over. Commerce had become more complex, requiring larger ships, more extensive connections at home and abroad, and greater capital resources than ports like Salem and New London could command; and they lost trade to greater neighbours. Even Boston, frustrated for so long by lack of transport connections inland, fell behind her southerly rivals New York and Philadelphia.

The prosperity of Philadelphia and New York was increasingly based upon trade with Europe. New York, especially, with her superb harbour and approaches, drew ahead of Philadelphia, to become the pre-eminent importing port in the New World. Liverpool merchants and textile manufacturers from the Pennines had been establishing agencies there since the 1790's; and it was the auction rooms of New York which were chosen for dumping goods from pent-up British warehouses after the War of 1812. In 1817 an expatriate Yorkshire merchant in New York called Jeremiah Thompson, taking advantage of the improved sailing powers of ships, established the first commercial packet line sailing fortnightly between New York and Liverpool. The "Black Ballers", together with other lines between New York or Philadelphia and European ports, revolutionized the carriage of freight, emigrants and business intelligence and the North Atlantic trade became ever more concentrated on the New York-Liverpool run. The opening of the Erie Canal in 1825 tapped for New York a vast new hinterland.

Grains, flour and timber products from up the Hudson were not the only home-produced cargoes loading at New York. Liverpool merchantmen had brought British manufactures, prominent among which were the cotton textiles of Lancashire; and by 1820 Lancashire's almost sole source for raw cotton was the plantations of South Carolina and Georgia. For forty years cotton was king, not only of the American South, but of the Atlantic economy. Cotton gin and slave-plantation were linked with spinning-frame and power-loom in a vast commercial venture which quickened Atlantic trade. Between 1821 and 1851 the value of raw cotton in American exports rose from nearly 40% to nearly 60% of the total. The seemingly insatiable demand of the Liverpool exchange for American cotton stimulated a cotton-growing boom which sent seaboard planters inland to cultivate the rich cotton belt of Alabama and Mississippi. And New York, because of her financial power, her commercial connections, her shipping, and her need for outward-bound cargoes, quickly dominated the American end of the Liverpool cotton trade. New York and Philadelphia houses negotiated with Southern planters for their crops, financed, and even came to own, plantations. The bales were shipped in a triangular movement from New Orleans, Savannah and Charleston either direct to Liverpool or by coastal vessels to New York or Philadelphia for trans-shipment to an Atlantic freighter; and to the growing dismay of Southerners, Northern merchants reaped the commissions, as well as the profits of a highly speculative market for the South's great export staple.

Cotton, raw and manufactured, was only the most important staple in an Atlantic exchange of raw materials for manufactures which grew in importance with the rise of the Cotton Kingdom and the multiplying of a commercially ambitious people in the New World. That trade was governed by the decisions of some half-dozen merchant houses in English and American ports. Some, like Peabody and Co., were run by Americans in England; others, such as Brown Brothers of Liverpool, Baltimore, Philadelphia and New York, were truly Anglo-American; but the majority and especially the most powerful of all, Baring Brothers, were English and the dominance of the group derived from the City of London. Americans resorted to many devices, including lotteries, to increase their stock of liquid capital. Banking institutions also became established. In 1790 there were only three rudimentary banks; but by the 1820's the growing multiplicity of business had induced a rash of local banks, each issuing its own notes and conducting its own deposit and commercial business. Lack of expertise and heady optimism created a banking chaos which wildly exaggerated the fluctuations of confidence and trade. The more knowledgeable and conservative business communities of the great ports, like that of Boston whose Suffolk system provided stable clearing-house facilities for northern New England, imposed more ordered arrangements which greatly aided commerce. But despite such facilities, loanable funds remained scarce and interest rates were prohibitive. Commerce would have been hobbled had it not been for the commercial credits, at long terms and low rates of interest, which the Anglo-American houses were prepared to extend to American merchants. For behind the commerce of the Atlantic ports lay the great financial power of Lombard Street which under-wrote not only Anglo-American trade, but American trade with the Orient, and through American merchants and wholesalers reached back to remote country storekeepers in Ohio and cotton planters in Alabama.

The power of the City of London went further. Most of the Anglo-American houses began as dry goods merchants. But through their financial connections and the profits of trade they came to act as merchant-bankers for lesser firms and individuals. From this it was only a step to marketing American securities in London. By 1850 the growth of American insurance companies and savings banks, the passing of general incorporation laws which made it easy for public companies to be floated, and the development of the New York and Philadelphia stock exchanges which enabled promoters to reach a wider public of small investors, combined to make possible the accumulation of domestic investable funds. But these were by no means sufficient to supply the capital needs of a dynamic economy. For another generation or more, investors had to look abroad for the large drafts of capital needed for ambitious undertakings; and in the field of transport especially the New York stock market played only a subsidiary role to that of its elder brother in London. By means of the Anglo-American Houses and the New York stock market there was funnelled to the United States a stream of British and Continental capital for investment in Federal, State, municipal and private securities. And among the chief objects of this investment, direct and indirect, were those enterprises, notably in cotton-planting and in canal and railway construction, which were successively to lead the economy into new paths. In 1860 foreign investment, largely British, amounted to probably $400,000,000, about 20% of the total funded indebtedness. In the last analysis European capital primed the pump of the American economy; and these investment funds preserved the American balance of international payments by bridging the gap between American demands for overseas products and the immediate means of paying for them.

By the 1840's foreign trade was declining in importance for Americans. The long predominance of the American merchant marine was coming to an end. British sail was taking an increasing share of Atlantic freight; and although swift and beautiful American sailing clippers, whose design was perfected only in the fifties, held the palm for the carriage of express freight and passengers, the arrival at New York in 1838 of the British steamer *Syrius*, and the start two years later of Samuel Cunard's steam-packet line, foretold a new age when iron, screw-driven vessels from industrial Clyde and Mersey would take over more and more of this traffic.

However, a principal cause of the relative decline in overseas trade lay, not in foreign competition, but in the greater attraction of domestic enterprise. American merchants were looking westward; they had become continental-minded. New York and Philadelphia had grown into great metropolitan cities and their merchants had interests which far transcended port business. Dealings in up-country produce had led to commitments to internal markets; and as population moved west, seaboard merchants had become increasingly pre-occupied with extending their commercial territory inland.

In 1800 Americans, even on the seaboard, still lived in scattered townships linked by a few local roads which were no more than muddy or dusty trails, and by arduous coastal sailing; and the newer settlements, in the Appalachian highlands, in western New York and, beyond, in the Ohio valley, were stunted through lack of communication with the seaboard cities. Merchants who had been trained to a close calculation of prices in distant ports turned their minds to the profitability of landward connections which would make it economic for isolated, homespun communities to produce commercial crops and minerals, and to buy the manufactured amenities of civilization. Here in a continental market was the prospect of greater prosperity; and the key to that market lay in transport. A growing proportion of American enterprise was directed towards the creation of transport links up and down the coast and towards the West. Baltimore fought with Philadelphia, Boston with New York, in the attempt to broaden its hinterland at the expense of its rival by means of improved waterways, canals, turnpikes and railways. Hundreds of small seaboard towns and hopeful inland settlements clamoured for transport connections which for them were a matter of life or death.

From early Federalist days, but chiefly after 1816, groups of merchants and promoters were obtaining charters from State governments to build and operate toll bridges across the endless river barriers of the shore line and toll roads of stone and gravel which would bear heavy waggons. By

1830 a turnpike mania had created a spidery system of improved roads converging on the principal seaboard cities; and back-country farmers in Pennsylvania and southern New England began to find it worth while to grow produce for urban markets. In 1815 a much greater project was under way: the building of a Federal turnpike, known as the National Road, westwards from Cumberland, Maryland, through the Alleghenies to the Ohio (1818), and on by stages across Ohio and Indiana to Vandalia, Illinois, which it reached about mid-century. This important road was the first means of linking trans-Appalachian west and seaboard. Along it passed a heavy traffic by stage, horse and foot, westward of travellers and emigrants, of pedlars and waggoners taking eastern merchandise, and eastward of drovers driving cattle to urban butchers and traders in whisky and furs. In response to turnpikes there developed a new field of enterprise in waggoneering, coaching and in tavern and livery-stable keeping.

But even improved roads were of limited value. Normally financial failures, they only made possible a limited traffic of travellers and light merchandise. The first solution to the carriage of heavy freight was sought in the natural waterways which channelled the littoral and provided an age-old line of communication to the West. Rivers like the Hudson, the Susquehanna and the Delaware brought heavily-laden barges to port. Across the mountains, the great river system of the Ohio provided almost the sole means of transport. Migrating families floated down the Ohio and its tributaries; and at river-side settlements the first wilderness surplus was collected for market. Potash, staves and corn were loaded by farmers and river men on to flat- and keel-boats and poled the long voyage down the Ohio and the Mississippi to New Orleans, the West's first great market town. The trade of the Ohio, Tennessee and Kentucky settlements with New Orleans was sizeable even before the War of 1812. But it was a hazardous business. Rivers were dangerous to navigate, and the seasonal journey caused gluts and losses at market. Above all, like the river trade of the east, it was largely one-way. Some means had to be found to propel boats upstream if American rivers were to be true arteries of commerce.

The answer was the steamboat. Experiments by American engineers like Evans, Stevens and Fulton perfected the steamboat which, after the War of 1812, became a principal means of travel. Steamboat lines linked coastal ports by sheltered waterways, up the Delaware and Raritan from Philadelphia, along Long Island Sound from New York to Providence and Boston. In the West by 1820 scores, and by 1840 hundreds, of steamboats plied a speedy, if still dangerous, trade up and down the great waterways of the Mississippi system, penetrating into the most remote reaches from St. Louis to Pittsburgh, from the Gulf to the head of navigation on the Missouri in far-off Dakota. Steamboats made the internal waterways the basis for the first great regional market. Corn from Kentucky and Ohio, wheat from Illinois, lumber and cotton bales from Tennessee and Mississippi, forwarded by the country storekeepers of a thousand settlements, were delivered at the quays of thriving river ports such as Pittsburgh, Cincinnati, Louisville, St. Louis, and shipped by steamboat downstream to the ocean port of New Orleans, only to be trans-shipped into coastal vessels for the Atlantic seaboard or into freighters bound for Liverpool or Havre. With receipts from these sales, merchants and storekeepers in the remote interior could draw on eastern merchants and banks for manufactures and other necessities which returning steamboats delivered, along with their complement of emigrants and travellers, to upstream landings. The river steamboat enormously enhanced the prospects of a diversified commerce. Farmers north of the Ohio could earn credits from supplying corn and salt pork to planters in Mississippi, Alabama and Louisiana; and these in turn could concentrate their slave forces on raising cotton and sugar for the New Orleans and Mobile markets. As a result of this traffic New Orleans became the greatest exporting port in the United States.

But although the business of New Orleans expanded steadily until the Civil War, the proportion of her receipts from the products of the upper Mississippi Valley diminished from the 1840's onwards; and for a significant reason. The steamboat had solved one problem for the West; but although New York cotton brokers, through their correspondents in New Orleans, might control much of the Mississippi cotton trade, the mercantile fraternity of the Atlantic coast was by no means satisfied with a communications system which funnelled trade southwards to the Gulf, rather than directly east to the Atlantic coast. In the 1820's they strove to overcome what the merchants of the lower Mississippi valley assumed to be the natural flow of trade by building a new east-west transport link which was to short-circuit the river system and bring the old North-west within the hinterland of Baltimore, Philadelphia and New York.

The first means of accomplishing this was by building an artificial waterway. American capitalists had speculated about building canals long before George Washington and his partners had promoted a scheme to link the Potomac-Kanawha watershed by a water course in 1787; but it was only after the War of 1812 that the first effective canals were dug. Of immediate impact on the coastal cities were those linking Piedmont with Tidewater, like the *Susquehanna and Tidewater*, designed to draw off produce from Philadelphia to Baltimore, or the *Delaware and Hudson* and the *Lehigh* which in the 1820's made it profitable for settlements of miners in Pennsylvania to sell their coal to householders in New York and Philadelphia. But the most ambitious schemes were for canals which would circumvent the Appalachian barrier. The greatest, as it was the first, of all American canals was the *Erie*, completed in 1825. Prosecuted with characteristic American enterprise by men who knew nothing of canal engineering, financed by the State of New York with securities which were bought up largely by British investors, and dug by Irish navvies, "Clinton's big ditch" ran for three hundred miles along the "water-level" route from the Hudson at Albany to Lake Erie. It was designed to bind to New York City the fertile farming region of western New York whose produce was being drained off down the Susquehanna and Delaware. It succeeded far beyond the dreams of its promoters. The reduction in the cost of transporting a ton of produce from Buffalo to New York, from $100 to $8, transformed the commercial prospects of the rich Finger Lake country of Western New York.

But the *Erie* proved to be even more fruitful for American enterprise; for by establishing a water connection with Lake Erie it opened up the continental region bordering the Great Lakes. An immediate commercial success, the *Erie* induced a rage for canal-building among New York's rivals and especially in the State of Pennsylvania which constructed its own canal system through infinitely more difficult terrain across the mountains to Pittsburgh, and in Virginia where the *Chesapeake and Ohio* never reached further west than Cumberland. It also encouraged the distant farmer-legislators and land speculators of Ohio, Indiana and Illinois to dig canals linking the Ohio and Mississippi Rivers with the Great Lakes, and hence by means of the *Erie* with New York. The canals were built, with State bonds floated in Europe; and although they never paid their way, they proved a valuable adjunct to the Erie-Great Lakes system. In the 1840's, a new spurt of land development settled the Ohio and Indiana prairies and stimulated a new type of agriculture. Instead of the semi-subsistence, woodland farming of the river settlements, farmers on the prairies began commercially to raise corn, wheat, cattle and hogs which, in the form of flour milled in Buffalo, and meats canned in Cincinnati, could be shipped by Great Lakes waterways to eastern markets. In 1838 the infant settlement of Chicago, Lake Michigan terminus of the Illinois canal, sent its first grain sloop along the Lakes to Buffalo. During the forties a growing volume of wheat, corn and meat products, raised cheaply on rich frontier soils, flooded eastern markets and caused an agricultural depression in the stony uplands of New England whose sons and daughters went to town to work or west to take part in the new farming bonanza.

For the Great Lakes-Erie waterway was a two-way system. Grain and timber barges and sloops returned from Albany and Buffalo packed with migrants from New England and the Mid-Atlantic States and, further afield, from England, Germany and Scandinavia, intent on settling on new frontier lands bordering the Lakes in Michigan, Illinois and Wisconsin. This new wave of settlement, coming direct from the East, populated the Northwest and altered the geographical balance of the economy. Henceforward the communications and commercial allegiance of Midwestern merchants and farmers lay with New York, Philadelphia and Boston which provided markets and manufactures, commercial credits, and capital for major transport undertakings.

But waterways were not the complete answer to the problem of continental communication. Canals, frozen in winter, permitted only a seasonal freight; and travel by winding water levels and locks was slow and tedious. Railways, which could reach more directly across country, had been projected in the 1820's—the first stretch of the *Baltimore and Ohio* was in operation in 1830—but it was only after the canal boom had spent itself that promoters turned their attention seriously to their construction. The first lines, as in England, were designed to serve quarries and mines, and to act as feeders to canals and ports. John Stevens' *Camden and Amboy*, built by 1833, linked the New York-Philadelphia steamboat services across the neck of New Jersey; and gradually small, local companies pushed south from New England cities and east from New York to meet the steamers on Long Island Sound. In the 1840's New England was cross-hatched with such railroads; and by 1851 a series of short lines, not all the same gauge, provided a continuous link between New York, Albany and Buffalo.

The backing for such ventures was variously recruited. Civic patriotism and commercial interest prompted terminal cities to raise capital by issuing municipal bonds; local merchants and men of property bought stock, and their like in intermediate towns lobbied for the tracks to be routed favourably. Landowners and farmers contributed funds and sometimes grading-labour to a road which would raise property values. Business leadership was equally various. Some of the early railroad operators moved over from engineering, like the Stevens's, from carriage-making or stage-operating, from ferry-boating, like Commodore Vanderbilt, or from the U.S. Army Corps of Engineers. But the majority were recruited from the established mercantile and legal fraternity of the great cities, to whom railroads appeared a more profitable investment than foreign commerce. John Murray Forbes and W. H. Osborn had been in the China trade, James Boorman an iron importer, J. N. Denison a Boston dry goods merchant. These men, educated, with good family and business connections, and living in the great cities, conducted the strategy and provided the link between local enterprise and the sources of large-scale investment which were essential for such unprecedented construction. As in the case of the canals, most of this capital had to come from overseas. A local company scraped together enough funds and direct labour to grade the track; but railway iron and the means to pay for it came from England. Companies paid for iron rails imported from South Wales with railroad bonds which found their way to the London market. From the early days of the *Baltimore and Ohio* and the *Camden and Amboy* to the boom times of the *Erie* and the *Illinois Central*, the London money market played a decisive role in American railway construction; and the middlemen who made it possible were the merchants of Boston, New York and Philadelphia, known and trusted in the Anglo-American mercantile world.

The completion of the eastern, and the construction of the western, railway network lie beyond the scope of this essay. The railway boom of the fifties, with its revolutionary impact on markets and on the manufacture of iron, takes us out of the mercantile, and into an industrial era. But by rapid and cheap construction a skeleton system had come into being by 1853 which, forcefully supplementing the waterways, had established the lines of communication of modern America. Although, with the exception of the *Baltimore and Ohio* and the *Erie*, trunk lines could hardly be said to have existed, the *Pennsylvania* had just linked Philadelphia with Pittsburgh, and Erastus Corning was in the process of unifying the water-level route from New York to Buffalo as the *New York Central*. All these lines pointed towards the Mississippi Valley; and over five hundred miles away the thrusting businessmen of Chicago were reaching out to Washington, New York and London for capital to build the *Illinois Central*, and local lines and terminal facilities in readiness for the trunk routes which were to provide speedy Atlantic connections. By their energy and enterprise the men of the windy city were to make Chicago, with its converging railways, a Midwestern metropolis. It was Chicago which wrested the leadership in lumbering from Bangor, Albany and the Susquehanna, in meat-packing from Cincinnati, in flour-milling from Buffalo and Rochester, and in merchandising from St. Louis, whose complacent merchants still comforted themselves with the dogma that the natural flow of trade was downstream.

Until the 1850's lack of cheap transport inhibited the growth of industry. As late as 1820 it was often cheaper to import coal from South Wales than to transport it from mines thirty miles inland; even after the canals were built coal remained expensive; and the primitive state of the iron trade kept American industry to the methods of a pre-industrial day. Americans were still only scratching the surface of their rich continent. Their houses, for the most part, were heated by wood and lit by whale oil and tallow candles; their machinery was built of wood and wrought iron, harnessed with leather and hemp rope, greased with vegetable or animal oils, and turned by water-power; and their principal form of enterprise, after trade, transport and agriculture, remained the extraction of raw materials from the forests and their wild life, and from the sea.

The largest fortune made by an American before 1850 came from furs. John Jacob Astor arrived in New York as an immigrant in the year of American victory, 1783, and soon became prominent in that most ancient of all North American activities, fur trading. By this time the Appalachians were already depleted of beaver and the trade was dominated by Canadians who controlled the vast fur-bearing region of the upper Great Lakes. But by dealing with Montreal and, after Jay's Treaty had settled disputed boundaries, by establishing their own stations at Detroit, in the Ohio country and on the Missouri, American fur traders laid the basis for an empire which, at the turn of the nineteenth century, reached out to the

Rockies and the Pacific Northwest. Astor used furs as the means of building a complex merchandising business in New York which enabled him to assemble trade goods from all over the Americas and Europe. By this means he acquired an ascendency in the United States fur trade, organizing subsidiary companies and agencies at Michilimackinac, Detroit, Montreal, St. Louis and New Orleans. After the War of 1812 he had established a quasi-monopoly of the United States fur trade and, through his dealings in Pacific furs, he was a powerful influence in far-away Canton. But by the late 1820's the fur trade, that arch-robber of natural riches, was reaching the limits of profitability in the United States and shifting fashions of dress prompted Astor to retire in 1832 and sink his already enormous fortune in that characteristic new field of investment, New York City real estate. Astor's retirement marks the end of the fur trade as a major force in American economic life.

Similar to the fur trade was a second extractive industry which pushed its own, independent frontier across the American continent. The demand of Americans for forest products was insatiable. As population grew and spread inland the great stands of oak, chestnut and pine were cut, dragged over frozen snow, logged down spring rivers and through the canals, to provide frame-houses, barns and stores, wagons and even roads, for wood was the almost universal building material. Like furs, the timber industry was a Canadian-American affair, with origins in the New Brunswick-Maine forests as well as in those of western New York and Pennsylvania, where in the 1820's on the Susquehanna alone as much as 40 million feet a year was shipped downstream. When in the 1830's these forests became depleted and settlements grew up on the treeless country of Ohio and Indiana, lumbermen appeared in the forests of Ontario and Michigan to cut timber for prairie farmhouses. The timber industry was of rapid and continuous growth, production multiplying fourteen times in forty years; and although, unlike furs, it did not produce in this generation any towering monopolists, it was a major force in economic growth.

On the forested slopes of the Appalachians, the Adirondacks and else-where "pioneers" of a different kind were working the first shallow tunnels into seams of mineral wealth. Americans had smelted bog iron from colonial days, and their successors continued to develop seams of ore which could be easily turned into pig iron for local use. Until the 1840's the iron trade was a primitive affair of charcoal furnaces burning the fuel of the forest and supplying malleable iron which local black-smiths could turn into nails, horseshoes and farm implements. But improved transport and brisk demand prompted ironmasters to experiment with improved methods, with rolling mills, and with the puddling process which allowed the use of coal as a fuel. Coal miners, largely from England and Wales, were at work on bituminous and anthracite outcrops in the Alleghenies; and in nearby ironworks, especially after 1838 when a Welsh furnace-master, David Thomas, was imported to teach the technique, ironmasters began to manufacture anthracite-fired iron which, rolled into bars and railway rails, was suitable for heavy industry. But only in the late forties could it be said that the nucleus of a modern iron industry had been established, and only in the fifties did American railway constructors, the great users of iron, obtain the greater part of it from domestic sources. The story of the iron industry, like that of its twin, the railways, properly belongs to the later age of American industrialization.

Before 1850, with one prominent exception, American industry remained an affair of mill, cottage, shop and foundry, producing goods by craft methods for parochial markets. The problem of the market, the solution of which attracted enterprise and capital, discouraged those very forces from revolutionizing production.

Without cheap transport, industry was limited to local markets. The Atlantic ports and to a less extent an inland town like Pittsburgh were centres of industry supplying local needs. The last three decades before 1850 were years of rapid growth for Philadelphia, New York, Boston and Baltimore. The mercantile wealth and opportunity of a great port attracted to it the enterprise of lesser neighbours as well as an influx of immigrants from Europe who settled down to trades or manual labour in their port of entry. Between 1820 and 1850 the population of New York grew from 123,000 to over 500,000, that of Philadelphia from 112,000 to 400,000. The greater part of this urban population were jobbers, merchants, storekeepers, tradesmen or builders, or were engaged in the multifarious activities of the port, as ship-builders, ship wrights, ship-chandlers, dock labourers and seamen; but a sizeable proportion—in Philadelphia in 1860 as great as 17%—was engaged in manufacturing of various kinds from shoe-making or carriage-making to engineering and textiles. But even in the ports domestic manufactures still had to struggle hard to compete, not merely with imported luxuries, but with cheap standard lines of textiles, crockery, cutlery and hardware from the English midlands; and outside these urban centres specialization was slow. Here and there a local industry established its hold upon a regional market, like the hatters of Danbury, Conn., or the shoemakers of Lynn, Mass. But throughout the period, manufacturers of consumers' goods struggled with the problems of competing in wider markets with limited capital and primitive technique.

The great exception was textiles. In the early years of independence Americans of the poorer sort continued to dress in home-made clothing: in skins and in woollens spun and woven in cottage and homestead. Because of the rapid spread of population in advance of communications the production of homespun woollens probably increased down to 1830. But no sooner had the Revolutionary War ended than a few enterprising merchants sought to augment their stock of goods by assembling spindles and looms with the object of manufacturing textiles commercially.

These early "manufactories", sited on the rapid-flowing rivers of New England, New York and New Jersey, were almost totally handicapped by lack of knowledge of the new techniques of spinning, weaving and finishing which were transforming Britain into the world's first industrial metropolis. This knowledge was difficult to obtain, owing to the British ban on the export of artisans and machinery. But so great was the lure of America that from 1790 onwards an increasing number of British spinners and weavers took clandestine passage across the Atlantic in order to sell their knowledge and skills along with their birthright in the United States. Among the first there were a few so mechanically gifted that they were able to reproduce the machinery they had worked at home. In 1790 Samuel Slater, at the expense of Almy and Brown, Quaker merchants of Providence, Rhode Island, constructed the spinning frame he had learned to tend under Strutt at Belper, Derbyshire; and the mills he subsequently built, the influence he spread and the fortune he made entitle him to be regarded as the "father" of the American cotton industry. The Scholfield family of Saddleworth, Yorks., performed a similar office for woollens. The trail of such innovators was followed by scores and, later hundreds, of skilled operatives from the Pennines, a few contributing new techniques, most simply exercising their skills on familiar machinery.

The Embargo and the War of 1812, by cutting off British textile imports, induced more New England merchants to invest capital in textiles. In particular, Francis Lowell, a member of the Boston mercantile dynasty of Lowells, Jacksons, and Lees, persuaded two of its partners to put up funds for the construction of the most radical cotton mill yet seen in either hemisphere. Lowell, who constructed the first workable power-loom in the United States on the basis of experimental models he had inspected in Britain, was not content with the limited mill and outwork arrangements of Lancashire and Rhode Island. Adapting Robert Owen's New Lanark to American conditions, he constructed at Waltham on the Charles River a water-powered factory in which all the processes of spinning and weaving cotton took place under one roof. Here, and later in the daughter factory-towns of Lowell and Lawrence on the Merrimac, Lowell and his successors created a characteristically American innovation: the large-scale manufacture of a few counts of cheap, standard cloths in a rationalized factory-layout, operated by a few skilled workers and a large amateur force of New England farm girls, attracted to temporary jobs by prospects of pin money and lodging in respectable company boarding-houses.

From Lowell's day, the textile industry began to forge ahead on lines of its own, and already in the late 1830's was contributing inventions, such as ring-spinning and the Goulding condensor, which were later to find their way back across the Atlantic. Although woollens remained backward, the cotton industry, behind a protective tariff, made extensive inroads into the American market for cheap English cottons, particularly the denims and corduroys which were the staple clothing of farm hands and slaves. But throughout the period, especially in southern New England, the industry remained largely a colony of Lancashire. New processes, like the self-acting mule and calico-printing, continued to be imported along with the British operatives who, despite dilution by Irish and French-Canadians, were the backbone of the skilled labour force until well after the Civil War. The Yankee mill-owners who put up the capital, made sure that few of the immigrants, however enterprising and skilled, should rise higher than factory superintendent. But in terms of skill and operation the rise of the American cotton industry is a phase of Lancashire's expansion. The Cotton Kingdom was basically an exchange of American raw material for British manufactures. However, the exchange was so productive that British and American capital not only created a continental market in the United States, but released further American capital to finance an American offshoot of the prime British industry nearer to markets and to sources of supply. And because of contrasting industrial and social conditions on the two sides of the Atlantic and of the ease of travel along the North Atlantic trade route, British industrial labour was easily induced to migrate westwards and to colonize the new industry. As in other industries, from pottery to steel, the rise of American textiles is best regarded, not as an autonomous venture, but as a process of migration within the Atlantic economy: the first major phase of American progress from "colonial" to "metropolitan" status.

Slater, Lowell, Lawrence, Appleton and their rivals were fully-fledged manufacturers. However, most of them, even in this exceptionally advanced industry, had begun as merchants; and in general it was the enterprise and capital of merchants, jobbers, land speculators, transport promoters, lumbermen, millers and farmers which determined the thrust of the American economy during the period.

Apart from textile manufacturers and a few ironmasters, industrial capitalists, as a separate class, had hardly come into being. The "manufacturer" still bore a recognizable resemblance to the master craftsman of colonial times. Often himself a promoted journeyman, "the boss", in the old dutch slang of New York, presided over a small shop or put out materials to cottages in which other journeymen turned out custom-made or small-batch market wares to the order of wholesaler or merchant. It was the merchant who, by means of his entrenched position and his capital, controlled the access to markets, determined the flow of orders and provided the credit for raw materials, wages and rent. And because the merchant was pre-occupied with holding his own in rapidly expanding markets for numerous commodities, he had neither the knowledge, the time nor the capital to devote to improving manufacturing techniques in one commodity. Here and there capital was employed to cheapen the processes of manufacture. Cotton textiles was not the only industry in which devices were invented to rationalize production in ways best suited to American conditions of a scarcity of skill and a mass utility market. From the day in 1800 when Eli Whitney first manufactured rifles by means of inter-changeable parts put together by relatively unskilled workmen in a series of simple operations, small New England machine-shops had been pioneering new engineering methods which were to be the basis for a machine-tool industry; and already in 1851 characteristic devices from Elias Howe's sewing machine to Cyrus McCormick's reaper demonstrated at the Great Exhibition in London that Americans were more advanced than Englishmen in getting tedious operations done by machinery. But the fruits of such inventiveness were for the future. Industry as a whole was backward by English standards.

Manufacturers were, indeed, severely handicapped by their lack of control over markets and capital. With reduced transport costs, markets expanded and competition from more distant producers forced merchants to cut prices. These cuts were passed on to the manufacturer who was forced to turn from the production of custom-made and small-batch goods at "conventional" prices for local sale to the manufacture of cheap and more standard articles for distant markets. Without the means of in-creasing his productivity through the use of more advanced machinery, he had no alternative to cutting piece-rates. In the 1820's and '30's a journeyman was forced to produce more piece-goods to make both ends meet. Instead of working in his own time and combining a cottage craft with a small-holding or, like the cordwainers of Lynn, with deep sea fishing, he found himself working from "sun-up to sun-down" as a full-time wage earner in sweat-shop conditions. At the same time the coastal cities were thronged with immigrants from the countryside and from Europe, prepared to work for lower wages, and crowding the poorer tenements until rents were at a premium and craftsmen as well as labourers had to make shift with miserable lodgings in cellars and attics. In the 1830's Boston, New York and Philadelphia already suffered a slum problem which during hard times strained the resources of charity.

Such conditions bred unrest. From the 1790's masters and journeymen had moved to protect their craft by forming trade societies which on occasions had organized strikes for higher payments. Despite hostile courts which treated them as conspiracies against trade, such combina-tions won temporary concessions during good times, and in the 1820's the trades of Philadelphia, New York and lesser centres formed local unions of crafts, "city centrals" which in the 1830's sent delegates to a series of national conventions of trades. This activity was closely con-nected with the rise of political parties, the object of which was to use the votes of the newly enfranchised working men to promote political reforms which would better their status. The disparate programmes which in-cluded a ten-hour day, a hard currency, universal education, abolition of imprisonment for debt and freedom to settle on the public lands, together with the eligibility for membership of their "bosses" and farmers, indeed of all save bankers and merchants, illustrate the workers' bewilderment at the cause of their plight. It was not clear to either worker or "manufacturer" that their interests might conflict. Both were united in opposition to the privileged classes, bankers, merchants and lawyers who appeared to manipulate the economy against the "producers". They looked, not forward to an industrial age, but back to an age when craftsmen enjoyed independent status. Disillusioned by the failure of the workingmen's parties, the journeymen returned to industrial action; but it was to be a long hard fight. Only in 1842 did an important court decision in Massachusetts recognize that trades unions were lawful and strikes for a closed shop legal, and only subsequently did the spinners of New England organise the first, clearly-conceived drive on the part of factory workers for a ten-hour day.

From the days of the Federalists the mercantile fraternity of the Northeast had worked for the systematic development of American resources. Some among them had read Adam Smith, and most hoped for the freest possible trade with commercial nations like Britain. But the exposed position of the infant Republic abroad, and the poverty of capital at home, reinforced an inherited mercantilism which made it natural for them to look to the State to provide protection and initiative in economic affairs. Hamilton had hoped to bind mercantile wealth to the Republic by reciprocal interest. Jefferson had shown that the interests of the Republic were broader than those of commerce; and after the collapse of the Federalist party, the mercantile communities no longer expected to dominate the policies of an increasingly continental-minded nation. But they continued to look to the cities, the States and the Federal Government to provide backing for commercial enterprise by means of the whole battery of devices characteristic of the mercantilist age.

Direct action by individual States seemed the only solution to the unprecedented financial and legal problems of transport undertakings. Some of the earliest of the turnpikes and bridges were built and operated directly by State-owned corporations governed by acts which authorized the issue of State bonds and the appropriation of taxes. This solution was found even more suitable for the formidable problem of canals. The *Erie* was a public work of the State of New York, and its example was followed by Pennsylvania, by other eastern States, and by those of the upper Midwest. But after the first phase of direct State innovation, the more characteristic form of enterprise in transport and banking was the mixed or private corporation. A chosen group of merchants and promoters would be granted a State charter to form a public company to build and operate a turnpike, a canal or a railroad, or to conduct a banking or insurance business. In many cases such franchises would carry monopoly rights; but often even the most favourable charter was not sufficient

I

without the promise of public funds; and many of the corporations were financed, in part, by State capital provided by the issue of public securities, and governed by a mixed board of public and private directors. By this means, powerful and politically influential capitalists in the eastern cities were in a position to enjoy a protected investment and to command the economic development of important communities.

At this time the State was the most important unit of economic policy. But in the early days the Americans also looked to Federal Government to give a lead in enterprise. Hamilton's thoroughgoing programme of economic development had never found full acceptance; but from the days of the National Republicans to those of the Whigs the mercantile communities continued to press for active Federal control. The National Road was built at the expense of the Federal Government into the heart of the Old Northwest. The Federal Government also persisted in a banking policy, despite the hostility of the Jeffersonians who had allowed the charter of Hamilton's United States Bank to lapse in 1811. In 1816, after the chaotic experience of government finance during the War of 1812, and through the efforts of prominent merchants like Stephen Girard and Astor, a second Bank was instituted along the lines of the first. The Bank's object was to aid the Federal Government's fiscal transactions, to support government securities and to act as a central bank. Like its predecessor and the State-chartered banks it was a mixed corporation, with a combination of public and private capital and direction. Under the enlightened administrations of Cheves and Biddle in the 1820's the Bank was a positive force in restraining the fluctuating credit policies of private banks and in acting as a flywheel for the economy as a whole.

But the late 1820's was the high-water of Federal action in the economic sphere. In those days of rapid territorial expansion political power was dispersed and the rights of States were asserted at the expense of the Federal government. There grew up, especially in the new West and South, a multitude of small entrepreneurs, planters, farmers, merchants, bankers, millers, lumbermen, transport operators, with local interests which conflicted at the Federal level; and as a result national economic policy was neutralized. The tariff ceased to reflect any clear economic objective; land policy was progressively liberalized in the interests of speedy settlement; and by vetoing, on constitutional grounds, a Bill providing Federal funds for a new section of the National Road, President Jackson put an end, for a generation, to the use of Federal funds for transport improvements. But the greatest defeat for Federal power came with the Jacksonian attack on the United States Bank. The defeat of the attempt to re-charter the Bank in 1833 was the result of political conflict in which economic issues were confused. Opponents of the Bank included westerners who objected to its credit-controlling policies and its eastern, privileged character, eastern working men for whom it was an inflationary instrument and the symbol of an oppressive merchant capitalism, and even eastern private banking interests. But the result was the virtual abdication of the Federal Government from the exercise of positive economic direction. Henceforward, until land grants for railroads, *laisser faire* was the rule in the Federal sphere.

Similar tendencies were to be discerned at the State level. By 1840 State mercantilism had built a transport network and subsidized a banking system. But public opinion was beginning to turn against quasi-state enterprise. The canal mania had ended in financial disaster, with the economic collapse of 1839-42 and repudiation of State bonds. In the east, as in the west, a growing number of small entrepreneurs resented the control exercised over the economy by the established mercantile community. The Jacksonian party in the east included, not only working men, but small businessmen convinced that privileged groups of merchants, bankers and lawyers were acquiring a stranglehold on the country. Such men were particularly jealous of the hegemony of great merchants over markets and of the facility and security with which they could obtain public capital, and exclusive rights of incorporation. Among these were a growing number of small manufacturers who needed capital in order to expand production and establish their own contact with markets. As a result of these shifts in opinion, State legislatures began to divest themselves of their commercial responsibilities and to assume a more neutral role in economic matters. At the same time they began to give heed to the growing demand of small businessmen for equal privileges. From 1837, when Connecticut passed the first general incorporation act, the eastern States began to grant blanket authority for the forming of public corporations. This step made it easier for new men, without the influence to put through special Acts and without the capital to function as a simple partnership, to acquire corporate privileges and to attract capital on the open market. The gradual extension of limited liability, the abolition of imprisonment for debt and the regulation of bankruptcy opened new vistas for business and liberated innate American desire for speculative profits.

In short, in the States as well as in the nation at large, *laisser faire* was becoming the rule by the close of our period. The change reflected the passing of a mercantile age, in which a powerful commercial oligarchy commanded capital and enterprise. Henceforward, in the fifties, a new generation of railway promoters, ironmasters, textile, and other manufacturers, were to make the running; and at their heels was a crowd of thrusting industrial capitalists who were to hold the power and take the major decisions in the second half of the century. In the fifties the shift from mercantile to industrial capitalism was not complete; and it was only after the Civil War that it was reflected in political life. But already in 1853, at the start of the first great railway boom, all the signs were there. And with the rise to power of a class of industrial capitalists bent on establishing behind tariff walls a range of modern industries geared to manufacturing commodities on a mass scale for a continental market, the mercantile economy of the Atlantic was to take on a secondary importance. The United States still needed European capital and labour, but the Atlantic gave precedence to the Continent.   America was turning inward.

MANIFEST DESTINY

By John A. Hawgood

★

THE desire of the people of the United States to extend the territory under their sovereignty until it comprehended the whole of the mainland of North America and certain strategically placed islands both to the east and to the west of that continent was first given its classic and forceful definition as the pursuit of "Manifest Destiny" in the year 1845, but the aspiration and indeed the policy implicit in that term go back much further, to John Quincy Adams, to Thomas Jefferson and even to Benjamin Franklin. It is a term of much flexibility, as indeed it needs to be to describe alike the ideas of the expansionists of 1782, of 1812, of 1844, of 1898 and of 1911. It has undergone many changes of meaning and has many facets. One scholar, Albert K. Weinberg, has discovered in it fifteen different aspects, to each of which he was able to devote a chapter of a very big book. In Manifest Destiny he saw Natural Right, geographical predestination, the destined use of the soil, extension of the area of freedom, the true title, the mission of regeneration, natural growth, political gravitation, inevitable destiny, the white man's burden, paramount interest, political affinity, self-defence, international police power and world leadership. This formidable list is by no means exhaustive. Manifest Destiny can mean whatever any generation, or indeed any man, cares to make of it, in the course of justifying the acquisition of territory.

What the Americans have chosen to call "Manifest Destiny" is of course a concept and a policy by no means peculiar to them or to their country. Almost all peoples have, at one stage or another in their history, felt and expressed the need to extend their territory and also to explain and justify this need both to the world and to themselves. The Americans, both a highly articulate and a highly-strung people, have talked about their Manifest Destiny even more consistently than they have followed it, and at times the vacuum during a generation of relative territorial stability has been filled, by way of compensation, with an inordinate amount of talk about their need and their right to expand.

In the first hundred years of the history of the United States (to which this particular essay is confined) the doctrine of Manifest Destiny received its final definition—though many glosses were subsequently added thereto—and achieved remarkable successes, the two most spectacular being the Louisiana Purchase of 1803 and the acquisition by very different

123

methods of Texas, Oregon, California and New Mexico, between 1845 and 1848. Each of these two great accessions of territory nearly doubled the area under United States sovereignty, while the purchase of Alaska in 1867 added more than another half-million square miles to the three million already possessed. For a country which had emerged from the Revolution with only 892,135 square miles this was indeed remarkable. These striking results were achieved largely through the intense conviction of the Founding Fathers and of the leaders of two succeeding generations of Americans, such as John Quincy Adams, Andrew Jackson, James K. Polk and William H. Seward, that the United States must expand until they comprehended, if possible, the whole North American continent. It is true that Canada was not annexed, that the major part of Mexico remained independent, and that certain islands lying off the coasts of North America which were also deemed to lie in the path of "Manifest Destiny", remained and still remain outside the political sphere of the United States; but they were under almost constant pressure up to about the year 1872. In that year, with four times her area of the year 1783, the United States had a population of over forty millions, compared with barely four millions at her first census in 1790, and her people were spread in places thickly, in other places sparsely, over the length and breadth of her three million square miles. The Mississippi had long since been crossed, the prairies put under cultivation, the rich mineral resources of the Rocky Mountains exploited and the fabulous wealth of the Pacific Coast area discovered and garnered. The acquisitions of land between 1803 and 1867 had created a whole new series of American frontiers, the last of which were still, in 1872, in process of being called into existence. Not until after the Census of 1880 (but before that of 1890, according to F. J. Turner's famous definition) did the classic "American frontier", the unbroken belt of unsettled land stretching from the Mexican to the Canadian border, cease formally to exist.

The year 1872 is therefore an appropriate vantage point to look back upon this century of territorial expansion, for there was to be no further acquisition of territory by the United States upon the American mainland from that day to this, though an island empire was soon to be secured both in the Atlantic and in the Pacific oceans. The continent had by 1872 been spanned, not only by the overland pioneers, on foot, on horse and mule back and in their covered waggons and prairie schooners, but by the Pony Express (in 1860), the electric telegraph (in 1861) and finally by the fast transcontinental railway (which was completed in 1869). In 1872 the Indian menace was all but extinguished, and the great Civil War which had briefly checked both North and South in the process of occupying and exploiting the West (but had not appreciably slowed up the development of the West itself) was over and had released thousands of its unsettled veterans into the new lands. Immigration was climbing to new statistical heights and was beginning for the first time to include large numbers of eastern and southern Europeans. Above all, the industrial revolution had at last reached the United States in full flood. A young Scottish immigrant of the year 1848, Andrew Carnegie, was in 1873 to turn his attention to steel production, with decisive effects upon the American and, indeed, world economy. The United States was, in the popular phraseology of the day, "coming of age" as a great power. Manifest Destiny had not only put her on the map but had spread her all over it.

The dubious honour of having actually coined the term "Manifest Destiny" belongs to the Irish-American editor, John L. O'Sullivan, who first put it into print in the July 1845 issue of *The Democratic Review* with reference to the proposed reception of the Republic of Texas into the Union. It has, however, a number of foster-fathers, and the latest and strongest claim in this category is that made on behalf of John Quincy Adams (by no less an authority than Samuel Flagg Bemis). Adams could easily have written John O'Sullivan's words, asserts Dr Bemis. In fact "he had all but coined the magic-making phrase". Perhaps, indeed, O'Sullivan should be given the credit also for having "all but coined" the phrase six years before he actually did so, for in 1839 he had written in the *Democratic Review*, "The far-reaching, the boundless future will be the era of American greatness. In its magnificent domain of space and time the nation of many nations is destined to manifest the excellence of divine principles. Its floor shall be a hemisphere, its roof the firmament of the star-studded heavens." For John O'Sullivan, indeed, the sky was the only limit.

A very strong and widely held sentiment was thus forged by grandiloquent phrase-mongering in the 1830's and 1840's into the spearhead of a new burst of expansive energy. But the urge had long been present, almost since the first settlers landed on Roanoke Island and lost themselves or were destroyed, through wanting to find out (in all probability) what lay beyond. This urge was already very strong in the generation before the American Revolution, when such men as Benjamin Franklin and John Adams strongly supported Britain's policy, in the French and Indian wars which broke out in 1754, of removing the barrier imposed by France to the expansion of the British mainland colonies across the Alleghenies and into and down the Mississippi Valley. George Washington made his military and administrative reputation on the Virginia and Pennsylvania frontier between 1753 and 1758 in the series of operations which culminated in the abandonment by the French of Fort Duquesne (Pittsburgh), a key-point in this French barrier.

When the war was over in 1763 and the French had been defeated and driven from Canada and the whole Mississippi Valley—for Louisiana was transferred to Spain while Britain took Florida—the colonists were understandably incensed by the policy of the notorious Royal Proclamation of that year. It sought to deprive them of the hinterland, an area for future westward expansion which already they considered their heritage, by drawing a line along the crest of the Appalachians beyond which white settlement was in future to be prohibited. This primary cause of the revolution was given even more irritant force by the British government's Quebec Act of 1774, which, while retaining the barrier to settlement westward (from all of the thirteen colonies except Georgia) at the crest of the Appalachians, gave to the Canadian colony of Quebec the rich hinterland north and west of the Ohio River right to the Upper Mississippi, a huge V-shaped area later to be known as "the Old Northwest", which was claimed by several of the colonies under their charters. Only through Georgia could the thirteen colonies now expand to the Mississippi (beyond which lay the barrier of Spanish Louisiana), and from South Carolina to Massachusetts the interposition of a great Indian reservation erected a double barrier between them and the great river. When the policy of giving no further grants of land to western settlers in the rebellious colonies was advocated in the British Parliament early in 1775, Edmund Burke, who had already vigorously criticized the Proclamation of 1763 and the Quebec Act, exploded in high indignation and in prophetic vein in his great speech on Conciliation with America. He said:

But if you stopped your grants what would be the consequence? The people would occupy without grants. They have already so occupied in many places. You cannot station garrisons in every part of these deserts. If you drive the people from one place they will carry on their annual tillage and remove with their flocks and herds to another. Many of the people in the back settlements are already little attached to particular situations. Already they have topped the Appalachian mountains. From thence they behold before them an immense plain, one vast, rich, level meadow; a square of five hundred miles. Over this they would wander without possibility of restraint; they would change their manners with the habits of their life; would soon forget a government by which they were disowned; would become hordes of English Tartars; and pouring down upon your unfortified frontiers a fierce and irresistible cavalry, become masters of your governors and your counsellors, your collectors and comptrollers, and of all the slaves that adhered to them. Such would, and in no long time, must be, the effect of attempting to forbid as a crime, and to suppress as an evil, the command and blessing of Providence, "Increase and multiply". Such would be the unhappy result of an endeavour to keep as a lair of wild beasts, that earth, which God, by an express Charter, has given to the children of men . . .
. . . I think this new project of hedging-in population to be neither prudent nor practicable.

Here, in Edmund Burke's eloquent phraseology, is perhaps the earliest explicit statement of the doctrine of the manifest destiny of the Americans to expand over "that earth, which God, by an express Charter, has given to the children of men". With this passage perhaps in mind, Benjamin Franklin and John Jay, during the peace negotiations of 1783, were to reject with equal violence a French suggestion that an Indian state under Spanish protection be interposed between the territory of the former thirteen colonies and the lower Mississippi and Ohio. (This would even have deprived the United States of Georgia's former Mississippi frontier under the Proclamation of 1763 and the Quebec Act.) Such a boundary, said Franklin, would have "cooped us up within the Allegheny mountains". In such homespun phraseology, redolent of "Poor Richard" rather than of the words of those two eloquent Irishmen Burke and O'Sullivan, did Franklin nail his colours to the mast of Manifest Destiny. He also coolly suggested (though without success) that it would be "desirable" for Britain to give up "every part of Canada" to the United States. Though this was a bargaining move which was not pressed very hard, Franklin was nevertheless staking a claim that was to be repeated again and again in future years by American expansionists, and to be re-enforced more than once by invasion or the threat of invasion of the northern neighbour.

Thanks to the efforts of Franklin, Jay and Adams, the new republic was not born "cooped up" in 1783, but obtained the Mississippi river as its boundary from its source (wherever that might be) to the southern extremity of Georgia at the line of 31° north latitude. But, to pursue Franklin's metaphor, it was not long before the United States began to flutter her wings. As early as 1787, John Adams, one of the American signatories of the treaty of 1783, opined that his country was "destined" to spread over "the entire north part of this quarter of the globe". Such a destiny was as yet hardly manifest in a confederation of bickering states which had all but gone to war with each other over conflicting claims and interests, which were bankrupt and militarily weak now that the revolutionary levies had been disbanded, which had not yet created an effective national government and which indeed were finding it difficult to maintain in the Northwest and the Southwest even the boundaries they had obtained in 1783. Such, however, was (and is) the invincible optimism of American statesmen that none of his compatriots challenged Adams's statement, while any foreigner who heard of it would have dismissed it as mere empty bombast. One is reminded of the words (uttered in the year 1902) by a then little-known Princeton University professor named Woodrow Wilson to the effect that "a new age is before us in which, it would seem, we must lead the world".

The eastern half of the Mississippi Valley had been saved for American democracy by the negotiators of 1783 not only from their British enemies, but also—and with even more difficulty—from their French and Spanish allies. The settlers were already flooding through the Cumberland Gap and fanning out into the territories of Kentucky and Tennessee before the ink was dry on the treaty of peace, to join those pioneers taken through "illegally" (in the eyes of the British Crown) by Daniel Boone

in and after 1775. George Rogers Clark had begun to open up and pacify
the Old Northwest across the Ohio river during his successful campaign
against the British and their Indian allies during the war; and now the
first flatboats were beginning to float down that river to Marietta (1788)
and points west. Zanesville (founded in 1799) was named for the maker
of Zane's Trace, that pioneer cart-track to the west that was later to be
followed by the famous "National Road", short-cutting the winding
Ohio river route across into the Indiana and Illinois country to the old
French settlement of St. Louis, where the Missouri river joins the
Mississippi. From 1763 to 1803 St. Louis was in Spanish hands and the
whole Missouri Valley belonged (until its forcible re-transfer back to
France at the dictate of the First Consul, Napoleon Bonaparte, in 1800)
to his Catholic Majesty. It was as yet only very inadequately explored
and almost unexploited, except by occasional trappers and *voyageurs*.

All this wilderness going to waste was a challenge to the roving
imagination of another of the Founding Fathers of the American republic.
Thomas Jefferson, a frontiersman himself, born at Shadwell in Albemarle
County, Virginia, within sight of the Blue Ridge of the Alleghenies, was
a strong upholder of the rights of the western settler. Furthermore he
pictured the ultimate spread to the west coast of North America of "free
and independent Americans, unconnected with us but by ties of blood and
interest, and employing like us the rights of self-government". At that
time the United States had no shred of a claim to any territory on or
even near to the west coast of North America. Jefferson had tried to
interest George Rogers Clark in an expedition to the West in 1783; and,
while American Minister in Paris, he had listened with sympathy to the
schemes of John Ledyard, an American seaman who had been one of
Captain James Cook's crew on the famous voyage round the world and
who had conceived the idea of reaching the coasts of Oregon and California by travelling eastwards across Siberia. Encouraged and financed
by Jefferson, Ledyard was half-way across Asiatic Russia in the direction
of Kamchatka and the Behring Straits when Catherine the Great refused
to let him proceed any further. Back in the United States in 1793 as
Washington's first Secretary of State, Jefferson tried to organize an
exploring expedition, under Michaux with young Lieutenant Meri-
wether Lewis as his *aide*, to the great river of the West. An American
sea captain named Grey had just entered it from the Pacific, had named
it the Columbia, and had formally claimed it for the United States. But,
by the year 1800, although the Jay and Pinckney treaties of 1794 and
1795 had reinforced the claims of the United States to her frontiers of
1783 and had kept the Mississippi River open to her traders, not one
inch had been added to her territory. It was Jefferson's roving imagination,
again, which sensed the danger that would arise for the United States if
the weak and decaying Spanish monarchy should give back the great
Louisiana territory to a rejuvenated Republican France, now under the

leadership of the boundlessly ambitious Napoleon Bonaparte. The First Consul did in fact insist on this transfer of territory in the year 1800 (though Jefferson was not to hear the terms of the secret treaty of San Ildefonso until two years later) and had plans to re-establish a French Empire in the Mississippi Valley, which would seriously have hindered American expansion across that river. A French expedition to the island of Santo Domingo (half of which Napoleon had forced Spain to cede to France) was, after putting down the slave-rebellion there, to move on to Louisiana through the port of New Orleans. The prospect for the United States, only uneasily in control of the new states of Kentucky and Tennessee (which had shown some signs of breaking away from the Union almost as soon as they became part of it), was alarming.

Thomas Jefferson's government snatched at an opportunity, provided by the outbreak of war again in Europe in 1803 and by the failure of the Santo Domingo expedition, of exploiting a hint from Napoleon Bonaparte that he might be prepared to sell Louisiana and the colony of New Orleans to the United States. Napoleon undoubtedly feared that Britain, in command of the seas, might capture Louisiana if he did not get it quickly into the safe, neutral hands of the United States. He may well have been influenced by Jefferson's threat (which was allowed to "leak" through the gunpowder manufacturer Dupont de Nemours to the First Consul) that the existence of a French army in Louisiana would cause the United States to conclude an alliance with Great Britain, "to marry ourselves", as the author of the Declaration of Independence brought himself to say, "to the British fleet and nation".

The great Louisiana territory, not much short of a million square miles in size, extended the boundaries of the United States to the Rocky Mountains in the west, to the headwaters of the Missouri river in the north-west, and to the Sabine River (some said the Rio Grande) in the south-west. Virtually none of this territory was settled except the territory of New Orleans, at and near the mouth of the Mississippi River, and the area around St. Louis. Most of it was entirely unexplored and the exact location of its western limits had yet to be determined. The Spaniards in New Mexico had outposts in the Rocky Mountains to the north of Santa Fé (and beyond the Continental Divide) but had not penetrated into what is now the state of Colorado; a few *voyageurs* had pushed up the Missouri to the villages of the Mandan Indians in what is now North Dakota, and the men of the Hudson's Bay Company had traded down from Canada to those same villages, but nobody had found a way for settlers to follow through the mountains to the Columbia and to the South Sea or Pacific Ocean which lay beyond, connecting America with China.

In the very year that the Louisiana Purchase was made (1803) Jefferson sought to fill this gap in geographical knowledge and also to stake a further American claim to the Pacific Northwest which men of the Hudson's Bay Company and its competitors were beginning to explore and which one of them (Alexander Mackenzie) had described in a book, published in 1801, and read by Jefferson at this time. He sent out Lewis, with William Clark, to find a route to the Pacific by travelling up the Missouri and down the Columbia. By December 1805, after many adventures, they achieved their objective and wintered on the shores of the Pacific Ocean. When the supply ship which Jefferson had said he would send around Cape Horn to meet them failed to materialize, they set off eastwards again in April 1806; finding a quicker way back through the mountains (and aided by being able to travel downstream on the Yellowstone and Missouri rivers) they were back in Washington to report in person to Jefferson before the end of that same year.

Meanwhile Jefferson had sent out another army officer, Lieutenant Zebulon Montgomery Pike, to explore the Mississippi River to its source, which he succeeded in finding and mapping in 1805—to the great advantage of American claims in the negotiations with Britain in 1819. Pike the next year made the longer and more hazardous journey across the plains to Santa Fé, there to be arrested as a spy by the Spanish authorities and conducted by a roundabout route, which enabled him to see and describe Texas, back to the Sabine River at Nagadoches, the first American frontier and trading post. A third expedition by Pike failed to penetrate far into the Colorado Rockies and he pronounced the Peak which bears his name to be "unscalable". A motor road now runs up to its summit, 14,000 feet above sea-level!

Nevertheless, the expeditions of Z. M. Pike, and the books in which their reports were published, began to familiarize men with the routes across the plains, though another official explorer, Stephen H. Long, was to describe a "Great American Desert" in such exaggerated and forbidding words that it was believed that the high plains were permanently incapable of agricultural development and could only be exploited by the hunter and the trapper. Not until the 1840's, when the fur-trapping era was nearly over in the beaver-denuded streams pouring down from the Rocky Mountains, both to the east and to the west, did tales of fertile valleys in the Oregon Country and in California, far beyond the mountains and the desert, begin to attract settlers in any large numbers; men who would make the great trek across to the Pacific Coast into territory the United States did not yet own, and where, therefore, their title to the lands on which they settled could only be precarious. But land hunger drove them on; the soil of New England, never over-fertile, had been overworked and mercilessly subdivided, while the best lands of the Mississippi Valley east of the line of semi-aridity were already taken up and could only be obtained at "improved" prices. The movement of agricultural settlers from the United States into Spanish Texas had started a quarter of a century earlier, because there no natural barriers except easily fordable rivers stood in their way.

The United States had a claim to Texas up to the Rio Grande, by an interpretation of the Louisiana Purchase Treaty which Spain strongly denied. She had, also, a claim to the Oregon country by virtue of the voyage of Captain Grey, the expedition of Lewis and Clark and the founding of the trading post of Astoria in 1812. But to Upper California she had not a shadow of a claim, and she recognized this explicitly in the treaty of 1819 with Spain, which admitted that Spanish territory on the western side of North America ran up to latitude 42° north. In that same Adams-Onis treaty (under which the United States purchased Florida from Spain) the frontier-line of the Sabine River was agreed upon, and the somewhat shadowy claim to Texas was thus abandoned.

Manifest Destiny had not yet been coined as a "magic phrase" but an outburst of expansionist energy had already, before 1819, occurred in the United States. This was the outcry to obtain possession of Canada and end for ever the vexatious raids on American settlements of Indians subsidized and armed—or thought to be—from across the northern border. The "War Hawks" of 1811 and "the Expansionists of 1812" had used the friction with Great Britain, which resulted in the outbreak of war between the two countries in the latter year, to whip up the movement for an attack on Canada, but the invasion had been no more successful than was a British invasion of the United States from Canada during that same war, and the treaty of peace signed at Ghent in 1814 left the boundaries between American and British territory exactly where they had been before. In 1818 a further treaty was to give the United States the 49th parallel as its northern border from the Lake of the Woods to the Continental Divide and thus eliminate a British claim to part of what is now Minnesota, but this was territory far to the west of the older provinces of Upper and Lower Canada, Ontario and Quebec, which the American expansionists had coveted in 1812.

While it was a group of men most of whom were new to national politics, like Henry Clay of Kentucky, who led the expansionist clamour in 1812 and after, it was in fact two old hands at the helm of United States policy, John Quincy Adams and James Monroe, who negotiated the treaties of 1818 and 1819 with Britain and Spain and that of 1824 with Russia, which so well prepared the way for the next great expansion of United States territory in the 1840's. These treaties, between them, only gave to the United States East Florida and Northern Minnesota in addition to territory she already held, and they saw her abandonment of her claim to Texas, but, nevertheless, they forced Spain, Britain and Russia all to recede from extreme positions or claims to which they had previously clung. Spain, who had claimed the Pacific Coast up to 54° 40′ north, was now down to 42° N; Russia (in treaties both with Britain and with the United States) abandoned her claim to any territory south of 54° 40′ north; Britain had given up least, refusing to abandon her claims in Oregon, in the north-east, and between Lake Superior and the Lake of the Woods, but had at least recognized the 49th parallel from the Lake of the Woods to the Rocky Mountains. The Anglo-American "condominium" in Oregon was extended indefinitely in 1828 and continued to work perfectly well until the "Oregon fever" began to sharpen the claims of the United States to the whole of the Pacific Northwest.

The Monroe Declaration of 1823 really plays no conspicuous part in the history of Manifest Destiny or in the expansion of the United States during the generation in which it was first formulated. Restated and sharpened by President Polk in the 1840's, it only then began to have teeth, more of which grew in the days of William H. Seward, while it became almost nothing but teeth as interpreted under the Roosevelt Corollary at the beginning of the twentieth century.

The Simon-pure Monroe doctrine, largely drafted by John Quincy Adams and announced to the world by the President of the United States in his message to Congress on December 2, 1823, was in essence a negative and a defensive rather than an expansionist or aggressive statement. It simply denied the right of non-American powers to establish further colonies on the American continents, or to intervene by force of arms in the affairs of American states which had won their independence. While John Quincy Adams believed that the United States would one day rule over all of the North American continent and that all European colonies therein would be eliminated, he did not state or even imply that in the famous message of 1823. In 1821 he had said to the British Minister in Washington "Keep what is yours, but leave the rest of this continent to us", a statement more blunt than anything to be found in the Monroe declaration itself.

"With a few striking exceptions" claims Richard Van Alstyne "the United States shifted the emphasis in its foreign policy from security to expansion for the balance of the century after 1823." The original Monroe Doctrine was a measure of security, but every extension and re-interpretation of it until Woodrow Wilson's return to the "security" aspect in 1913 was essentially expansionist. In and after the year 1843, when "Mr Monroe's Doctrine" was first talked of as such, it began to be used by the Democratic Party as a tool of Manifest Destiny. By the middle 1850's "the Monroe Doctrine", as it was now being called, had become bi-partisan, for the Whigs had accepted it—and many of them Manifest Destiny too—and thus the new Republican Party was born (in 1854) with Manifest Destiny in its bloodstream. William H. Seward, Abraham Lincoln's Secretary of State, was, after the end of the Civil War, to become one of the most active proponents of expansion in American history, despite the fact that Lincoln—preoccupied with other things— cannot be classed with J. Q. Adams, Jackson, Polk, Pierce or even Buchanan as a White House expansionist.

It cannot be too often reiterated that by the year 1819 the United

States had renounced formally and by treaty any claims she might have had to either California or Texas. President Monroe seems fully to have accepted this as a permanent bar to further westward expansion (except into the Oregon country) on the part of the United States. In so far as he was interested in further expansion himself, it was expansion *eastward* —into Cuba now that Florida had been secured, for "I consider Cape Florida and Cuba as forming the mouth of the Mississippi" he wrote to Thomas Jefferson in 1823, a view no doubt acceptable to the latter, who (in 1807) had opined that "we consider the whole Gulph Stream as of our waters". Florida had been thought desirable by the young Henry Clay "because it fills a space in our imagination". So now, apparently, did Cuba, even for the most conservative of American statesmen.

The less conservative let their imaginations rove more widely—even in 1823. "Sir," said Representative Bayliss in the House, when Senator T. H. Benton (who afterwards changed his mind) had talked about the Rocky Mountains as the "terminus" of westward expansion, "our natural boundary is the Pacific Ocean." Benton at this time thought that the United States had bitten off just about as much as she could chew. It was difficult to conceive of him then as a potential father (or, at any rate, father-in-law) of that Manifest Destiny which, at full flood, carried United States sovereignty to San Francisco Bay, Monterey and San Diego. Benton's gifted daughter, Jessie Frémont, was embroidering the truth more than a little when she wrote in the memoir of her father which is appended to her husband's *Memoirs* (also tastefully embroidered by the same fair and fine hand), "In 1820 commenced in the Senate his championship of a quarter of a century for our new territory on the Pacific." In 1820 nothing had been further from Benton's thoughts. His own new state of Missouri still stood upon the frontier and the supposed Great American Desert lay between it and the Pacific. The overland routes had not yet been opened.

But if Benton had not taken the road of Manifest Destiny by 1823, there were two men who very definitely had already done so. These two men were Andrew Jackson, who had lately filibustered his way into Florida, and John Quincy Adams. These two fought each other bitterly in the Presidential elections of 1824 and 1828, but as regards the future expansion of United States territory their hearts beat as one. They differed somewhat respecting the methods that should be used. Andrew Jackson, having tried it already with success, was all for what the twentieth century would call the Fifth Column technique. Mid-nineteenth century Americans were soon to designate it as "The Texas Game". "This [the seizure of Florida] can be done without implicating the government," he wrote cheerfully on January 16, 1818. John Quincy Adams, no less anxious (as early as 1819) that "the world should be familiarized with the idea of considering our proper dominion to be the continent of North America", advocated the method of "fair purchase for a valuable consideration", a principle on which the Yankee politician as well as the Yankee trader could regulate his way of life without undue strain on his conscience. "Old Hickory", lacking both the Yankee conscience and Yankee principles, was prepared to try rougher methods.

Yet the 1830's, within which decade Andrew Jackson's two presidential terms were confined (except for the year 1829), was not a decade of expansion for the United States, but rather a decade of preparation. The twenties had seen a halt called to further European expansion on the American continent—both by the enunciation of the Monroe Doctrine and by the Treaty with Russia of 1824, in which the Russians renounced any claim to territory south of 54° 40′ N latitude and thus left what were to become British Columbia, Washington and Oregon for the British and Americans to bicker over and finally to partition in 1846. Andrew Jackson was not responsible for the treaties of 1824 and 1828, which were Adams's handiwork; at that time he was much more interested in the possibilities of south-western than of north-western expansion. While it did not become part of the United States for another ten years, Texas (which Jackson looked on as a potential Florida) achieved independence of Mexico in 1835 under a government manned by immigrants from the United States.

In that same year (1835) a very acute foreign observer, Alexis de Tocqueville, wrote: "At a period which may be said to be near . . . the Anglo-Americans will cover the immense space contained between the polar regions and the tropics, extending from the coasts of the Atlantic to those of the Pacific Ocean." He did not know that at that very time the ambitious intriguer Anthony Butler, Andrew Jackson's official representative in Mexico, was attempting to bribe Mexican leaders to cede to the United States "the whole of that tract of territory known as New Mexico and higher and lower California, an empire in itself, a paradise in climate . . . rich in minerals and affording a water route to the Pacific through the Arkansas and Colorado rivers". Butler thought that about $500,000 would do the trick. His geography may have been rather weak but his enthusiasm and his optimism were beyond doubt. Andrew Jackson (who had the enterprising Butler returned to him empty-handed by the Mexicans as *persona non grata*) was less niggardly but almost equally weak in geography when he proposed in 1837 to the Mexican leader Santa Anna—recently captured by the Texans at San Jacinto and sent to Washington to see the President but now magnanimously released—that in return for a payment of $3,500,000 Mexico should cede Texas and all other territory north and east of the Rio Grande to the United States, and then accept the 38th parallel as a boundary (instead of the 42nd, as agreed in 1819) between the headwaters of the Rio Grande and the Pacific Coast. This would have given Utah, Northern Nevada and Northern California to the United States but not San Francisco Bay, which was what she most wanted. The Mexicans saved Jackson

from the consequences of his geographical *gaffe* by repudiating Santa
Anna's bargain and sending him—their perennial bad penny—back into
exile. This was Jackson's last chance to win California and to secure a
clear title to Texas, for in March 1837 he was succeeded by his henchman
Martin Van Buren as President. Van Buren, a northerner, was suspicious
of all further expansion for fear that it would only serve to extend the
area of slavery. Americans had already taken their slaves with them
into the Texan Republic, whose government legalized slavery there even
though it had been prohibited when Texas was a province of Mexico.
It was feared that they might also take them into New Mexico
and California should these territories be acquired. Little was then
known about the climate and economic possibilities of those remote
areas.

Thus, during the presidency of Martin Van Buren, Manifest Destiny
marked time. But if the politicians were inactive, the publicists were not.
John L. O'Sullivan already had the "magic phrase" on the tip of his
tongue in 1839, as has been seen, and his fellow-editors, J. Gordon
Bennett, Moses Beach and Thomas Ritchie, were beginning to beat their
drums too. After the election of President Harrison in 1840, Andrew
Jackson began once again to assert his great influence (in eclipse for a
time on account of his quarrel with Van Buren) and to urge Tyler—who
stepped up to the Presidency after Harrison's death in 1841—to conclude
a treaty of annexation with Texas. Jackson had gone out of office before
Texas (the independence of which the government in Washington
recognized somewhat tardily on March 3, 1837, the last day of his
Presidency) could be annexed by the United States. When the Republic
sought admission to the Union in August 1837, Van Buren—already
moving toward his later "free soil" attitude—stalled by treating the
request as "inexpedient", while John Quincy Adams, who was still for
expansion in all other directions, now set his Yankee conscience against
swallowing the slave republic and filibustered for three weeks in Congress
against any such action. The disgruntled Texans withdrew their application and started coquetting with Britain, who at least was thought to
be willing to give the Lone Star Republic protection against reconquest
by Mexico, at the price of their abolishing slavery and promising never
to revive the idea of becoming part of the United States. Even General
Sam Houston, the first President of Texas, who had been sent down
there "to play the Texas game" by Andrew Jackson in 1832 and who
had led the movement for independence from Mexico, lent himself to
this intrigue—as it was regarded in Washington—with Palmerston and
Aberdeen. In 1842 the Texans were again rebuffed by President Tyler's
Secretary of State, Daniel Webster, another New Englander who, even
if he did not have much of a conscience, was not prepared to swim
against the current of northern opinion. Only after Webster had gone
out of office did his successor, Abel P. Upshur, a gentleman from Virginia,

K

announce the intention of the United States government to annex Texas. Andrew Jackson had worked effectively to this end upon President Tyler (now a renegade from the Whig Party) and it was at this time that the formidable ex-President spoke of Texas as being "presented to the United States as a bride for her espousal"—a bride, incidentally, who had already been left at the church door by the hitherto reluctant groom no less than three times. Senator Benton, not to be outdone, was even more explicit. "Man and woman were not more formed for union by the hand of God than Texas and the United States are formed for union by the hand of nature" he declared on August 29, 1844. Jackson had already both clouded and clarified the issue (and somewhat mixed the metaphor) by referring in 1843 to the proposed annexation of Texas as "extending the area of freedom". This was interpreted by the extreme southerners of the school of John C. Calhoun as "freedom" to join the Union and thus to increase the pro-slavery vote in the Senate, as well as "freedom" to reject the overtures of abolitionist Britain. They were all for this sort of freedom. By this time the abolitionists of the North and the extreme pro-slavery element in the South were chasing their own tails on the subject of Texas, the former regarding annexation as a "slave-holder's conspiracy" and the latter treating it as an anti-slavery intrigue, especially after Great Britain recognized the independence of Texas in 1842. The Senate was divided so completely on the issue that a two-thirds majority in favour of a treaty of annexation proved impossible to secure. Calhoun, the new Secretary of State (after Upshur's untimely death), anxious to bring Texas in as a slave-state before she struck any corrupt abolitionist bargain with Britain, quickly signed a treaty of annexation with the somewhat bewildered Texan representatives on April 12, 1844. Both Van Buren (an ex-Democrat) and Clay (a Democrat in good standing) came out against annexation, along with the Whigs John Quincy Adams and Daniel Webster, and the treaty was rejected. Still standing at the church door, the bride cast yet another sidelong glance at that ogling *boulevardier*, Lord Aberdeen, especially when Britain persuaded Mexico (still extremely reluctant) to recognise the independence of Texas on the understanding that she should stay independent. Only the by-passing of the Senate impasse (largely through T. H. Benton's intervention) by the device of annexing Texas by a joint resolution of both Houses of Congress—which merely required a simple majority in each—brought the reluctant wooer up to scratch, and Texas was at last brought into the Union on December 29, 1845, if not a blushing, certainly a somewhat red-faced bride. If there had been anywhere else for her to go and if she had not been bankrupt and more or less defenceless, she would certainly not have submitted so meekly (for her) to this series of pre-nuptial humiliations.

"Manifest Destiny" thus started somewhat raggedly as a magic phrase first applied by John L. O'Sullivan (in his July 1845 article) to the extremely confused Texas situation. But he at least made his meaning clear. He wrote:

Why, were other reasons wanting in favor of now elevating this question of the reception of Texas into the Union, out of the lower region of our past party dissentions, up to its proper level of a high and broad nationality, it surely is to be found abundantly in the manner in which the other nations have undertaken to intrude themselves into it between us and the proper parties to the case, in a spirit of hostile interference against us, for the avowed object of thwarting our policy and hampering our power, limiting our greatness and checking the fulfilment of our manifest destiny to over-spread the continent allotted by Providence for the free development of our yearly multiplying millions.

O'Sullivan asserts that the "hostile interference" of other nations had been a principal factor in sharpening the appetite of the United States for further expansion. This fear of hostile interference dated only from around 1841 when, according to Dexter Perkins, "In Texas, in California and in Oregon the ambition or the intrigue of European nations seemed to the dominant political generation of Americans to threaten fundamental American interests." In 1842 an American naval squadron had prematurely occupied (and immediately afterwards evacuated) Monterey, the capital of Spanish Upper California, out of a mistaken fear that Britain was about to do so, and, in that same year, Daniel Webster and Lord Ashburton had been forced to exclude a settlement of the Oregon question from their treaty owing to a complete failure to agree on a permanent boundary in the Pacific Northwest.

It remained for James K. Polk, elected President in November 1844 while the Texas problem was still hanging fire in the United States Senate, to settle, in a fashion highly satisfactory to the United States, all three of the territorial threats mentioned by Dexter Perkins. It is true that this was achieved at the expense of a war with Mexico and of risking a war with Great Britain, but the prizes were glittering ones and the fact that the United States had come opportunely (in the winter of 1844 and the summer of 1845) to the crest of a new wave of expansionist sentiment greatly helped the administration. Like the negotiations with Texas over annexation, the negotiations with Great Britain over the partition of Oregon dragged on through 1845, the Americans vacillating greatly regarding their minimum terms. In 1842 Tyler and Webster had been prepared to accept the Columbia River as the boundary (giving the whole of the modern state of Washington to Great Britain), had Britain been prepared to help to bully Mexico into giving up Texas and Upper California to the United States. Indeed Waddy Thompson, American Minister to Mexico, almost brought off this deal without the aid of Great Britain and might quite easily have done so but for the precipitate action of the egregious Commodore Thomas Ap Catesby Jones at Monterey, in California, that autumn. By 1844, after the "Western Agitation" and the "Oregon fever" of 1843 had hardened and inflamed American opinion, the demand was for "Fifty-four Forty or Fight", a slogan that the Western Democrats used in the Presidential campaign of 1844 and to which Polk, their chosen candidate, was himself committed. The Democratic party platform of 1844 also spoke about "the re-occupation of Oregon and the re-annexation of Texas", thus blandly assuming that Oregon and Texas had both previously belonged to the United States, which would have been hard to prove in a court of international or any other law.

Once elected, Polk and his Secretary of State, James Buchanan, were more realistic, though Buchanan was too much of a politician to be statesmanlike without a certain amount of backing and filling, which disgusted the President—as his remarkable *Diary* shows. The demand for 54° 40′ was quietly dropped and the 49th parallel (including the giving up of the whole of Vancouver Island) was once again proposed by Buchanan in July 1845. With the Texas question still unsolved, it was worth a lot to the United States to remove the danger of war with Britain over Oregon. The stiff-necked British Minister in Washington, Sir Richard Pakenham—who had been forced to live in the United States through the "Fifty-four Forty or Fight" agitation, and whose temper must have worn very thin by this time—rejected this overture without even consulting his government, but Lord Aberdeen instructed him to re-open negotiations along very similar lines soon afterwards. Now it was the turn of Polk to be stiff-necked, but in February 1846 he finally abandoned the idea of going back to the demand for 54° 40′. Meanwhile, the annexation of Texas had been achieved, and Mexico was beginning to talk about it as a *casus belli*. If there was going to be a war with Mexico there was all the more reason for a peaceful compromise with Great Britain; after all, there were virtually no American settlers north of the Columbia River, in 1846, so that the attainment of a boundary along the 49th parallel was a very considerable diplomatic success for the United States. Congress discussed the proposed settlement in its great "Oregon Debate", in which the sentiment on Manifest Destiny was given a very thorough airing indeed. Such ill-assorted figures as Calhoun, Webster, John Quincy Adams, Henry Clay, T. H. Benton and the veteran Gallatin (Jackson was now dead) supported the settlement, and although Senators Hannegan and Allen still kept up their sing-song of "Fifty-four-forty-or-fight", they were now generals without an army. On August 5, 1846, the Oregon Treaty was proclaimed.

Meanwhile (so completely did the different phases of the onward march of Manifest Destiny overlap each other in this "Year of Decision") the Mexican War had broken out. Though the news had not yet reached Washington, California had been occupied by American naval parties, co-operating with American irregulars recruited from among settlers and recently arrived immigrants in the Sacramento Valley, to whom that resourceful and ambitious topographical engineer, John Charles Frémont, had lent encouragement and clandestine leadership in the Bear Flag revolt of June 15, 1846. It was not then known in California that the United States and Mexico were already at war, though the news of border clashes on the Rio Grande had been received. The Americans in California who ran up, first the Bear Flag of an independent Californian Republic (truly "the Texas game" all over again), and then the Stars and Stripes in June and July 1846, were taking the considerable risk that, should the United States and Mexico not be at war, or a peace be quickly concluded, California would be handed back again, with apologies, to the Mexican authorities, as Monterey had been in 1842. Several of the most important and most prosperous Yankee settlers in California expressed this fear in forcible terms to the United States Consul at Monterey, Thomas Larkin, and he was even worried about the possibility himself, as his reports to the Secretary of State, James Buchanan, clearly show. The strength of the sentiment of Manifest Destiny in Washington was not properly appreciated in far-off Monterey or in the hamlet of Yerba Buena (soon to be renamed San Francisco) or in the "City of the Angels" down in the south. Once they had Upper California the Manifest Destinarians of the United States were not likely to let it go. Nevertheless it should always be remembered that as late as February 1848, when President Polk sent the Treaty of Guadalupe Hidalgo to the United States Senate, Daniel Webster and no fewer than fourteen other Senators voted to hand back to Mexico all territory west of the Rio Grande. "New Mexico and California are not worth a dollar" argued Webster. Yet as recently as 1846 that versatile statesman had written to his son "The port of San Francisco would be twenty times more valuable to us than all Texas." This made all Texas worth rather less than five cents, which was truly cutting her down to "little giant" size.

It was perhaps only to be anticipated that the supporters of "Manifest Destiny", having achieved such heady triumphs within three short years for the United States, should have become intoxicated with the implications of their own words, which every day became more extravagant. When, in his annual message of December 1845, President Polk re-asserted the Monroe Declaration (the first mention of the message by an American President for twenty-two years), he added his famous corollary to the effect that "The Peoples of this continent alone have the right to decide their own destiny" and the right, also, to join the American Union "without any foreign interposition". This was a significant step beyond Monroe's simple assertion that the peoples of the American continent, having once won independence of European domination, should not be re-conquered by force of arms, and brought the Monroe Doctrine into step with Manifest Destiny. During the course of the war with Mexico a sentiment in favour of the acquisition of all Mexico grew up.

At first it was fought with distinctly limited territorial objectives, summed up in the instructions to Slidell, who was sent to Mexico before the war had started in a last effort to purchase the territory desired, and to Trist, who was sent into that country with General Scott's invading army to try to conclude a peace with the Mexican government based upon very similar objectives. James Buchanan, who had, at the outbreak of hostilities, urged upon President Polk the issue of a pledge that Mexico would not be dismembered, characteristically changed his mind, much to the exasperation of Polk, and joined the "Continental Democrats" who clamoured with the *Democratic Review* (once again) in October 1847 that "until every acre of the North American continent is occupied by citizens of the United States the foundations of the future Empire will not have been laid". The invitation to the United States from the authorities in the remote, tropical Mexican province of Yucatan to take it, plagued as it was by a serious Indian uprising, under American protection, was a most tempting prospect. Lewis Cass, who was to be the Democratic candidate for the Presidency in 1848 and who was already looking for good publicity angles, came out at the beginning of that year in favour of the annexation of Yucatan. "Providence" he declared "has placed us, in some measure, at the head of the republics of this continent, and there never has been a better opportunity offered to any nation to fulfil the high duty confided than the present." Later that same year he turned his eyes in the direction of Canada too, and one German diplomat in Washington reported to his government that Cass's election would probably have led to an invasion of Canada and a war with Great Britain.

But it was not always wise to take the words of the Manifest Destinarians at their face value. *Niles Weekly Register* printed at the time (January 1848) a whole column of typical "Manifest Destiny Doctrines", such as would have taken the United States half a century of war with about half the world to implement. Indeed, as the demands upon Mexican and Canadian, Caribbean and other territory in the western hemisphere became over-extravagant, a reaction set in. Calhoun, John Quincy Adams and Daniel Webster had all, for their various reasons, opposed the aggressive policy of the Polk government in the Mexican war and now all three argued against the annexation of more than a limited amount of Mexican territory, Webster going so far as to want only Texas and New Mexico east of the Rio Grande—which had been claimed by the independent Republic of Texas for a decade anyhow. The veteran Adams even uttered a pro-Mexican sentiment in a letter to the yet more venerable Albert Gallatin on December 26, 1847. "The design and purpose to dismember Mexico . . ." he wrote "has been pursued by means which gave to Mexico from that time [the year 1830] ample cause of war in self-defence against the United States."

The moderates (or the extremists of other types, like John C. Calhoun) who feared by the beginning of 1848 that Manifest Destiny was getting out of hand, were relieved to hear the terms of the Treaty of Guadalupe Hidalgo, concluded by the repudiated State Department clerk Trist on February 2, 1848—just a week after the discovery of gold in California, though nobody knew about this in Washington D.C. or in Mexico City for some months to come. By this treaty Upper California and New Mexico were transferred to the United States and the annexation of Texas was recognized. The provinces of Lower California, Sonora and Chihuahua, and all her remaining territory (much of which the expansionists had claimed) were left to Mexico, and no extra-territorial rights in the Isthmus of Tehuantepec were accorded to the United States. Grumbling, Polk sent this treaty (without his blessing, for even he had wanted more) to the Senate, which, already involved in the early manoeuvres of the Presidential campaign of 1848 (in which a number of Senators were active candidates for nomination) and anxious to get this more remote struggle out of the way, finally ratified it on May 30. The fact that 26 Democrats and 12 Whigs voted for it, and 7 members of each party against it, is interesting. President Polk noted in his *Diary* on February 25, 1848, that "Mr Webster is for *no* territory and Mr Hannegan for *all* Mexico and for opposite reasons both will oppose the Treaty. It is difficult upon any rational principle to assign satisfactory reason for anything Col. Benton may do . . . The truth is the approaching Presidential election absorbs every other consideration".

Nevertheless, the Democrats were the Manifest Destiny party still, and they suffered in the election campaign of 1848 from the surfeit of Manifest Destiny talk to which the country had been subjected. The Whigs found a strong candidate in General Taylor, a hero of the Mexican war (and a Whig in good standing even before the war) whom President Polk, who was not a candidate for re-election, was known to detest, a fact which helped the General considerably. The Whigs came into office in 1849 and Lewis Cass was saved from the temptation to send expeditions into Yucatan and Canada. Until nearly the end of the four years of the Taylor-Fillmore administration (Taylor died in office) Manifest Destiny was damped down. But it soon became evident that it was only gathering strength for fresh claims and new extravagances. Out of office, the Democrats could abandon all verbal caution and talk in terms of "tomorrow the world". The ultra-nationalist "Young America" movement was a by-product of all this, and not to be outdone by native Americans, two enterprising German immigrants, G. Poesche and A. Goepp, produced in 1853 a pamphlet entitled *The New Rome—or the United States of the World*, outlining a plan whereby the United States of America, by a process of "natural growth", might ultimately absorb every quarter of the globe into the Federal Union.

Even the Whigs now began to catch the infection. Both Henry Clay and Daniel Webster were caught publicly boasting, in the year 1850, of the size and strength of the United States, thus by implication approving of past, even if they did not advocate further, expansion. Then, the last Whig Secretary of State, Edward Everett, produced on December 1, 1853, a remarkable state paper in which he enunciated the doctrine of the "natural growth" of the United States, in the course of refusing a sly Anglo-French proposal that all three powers should sign a self-denying ordinance regarding the annexation of the island of Cuba, which was then in the midst of one of its numerous revolts against Spain. "America" said Everett ". . . but lately a Waste, is filling up with intense rapidity, and adjusting on natural principles those territorial relations which, on the first discovery of the continent, were in a good degree fortuitous." The cynical reaction of Lord John Russell to all this compares interestingly with the glee with which American Senators and Congressmen fastened upon it. Senator Soulé took it as a justification for those filibustering expeditions he was helping to promote; Senators Mallory and Cass found it the perfect statement of Manifest Destiny; Senator Douglas discovered in it an excuse for breaking treaties at will. Every expansionist read into it what he himself believed.

But the Whigs (whose one concrete piece of expansion had been the modest Gadsden Purchase of some 50,000 square miles of territory, mostly desert, on the Mexico-Arizona border in 1853) were not to be given a chance to show exactly how far their espousal of the doctrine of national growth could take them along the line of Manifest Destiny, for the Democrat Franklin Pierce had been elected President in November 1853. In his inaugural address, stealing some of Everett's thunder, Pierce went on to take up a much more positively expansionist attitude than had any previous President of the United States. His administration, he declared, was not to "be controlled by any timid forebodings of evil from expansion". Four years later, his successor as President, James Buchanan (at last taking up a firm attitude on the subject—his life-long ambition now having been achieved) went even further and declared, in his inaugural address: "Expansion is in the future of our country and only cowards fear and oppose it."

Alas, despite all this brave talk the eighteen-fifties proved to be a decade of frustration after frustration for the irresistible force of natural growth toward a Manifest Destiny having no limits, and were to end in a sectional struggle that, for the time being, removed from the minds of Americans all ideas of acquiring more territory, so preoccupied were they with trying to hold together what they already had. The sixties were a decade of civil war and reconstruction, of Indian counter-attacks, of the construction of transcontinental wagon and stage roads, telegraph lines and railways to bind Atlantic and Pacific states more closely together— and not of further expansion. Not one square mile of territory was added to the United States between the Gadsden Purchase of 1853 and the Alaska Purchase of 1867. This was not, however, despite the preoccupation of the sectional struggle, for want of trying.

Great Britain, while not challenging the basic principles of the Monroe Doctrine, continued to attempt, in a number of subtle ways, to check American expansionism by diplomatic action. The Clayton-Bulwer treaty of 1850, which was very unpopular in the United States, saw both powers agree not to annex any territory in Central America—the United States of course had none there yet—and to act together over a canal through Nicaragua. The reciprocity treaty of 1854 removed the irritant of the north-eastern fisheries dispute—*Punch* had sensibly declared "We can't think of quarrelling with Jonathan about fish"—and the trouble over recruiting men in the United States to fight for Britain in the Crimean war (which resulted in the expulsion of John Crampton, the British minister in Washington, in 1856) was successfully ironed out. American filibustering expeditions to Nicaragua under William Walker and other adventurers continued through the 1850's, and the failure of the United States government to curb these unhallowed expansionists continued to make the British government doubt its good faith. Even more annoying was the continued American interest in the annexation of Canada. The expansionists of 1782, of 1812, of 1837 and of 1849 had all been disappointed in their belief that this particular pear was ripe, and that the natural force of gravity (as John Quincy Adams had once put it) would at any moment bring it down as a windfall to the American Union. There were always disgruntled elements in Canada which lent encouragement to American hopes only to fail to deliver the prize. William L. Mackenzie, the leader of the 1837 rebellion in Canada, was unkind enough to say, after a subsequent visit to the United States, that he could not have wished a worse fate for his country than to become part of the American Union. The most egregious and annoying attempt to gain Canada for the United States was to come in the eighteen-sixties, in the very year of the British North America Act, when Senator Charles Sumner of Massachusetts coolly proposed that Canada should be handed over in settlement of the *Alabama* and subsidiary claims (which his peculiar arithmetic inflated into billions of dollars). The opinions of the Canadians themselves were not sought by Sumner; if he had paused to think he would have realized that the series of pinpricks caused by the recent Fenian "invasions" of Canada from United States territory had not helped to make them more favourable to what he demanded. Only after 1871 may the Americans be said to have come for the most part to accept the idea that the Dominion of Canada actually preferred retaining its allegiance to the British Crown to the alternative of seeking admission to the American Union. Only after the *Alabama* settlement was it considered safe by both countries to leave a really "unguarded frontier" along the border of the Great Lakes and the forty-ninth parallel. As recently as 1868 the *New York Herald* had considered Canada's monarchical institutions "an irritant" to free Americans.

William H. Seward, the able Secretary of State under Presidents

Lincoln and Johnson, had nailed his colours to the mast of Manifest Destiny many years before, by stating in 1846 that "the popular passion for territorial aggrandisement is irresistible", but during his period of office he was more interested in the possibility of expansion in the Caribbean area than anywhere else. The acquisition by purchase of Alaska in 1867 was an unexpected bonus first proposed by the Russians themselves. American filibustering in Cuba and Santo Domingo in the fifties had greatly annoyed Spain and other countries without benefiting the United States, and the sending of John O'Sullivan and Senator Soulé to Portugal and Spain as American Ministers, when both were known supporters of filibusters such as Lopez, had not been the most tactful of actions. Seward was more adroit than this, but he failed to restrain Andrew Johnson from making expansionist claims, and indeed, the President's expansionist message of December 8, 1868, was drafted or at any rate inspired by his Secretary of State. Johnson's successor, Ulysses S. Grant, was no more restrained, and continued to hope to secure Santo Domingo either by intrigue or by purchase, but by this time Congress had turned unco-operative and at last seemed to be growing tired of all the alarms and excursions of Manifest Destiny. Canada, Central America and the West Indies, Hawaii, Japan, Formosa and the China coasts were, in addition to Mexico, continuing to catch the roving eyes of American statesmen. It was the legislature (which in the forties and fifties had tended to egg them on) which now, from its position of greatly enhanced post-war strength, at last called a halt—for a decade or so—to the heady and intoxicating game. Grant was told by Senator Bayard of Delaware that his plans "would embark the government of the United States upon the vast and trackless sea of imperialism", and Senator Carl Schurz (an exile of the German revolution of 1848) said that further expansion would "demoralize and corrupt our political life". He called it "Manifest Doom" rather than "Manifest Destiny".

After being in the saddle for over a quarter of a century, Manifest Destiny had at last fallen upon evil times. President Grant discontinued his efforts to obtain Santo Domingo, and watchdogs like Carl Schurz prevented any serious revival of expansionist sentiment until the eighteen-nineties. Perhaps the best epitaph on that early type of Manifest Destinarian, who flourished from 1812 to 1871, and had his heyday between 1844 and 1856, was uttered by an astute British diplomat, Sir Henry Bulwer, writing to Lord Palmerston from Washington D.C. on August 12, 1851. He wrote:

The hold which their government has over them [the expansionists] is exceedingly weak and uncertain; and it has been their habit to pour into and occupy territory contiguous to their own; and then, assuming the character and position of its natural inhabitants, to claim its annexation to the Mother State . . . Some of the traits I have noticed have always constitutionally marked the early history of a powerful race; and have been conspicuous in the history of our own.

F. J. TURNER AND THE FRONTIER IN AMERICAN HISTORY

By H. C. Allen

★

THE most significant as well as the most striking theme in the first three centuries of American history is the seemingly irresistible westward movement of the American people:

> For now the flood goes west, the rushing tide,
> The rushing flood of men . . .

From the foundation at Jamestown in 1607 until the official statement by the Superintendent of the Census for 1890 that the "frontier of settlement" no longer existed, that frontier was one of the dominating facts in American life.

The great land which was thus conquered—men were wont to use the biblical term "wilderness" to describe it—had only been sparsely inhabited by the fierce partly nomadic Indian tribes, and their opposition to the advance of the Europeans was neither as formidable as that met with in the wars on the densely populated European continent, nor as unimportant, for instance, as that encountered from the aborigines to the settlement of Australia. Although Indian warfare always remained a grim reality to those actually on the frontier, it had ceased by 1783 to be more than an inconvenient obstacle to the expansion of the United States as a whole. The increasing margin of superiority in technology and social and political organization enjoyed by the white men over the Indians, who were unable to adopt the methods of Western civilization quickly enough to affect the outcome of the struggle decisively, made the victory of the American people certain; and if a full utilization of the resources of the land be in itself a desirable end, there can be no doubt that they deserved their triumph, for they developed and exploited the great bounty which nature has vouchsafed to the continental United States with an energy unmatched perhaps in any place or at any time in human history.

The importance of the frontier in American history is illustrated by the fact that the Americans use the word itself in quite a different way from the English; to the European it is a boundary, which is as clearly defined on the ground as on the map (often with barbed wire and armed guards to boot), but to the American it has been a far less definite "border of

145

settlement", abutting on (and usually in the process of moving into) the wilderness. To the one it is a precise line, normally fixed: to the other it is a fluid zone, generally in movement across a continent. The American term thus has overtones which are not at first easily distinguishable to the Briton's ear, but once he has grasped its meaning, this open, moving frontier makes an immediate and vivid appeal to his historical imagination.

The first historian clearly and comprehensively to formulate the concept of the significance of the frontier in American history was Frederick Jackson Turner, perhaps the most influential figure in American historiography. This influence was all the more remarkable because he actually wrote so little history. He was one of those historians who are held in high esteem despite the fact that they produce no massive works of historical scholarship: he was an Acton rather than a Gibbon, or in American terms a Carl Becker rather than a Francis Parkman. His was a seminal mind, which expressed itself in what were for the most part little more than essays, and of these one of the very earliest far outshone all the others, for his "Significance of the Frontier in American History", read before a session of the American Historical Association at Chicago in 1893, gave extraordinarily complete expression to the essentials of his whole frontier thesis.

In it he maintained that "The existence of an area of free land, its continuous recession, and the advance of American settlement westward, explain American development." This "advance of the frontier has meant a steady movement away from the influence of Europe, a steady growth of independence on American lines"; the "frontier is the line of most rapid and effective Americanization". The frontier processes tended to be repeated by each new generation, with modifications necessitated by different geographical circumstances, in a sort of embryological recapitulation of the growth of civilization. The West which the moving frontier brought into existence dominated the American way of life; it promoted the sense of nationality, freedom to rise, individualism and democracy; it bred strength and coarseness, practical inventiveness and quickness of mind, restlessness and nervous energy. The freedom from the hampering garments of traditional society which made these developments possible owed its existence to the vast readily available tracts of land upon which the frontier fed as it moved inexorably westward.

It was not really until the closing of the frontier that its full importance in the history of the United States was perceived. Of course, this idea, as always, had its precursors; Turner was to some extent forestalled, to quote one example, in his interest in the frontier by Theodore Roosevelt with his *Winning of the West*. But the historians of Turner's day were to a remarkable degree obsessed with the importance of the eastern seaboard and the colonial period in American history. This was not unnatural, for nearly all the active university history departments were still in the East, and nearly all the historians (although many of them were not professional academics at all) were Easterners, while the longest span of America's history still lay in the years prior to the Revolution. Moreover, the ascendancy of New England, which had recently been not only paramount but almost exclusive in the cultural life of the United States, remained powerful, and the Eurocentricity and Anglophilia of its intellectual bent maintained the influence of English historians, who were at this time in the heyday of their medieval studies. The whole Anglo-Saxon world, moreover, was peculiarly under the spell of the Germanic constitutional theories associated with the idea of the importance of "the mark" in the development of Western democracy, and its historians, with many of the Americans among them, were fascinated by the long slow growth of its political institutions, largely in the English sunlight, from their Teutonic seeds or germs. The leading centre of historical research in the United States, The Johns Hopkins University at Baltimore where Turner himself was trained, was also Germanic in academic method as well as historical inspiration.

Most academic American historians were thus intensely pre-occupied with the element of heredity in American development, a pre-occupation which amounted almost to a fixation on the remote European constitutional origins of the institutions of the United States. This was a cause of deep dissatisfaction to Turner. Others were also dissatisfied with this one-sided view of the growth of the American republic, which excluded the West from its consideration, but they none of them saw as clearly as he did where precisely the trouble lay. C. H. Shinn, for example, wrote in his *Mining Camps: A Study in American Frontier Government* published in 1885: "But if our institutional studies cease at the summits of the Alleghenies, we have learned only a part of the lesson that America has to teach." He continues, however, in a vein which shows clearly how deeply he was in thrall to the "germ theories" of the day (he, too, was a student at Johns Hopkins): "In that New West beyond the rocky borders of Nebraska and the remote sources of the Missouri, American pioneers have shown their hereditary fitness for self-government under exceptionally trying conditions. They have wrought out . . . local institutions in the highest sense their own . . . 'the mining era' deserves to be called a stanza in the political epic of the Germanic race to which we belong." So instinct indeed is his thought with the preconceptions of the nineteenth-century medieval historians that he writes of the application of the ideas of *folk-land, common-land, heir-land* and *book-land* to the land system of California, and even refers at one point to the "folk-moots of the Sierra". He could not wrest his ideas free from the prepossessions of his age: it is the measure of Turner's greatness that he did. He saw clearly that what American history needed was far less emphasis on heredity and far more stress on environment. In this he was closely attuned in his turn to the latest trends in European, and indeed Western, historiography, where the influence of environment was in the future to be increasingly emphasized at the expense of inherent qualities.

Turner himself was, as an individual, stimulated by his environment to formulate the frontier concept, for he was born and raised in the Middle West. It seems probable, too, that his personal interest was further aroused and sharpened by his reaction against the scepticism with which the subject of his doctoral dissertation, *The Character and Influence of the Indian Trade in Wisconsin*, tended to be greeted at first by his seniors at Johns Hopkins. Indeed its sub-title, *A Study of the Trading Post as an Institution*, suggests a concession to the dominant school of institutional historians. It is not unreasonable to suppose that a young historian of such character and ability would be fortified in his interest in the West by a predominant academic orthodoxy which could not regard this as a respectable or worth-while subject of study except under the guise of a piece of institutional history.

But there were also wider influences at work upon Turner. His ideas were plainly a manifestation of American nationalism, which was, in the very decade which saw the publication of his most influential essay, to burst forth in the acquisition of the first extra-continental imperial possessions of the United States. His works were pre-eminently a vigorous assertion of the importance of what was new and native in American history. In the more strictly technical sphere of historical thought, too, Turner was influenced deeply by the rising tide of economic history; he was well in the van of the characteristic twentieth-century movement towards the economic interpretation of historical data. As he wrote in 1891, "Today the questions that are uppermost, and that will become increasingly important, are not so much political as economic questions." Turner's whole thesis was in a sense a rejection of the political and constitutional assumptions of his predecessors in favour of broader social and economic principles.

Turner, however, was not only influenced by the general historical thought of his day: he contributed a good deal to it. His concern with environmental factors led him to lay especial stress upon physiographical influences, and this emphasis on the formative effect of geography constituted a particularly American contribution to historical thought. Only in a body politic large enough to contain such wide geographical differences as those between the great sections of, for instance, the Deep South, the Great Plains and the Rocky Mountains, does the historian easily perceive the full importance of men's geographical environment in their history. Even the imperial history of Britain does not bring it home to the student as forcibly as does the history of the United States. That this is so was to a considerable degree Turner's doing, for he did much to inaugurate not only the frontier thesis, but also a wide realization of the continuous and vital importance in American development of the great geographical sections. Sectionalism indeed, of which the moving frontier was only a single, if unique, manifestation, has been of profound importance in American history, and is still the key to our understanding of many of the processes in the political life of the United States.

Turner was in fact an historian of great penetration of mind. Nothing could be farther from the truth than the view which has developed in many quarters during recent years that his ideas were naïve, for his conception of history was intellectually sophisticated in a high degree. This is demonstrated by his little-read essay on *The Significance of History*, for it was no mean thing to be able to perceive as early as 1891 that "Each age writes the history of the past anew with reference to the conditions uppermost in its own time." But this sophistication was combined with an equal common sense, for his idea of the purpose of history was severely practical and utilitarian: "The aim of history, then, is to know the elements of the present by understanding what came into the present from the past." His grasp of the way this has to be done was masterly, for he did not neglect the fundamental truth that the simpler a historical thesis is the better: the most influential and profound historical interpretations are often those which have the greatest simplicity. All human knowledge can perhaps be regarded as the apprehension of relationships between phenomena, and the function of the historian, like that of the scientist, is to try and see the true relation in which facts stand to one another. One of America's ablest young historians, Norman A. Graebner, may feel justified in writing of an analogous thesis, "Like most broad generalizations, it does not bear close scrutiny", but this must not divert the historian from his first duty—to generalize as broadly as possible, subject only to the truth. It still is the case that he is the best historian who can generalize most widely and most simply within the framework of the facts. When judged by this criterion Turner ranks very high, for it was the splendid simplicity of the frontier theory which was its strength.

So far is this from being universally acknowledged that in all probability most contemporary American historians would strongly disagree with any such opinion. Turner, like many great men, was no hero to his seniors; it was not uncharacteristic that one of them commented, after receiving an offprint of his great essay of 1893, that he must be a "very provincial man". But in fact he was to dominate the development of American historical studies for the next forty years, for he was the prophet of that Middle West which was during this period to come into its own in many branches of national life besides history (it was, for instance, to be the area of greatest university development), and his influence extended far beyond academic circles, for he had a direct effect upon Wilson and probably Theodore Roosevelt and an indirect effect upon a whole generation of his countrymen. Turner reinforced his vague and unclaimed, yet real, ascendancy in American history, by his genius as a teacher, for as the years passed the United States became sprinkled with historians who had been under the wand of the magician. Indeed his ideas became the object of a somewhat excessive adulation, which defeated its aim by provoking a reaction against them. Turner himself over-emphasized his own thesis upon occasion—few historians are in a position to cast the first stone at him for that—but the worst exaggerations of it were the work of his followers; such theories, for example, as that which regarded the frontier as a social safety-valve for the urban discontent of the East was never fully propounded by Turner at all. This was partly the result, it is true, of the limited quantity he wrote, which laid his views exceptionally open to amplification, modification and misinterpretation, even by those who were his admirers; but he himself (it was in a sense the virtue of his vice of non-productivity) always retained a remarkably open mind. As one of his pupils, Avery Craven, wrote, "I one time asked him why he did not answer a critic who had distorted in order to criticize. He only chuckled and said: 'I've always been surprised that there has not been more criticism.' He was too eager for truth to care for praise or blame."

But a reaction from his influence was no doubt inevitable, and it has certainly not lacked in vigour. For the past twenty-five years he has been assailed from all sides by an increasing army of critics, two of the more vehement of whom (Louis M. Hacker and James C. Malin) have not hesitated to describe the Turner tradition, the one as "not only fictitious but also to a very large extent positively harmful", and the other as having "unsound and vicious methodology and philosophy". This was not merely the customary revolt of one generation against its predecessor, but was also a product of the development of increasingly specialized historical research; Turner was one of the great historical generalizers, and none of them has escaped altogether from the assaults of the specialists. In the same way, for instance, did the once venerable Whig interpretation of English history fall into disrepute. This constant process of contemporary correction of historical error is entirely proper, but it should not be conducted with such violence or venom that the right conclusions disappear along with the wrong ones and that future historians are frightened to try and replace bad generalizations by good. There are firm grounds for thinking that the reaction against Turner has gone too far, and that his critics have in their turn laid themselves open to criticism. Indeed there are already signs of a counter-attack; as Robert E. Reigel suggests, "The time seems to have arrived when the bickering over Turner . . . should be replaced by the formulation of a new set of generalizations based upon the researches of the past half century."

This process is already under way, and one aspect of it should be a rehabilitation of Turner himself. In a number of cases a general reconsideration of Turner's view and that of his critics on a particular issue leaves a remarkable proportion of his thesis standing—far more indeed sometimes than of the critical antithesis. "Simplest of the accusations against Turner", for example, in Riegel's words, "was that he had used his terms so vaguely and with so many different meanings that precision was impossible." As the most specific of his critics on this score, George Wilson Pierson, complained, "the frontier was not merely *place* and *population*, that is to say a savage wilderness and a sparse society of trappers, herders and pioneers. It was also *process*, or more specifically the processes of conquering the continent, of moving westward, of changing from Europeans into Americans. Whether such irregularity in definition can any longer be tolerated is a question" for very serious consideration. But does such criticism really invalidate Turner's thesis? The use of a single term with many meanings is not necessarily a loose usage, and if it corresponds with reality, the more compendious the meaning and the more succinct the word the better. There does not seem to be anything wrong or really confusing about associating the place, the people and the process with the single name "frontier"; indeed, the very reverse appears to be the case, for it was Turner's real achievement to make this single word the key to so much in American history. An analogous term much used by medieval historians seems to be very similar and also very satisfactory—"the marches". It conjures up, without difficulty and with illuminating effect, an image not only of a kind of place, but also of the kind of people who were important in that place, and even of the process by which they developed a new and special kind of social structure. In fact, the concept of the American frontier can sometimes be more easily understood by the English student in terms of the medieval march than in terms of any more modern parallel. Yet this semantic criticism of Turner has been widely accepted in practice as undermining his whole thesis, a sweeping result which does not seem to be entirely justified by a reconsideration of the evidence: on the contrary, it seems to leave Turner's original use of the term remarkably unscathed.

Indeed what seems in some ways most remarkable about his ideas, sixty years after they were first put forward and thirty years after his death, is how extraordinarily right they are in their major contentions. By no means all the criticisms were, of course, too severe and not many of them can be disregarded altogether: most of Turner's ideas have needed filling-out and a number have needed correction. But when all is said and done, they contained a very small proportion of dross. This is true even of such a very general question as the whole context in which he saw the importance of the American frontier. Perhaps the most important dis-service done to Turner by his followers was to exaggerate his emphasis on the uniqueness of the American frontier experience by studying it almost entirely in isolation. (It was no coincidence that in political, as well as historical, affairs, Turner's followers were of a generation that was far more isolationist than Turner.) This subtle twist which was given to the background of the frontier as Turner saw it was also characteristic of the process by which words were put into his mouth by

L

others. There is no doubt that in his mind the development of the American frontier remained an integral part of European and Western history, although it is not so immediately apparent in his writings that he felt it to be so.

This was the case even though he was primarily concerned to demonstrate that the importance of the European origins of American society had been grossly over-emphasized in the past. It came out very clearly in his teaching, one of the great virtues of which was that he brought his students to a fascinated realization, as Craven wrote, that "local history was human history". Turner's mind had been stimulated by, and was well furnished with, a wide knowledge of the development of the ancient and modern world. In his early years he even taught courses on ancient and general European history as well as on European history in the nineteenth century, and it was not uncharacteristic that he wrote in 1891: "Even here in young America old Rome still lives . . . not only is it true that no country can be understood without taking account of all the past; it is also true that we cannot select a stretch of land and say we will limit our study to this land; for local history can only be understood in the light of the history of the world." This broad sense of perspective was lost in the parochialism and indeed chauvinism of some of the agents of the reaction against the "germ theory" of political history which Turner began.

We are now in a position to restore that sense of perspective and to see the American experience as part of the experience of mankind. The frontier of the United States was one among many; it was but a part, as W. P. Webb has pointed out, of "the great frontier" of Western civilization. The expansion of the United States was merely one aspect of the huge expansion of the European peoples into the sparsely settled areas of the globe, which took place between the fifteenth and the twentieth centuries. American beef, Southern cotton, and Northern wheat were the counterparts of Australian wool and New Zealand mutton. In many respects, however, the American was the most remarkable of the frontiers, and it was the good fortune of the American people that their land was both potentially rich and actually thinly populated and that their lines of communication with Western Europe were relatively short and direct. The great Atlantic waterway nurtured the growth of the United States in an economic sense long after political separation had taken place, and the link between British capital and manufactures exported to the United States and the westward movement of the American people was much closer and lasted far longer than American historians have sometimes recognized. Without the Industrial Revolution, which had its origin and for a long time its centre in Britain, the expansion of the American frontier could never have proceeded at the speed which it in fact attained. Although of unique significance it has nevertheless been an integral part of Atlantic history, which by the date of its closing was fast becoming (although the fact has not even now been recognized by many historians) the only fully significant form of Western history. Such a development was not as alien to the thought of Turner as to that of some of his followers.

Thus it is that in other respects also Turner's views stand up much better to the criticism to which they have been subjected than has often been admitted. It is not possible here to analyse his views in detail, but it may be useful tentatively to suggest a few conclusions about the frontier which can be maintained today even in the face of Turner's critics; and it will be found that in outline these conclusions still follow with notable fidelity the contours of his original work. This was, of course, that of a pioneer, and his map lacks much of the detail which has been found necessary by later cartographers; it was a sketch-map which needed checking and augmenting. A great deal of this has been done, but little overall reconsideration of his thesis has been attempted. The complexity of frontier history, the variegated forms which the opening up of the West took, has made and still makes generalization hazardous. Yet a certain majestic uniformity does characterize the westward movement as such, albeit in the early years of the republic the drives north into upper New England, and, even more particularly, south into lower Georgia and Florida were also of great importance. But although the main flow of the current was unmistakable and apparently irreversible, when observed more closely even the periods of swiftest impetus to the West can be seen to have incorporated many diverse types of frontier and of frontier activity: each wave upon the shore was at once similar in outline to its successor yet vastly different in detailed structure. Of these many different forms of frontier, some tended to recur frequently, and sometimes to do so in similar sequence, though this repetitive pattern was, as is the way of human history, never uniform or exact.

It is not possible here to recount all the manifold modes of frontier life —the fishermen's frontier, for example, which always reaped such liberal harvests from the eastern ocean but which has spread also to the waters of the once distant Pacific. The main forms of frontier, however, may conveniently be grouped under five heads, those of the hunter, the miner, the pastoralist, the plantation owner, and the pioneer farmer.

First the frontier of the hunter, the trapper, the fur-trader, who was usually the first upon the ground. Of such as these, the Daniel Boones, the Davy Crocketts and even the Buffalo Bills, was one of the most potent elements in the romantic legend of the American frontier made. And rightly so, for upon them there mostly fell the burden of exploring and opening up the Indian hunting grounds which lay always beyond the areas of settlement. In this way, for instance, New York became the greatest base for the fur trade because of the easy access to the West afforded by the Hudson-Mohawk valley through the Appalachians. The task of the hunter and trader was not always made easier by the fact that he was often followed closely by the settler, whose insatiable appetite for land was the fundamental cause of bad relations with the Indian. Not that the trader himself was without blame; the fur trade could certainly be profitable to both parties, but the Indian was often cheated, and he was almost always debauched by the sale of alcohol, while the settler had every reason for complaint against traders who put fire-arms in the hands of the tribes.

But as long as there were animals to hunt whose skins or hides fetched a high price in the eastern states and in Europe, the fur trade prospered. The game which was to be found differed with the physical background of the frontier, although the forested areas of the East and later of the Far West afforded broadly similar hunting, and the pursuit of the buffalo on the Great Plains presented quite new problems. But the profits to be derived from furs, which were of relatively small bulk for their price and thus easy to transport where all communications were poor, remained high, while with the growth of urban America and the building of the railways in the nineteenth century even the less valuable buffalo hide proved an economic commodity.

Furs, indeed, admirably met the classic need of the frontier, a so-called "cash crop". The frontier zones of the Western world were perennially debtor areas; the cost of breaking new ground was high in money as well as in men, and to meet that cost the pioneer went into debt to the inhabitants of the settled areas behind him, who had capital available for investment. This was a vast economic problem with distant ramifications and important social and political implications. The thirteen colonies as a whole had been in debt to the mother country, and the adverse trade balance produced an acute shortage of specie in America, which played an important part in bringing about the American Revolution. In the same way, within the United States and throughout the whole of American history, frontier areas, which were usually in the West, tended to be in debt to those farther east, and to be in favour of inflationary monetary policies which eased the burden of their debts. At first, following the object lesson of the inflation of the Revolutionary period, they tended to support movements for a plentiful paper currency, such as the Greenbacks of the Civil War years, but by the end of the century their zeal took the form of the demand for a bimetallic currency—for the free coinage of silver, in opposition to the orthodox deflationary gold-standard policies favoured by financial interests which had their greatest strength in the East. But the basic debtor condition of the frontier areas could only be palliated by currency manipulation: the sole cure lay in the production of a surplus for sale. The quicker the cash crop came along the swifter the progress of the area towards economic maturity; the abiding merit of the fur trade from the point of view of the frontier was the relative speed and size of its return.

But the perfect frontier cash crop, and the one which added to the wealth of the United States in the most spectacular and flamboyant manner, consisted of precious metals. The miner's frontier has a glamour of a more glittering, if meretricious, kind than that of the hunter and a much more direct appeal to man's economic appetites, and particularly to his cupidity. Semi-precious metals such as copper, and even minerals such as salt and coal, could be important in opening up the West, but at the heart of the American miner's frontier was the pursuit of silver and gold.

From the first Spanish discoveries of gold in Latin America, the lure of El Dorado remained a potent feature of the American dream, but in fact relatively little gold or silver was found in the territory of the United States until the great discoveries which began in California in 1848, just after its conquest from Mexico by the United States. For the next twenty years the miners did more than anyone else to open up the lands of the Far West. The demand for gold, which was maintained by the nearly universal acceptance of the gold standard among the nations of the world, provided a continuous incentive for its production, but during the same period the United States also became the world's leading silver-producer. With the exploitation of the huge silver deposits of the West, such as the Comstock Lode, in the sixties and seventies, the value of silver in terms of gold steadily declined, and when the United States in 1873 ceased to coin silver the question of a bimetallic currency became a political issue which grew in importance for the next quarter of a century. The physical location of the silver mines in the West (where also lay some of the greatest areas of discontent among the farmers, who were very ready to support an expanded currency), combined with the liability of the American political system to the influence of "pressure groups", which often have a geographical and sectional basis, helped to make possible the rise of the powerful Populist party—the last of the true radical frontier movements in American history—and its capture in 1896, under the leadership of William Jennings Bryan, of the Democratic political organization.

The miner's frontier was thus very largely confined to the West and to the second half of the nineteenth century; to a lesser extent this was also true of what may be called, though the term is not often used in this sense by American historians, the pastoral frontier, for this reached its apogee with the "cattle kingdom" in the years between the end of the Civil War and the closing of the frontier. By this time the term "rancher's frontier", derived from Latin American practice, fully describes it, but cattle raising as a specialized economic activity was a feature of frontier life in quite other places, such as the foothills of the Appalachians, and quite other times, such as the colonial period. Sheep herding was rarely a frontier activity proper in the United States, as it was in Australia, and sheep never in any case occupied a place comparable in importance with cattle in national life. It was in the vast open areas of the West, semi-arid and sparsely vegetated, that cattle raising really came into its own. It was as important in opening up the Great Plains—hitherto shunned as "The Great American Desert"—to human habitation as mining had been in opening up the mountain areas farther west twenty years before. Then the plains had been hastily traversed, or indeed avoided altogether by taking the long sea journey round the Horn or the sea and land journey across Central America, for California, which was settled in the first instance more from the west than the east, was the base from which most of the miners pushed eastward to exploit the further mineral wealth of the Rocky Mountain area, thus constituting the only major exception to the persistently westward movement of the American people.

The area between the 100th meridian and the Sierras still remains that part of the United States in the economy of which cattle are proportionately most important, but the open ranges of the cattle kingdom in its heyday have long since gone for ever. The extension of the railroads put an end in the last decade of the nineteenth century to the "long drive" of the cattle herds from Texas to railheads fifteen hundred miles away to the north; the growing competition for land from the advancing sheep herder and the farmer, as well as among the cattle men themselves, rendered the enclosure of ranches desirable, and the invention and large-scale production of barbed wire made it economically possible. The era of the cowboy was necessarily a transitory phase in American frontier development. Yet it, more than any other aspect of that frontier, has left a deep imprint on the imagination not merely of the Americans but of many other peoples; the hunter and scout in the coonskin cap was the hero of a number of nineteenth-century novels and has more recently been rediscovered by Hollywood, but the romance of the cowboy has made an appeal to many millions of mankind for half a century. Perhaps because it flourished just at the dawn of mass literacy and mass media of communication, it caught the popular fancy and held it. Through its innate merits as drama and story, its vicarious tang of the open air, and its appeal to all age-groups, it has a timeless contemporaneity. Whereas the concurrent crime story depended for its impact upon the intensification of the realities of an industrial society, the "western" made its even more powerful appeal to the desire of an urban population not merely for excitement but for escape. However brief the life of the cattle kingdom in historical reality, it will not easily lose its place in the popular mind as the best known American frontier.

The remaining two broad types of frontier which need discussion are both agricultural, and necessarily have less of the romantic about them; but the Southern planter does have a certain glamour: at first glance the pioneer farmer of the North has very little. The exotic element in the slave South has perhaps a greater appeal to the Englishman, who is not instinctively repelled by an oligarchial society, than to the American of the North, yet even for the latter it has a certain romance. Although on

investigation the charms of the ante-bellum South turn out all too often
to be

The sick magnolias of the false romance,

their appeal to the sympathy and the sensibilities of the historian dies
hard, much harder than that of the plantation system upon which the
social structure of the South was in part based.

This system of growing staple crops by slave labour upon plantations
was a vital feature of Southern frontier development. The first of these
cash crops for which there proved to be a ready market in Europe was
tobacco, the cultivation of which put the early Virginia settlements
economically on their feet and enabled the Upper South to maintain a lead
in colonial expansion westward until the end of the eighteenth century.
Early in the nineteenth, the frontier of the Deep South began to move
westward very much faster, through the development of cotton culture
on the lands of the great Black Belt of Georgia, Alabama, Mississippi,
Arkansas and Texas; for raw cotton there was a far more remarkable and
more prodigiously expanding market in Europe, and particularly Britain
where the Industrial Revolution was at its most vigorous, than there had
ever been for any of the other staple crops. The fact that it, even more
than tobacco, rapidly exhausted the soil, combined with the unprecedented
growth of the market, resulted in an expansion so swift that by 1860 the
frontier of the South had reached the edge of the Great Plains and, as it
seemed, the end of all land suitable for the production of cotton.

Though the South had at first expanded its frontier to the west more
rapidly than the North, it had never been unrivalled, and by the Civil
War it had become clear that it had been, and would continue to be,
outclassed. This was the work of the small pioneer farmer of the North.
Not that there were no small pioneer farmers in the South, nor even that
the large plantation was the most characteristic form of Southern husbandry; but on the Northern frontier the small man was without peer.
Beginning as a subsistence farmer, he (or, if he was one of the many who
spent their lives moving on with the frontier, the successor to whom he
sold his land after it had appreciated in value) began in time to produce
a surplus for sale. By this date, however, the area had nearly always
ceased to be on the frontier, which had swept onward to the west, at a
speed which gave to the victorious society of the North after the Civil
War a rapidly increasing preponderance in American life. But the
pioneer farmer left his mark upon the territory over which the frontier
passed.

Cultivating for the most part an acreage much less than the normal
Southern plantation owner, but much more than the average European
peasant or yeoman, he was the predominating figure in the development
of the American frontier. He it was who first really broke the crust of the
wilderness, over the surface of which the hunter had lightly passed or

beneath the surface of which the miner had occasionally dug: he it was who truly planted Western civilization in the soil of the West, where it was to strike deep roots and to bear such lush fruit. And he was not only predominant in a figurative sense: it is not too much to claim that he constituted the norm of American frontier development. The most characteristic American frontier was that of the great Northern and Western belt of the continental United States, bounded very roughly on the South by the 38th parallel. This area long contained and still contains the vast majority of the American people, and historically its form of frontier was by far the most important. It was from Wisconsin in its heart that Turner came, and it may well have been this fact which led him instinctively to depict its type of frontiersman as the American prototype. But the instinct was sound, and he had good and solid historical reasons on his side, for when the tumult and the shouting of the critics dies it still remains true that the image of it which Turner carried in his mind was closer to the norm of the American frontier than any other would have been.

He was right also when he pointed out the importance of "free land" in American development. It may be that Turner paid too little attention to the land speculator and that he sometimes seemed to imply that the exploitation of the unsettled lands of the West by an overflowing population from the East was more direct than at times it actually was, but the availability of vast and virtually unoccupied lands on the frontier must obviously have been one of the most important conditioning factors in America's growth, as a glance at the contrasting situation in the older and more settled countries of western Europe shows. Turner was very aware of the economic and political importance of the issue of cheap land in the first century of American independence, and subsequent research has in fact shown clearly that the years 1800-1862 in American land legislation saw an increasingly successful series of efforts to replace the Hamiltonian idea of land as a source of Federal revenue by the Jeffersonian belief in cheap land as the birthright of a democratic people, which took legislative shape in progressive provisions for the acquiring of smaller and smaller minimum lots of public lands at lower and lower prices. That this movement had at heart the interests of the small pioneer farmer is indicated by the tendency of both large Southern planters and great eastern employers of labour to oppose it, and by the fact that the Homestead Act of 1862 allowed virtually any adult to apply for a quarter-section, or 160 acres, of public land for a fee of $10, designed to cover only administrative costs. Even though conditions were to change radically as the frontier entered the arid West, and thus to render the Homestead Act itself much less important than had been hoped, or than has sometimes been supposed since, the type of frontiersman whom Turner had in mind was able to dominate the land legislation of the nation in the most critical years of its development. This historical figure, the small pioneer farmer, is, if not quite so unchallenged in importance as Turner's followers supposed, a much more real one, and a much surer foundation for generalizations concerning the American frontier, than his critics have allowed.

These generalizations are many, and they are so important because the frontier deeply affected the lives and habits and also the personalities of those who lived upon it, and through them of their children and their children's children, for, as Turner pointed out, the frontier influence passed insensibly from father to son, until it became part of the American heritage. There is no corner of the United States that has not been on the frontier at some time in the last three hundred and fifty years, and perhaps a half of its territory has been subdued within the last century. Although only a relatively small part of America has been frontier at any particular moment (indeed, as G. W. Pierson has pointed out, the proportion of the American people who actually lived on the frontier decreased steadily throughout American history), until about 1890 the frontier tradition profoundly modified the way of life even of those Americans who spent their lives far away from it in great cities. Since that time other factors, such as American industrial might and the increasing pressure of foreign affairs, have altered the inherited pattern of American life, but even in the case of nations the character and ideas acquired in youth are very difficult to alter, at all events with any speed, so that the significance of the frontier in American history must still be reckoned almost as considerable as Turner believed.

Nor need we reject his views as to the way in which the frontier affected America quite as absolutely as some of his critics would have us. Modifications of his thesis are certainly necessary, but it still contains a solid stratum of truth. One of his primary contentions, for example, was that the frontier was the line of most rapid and effective Americanization. In the colonial period this seems very likely to have been true, because few parts of the colonies were in fact far away from the frontier and its influence, as the western experiences of a Tidewater Virginian like Washington may serve to illustrate. After independence the frontier began to move more swiftly and to leave ever more extensive settled areas behind it, but it had already made an indelible imprint upon the American character. The predominantly North-European immigrants of the first half of the nineteenth century seem to have found their way in considerable numbers to the developing rural areas of the Middle West; the South absorbed relatively few of the newcomers, because of the existence of Negro slavery, although the frontier even of the lower Mississippi valley certainly remained a line of effective Americanization in the days of Andrew Jackson. But, setting aside the Irish who tended often to gather in the urban areas, the characteristic new American, even as late as 1860, probably settled in regions where the pioneer farmer or his immediate successor was the dominating figure, as in Wisconsin in the days of Turner's youth. After the Civil War the huge waves of "new immigrants" went overwhelmingly to the great cities, and it was here that the process of assimilation had increasingly to take place, but it was a good deal slower and less effective than it had been, while rural America still provided, under the influence of Jefferson, the ideal pattern for American society, certainly down to the Populist era and perhaps even to that of Wilson. The Jeffersonian idolum was not effectively replaced by one more suited to the realities of life in a great industrial community until the days of the New Deal. Thus it can be maintained that the frontier was *a* line of rapid and effective Americanization throughout its existence, and *the* line of most rapid and effective Americanization during the formative years of American history.

In the same way Turner held that the frontier had a nationalizing tendency, that it strengthened the hands of the federal as opposed to the state governments, because almost all the states except the original thirteen grew up under the aegis of the Union and therefore their citizens had more feeling for the nation as a whole than for their particular states. This opinion has been little criticized and seems valid still. Equally uncontested is his view that the frontier helped to make Americans prodigal, indeed wasteful, in their use of the seemingly inexhaustible natural resources of their country. Here, despite the rise during his lifetime of a conservation movement of which he strongly approved, the mark upon American life, both in city and country, is still plain to see: never perhaps has there been a whole society so uninhibited and so ruthless in the exploitation of the bounty of its natural environment. Yet another of Turner's theses has not been very seriously disputed, that which pointed out that the harsh and pressing realities of frontier life left little time for the refinements of civilization, so that there was a certain crudeness in the American way of life. That a reaction against this set in, in favour of the cultivation which prosperity made possible, was natural and does not invalidate the main argument, which receives ample support not only from the offensive comments of many British visitors to the West in the nineteenth century, but also from the long cultural dominance of the East.

Much more contentious has been his assertion that the most important effect of the frontier has been the promotion of democracy in the United States and in Europe. Critics have pointed out that not many democratic processes were invented in frontier areas, and that many reforms had their origin in the East. This is true, but less harmful to Turner's contention than has been maintained. The history of older societies in Europe clearly shows that it was not so much the invention as the adoption of democratic ideas that was difficult: the seeds of most new ideas have long existed in some form or other, and their need is always a fruitful soil and a favourable climate in which to germinate. This the frontier provided. There was some democratic thought in England in the seventeenth century, and much by the early nineteenth, but many years were to pass before it was generally accepted or actually put into practice. The fundamental reason for this was the power of vested interests, and even more of fixed habits and prejudices, and Turner rightly claimed that the effect of the frontier was to destroy many of these, and to reduce man, as an economic and political animal, to his simplest basic elements. The result was a national atmosphere in which increasingly one man tended to regard himself as the equal of the next and in which the ideas of democracy naturally flourished; thus it has yet to be demonstrated that any narrow oligarchical constitutions existed in the Middle West (even in the south of which democracy was for the white man a powerful reality) whereas it has been clearly shown that plenty of the new states in the area had democratic governing processes from their first entry into the Union. Even more striking is the fact that a number of western states held second constitutional conventions within two decades of their admission to the Union, and that the new constitutions produced by them tended to be more democratic than the original ones, partly no doubt because they embodied the western experience of the settlers. Indeed it is still hard to see how it can be disputed that the adoption of democratic ideas proceeded very swiftly in the West and that the great popular movements found much of their support in areas where frontier conditions had recently prevailed. Few Europeans, for instance, who have visited the excellent reconstruction of the village at New Salem from which Lincoln sought election to the legislature of Illinois as the representative of Sangamon County in 1832, can have any serious doubt of the reality of frontier democracy or the depth of its influence. From it grew Lincoln's profound conviction that the future of popular government in the world depended peculiarly upon the United States, and in this sense it is still possible to maintain that one of the most significant effects of the frontier has been the promotion of democracy.

Among the most influential of Turner's dicta was that which declared that the frontier encouraged self-reliance and individualism. Of the pioneer farmer, the dominating frontier figure of the years before the Civil War, this was intensely true; this independent practical landowner was the classic Jeffersonian and Jacksonian democrat. Turner and his followers may have over-emphasized these qualities; some critics have pointed out, for instance, that in many ways the life of the frontier essentially depended upon mutual assistance. But this has never really been denied; it has seldom been asserted that many men (let alone women) actively enjoyed the hardships of frontier existence, but the fact remains that they endured them, and if they survived no doubt took a good deal of pride in the fact that they did so. Nor is it reasonable to compare the occasional, although essentially necessary, co-operation of individuals on the frontier—in the log-rolling and other assistance, for instance, without which a log-cabin could not be built—with the insensible everyday dependence of the individual upon society which is characteristic of more settled areas; to do so implies a certain lack of sense of proportion, for to emphasize the self-reliance of frontiersmen is not to assert that they were self-sufficient. Nor must too much be made of the criticism of the reality of frontier individualism which points out that the individuals were in fact remarkably alike, that all along the frontier these individualists were asserting their independence of each other in precisely similar ways. Individualism need not necessarily be eccentricity, and if individuals, even in isolation, did not react in similar ways to similar stimuli, any form of society, and in particular any democratic system of government, would be quite impracticable. Fine distinctions between shades of red must not blind historians who make them to the more important difference between red and blue; if we compare it for a moment to a closed society like that of many countries in Europe, we can still agree that, at least up to the Civil War, the American frontier was a breeding ground for self-reliance and individualism.

After this date a change did take place. The pioneer toughness, the readiness to resort to direct and even violent methods to attain political and economic ends, which was characteristic of all frontier life in America —and indeed to some extent elsewhere—remained; but nature decreed that the ratio of individual to social effort should alter radically, so that the individual found himself able to achieve far less than he had been able to heretofore without calling society to his aid. As Webb has pointed out, men were forced when they launched forth upon the Great Plains to adjust the habits which they had acquired in a forested area to suit the treeless prairie, and as they entered the zone between approximately the 96th and the 100th meridians they began to feel the full effect of an even more formidable change, that of increasing aridity. For a period it was concealed by a cycle of years of better-than-average rainfall and by the highly fluctuating nature of that rainfall, but, at the cost of great hardship and suffering in such states as Kansas, the lesson was in due course learned that the small pioneer farmer could no longer function as he had been able to do farther east, and that even the large-scale farmer needed more and more help from society the farther he moved into the arid and later mountainous regions of the West. Men could only prosper on the land by enlarging their holdings and relying increasingly upon pastoral husbandry, or by calling upon society for aid in the form of improved agricultural techniques or of irrigation. Thus, whereas in the fertile lands over which the frontier had previously passed a man could make a very satisfactory living off 160 or even 80 acres, in the West it was pretty nearly impossible on 320, let alone 160. Unless his land was irrigated, a farmer on the Great Plains needed between 360 and 640 acres and a rancher there or farther west anything between 2000 and 50,000 acres. This inexorable fact was reflected in the general tenor of land legislation after the Civil War, by which the long Jeffersonian trend towards smaller holdings was surely, if covertly, reversed. Between 1873 and 1889 a number of measures were passed by Congress which made greater maximum holdings possible without greatly increasing their price. At the same time there developed an increasing reliance on the co-operation of farmers one with another, as in co-operatives, and on the new scientific methods developed by the technicians of society at large, such as those for dry farming.

Although it only began to develop on a large scale after the frontier was officially closed, it is the history of irrigation which most clearly illustrates this increased reliance of the individual pioneer upon society, as soon as he enters an arid zone, for it is only possible where there is centralized control over the actions of many persons. Normally this can only be exercised by one authority, the state, and in mid-nineteenth-century America, even more than mid-nineteenth-century Britain, there was very general aversion from state interference in economic affairs. It is thus most interesting that the great pioneers of irrigation were the Mormons. This was not only because they moved much farther into the semi-desert lands much earlier than any other settlers, but also because their Church of Jesus Christ of the Latter-day Saints exercised a very close supervision over the whole life of the community, so that Brigham Young in his wisdom was able to invest ownership and distribution of the vital waters running down from the mountains of the Wasatch Range in the church. This produced a uniquely successful system of irrigation many years before the pressure of circumstances had forced Americans to accept large-scale state action to alleviate, among other things, the difficulties arising from the aridity of the West. This acceptance by the state of a positive economic role in the life of the people owed much to the harsh conditions of life in arid frontier regions; it was promoted, too, by the growth of industrialism and the rise of socialism and trade unionism which began in Europe, but it also had grass roots, for the fundamental basis of Populism was agrarian. The Granger movement, which started as a non-political alliance of farmers for economic ends, before long fostered in the hearts of its members a determination to assert their political power to attain those ends. By capturing a number of state governments, the outraged farmers were able to enforce government control over some of the economic practices which they disliked, as for example by the regulation of abuses arising from the existence of great railroad monopolies. The difficulties of the frontier in the West in the last quarter of the nineteenth century forced men to rely less on themselves and more upon one another and upon the state.

Critics of Turner have objected vigorously to his elastic use of the term frontier to cover the settled areas of the West, such as, for example, Kansas in 1890; this identification of the frontier with the West seems to them unjustified. But this objection not only shortens the perspective of history; it ignores Turner's point that the United States is like a palimpsest, with the influence of the frontier embedded at each level. The frontier, for instance, was not far below the·surface in Nebraska in 1896; in 1860 its population had been 20,000, and by 1890 was over a million, yet many a young man of the former year was still in the prime of political activity in the campaign of 1896. To ascribe to such areas the character of frontier societies seems far from unreasonable, and it is not wildly absurd to do so even to certain areas of the South which played a part in the Populist movement.

Of this lessening of the degree of self-reliance and individualism which was possible on the frontier, Turner was well aware; he saw that the small pioneer farmer could no longer succeed unaided in the arid West, and that, with the channelling of frontier energies into political agitation, the state would have to play a much greater part in the economic development of the country. He was too close to the event to appreciate, as can now be done, how greatly the peculiar conditions of aridity in the West, by encouraging economic reliance on the state, prepared the way for the new position of government in the American industrial society of the twentieth century. The ease of transition from the overwhelmingly rural Democracy of Jackson and the predominantly rural Democracy of Bryan to the largely urban Democracy of Woodrow Wilson and Franklin D. Roosevelt owed much to this historical chance, for although it is possible to exaggerate the reluctance of state, and even federal, authorities to play an active economic role in the first century after independence (as the whole history of the demand for internal improvements shows), the transformation of a *laisser-faire* rural nation into an industrial society with an increasing element of government control would have been much harder without the particular preparation afforded by the Populism of the West.

Turner was greatly concerned to point out that the closing of the frontier could be expected to have—as it has had—profound effects upon the development of American life, and it is on one notion arising from his ideas on this subject that he has been most powerfully attacked, the safety-valve theory; but it should be remembered that he himself never fully or explicitly formulated this concept which was greatly—and sometimes rashly—elaborated by his disciples, and which had in any event existed in an inchoate form even before his time. It is now clear that after 1860 only relatively minute numbers of settlers went from the industrial areas direct to the frontier in the capacity of farmers, though the situation before that date is by no means so clear, and in all periods the extent to which non-farmers were able to move west as the basic development of agriculture made possible more complex economic growth (acting in fact as a kind of economic multiplier) needs careful investigation. But whatever the reservations one must make, for many thousands of families the frontier in America offered better possibilities for a good and growing livelihood on their own land than anywhere else in the world, a fact which sank deep into the American consciousness, so that even after 1860 most of his fellow-countrymen believed with Turner that free land meant free opportunities. The myth, if such it be, associated with the words, "Go west, young man", was possibly almost as success-ful in allaying discontent as the reality would have been, for what men believe is usually the decisive factor in their actions; many Americans no doubt more patiently bore those evils that they had because they believed that a way of escape always existed for them, although they could never actually bring themselves to take it. In any case, as Riegel writes, "While a good case can be made that the frontier had no real effect on eastern population concentration, such a conclusion seems to affront common sense . . . The occupation and exploitation of an entire continent with no effect on population concentration seems incredible."

In the same way Turner has been attacked by some historians, parti-cularly those influenced by Marxist ideas, because his thesis largely ignored the importance of class in the development of American society. Most of this criticism came in the thirties when the Great Depression had undermined faith in the traditional "American" virtues, and it was very unhistorical, for when Turner published his most influential essay in 1893 it was, despite the growing inequalities of wealth which sprang from the new industrialism, emphatically still true that the remarkable thing about America had until quite recently been the political and social democracy which the abundance of land had chiefly made possible. Even to the present day the habits of mind acquired in those early years have done much to prevent that stiffening of the nation's social and economic joints which is often the bane of older societies. In modern America social equality is a potent ideal and class distinctions are less important than in the life of most other peoples. For this fact the frontier was in part responsible. If Turner is to blame here it is because he did not sufficiently modify his own views in later life when circumstances had changed, but there was in any case no call for him to do so except of the most recent years, for before then he was on solid ground.

Broad generalizations about whole societies are always difficult and seldom absolutely true, but it is not really possible to doubt the deep and lasting influence of the frontier upon the history of the United States, nor to question that it directly contributed to the formation of many of the most pronounced characteristics of the American people. It cannot be doubted, to give another instance, that it encouraged their optimism and their idealism, as Turner claimed. Because that optimism was usually justified it does not mean that there have not always been more gloomy traits in the American character: it simply means that cheerfulness was normally uppermost, if only because the pessimistic and the weak had often gone to the wall already. Idealism, too, was a vital force in their lives, even if their primary objectives were, as critics have pointed out, largely economic; few men are not deeply, often fundamentally, motivated by material needs, and what was important about the Americans was that they were also moved by political and social ideals of a high order. Both idealism and optimism were in the end encouraged by the frontier, despite the pessimism of such observers as *Martin Chuzzlewit* and the "realistic" novelists of the Great Plains; indeed, as the story of Per Hansa in *Giants in the Earth* so clearly shows, conjoined in the form of hope (which never had greater call to spring eternal in the human breast) optimism and idealism *had* to be part of the equipment of those who successfully braved the terrible rigours of the frontier.

> And the west wind blew in the faces of Dickon's sons
> And they looked to the West and searched it with their eyes,
> And there was the endless forest and the sharp star.

But they needed more than that to conquer and subdue a continental domain of three million square miles. They needed great ingenuity and prodigious energy, and Turner was right to call attention to the existence of both among the frontiersmen. Concerning his claim that they displayed ingenuity in adapting themselves to changed conditions of life on the frontiers of civilization, critics have declared that in fact they only adapted themselves slowly to changes in physical environment, and cite their delay in leaving the forests to tackle the Great Plains as an instance. Yet the whole process, not merely of adaptation but of complete occupation, took barely half a century. Half a century! Let them see the Frenchman still ploughing with his ox! None but an American could have thought of such a comment, a fact which is in itself a tribute to the depth of the frontier influence. If the criticism is taken further and it is claimed that very few inventions were actually made on the frontier, let it be remembered that, in economic as in political affairs, it is not the devising of new techniques, but the speed of their adoption—whatever their origin—which is the fundamental condition of great and rapid development. The frontier encouraged the existing Yankee virtues of ingenuity and resourcefulness.

Above all, however, it fostered that driving, furious energy which is perhaps the most striking and characteristic of all the features of American life. It not only pervades the history of every phase of the American frontier, but also permeates city as well as country throughout the land; even the South, with its "lazy, crooning, comforting tongue", swallowed up the vast Black Belt of cotton lands in little more than fifty years. The "rolling, resistless wave of seeking men", surging "westward and westward, killing down the day", is at the very heart of the American experience, and the indomitable expansion of the people of the United States across their continental domain has fired the imagination not only of the Americans but also of many foreign observers and historians. It is impossible not to believe with Turner that this consummate achievement has been of profound and enduring significance for America, and, through her, for mankind.

SECTIONALISM AND THE CIVIL WAR

By Maldwyn A. Jones

★

GOUVERNEUR MORRIS, addressing the Federal Convention in 1787, was in no doubt as to the reason for the impotent condition into which he believed the Union to have fallen. It was the jealousy and suspicion shown by the States towards the central government. "State attachments and State importance", he asserted, "have been the bane of this country." And if the Union was to survive some means must be found of limiting the authority of the States. As Morris expressed it, "we cannot annihilate, but we may perhaps take out the teeth of the serpents". These, it is true, were not the sentiments of all the delegates. Yet they described accurately enough the spirit in which the Convention went to work, for by a skilful redistribution of powers between States and Nation, it was able to frame an instrument that afforded an effective remedy for the weaknesses that had afflicted the Confederation.

The success of the new government, however, though providing an essential basis for the growth of American nationalism, did not imply that the Union had replaced the States as the chief object of American loyalty; and the stability of the Union continued to be threatened by conflicts of authority between State and Federal governments. Within a decade of the ratification of the Constitution, the legislatures of Virginia and Kentucky were asserting the right of a State both to judge of infractions of the Constitution by the Federal government and, where such infractions were deemed to have occurred, to interpose its authority so as to nullify the offending law. Little more than ten years later, these same doctrines were embraced in turn by the New England States; and in 1832 South Carolina gave them practical effect in her celebrated Nullification Ordinance. Similar, if less dramatic, examples of State resistance to Federal legislation continued to be forthcoming in the numerous Personal Liberty laws adopted in the 1840's by the Northern States. But the final proof that the "serpents" of which Morris had spoken had not lost their teeth came in the winter of 1860-61, when eleven Southern States insisted on exercising the right they claimed of seceding from the Union.

Yet in spite of the prominence achieved by the question of State Rights between the adoption of the Constitution and the Civil War, state particularism was not the source of the danger which threatened the Union throughout that period. The real threat came from the particularism of those great natural regions into which the United States was divided by geography, climate and economic activity, and which Americans came about this time to know as sections. During those decades sectional feeling and sectional rivalries were so intense that there seems hardly to have been a time when the secession of one section or another did not seem possible, if not imminent. And if the constitutional arguments which sectional conflict provoked were centred largely round the question of State Rights, that was not because the issue had any intrinsic importance but merely, as Turner pointed out, because such a concept afforded a convenient constitutional shield for sectional aspirations.

The difficulty of uniting within one political system the diverse regions of which the United States was composed was remarked upon as early as 1781 by the English pamphleteer, Josiah Tucker. Struck by the barriers to communication presented to Americans by "great Bays of the Sea, and by vast Rivers, Lakes and Ridges of Mountains", Tucker concluded that the "mutual antipathies and clashing interests" which resulted could only ensure that they would remain "a disunited people until the end of time". And while this conclusion might have seemed to most contemporary Americans unduly pessimistic, few of their leaders at least could have been unaware that the United States was a federation not only of States but of sections. The Founding Fathers certainly—despite the attention they necessarily gave at Philadelphia to the role of the States—were fully conscious of this fact, for it was only by recognizing the existence of competing sectional interests, and by working out compromises between them, that they were able to frame an acceptable Constitution.

That the division between sections was the really significant one was the belief of James Madison, who insisted to the Convention that the division between large and small States, which had appeared in its debates on the Virginia and New Jersey plans, was largely artificial. "Look to the votes in Congress", he exclaimed, "and most of them stand divided by the geography of the country, not according to the size of the states." The true line of demarcation, it seemed to Madison, was that between "the great southern and northern interests of the continent", the slaveholding and non-slaveholding States. And the great danger to the Union arose from the opposition of these two interests.

In the light of such evidence, and of the compromises over slavery that were embodied in the Constitution, it is tempting to conclude that the sectional division described by Madison was the outstanding one of 1787, and that the slavery issue, so prominent in later sectional controversies, was even at that date the true sectional touchstone. Yet while there was undoubtedly an antipathy between the "carrying" and the "planting" States, the question of slavery was not of paramount importance in the discussions of the Convention. And in any case, the sectional pattern was too complex to be reduced with any accuracy to a simple division between North and South.

Indeed, the most commonly accepted sectional division up to that time had been one that recognized New England, the Middle States and the South as separate sections. This threefold division had long seemed a natural one to geographers, and by the middle of the eighteenth century it had become sufficiently familiar to form the basis of plans for the political organization of the Colonies. Thus one writer of that period could propose that the English mainland colonies should be grouped into Northern, Middle and Southern unions since, he remarked, these represented "three distinct and separate countries, separated from one another by natural boundaries; different in situation, climate, soil, products, etc., while the several colonies included in these divisions, which we look upon as separate colonies, are all one and the same country in these respects". The Revolution, it is true, brought no attempt at political organization along the lines here suggested, for the circumstances of the break with Britain were such as to make a single Union imperative. Yet the decisions of the Continental Congress relating to Indian, naval and military affairs show that, for administrative purposes, the existence of three separate sections was nearly always assumed. And in the debate on the chief magistracy in the Federal Convention, George Mason proposed that, in order to reassure the people of each section that there would be "a proper attention paid to their concerns", the executive power should be vested in three persons, one from New England, one from the Middle States and one from the South.

The sectional pattern of the Revolutionary period was further complicated by the antagonisms that prevailed between the older-settled regions along the Atlantic coast and the newer, more primitive areas in the interior or back-country. Indeed, if the amount of violence it produced was any criterion, the cleavage between East and West was of greater significance than that between the three sections just referred to. In North Carolina, for instance, the discontent of the West had culminated in 1768-71 in the revolt of the Regulators; in Pennsylvania, in an armed demonstration by the Paxton Boys in 1764; and in Massachusetts, in Shays' Rebellion of 1786. Such outbreaks had a common origin in the resentment of the West at Eastern political domination. Denied adequate representation in the colonial legislatures by the existence of high property qualifications for the franchise and by unfair drawing of electoral boundaries, Westerners found their taxes disproportionately high, their demands for protection against Indian attacks ignored, and their hopes for better transport facilities and currency inflation disappointed. And where, as in the Southern colonies, there were also ethnic and religious contrasts between East and West, these formed an additional source of Western hostility towards the tidewater.

These antipathies were to some extent diminished by the Revolution, which brought in nearly every State a considerable gain in the political power of the West, a gain reflected by the transfer of a number of State capitals from tidewater to inland towns. Yet that resentment persisted between the two sections was evident not only from Shays' Rebellion, but from the fears expressed in the East that the spread of settlement beyond the Alleghenies would eventually mean the control of the Federal government by the new States of the West. It was because of these fears that Gouverneur Morris, for instance, proposed to the Federal Convention that "the rule of representation should be so fixed as to secure to the Atlantic States a preponderance in the National Councils". With perhaps a vision of the War of 1812, Morris asserted that new Western States would be "little scrupulous of involving the Community in wars the burdens and operations of which would fall chiefly on the maritime states".

Given the sectional rivalries that had developed by 1787, a struggle between the sections for the control of the new Federal Government could hardly be avoided. Yet so little was this apparent at the time in some quarters that even Washington was reluctant to acknowledge it. In his Farewell Address he deplored "that any ground should have been furnished for characterizing parties by geographical discriminations, Northern and Southern, Eastern and Western". Moreover, Washington went on to imply that the appearance of such parties was attributable simply to the efforts of "designing men . . . to excite a belief that there was a real difference of local interests and views". Yet this was not only to deny that sectionalism had any valid basis; it was also to ignore the sectionalizing effect of policies that Washington himself had championed.

For the truth was that the very measures which had been found necessary to place the Union on a firm foundation had—though succeeding in this object—a markedly unequal impact on different parts of the country. Especially was this so of Hamilton's fiscal policy, of which practically every measure, from the assumption of State debts to the granting of a bounty on dried codfish, had benefited the Northern financier and merchant at the expense of both Southern planter and Western farmer. Thus while Hamilton's policy succeeded brilliantly in its immediate aim of restoring public credit, there was never any real hope that it would achieve its ultimate object of "cement[ing] more closely the Union of the States". On the contrary, it led only to the birth of political parties predominantly sectional in form.

Yet the sectional character of the Federalist and Republican parties would have been less marked but for the impact of the French Revolution. For this event both deepened and embittered the geographical division of opinion resulting from the Hamiltonian programme. That New England should side with England against France in the war that broke out in 1793 was easy enough of explanation. The Congregational clergy, their authority still supreme in New England life, and always ready to oppose any threat to the established order, were so alarmed by the democratic and atheistic aspects of the Revolution in France that its principles became the subject of their most violent condemnation. The merchants of New England, moreover, waxing fat on the profits of neutral trade, were of no mind to question the pretensions of British sea-power when submission had such fruitful results. That the South should be just as enthusiastically in favour of France was due to more complex causes. Being exempt alike from the philosophical fears and material hopes that swayed New England, the South was free to indulge its sentimental attachment to France that had been the legacy of the Revolution, and its dislike of England as a stronghold of reaction and capitalist finance. For these reasons the transference of European issues to America gave to the conflict of parties and sections a virulence it had formerly lacked but which it was to retain until the "era of good feelings".

While sectional feeling between New England and the South was thus increasing, the "heartburnings and jealousies" of Westerners towards the East ebbed and flowed with circumstance. Thanks to the spread of settlement beyond the Alleghenies, the Piedmont area could no longer after the Revolution be referred to as the West; and this term came to be applied instead to the region comprised by Tennessee, Kentucky and the Territory north of the Ohio River. Debarred by the Alleghenies from easy communication with the Atlantic coast, the inhabitants of this area were obliged to turn to the Mississippi as the outlet for their peltry, grain and tobacco, and they thus came to look upon the unimpeded navigation of that river as an indispensable condition of their prosperity. Yet the lower reaches of the Mississippi from Natchez to New Orleans, besides the whole of the river's right bank, were under Spanish control; and in the absence of any formal right of navigation, access to markets for Westerners depended on the goodwill of the Spanish authorities in Louisiana and the Floridas.

Faced with this situation and feeling under the Confederation that the United States government was unable, if not unwilling, to secure their vital outlet to the sea, some Westerners began to contemplate disunion as a remedy. By 1787, a group of Western politicians, headed by General James Wilkinson of Kentucky, was deeply involved in a conspiracy hatched by the Spanish governor of Louisiana and aiming at the formation of a separate Western confederacy under Spanish protection. For the time being the plot came to naught for want of popular support. But Wilkinson and his friends continued for the next ten years to be pensioners of Spain, and unless the Federal Government could succeed in redressing Western grievances, the revival of their intrigues was highly likely.

The first effect of the new government's policies, however, was to increase Western particularism rather than to diminish it. And once again the blame for sectional discontent could be laid on one of Hamilton's measures. This time it was the Excise Act of 1791 that caused the trouble by levying a tax on distilled liquor. The distillation of whisky provided Westerners not only with an additional medium of exchange to supplement their scant supply of specie, but with a convenient method of disposing of their surplus corn, a commodity whose bulk made it difficult to transport. Thus the new tax was extremely unpopular with the frontiersmen, and in western Pennsylvania it even provoked the Whisky Rebellion of 1794.

Two years later, however, not only had the discontents aroused by the Excise Act subsided, but it was possible for Washington to make the somewhat extravagant claim that, thanks to the successful diplomacy of the Federal Government, Westerners now had "everything they could desire . . . towards confirming their prosperity". That Washington should cite Jay's Treaty as one of his administration's diplomatic successes was surprising in view of his private opinion of its terms. But at least there was ground for satisfaction at Pinckney's Treaty, by which Spain had granted to the United States the free navigation of the Mississippi and the right of deposit at New Orleans. In this treaty the President saw "a decisive proof [of] how unfounded were the suspicions propagated among [Westerners] of a policy in the general government and in the Atlantic States unfriendly to their interests in regard to the Mississippi". This success, Washington hoped, would induce Westerners to turn a deaf ear "to those advisers, if such there [were], who would sever them from their brethren and connect them with aliens".

Yet Washington's claims for his diplomacy were largely founded on sand, for the right of deposit granted by Pinckney's Treaty had been guaranteed for only three years. Thus, when at the end of 1802 the Spanish authorities at New Orleans suddenly withdrew the privilege— as it had by then become—Western commerce was so obviously in jeopardy that the West was more than ready to plunge the United States into war to safeguard it. By that time, moreover, a much graver threat had arisen to the future of the West—though not of the West alone— from the retrocession of Louisiana to France. But Jefferson was fully alive to the implications for the United States of having a powerful instead of a decadent Western neighbour and, prompted to attempt the purchase from France of New Orleans alone, found himself in consequence the possessor of the whole of Louisiana.

At this one stroke, all prospect of a popularly-based separatist movement in the West vanished for ever. For a year or two more, it is true, such inveterate plotters as James Wilkinson and Aaron Burr clung to dreams of empire which though shrouded in mystery, almost certainly included the detachment of the Western States from the Union. But such conspiracies were now mere expressions of personal ambition rather than of sectional discontent. Having secured its heart's desire in respect of the Mississippi, the West now had nothing more to demand of American diplomacy except the acquisition of West Florida; and for this boon, too, it had not long to wait.

The full implications for American sectionalism of the Louisiana Purchase did not become apparent for some time; not, indeed, until the status of slavery in that vast area became the subject of sectional disagreement. Yet even in its immediate effects the acquisition of Louisiana was fateful enough, for besides reconciling the West finally to the Union, it provoked such a countervailing response from New England that, in conjunction with other factors, it proved almost sufficient to drive that section to secede.

The discontents of New England began with the election of Jefferson in 1800. To the New England clergy and educated classes this event had implied something more than the mere rejection of their spokesman in favour of one from a rival section. It had meant also the triumph of democracy, with all the evils of violence, popular frenzy and irreligion that the French Revolution had taught them to associate with that word. And however little Jefferson's conduct, during his first term at least, justified such opposition, New Englanders began, in Henry Adams's phrase, "for the first time . . . to extend to the National Government the hatred which they bore to democracy".

It could be argued, of course, that the position of New England after 1800 was no worse than that of the Southern and Western states had been during the twelve years of Federalist rule, and ought therefore to have provoked no more serious a threat to the Union than was implicit in the Virginia and Kentucky Resolutions. But whereas, during the administrations of Washington and John Adams, the Virginia Republicans had been buoyed up by the hope—which turned out to be justified—that the westward advance of population would in time bring in new states favourable to their interests, the New England Federalists, once out of office, seemed to have no prospect but that of being a permanent minority. And this was doubly the case after 1803, when the Louisiana Purchase promised to supply the South with a succession of new agrarian states eager to do her bidding.

Scarcely, then, had the American flag replaced the tricolour at New Orleans, than the bitterness and despair of New England began to turn to conspiracy. By the beginning of 1804 a group of Federalist members of Congress, led by Timothy Pickering of Massachusetts and Roger Griswold of Connecticut, was busy organizing a movement designed to take the five New England States out of the Union, and conspiring with Aaron Burr to attach New York to their proposed Northern Confederacy. Yet these machinations never had much chance of success. Opposed from the outset by most members of the Essex Junto, who felt that separation was not only impracticable but no remedy for what they regarded as the disease of democracy with which New England was already infected, this disunion scheme foundered in April 1804 upon Burr's failure to win election as Governor of New York. And a few months later, when the famous duel at Weehawken Heights had both removed Hamilton from the scene and destroyed Burr's political usefulness, the secession movement had so far collapsed that every New England state but Connecticut voted for Jefferson's re-election.

By the end of Jefferson's second term, however, the embargo and, still more, the attempts made to enforce it, had revived all of New England's hatred of him. Convinced by this measure that Jefferson was both the tool of Napoleon and the inveterate enemy of commerce as a New England interest, the inhabitants of that section moved with alacrity back to the Federalist camp. In point of fact, Jefferson's relations with France were never worse than between 1807 and 1809; while the burden of the embargo fell chiefly not on New England, which found in manufacturing a profitable substitute for commerce, but on the South, and especially on the President's own state which was not only deprived of a market for its tobacco, but lacked New England's capacity to turn to new pursuits. Yet neither this circumstance nor Jefferson's belated conversion to what had been Federalist constitutional principles gave any comfort to New England. Deaf to any explanation of the embargo that did not presume the tyranny of the agrarian interest, New England appeared to be ready to act on Timothy Pickering's advice that "those States whose farms are on the ocean and whose harvests are gathered in every sea should immediately and seriously consider how to preserve them".

The action that Pickering had contemplated involved, of course, the revival of his scheme for a New England Confederation. But in accepting the idea of concerted opposition to the embargo by the New England states, most Federalists had hoped for nothing more than the repeal of the hated measure and the discomfiture of its author. And when these objects were achieved, Pickering's hopes declined accordingly, despite the adoption by Madison of alternative forms of peaceable coercion that were equally distasteful to maritime interests.

The real test of New England's loyalty, indeed, came only when the policy of peaceful coercion was abandoned in favour of war. When the idea of a New England Confederation had been mooted in 1804, George Cabot, a leading member of the Essex Junto, had declared that the only hope of inducing the people of New England to agree to leave the Union lay in "a war with Great Britain manifestly provoked by our rulers". Eight years later this condition appeared to have been fulfilled when the United States Senate declared war on Great Britain by a markedly sectional vote. Except for Vermont, New England voted unanimously against the declaration of war, support for which came largely from the West and South. And despite the emphasis placed by Madison in his war message on impressment and other maritime issues, it was all too apparent that John Randolph was right in declaring that the real motive of the War Hawks was "agrarian cupidity and not maritime right".

That the long-discussed plan to hold a New England Convention did not materialise until almost the end of the war was due chiefly to the quasi-neutrality that the New England States were able to maintain for the first two years of hostilities. Not until the spring of 1814 was the British blockade extended to the ports of New England, and while that exemption lasted, Yankee merchants monopolized the still substantial volume of American trade, while Yankee manufacturers and contractors made fat profits alike from the enemy and from their own countrymen. During that period, therefore, New England went no further in its opposition to the war than to discourage contributions both of men and money to the Federal Government, and to assert in the face of American victories that it was "not becoming in a moral and religious people to express any approbation of military or naval exploits which [were] not immediately connected with the defence of [their] own seacoast and soil". But when British blockading cruisers brought commerce to a standstill, and a British invading army held the coast of Maine, the plans of the New England malcontents came to fruition in the calling of the Hartford Convention.

Since, however, most New Englanders still believed that the grievances of which they complained were capable of redress within the Union, the Hartford Convention did not become a mere preliminary to secession as the extreme Federalists had hoped. Instead, the Convention produced only an expression of frustration at New England's loss of political influence and a number of suggestions as to how this could be regained. New England's real complaint, indeed, was not against the embargo or the war, grievous though these things were, but against what the Convention report called "a deliberate and extensive system for effecting a combination among certain States, by exciting local jealousies and ambition, so as to secure to popular leaders in one section of the Union, the control of public affairs in perpetual succession". The remedy, the report suggested, lay in the amendment of the Constitution so as to restore in the Federal Government "a fair and equal representation" of all sections. To deprive the Southern states of the additional representation they enjoyed in Congress in respect of their Negro slaves, the three-fifths clause of the Constitution should be repealed; to restore the balance of powers which existed among the original thirteen states and which had been destroyed by the Louisiana Purchase, the concurrence of two-thirds of both houses should be required before new states were admitted to the Union; and to bring an end to the Virginian dynasty upon which was centred so much of New England's bitterness, no president should be capable of re-election, nor should the president be elected from the same State two terms in succession.

Whether New England would have been ready for more drastic action had these amendments been rejected and had the war continued for another six months can be only a matter of conjecture. In the event, the

Hartford proposals were never formally considered by either Congress or the state legislatures for, by the time the Commissioners sent by the Convention arrived at Washington in January 1815, the news of Jackson's victory at New Orleans had deprived New England of its imagined ability to dictate terms to a collapsing Federal Government. And when the news of the Treaty of Ghent arrived shortly afterwards, New England promptly forgot the second convention planned to meet in Boston in June 1815, and turned thankfully instead to the restoration of its prostrate commerce.

That the wave of nationalism provoked by Jackson's victory should find an echo even in New England was proof that sectional feeling could at times succumb to a wider sentiment. Tocqueville, visiting the United States twenty years later, when sectional forces were again in the ascendant, was nevertheless struck by the permanence of the conflict between nationalism and sectionalism, which he described as "two distinct currents flowing in contrary directions in the same channel". Thus to gauge correctly the strength of sectionalism it is necessary always to remember that powerful counter-influences were continuously at work on the American mind. Even in the period after 1815, which became increasingly one of sectional conflict, there were never lacking forces to promote national feeling among Americans of all sections.

Yet by 1850, under the impact of social and economic developments, a new sectional pattern had emerged and disunion was again on the agenda of a sectional gathering. The new sectional division was that between North, South and West, each having, in Turner's words, "its own type of people, its own geographic and economic basis, its own particular economic and social interests". And while, since 1815, the sectionalism of New England had waned, the Nashville Convention showed how far that of the South had mounted.

It was between 1815 and 1850 that it first became possible to regard the Atlantic States north of Mason and Dixon's line as a single section having common characteristics and interests. That the old distinctions between New England and the Middle States should have become less marked was due in part to the decline of those influences which had long set New England apart from the rest of the Union. The discrediting of the Federalist party and, still more, the loss of authority by the Congregational clergy could not fail to sap the distinctiveness of the New England temper. But even more important in promoting Northern homogeneity was the fact that new economic forces—industrial development, commercial expansion, urban growth and large-scale European immigration—affected New England and the Middle States in like degree, and thus produced in them a similarity of economic activity and social organization. These facts, together with an agricultural decline due to inability to compete with Western farm products, made of the North Atlantic States a section where industry and commerce were the paramount interests and where, incidentally, each census brought striking advances in population and wealth.

The South, meanwhile, not only remained an agrarian section but, thanks to the spread of cotton cultivation, became increasingly devoted to one-crop agriculture based on the plantation system. That industry should have failed to develop in the South was not due to lack of minerals or of water power, but to a dearth of capital combined with a deeply-held contempt for industry and commerce as mere money-grabbing occupations. Turning a deaf ear to all appeals to diversify its economy, the South sank practically all its available capital into land and slaves; and in response to the soaring demands of European and New England textile mills, extended the domain of King Cotton from the sea-islands of the Carolina coast to the borders of Mexico. And since the whole edifice of the cotton kingdom was erected on the labour of the Negro slave, there developed throughout the whole of this vast region a form of society which, from its rigidity and class-consciousness, was wholly at variance with that developing in the North.

While North and South were thus drawing steadily apart, the rapidity and scale of the westward movement were carving a new West out of the fertile valley of the Mississippi. Unlocked by the Indian defeats of the War of 1812, the frontier gates swung open to admit a swarm of land-hungry settlers. The West, as Turner remarked, was less a place than a stage of society, and in time the upper and lower halves of the Mississippi valley were to take on many of the characteristics of the older sections by which they were peopled. But in the interval before that happened—and that interval was considerably longer in the North-west than in the South-west—it was possible to speak of the West as a separate and distinct element in the sectional pattern. Schooled by frontier conditions to self-reliance and independence of thought, the Western farmer was palpably more impatient of restraint and less respectful of established forms than were the inhabitants of the two older sections. And even when the frontier phase was over, the influence of pioneer days remained, and the West continued to be the home of individualism, innovation and an aggressively confident democratic spirit.

The opposition of interests which thus developed between North, South and West could not fail, sooner or later, to express itself politically, and when each section began demanding of the national government legislation favourable to its welfare, divisions along sectional lines began to appear. Of the purely economic issues the tariff was, perhaps, the most productive of sectional discord. Though not a sectional issue when first adopted in 1816, the policy of protection became a bitter source of contention once the wave of nationalism that had inspired it broke on the rocks of an economic depression. Thus the raising of schedules by the so-called Tariff of Abominations in 1828 roused such feelings of opposition in the South, where the measure was denounced as a subsidy to the

North, that it resulted four years later in South Carolina's Nullification Ordinance. And although the nullification crisis marked the high tide of sectionalism over the tariff issue—for the compromise measure of 1833 went far to meet the South's wishes—every revision of tariff schedules between then and the Civil War revealed the persistence of sectional attitudes.

A similar cleavage existed over the desirability—and the constitutionality—of devoting Federal funds to internal improvement. Designed to promote sectional harmony by the construction of canals and turnpikes, which would facilitate the exchange of products between agricultural and manufacturing sections, the policy of internal improvement evoked instead the same sort of sectional response as protection, with which it was linked in Clay's American System. The reciprocal advantage to Northern manufacturer and Western farmer was obvious enough, but the South, blessed by nature with an excellent river system and exempt from the necessity of finding a domestic market for its staple crops, refused to be convinced by Clay's argument that all sections would benefit equally from the policy he proposed. Though it was a Western president who, by the Maysville veto, provided the internal improvement policy with its most effective check, it was the South which year in year out provided the spearhead of the opposition.

Toward the question of the public lands the sections exhibited a more malleable attitude. To this generalization the West was, of course, an exception, for it never wavered in its insistence that the public lands should be made available to settlers in small units and at low prices. Neither of the two older sections however, was at first disposed to agree to this programme; the South because it had little interest in the matter while the tariff engrossed its attention, the North because it feared that a liberal land policy would lead to a labour shortage in its industrial areas. But as time went on the South was led into opposition to cheap land by the realization that such a policy would open the West to non-slaveholders. And when the motive for Northern opposition disappeared a significant shift in the alignment of sections took place. Its fears of a labour shortage removed by the great increase in European immigration, the North could eventually afford to give its support to the land policy demanded by the West in exchange for co-operation on the tariff question.

On the issue of a centralized banking system, however, the alliance of South and West remained unbroken until the Civil War. Both of them debtor regions, anxious for easy credit in the form of a plentiful supply of currency, these two sections strongly resented the restraining influence of the second Bank of the United States on note emissions by local banks. There were, it is true, many Westerners like Jackson who as "hard money" men were far from anxious to see the amount of paper currency increased. Yet these men, too, were bitter enemies of the Bank, which appeared to them to be not only a dangerous monopoly threatening the interests of the common man, but as a body whose capital was held chiefly by Northern financiers, an instrument of sectional oppression. And although the Panic of 1837 soon made clear the unwisdom of allowing the Bank's charter to expire, nothing could persuade the two agrarian sections to agree to re-establish a centralized banking organization.

That economic issues such as these played some part in producing the sectional pattern that led to the Civil War is undeniable. Particularly significant was the fact that, as canal and railroad forged new links between the upper Mississippi valley and the States of the North-east, the old alliance of the two agrarian sections tended to give way to one which left the South in isolation. Moreover, the constant agitation of these economic issues could not but lead to heightened sectional consciousness and antipathies. The tariff issue, particularly, was of great importance in fostering Southern economic sectionalism. For, despite the generally downward trend of tariff schedules in the generation before the Civil War, the South found in the protection granted to Northern industry the explanation of her own relative decline; and that the South was almost certainly wrong in this belief does not alter the fact of her resentment. When secession occurred, moreover, the contrast between the heavily protective Morrill Tariff at once passed by the Republican majority in Congress, and the rejection of the protective principle by the Confederate Constitution was sufficiently marked for foreign observers like *The Times* to leap to the conclusion that the tariff issue was the real cause of the Civil War.

Southern economic sectionalism, however, was born not only of opposition to specific measures proposed in Congress but also of a vaguer feeling that the section was being exploited in other ways by Northern capital. This feeling, expressed in the meetings of the Southern Commercial Conventions and in such publications as Kettell's *Southern Wealth and Northern Profits*, arose from the control which Northerners were able to achieve over every aspect of Southern economic life. Dependent on Northern capital to finance the growing of its staple crops and on Northern commission agents to market them, the South also relied on Northern vessels to carry both its exports and its imports, of which the latter came almost exclusively through Northern ports. Asserting that the amounts it paid for these services were grossly excessive, and that the enormous profits said to accrue to the North were largely responsible for that section's prosperity, the South believed itself to be in Rhett's words, "the very best colony . . . that any country ever had". That this indictment was unproved, if not unprovable, was less important than that the South came increasingly to believe it to be true. And long before political independence became the major Southern goal, the advantages of economic independence had been widely realized and a variety of expedients suggested to achieve it.

The awakening of the South to a realization of its dependent position resulted, however, not from an absolute failure to advance in population and wealth but, as Tocqueville remarked, from a failure to do so at the same rate as the other sections. Speculating in 1835 on the chances of the duration of the Union, Tocqueville thought that the greatest peril to which it was exposed arose from the continual changes which took place in the relative strength of the sections. "The rapid and disproportionate increase of certain States", he believed, meant that they became the object of envy and suspicion to the others, and it was to this cause alone that he attributed "the deep-seated uneasiness and ill-defined agitation" which he had found so noticeable in the South at the time of the nullification controversy. To Tocqueville it was not difficult to understand that the South "which had given four Presidents to the Union", should have become irritated and alarmed when it saw "the number of its representatives in Congress . . . diminishing from year to year, while those of the Northern and Western States [were] increasing". And, he concluded, what added enormously to the danger to the Union was that such changes took place so quickly as to emphasize the contrast between the South's present weakness and its former power.

Yet if previous manifestations of American sectionalism were any criterion, the mere loss of political influence, even when accompanied by adverse economic consequences, was not sufficient to induce a section to attempt disunion. New England, in spite of its loss of weight in the national scale after 1800, had steadfastly refused its support to the separatist plans of the extreme Federalists—though New England's eclipse, in comparison with what befell the South a generation later, was both swifter and more complete, besides bringing in its train more serious economic injuries. That New England's discontent had not culminated in secession had been due in the first place to the uneven impact upon her of the measures which were the chief object of her complaint. For, while Jefferson's and Madison's policies proved harmful to some of New England's economic interests, they acted in contrary fashion on others. But another obstacle to united action was that, even among the discontented, there were many who were far from convinced that disunion was the only remedy for New England's ills. Thus, that the South should eventually have gone beyond the limits of opposition marked out by New England in 1814, and beyond, too, the even wider limits it had itself set in 1832, suggests that something more was involved in Southern sectionalism than mere pique at the loss of political influence. Indeed, the real reason for the Southern uneasiness that Tocqueville remarked was that the change in the sectional balance had placed in growing jeopardy an interest of such transcendent importance to the South as to unite the whole section in a determination to preserve it.

Without its great and peculiar interest of slavery, it is probable that, after 1832, the South like other discontented sections before it, would have become gradually reconciled to the Federal Government. After all, none of the economic issues on which sectional disagreements occurred involved a threat to any vital interest of the South; and in any case the economic policies of the Federal Government continued up to the Civil War to be largely dictated by Southerners. One should remember, too, that while clear sectional tendencies were almost always discernible in the Congressional votes on economic issues, those issues never became wholly sectional in character. For, as no section had a single set of economic interests, so none could act with complete unanimity toward economic questions. This was less true of the South, perhaps, than of the two other sections but even in the South there existed sizeable economic groups which dissented from the dominant sectional attitudes. Thus even as late as 1857 it was possible for a tariff bill to pass the House by a vote that was anything but sectional. Again, a comparison of voting on economic issues at different times shows that sectional attitudes toward them could change with circumstances. That between 1816 and 1828 sectional leaders like Webster and Calhoun should so far modify their views on the tariff as to exchange positions was perhaps the most striking proof of this tendency but, as we have seen, significant changes took place also in sectional attitudes both to the public land question and to internal improvements. Then, too, it was surely of significance that none of the economic issues on which the sections disagreed proved so intractable as to defy efforts at compromise. On only one occasion between 1820 and 1861 was sectional opposition to an economic measure so marked as to threaten the existence of the Union; and even then only one State could be found to carry its opposition as far as nullification. And that the threat should subside with the passage of the 1833 compromise tariff was proof that even on the most contentious economic questions Congress could legislate successfully without undue injustice to the interests of any section. The history of sectional conflict on economic questions before the Civil War, indeed, points not to the impending breakdown of the American federal system but to its successful working.

One might even assert that sectional quarrels over such matters had comparatively little intrinsic importance as causes of the Civil War, being mere reflections of a larger conflict over slavery. For, as the existence of slavery was chiefly responsible for the South's lack of industries, so it determined her attitude to the tariff and confirmed her in her opposition to internal improvements. It was slavery again, allied to one-crop agriculture, that kept the South a debtor section and moulded her views on banking and currency questions. And it was concern for the expansion of slavery that was the main cause of Southern opposition to the cheap land policy. Thus an explanation of the Civil War that concentrates exclusively on the economic rivalries of the sections deals only in superficialities; and to get to the root one is forced to return to the slavery question.

For here was an issue which, to a far greater extent than any other, was a sectional one. It was, moreover, the one issue on which sectional attitudes, far from changing, became with time only more stern and unbending. And, being an issue in which morals and economics were blended equally, and thus one of both emotional and practical significance for the sections, slavery proved at the last the one matter on which compromise was impossible.

The development among Southerners of a frankly-avowed pro-slavery attitude had its origin in the stimulus given to slavery by the spread of cotton cultivation. At the time of the Revolution, when cotton had been virtually an unknown crop in the South and even Southern tobacco production had been in decline, the perpetuation of Negro slavery had not yet come to be regarded as a vital Southern interest. Under the influence of Revolutionary liberalism Southern leaders like Jefferson and Patrick Henry had been ready both to deplore the institution's existence, and to contemplate its abolition as soon as circumstances should permit. But such sentiments did not long survive the introduction of the cotton plant and the invention of Whitney's cotton gin. Once the South turned to the large-scale cultivation of a crop for which there was an apparently limitless demand, and for which Negro slave labour was ideally suited, the preservation of slavery came to be thought of as the one indispensable condition of Southern prosperity.

The change from embarrassed apology to uninhibited defence came sooner than is sometimes realized. As early as 1806, when Congress was debating the abolition of the slave trade, a Southern Congressman could assert that, far from believing slavery to be criminal, as did some speakers from the North, "a large majority of people in the Southern States" did not even consider it to be an evil. And by the time of the Missouri controversy in 1819, this fact was all too evident from the violence of the Southern reaction to the attempt to exclude slavery from Missouri as the price of her admission to the Union.

Yet it was not until the 1830's that the elaborate web of Southern pro-slavery thought was finally constructed and a strident and aggressive note appeared in Southern defences of the peculiar institution. The chief cause of this was the virulence and, as it seemed to Southerners, the unfairness of the Abolitionist attack. It was only to be expected that the abuse of slaveholders appearing in *The Liberator*, and especially the sending of such organs through the Southern mails, should provoke an indignant response. Yet with slaveholders forming only a small minority of the Southern white population, it was obvious that there were other factors besides economic interest involved in the South's whole-hearted adoption of the "positive good" theory. The all-important fact about the Southern attitude, indeed, was that slavery was regarded not merely as a labour system but as a practical solution of a race problem. And by the 1830's it was becoming increasingly apparent to Southerners, slaveholders and non-slaveholders alike, that that problem was both permanent and acute. The utter failure of the plans of the American Colonization Society revealed the futility of the hope that the Negroes might be got rid of by sending them back to Africa. Simultaneously, the sanguinary visions of a racial war conjured up by the Nat Turner insurrection drove the South to reinforce the defences of slavery as a method of ensuring social peace.

Impelled by these circumstances to defend slavery with both passion and unanimity, the South drifted into acceptance of a philosophy directly opposed to the Jeffersonian liberalism it had professed during and after the Revolution. Indeed, having once laid as the corner-stone of its society an institution whose very essence was inequality, the rejection of the ideals of the Declaration followed as a matter of course. Thus, though becoming more democratic in form as a consequence of the political reforms of the Jacksonian period, the South was far from sharing the democratic spirit now common to the rest of the Union. Bemused and dazzled by the image of itself it saw reflected in the romances of Sir Walter Scott, flattered by the similarities it believed to exist between its own society and that of ancient Greece, and proud of its supposed descent from Cavalier stock, the Southern ruling class was led by its devotion to slavery into giving its allegiance to an alien aristocratic ideal.

That the South should be led also by that devotion into a defence of State Rights was, so far as the causation of the Civil War is concerned, of purely incidental importance. The attempt made by Confederate leaders after 1865 to elevate State Rights into a principle for which alone the South had seceded is singularly unconvincing. No one, looking at the way in which the South— like other sections—embraced State Rights when its interests were suited and rejected State Rights when they were not, could believe that any principle was involved. And in any case it was not State Rights but slavery that Alexander H. Stephens, in a celebrated speech in December 1860, described as "the cornerstone of the Confederacy"; while Jefferson Davis, in analysing the causes of secession in April 1861, left no doubt that concern for slavery was at the bottom of his insistence on a constitutional right to secede.

In the North, though passion was not lacking on the slavery issue, nothing approaching unanimity was ever achieved. In that same debate on the slave trade in 1806 that had given one of the earliest indications of changing Southern views on slavery, John Randolph had intimated his belief that to avert a disruption between slaveholding and non-slaveholding States—which he regarded as the most probable line of separation should disunion ever occur—all that was necessary was that the North "should not erect itself into an abolition society". Yet had this been all that was required disunion ought not to have occurred in 1860-61 for, whatever the South might believe to the contrary, the North up to that date had not as a section given its support to Abolitionism. The Abolitionists themselves had remained a small and unpopular minority, de-

N

nounced not only by the South but by Northern conservatives as dangerous fanatics; and even by many people who sympathized with their aims
they were regarded as impractical idealists. Moreover, as Beard pointed
out, no major political leader save John Quincy Adams committed himself
before the Civil War to the support of Abolitionist doctrines; and the
only political party to adopt Abolitionism as its programme attracted
but a negligible popular vote on its only two appearances before the
electorate.

Yet no one could deny the existence in the North of a great and
growing antipathy toward the institution of slavery. For proof of this
one had only to look at the adoption by nearly every Northern State of
Personal Liberty laws, at the extraordinary success of *Uncle Tom's Cabin*,
and at the amount of approval expressed for John Brown's raid—to
mention only a few manifestations of this feeling. Arising in part from
humanitarian concern for the welfare of the Negro, and from a feeling of
indignation at the cruelties supposedly inflicted upon him by the slave
system, Northern hatred of slavery drew also on other sources. It owed
much to a mortifying realization that the United States stood, in the
middle of the nineteenth century, almost alone in maintaining the institution of human bondage. But it owed more, perhaps, to a growing
consciousness of the degree to which slavery contradicted the ideals to
which the United States had been formally dedicated at its birth. "I
hate slavery", said Lincoln in his Peoria speech in 1854, "because it
deprives our republican example of its just influence in the world, enables
the enemies of free institutions with plausibility to taunt us as hypocrites,
causes the real friends of freedom to doubt our sincerity, and especially
because it forces so many good men among ourselves into an open war
with the very fundamental principles of civil liberty, criticizing the
Declaration of Independence, and insisting that there is no right principle
of action but self-interest." Here was evidence of that new conception of
the Union and that new loyalty toward it that, by the time of the Civil
War, had grown up in all sections except the South. Proud of their
country's rapid advance in material wealth, and believing that it had a
great and peculiar destiny to fulfil, the people of the North and West had
developed by 1860 an almost mystical devotion to the Union as the source
of their achievements and the symbol of their aspirations.

Indeed, it was the very strength of their Unionism that explained the
reluctance of the States north of Mason and Dixon's line to adopt a
radical attitude toward slavery. Fearful of giving the slave States any
pretext for attempting disunion, the North was prepared to go to great
lengths to conciliate them. Thus, in spite of their hostility to slavery, the
great majority of Northerners were ready to abide loyally by those
provisions of the Constitution by which the institution was guaranteed
and protected. Lincoln undoubtedly had behind him the great mass of
Northern opinion when in his first inaugural he specifically disavowed

any intention of interfering with slavery in the States where it already existed. Indeed, there would probably have been a Northern majority for making this disavowal both binding and permanent by means of a constitutional amendment. And if the enforcement of the Fugitive Slave Act caused many Northerners considerable heart-searching, most of them were prepared with Lincoln to "bite their lips and say nothing".

Thus if the controversy over slavery could have been limited to these aspects of the question, as might have been possible had not the westward movement exerted so vast an influence on the relation of the sections, secession and war might still have been averted. But with the frontier advancing with giant strides towards the Pacific, and with both North and South looking to the West as a possible source of support for their own aims, the slavery question necessarily obtruded itself into that of territorial organization. Some historians, contrasting the furore over slavery in the territories with the fact that the natural limits of slavery expansion had probably been reached by 1860, have echoed the witticism that James G. Blaine made famous, that "the whole controversy over the Territories related to an imaginary negro in an impossible place". And indeed it is difficult from a superficial view to see why North and South should have clashed so violently over a question that seemed of little practical importance to either. Part of the explanation lies in the fact that, because of the constitutional safeguards with which slavery was surrounded at so many points, the territorial question was practically the only one on which antislavery sentiment could express itself effectively; on this question, therefore, was concentrated the whole weight of sectional feeling aroused by the institution itself. Again, questions of sectional prestige were involved. It was intolerable to Southerners, for example, that they should be forbidden to take their property into territories which, at least in the case of those acquired from Mexico, had been won for the United States chiefly by Southern arms.

Yet there were more substantive factors involved. To the South, whose peculiar institution had to expand in order to survive—or so Southerners believed—the exclusion of slavery from the territories was tantamount to a death-blow at slavery everywhere. It would mean the end of those dreams of a "tropic empire" in the Caribbean and the Gulf of Mexico by which some Southerners hoped to redress the sectional balance. It would mean that in the Border Slave States, where slavery was already insecure, its strength would be still further sapped by the opportunities for escape afforded to slaves by adjacent free territory. And even if this threat to slavery could be averted, what defence was there against the prospect that there would eventually be sufficient free States in the Union to enable slavery to be attacked by means of a constitutional amendment? Small wonder that the South refused to be placated by Lincoln's assurance that, in opposing the extension of slavery, he intended no interference with it where it already existed. The only step that could have satisfied the South, indeed, was that Federal protection of slavery should be extended to the territories as well as to the States. And led by its position to advocate this step, the South came ultimately to insist upon it as the condition of its remaining in the Union.

Yet it was not only the South whose vital interests were at stake in the status of slavery in the territories. When that issue had first appeared, at the time for Missouri's application for statehood, the North's opposition had been due not to hostility to slavery on moral grounds—for the morality of slavery had not yet been seriously questioned—but to apprehensions of the effect new Slave States would have on the sectional balance. By the time the issue was revived at the time of the Mexican War, there had been added to this apprehension a conviction that the spread of slavery to the territories would close them to free labour. Yet it was not these circumstances alone that accounted for the outburst of fury that greeted the Kansas-Nebraska Act in the North. The principal cause of Northern anger was a realization of the threat which slavery presented to American democratic ideals. It had been permissible, perhaps, to profess those ideals while merely acquiescing in the existence of slavery within those areas where the Constitution protected it, and where it had been permitted to go by the compromises of 1820 and 1850. But it was manifestly a different matter gratuitously to allow slavery to spread wherever it might be found profitable. This fact, it is true, did not become apparent to all Northerners at the same time; and even among those to whom awareness of the threat came early there were many who might have found difficulty in giving clear expression to their fears. But by 1860 even those like Stephen A. Douglas, who had professed indifference as to whether slavery "was voted up or voted down", had become sufficiently alive to the danger to American ideals to reject outright the South's demand for the territorial protection of slavery. The majority of Northerners, moreover, believing that an even firmer stand was now necessary, gave their votes to a party whose purpose it was to place an insuperable barrier in the path of slavery extension, and in so doing to ensure that the institution as a whole "was placed in the course of ultimate extinction".

Being all too aware of the implications of Lincoln's election, the South turned to secession as the only method by which slavery could be protected and perpetuated. And, given the strength of American nationalism in the North, secession could end only in a conflict of arms. As Lincoln was to say in his second inaugural, "both parties deprecated war, but one of them would *make* war rather than let the nation survive, and the other would *accept* war rather than let it perish, and the war came".

The Civil War, "the most drastic and the most tragic of sectional manifestations", as Turner called it, had the paradoxical effect of stimulating the very spirit of sectional particularism that, on the part of the North, it was fought to destroy. Pride in the gallantry and devotion of the Southern people in their vain fight for independence gave to Southern sectionalism an intensity it could never have attained in any other way. And when to the nostalgic aura surrounding "the lost cause" there was added a bitter memory of wrongs endured in common during the period of Reconstruction, the Solid South became a permanent feature of the American political system. Even today, though almost a century has passed since the Civil War, the South still presents a distinctively sectional attitude towards questions of public policy, and especially toward that one overriding question to which the South owes its existence as a section.

Yet in spite of the persistence of Southern solidarity, and in spite, too, of those striking expressions of Western discontent that came after 1865 in the Granger and Populist movements, the Civil War marked an epoch in the history of American sectionalism. For the war, by ending once for all the long controversy over the nature of the Union, ensured that sectionalism had henceforth to operate within more circumscribed limits. Once Appomattox had provided a final answer to the question of whether a right of secession existed, sectional animosities and rivalries, though persisting, were transferred to an altogether lower plane. Neither the Civil War nor the period since have seen the fulfilment of the wish John Jay expressed in 1786 that "the people of America would become one nation in every respect". But thanks to the outcome of the War between the Sections, which is perhaps the most accurate description of the conflict of 1861-65, there have been no grounds since Appomattox for fearing, as did Jay and his contemporaries, that a narrow devotion to local interests would lead to a disruption of the Union.

RECONSTRUCTION AND THE COLOUR PROBLEM

By George Shepperson

*

I will say to the north, Give up; and to the south, Keep not back . . .
Isaiah, XLIII, 6

THROUGH a multitude of agencies, Americans have kept alive and interpreted the memory of the twelve years after the Civil War: "dark Raven Days" of Reconstruction to many whites, when the defeated South endured military occupation and the attempt was made to stamp on it the conqueror's pattern; "days of Jubilee, Jubilo" to the majority of the four million former slaves to whom the War had brought freedom, the taste of political power, the hope of land, and the prospect of a new and exciting life on equal terms with the white man. Though the remembrance of these years has obviously been felt most acutely in the United States, the interest which peoples in Europe—particularly the British—took in American slavery and allied questions during the nineteenth century has ensured that Reconstruction would not be forgotten on the other side of the Atlantic. Indeed, by the turn of the century, the prejudices and vocabulary of at least one interpretation of Reconstruction had become firmly established not merely in America but also in Britain, where responsibilities of the New Imperialism amongst the "fluttered folk and wild" made for attitudes akin to those of many Southern whites. These British echoes often occur in the most unlikely places. One of these is H. G. Wells's foretaste of *1984*, *The Sleeper Awakes* (London, 1899) in which the possibility of the importation of Negroes to discipline the rebellious whites of a futuristic London is considered with Aryan horror; and there is a fascinating glimpse of the "black multitude" brought in for this purpose by Wells's equivalent of "Big Brother", "craning their black necks . . . to see . . . the rich and splendid city to which 'Massa Boss' had brought their obedient muscles . . . They knew they were to have lordly times among the 'poor white' trash."

Such "lordly times" found illustration in the works of Thomas Nelson Page, pioneer of the novelistic school of Southern paternalism and romanticism, whose writings appeared in both English and American editions. His *Red Rock* (London, 1898) shows the problems Page encountered when he tried to depict Reconstruction. He discovered, as he began this novel, that he was, in fact, writing a pro-Southern political tract, destroyed a third of the manuscript, and proceeded thereafter in a gentler key: "the real facts" of Reconstruction seemed "so terrible" that he was "unable to describe them fully without subjecting (himself) to the charge of gross exaggeration". Yet this studied attempt at moderation did not prevent Page from contributing to the emerging stereotypes of the Negro during Reconstruction: for example, the malevolent mulatto, Moses, who was lynched after several crimes "sufficiently heinous to entitle him to be classed as one of the greatest scoundrels in the world"; and the embittered Negro statesman intent on raising the taxes "till we bankrupt 'em everyone, and then the land will go to the ones as ought to have it".

These characterizations were elaborated within the next six years in two novels by Thomas Dixon, Jnr. *The Leopard's Spots: A Romance of the White Man's Burden, 1865-1900* (New York, 1902) praised the Ku Klux Klan, lynching, and all attempts to put the Negro "in his place". Evoking every form of racial prejudice, it condemned Reconstruction as "an attempt to reverse the order of nature". Dixon's second novel, *The Clansman, An Historical Romance of the Ku Klux Klan* (New York, 1905), went further in its castigation of the short-lived political privileges granted to the Negro at this time: a "new mob of onion-laden breath, mixed with perspiring African odour, became the symbol of American democracy". The influence of these two novels in riveting one picture of Reconstruction and the colour problem on the Atlantic Community was profound, especially when in 1915 the first great full length film, D. W. Griffith's *The Birth of a Nation*, which was based on Dixon's books, was presented to the world. This stamped upon the cinema in its formative period an anti-Negro interpretation of Reconstruction. Its views of Negroes running amok on the Southern Piedmont, its depiction of Reconstruction legislatures, its portrayal of Mae Marsh as a frightened white girl chased by a rape-mad Negro, and many other instances led to race riots in several American towns, culminating in fierce, city-wide clashes between white and black in Chicago after the film's revival there in 1924. Since then, it has continued to disturb relations between Negro and white Americans. The Dixon-Griffith heritage, though shorn of its worst crudities, was continued in Margaret Mitchell's *Gone With the Wind* (New York, 1936), both as novel and film, with its pictures of Negro political aberrations during Reconstruction: "former field-hands . . . suddenly elevated to the seats of the mighty conducted themselves as creatures of small intelligence might be expected to do . . ."

It is not surprising that such attitudes should produce reactions to the Negro's side. Foremost among these must be set the novel, *Freedom Road* (New York, 1944) by the Left-wing American writer, Mr Howard Fast, in which the Negro is portrayed as a constructive influence during Reconstruction, intent on co-operation with the Southern poor whites to create "a fine, a just and a truly democratic civilization". Mr Fast was undoubtedly following here in the tradition of the veteran Negro American sociologist, Professor W. E. Burghardt Du Bois who, from the time when he replied to criticisms of the main Northern instrument of Negro rehabilitation during Reconstruction, the Freedmen's Bureau, in his pioneer contribution to Negro literature, *The Souls of Black Folk* (Chicago, 1903), to his passionately comprehensive *Black Reconstruction, An Essay Toward a History of the Part Which Black Folk Played In The Attempt To Reconstruct Democracy in America, 1860-1880* (New York, 1935) has striven to stimulate revision of anti-Negro tendencies, not merely in American novels and movies but also in the writings of many scholars on the dozen years after the Civil War.

In countless other ways, Reconstruction has been inflated and deflated to fit the changes of American life. For example, it has been claimed of Claude G. Bowers's *The Tragic Era* (New York, 1929), an anti-Republican picture of Reconstruction, that it is a veiled attack on the Republican enemies of Alfred E. Smith, 1928 Democratic Presidential candidate, behind onslaughts on Republican leaders of 1868, 1872 and 1876. And so the kaleidoscopic pictures of Reconstruction continue to emerge, until it becomes clear that there are two major "Reconstructions" in American history: the actual Reconstruction of the Southern states which, though it may be subject to the various view-points of historical interpretation and be assigned by differing historians to periods greater or longer than the conventional twelve post-Civil War years, is, nevertheless, a concrete process; and an epiphenomenal "Reconstruction", a series of shifting emotional attitudes and prejudices, an ideological reflex of the actual Reconstruction, which has exerted and continues to exert an influence on the American scene. If this influence falls mainly within the field of Negro-white relations, it is not bounded by this, as the interpretation of Bowers's book indicates, or as is clear from *Freedom Road* which is much more than a Reconstruction essay—nothing short, in fact, of a criticism of the whole structure of American society.

Thus, until one has a master key to sociology—particularly to the sociology of knowledge—perhaps the best way of appreciating the many "Reconstructions" that are offered is to set one's knowledge in history's main perspective, its major logic: the chronologic. Five, perhaps six, stages may be noted in the emergence of Reconstruction and its problems.

The first begins in the two decades before the Civil War when both protagonists and opponents of the American abolition movements failed to suggest anything better for the slaves when they should be emancipated than shipping them off either to Africa or to settlements in the Caribbean and Latin America. When, therefore, during and after the War, the problem of the emancipated Negro passed from theory to practice, Americans were ill-equipped to meet it. This tendency was strengthened by the fact that emancipation was not one of the original war aims of Lincoln's government.

The second stage was the complex of attitudes that emerged towards the seceded States and their Negroes during the Civil War. Too often, the problem of bringing the States back politically into the Union and the question of what to do with the slaves as, between 1862 and 1865, they were emancipated, were separated. Thus, a state of mind was created, even in the most conscientious Americans, which found it difficult to regard the problem as a single whole—which it was—and more convenient to treat it as if it were in two separate compartments. The haphazard way in which emancipation came about strengthened this dichotomy. Lincoln's considerate plan for gradual, compensated emancipation was set aside, and abolition, when it came, was largely the result of military necessity. Yet even though Lincoln's plan had the very real virtues of gradualness and compensation, he, like most Americans of his time, had little idea of what to do with the slaves when they were emancipated. Would it be unfair to say that what solution he could offer of this question was little more than a form of liberal *apartheid*? As early as the Lincoln-Douglas debates of 1859, he had spoken against the "social and political equality of the white and black races" and had declared against Negro citizenship. Lincoln carried this attitude further when he conferred with some coloured men on August 19, 1862, on a scheme for colonizing American Negroes in Central America. He spoke to them plainly: " . . . when you cease to be slaves, you are yet far removed from being . . . on an equality with the white race . . . I cannot alter it if I would. It is a fact. But for your race among us there could not be war, although many men on either side do not care for you one way or the other . . . It is better for us both to be separated."

The failure, however, of schemes for Negro colonization abroad, during and after the Civil War, through lack of capital, business chicanery, and the fact that over two hundred years of slavery had created for the Negro an attachment to America and its values as abiding as the white man's, meant that Lincoln and others like him had been deprived of their main weapon for solving the Negro question; and that after Emancipation, they would take few positive measures during the War to ameliorate the Negro's condition in his new, bewildering status. This was clear from the Emancipation Proclamation of January 1, 1863, in which the only provision for the freed Negroes was the good advice that they "abstain from all violence, unless in necessary self-defence"; that "*when allowed* (author's italics) they labour faithfully for reasonable wages"; and that for some of them a form of stopgap economic aid would be available as garrison troops and sailors in the American armed services. The difficulties which the Federal Government felt in the way of taking responsibility for the freed slaves was indicated by the implicit attempt to put the onus for them on the States in Lincoln's Proclamation of Amnesty and Reconstruction of December 8, 1863. The fracas during the next eight months between Lincoln and Radical members of Congress who were critical of his Reconstruction plan was largely a political quarrel in which the Negro took second place to the ambitions of competing groups of white men. But the unity of the Republicans was maintained—at the expense of keeping from the electorate in the 1864 elections clear consideration of the issues of Reconstruction. It is another illustration of how election excitement often diverts Americans' attention from important problems. To this excitement were added, for the North, the thrills of victory and the trauma of Lincoln's assassination. Therefore, at a time when a large share of the national interest should have been concentrated on what was to happen after the War, it was set rather upon immediate issues.

Plans for the Negro's future suffered accordingly. There was little more clarity at the end of the War than at the beginning about what should be done economically for the Negro. The vital question of land for the freedmen—a people for whom generations of plantation slavery had linked the idea of livelihood and land firmly together—was considered only by a small group. It is true that Thaddeus Stevens of Pennsylvania had introduced into the debates on the 1862 Homestead Bill the possibility of confiscating the estates of the rebel slave-owners and of dividing them amongst the Negroes; but Lincoln stood out determinedly against confiscation. The Freedmen's Bureau of 1865 made some attempt to settle Negroes on sequestrated land; and some had been given to them in South Carolina, particularly by Sherman's 1865 Field Order No. 15 which reserved for them a large tract of land on the coast and among the sea islands. But even this was hedged about with reservations. Thus, the Civil War attempts to cope with the problem of land for emancipated slaves were pitifully small. Nor had much been done to provide other types of employment for them, apart from that pre-eminently temporary form of work, military service.

This make-shift attitude towards the Negro was carried into the third stage of Reconstruction, a stage demarcated by the Presidency of Lincoln's successor, Andrew Johnson. The struggle for power between President and Congress to control the process of Reconstruction, which had emerged during Lincoln's last two years, now came to a head. Johnson, himself a former slave owner, adopted a policy like Lincoln's: re-admission of the former rebel States to the Union on generous terms, and a careful wooing of Southern whites on awkward questions of Negro civil rights, to the extent that responsibility for the coloured man was placed in the hands of the individual States. To the Radical factions which dominated Congress, it seemed a betrayal of all that the War had been fought for, and offered the dangerous possibility that the South would re-gain its pre-War political power in the national government. Johnson's opposition to the Congressional plans for Reconstruction showed no small courage; but Congress was in no mood to have its will over-ridden by one whose attitude, in the temper of the times, seemed anachronistic in the extreme.

To do him justice, Johnson claimed that, as a Southerner, he could feel that region's mood better than the Congressional theorists. He could appreciate keenly the white South's anger at its economic weakness at the end of the War: two billion (American) dollars of slave property gone without compensation; about a billion dollars of cotton confiscated; physical assets destroyed; no effective credit system, and discrimination against such Southern banks as did exist by the new Northern-dominated national banking system. Above all, there had been the overthrow of the former Southern pattern of labour relations and, with the encouragement to the Negro to assert his new independence by Northern agencies and individuals, a difficult and slow birth of a new pattern. Meanwhile, Southern whites could watch from afar the rapid growth of a prosperous system of industrial and financial capitalism in the North which did little to restore their equanimity. When, to ensure that the South did not regain its political power in the national government and thus hold back— as its pre-Civil War opposition to tariffs had threatened to do—the North's new economic system, the federal government, through the Radical Congress, took the vote away from large numbers of former Confederates at the same time as the franchise was given to the recently-emancipated slaves, Johnson could understand the Southern whites' anger. As he put it, when discussing the Negro question with a coloured delegation in 1866: "The query comes up right there, whether we don't commence a war of races." Furthermore, Johnson, with his Southern poorer whites' opposition to the "Money Power", could appreciate the irony of the situation—that most of the pro-Negro Radicals in Congress were not entirely disinterested in their campaign for freedmen's rights.

That there was much truth in Johnson's statements was undeniable. Unfortunately, the effect of his lenient policy in the South played right into the hands of his Radical opponents. Lacking any effective federal plan for the freedmen, the Southern States had taken the law into their own hands and had drawn up "Black Codes": harsh instruments, with few exceptions, to discipline the Negroes, which appeared to be restoring a state of slavery in everything but name. As if to back these codes, from the very end of the War, Southern whites formed secret societies aimed at making the Negroes understand that they should not aspire to equality with the whites. If the Ku Klux Klan was the most notable of these, it was by no means the only one. The total effect was to encourage Congress to tighten the screws of military control over the South. Moreover, for all his understanding of the white Southern attitude, Johnson appreciated little of the Negroes' feelings, and could suggest nothing more as a solution for the freedmen's economic difficulties than migration from the South.

This is not to say that the Congressional Radicals had any better plan. The death of Thaddeus Stevens in 1868, shortly before Johnson was due to give up the Presidency, symbolizes the emergence of a fourth stage of Reconstruction. Stevens, for all his bitterness, had stood for those Radicals who had some other aim than the manipulation of the Negro vote to detach the South from its former Western allies and to prevent it from using its potential political power to interfere with the political and economic ambitions of an expanding North. Stevens understood the importance of land for the Negro. His death meant that the similarly-minded small group of Radicals was swamped by the other Radical Republicans whose major aim was the advancement of that way of life which encouraged the extension of a Northern-dominated capitalism, and who looked upon the Negro as a pawn in their struggle with the South. It is to this stage, perhaps, that the term "Radical Reconstruction" may be most appropriately applied, for this period represents the rapid elimination of the last, faint vestiges of Congressional idealism on the Negro question. It is at this juncture that Booker T. Washington's estimate of Reconstruction becomes most applicable: "a white man's quarrel . . . the Negro was the tennis ball which was batted backward and forward by the opposing parties".

Under Grant's big business Presidency, the federal government allowed responsibility for the Negro question to fall more and more into private hands, so that confusion increased and the white Southern cry of "interfering busybodies" grew in intensity. The slight hope that the federal government would curtail the wandering tendency of the newly enfranchised Negro, which led to some of the abuses of which Southern whites complained, by providing him with land, soon disappeared. Much of the South Carolina land that had been granted to freedmen passed again into white ownership, and the 1866 Southern Homestead Act to open to Negroes all public lands in eighty acre lots in five Southern states only touched the fringes of the problem. Much of this land was swampy and poorly drained, and incapable of settlement without large capital expenditures. The freedmen, with few exceptions, could not put their hands on large or even medium amounts of money. Those who expected assistance from the Freedmen's Bank, which the federal government had set up in 1865 to help Negroes, were disappointed when, largely as a result of a rampaging capitalistic spirit which saw easy pickings amongst Negro money, it was closed in 1874. The Freedmen's Bureau, certainly, did something to ameliorate coloured men's land and labour difficulties. But its most conspicuous successes were the establishment of schools and the administration of relief. Yet, as a provider of more than a temporary contribution to the Negro's economic problems, its failure was most apparent in the field of its greatest successes: for what the Negro needed most was not relief but work—and work on better terms than the impoverished South could offer him. To have made this possible, the federal government would have had to enact a comprehensive programme of economic rehabilitation for the entire South, white as well as black. The impossibility of such a programme was exemplified in the kind of opposition which the Freedmen's Bureau received from North as well as South: an opposition which, in its criticisms of expensive national spending and its objection to federal interference in relations between employer and worker, anticipated the attacks on New Deal agencies. And when, in 1873, the Slaughter-House Cases indicated the spate of future attempts that would be made to defend property on an appeal to the "due process" clause of the Fourteenth Amendment to ensure Negro citizenship, it was clear that the wheel had come full circle: what had begun as an attempt to secure Negro citizenship was in rapid process of transforming itself into an agency for the protection of business. The logic of Radical Reconstruction was apparent.

This logic in recent years has caught the attention of an increasing number of historians, and has sometimes had the effect of depersonalizing Reconstruction and of veiling the very real conflicts of whites and blacks in the voting booths and legislatures of the South behind a relentless economic process. Nevertheless, if this tendency can obviously be taken too far, it is clear that economic changes in the early 1870's were both a cause and a consequence of the ending of Radical Reconstruction, and an expression of a fifth and final phase of Reconstruction which now begins. Influential elements in both North and South were tiring not only of the excesses of Northern Reconstruction of the South but also of disorders for which irresponsible Southern factions were themselves to blame. It seemed, almost a decade after the War, that the time had come to recognize that America's real business was business, and not the sponsoring of semi-secret Union Leagues to put the Negroes into State legislatures, or the organization of hooded men and fiery crosses to scare from the polls ignorant Negroes whose voting power, if properly handled, could be used as much against agrarian radicals in the South as against the Radicals of the North, and who, if necessary, could be deprived of the vote by less dangerous methods than melodramatic terrorism. The 1873 depression was to drive this lesson home to these influential Northern and Southern elements.

This does not mean that, before federal troops were withdrawn from the South, formal Reconstruction did not end, as it had begun, with violence. The bloody clashes between parading Negro militia and whites in Hamburg, South Carolina, on July 4, 1876, and the wave of violence which swept the state until Wade Hampton became governor in 1877, are not isolated examples of tensions at the ending of an epoch. Nevertheless, such actions as the final provision by Congress in July 1870 for the extension of the national banking system to the South illustrated the tendency towards reunion between the business elements north and south of the Mason-Dixon Line. The 1871 repeal of the "ironclad" oath of early Reconstruction against former Confederates; the 1872 general amnesty restoring the franchise to all but six hundred former Confederate officials; the return to power of Democrats in the South and, particularly, their winning control of Congress in 1874, showed which way the wind was blowing. In 1876 Supreme Court decisions indicated that the Southern Negro and his few remaining friends amongst Northern Republicans could expect little national protection to enforce the laws which had been passed between 1870 and 1875, as a kind of last stand on behalf of the coloured man, to ensure for him the benefits of the Thirteenth, Fourteenth and Fifteenth Amendments. The repeal of the Southern Homestead Act showed clearly—if such demonstration were necessary—that there was slight hope that large masses of Negroes would secure land outside the share-cropping system. As a natural outcome of all this, most Democrats and Republicans were agreed at the 1876 elections that Reconstruction should end; and when the victorious candidate, Hayes, withdrew federal troops from the South in 1877, the completion of the final phase of Reconstruction was obvious to all.

But had Reconstruction really concluded in 1877? Certainly the formal Reconstruction, with a capital "R", had ended at this time; but of the informal reconstruction, with a small "r", of the South, the end was not, and still is not, in sight. In this respect, the choice of titles for the 1942 Southern Historical Association presidential address was appropriate: "One Hundred Years of Reconstruction of the South." In this long period, the modern American Negro problem took root and developed. Yet how far is it true to say that it was caused by the shorter, formal period of Reconstruction, with a capital "R"?

At the turn of the century when the proscription, segregation and dis-franchisement characteristic of the Southern Negro's predicament were growing very rapidly, the picture of Reconstruction as the seedbed of all sorrows of Southern plural communities was widespread. The Thomas Dixon, Jnr., type of novel was only the most virulent expression of a widely-held attitude. Its elements were uniform: at a time when the newly-emancipated slave required the most careful tuition by those who knew him best (his former masters from whom political power had been taken) he was unwisely given the vote and thrust prematurely into important positions in local and national government. The result was chaos; Negro excesses and white counter-excesses. To prevent society from disintegrating utterly, there was but one course: separate the races. Segregation, according to this view, ensued.

That there was some segregation during Reconstruction is undeniable: in church, school and armed services. Much of it, however, was a matter of convenience rather than the result of an anti-Negro drive. Some of it, such as the rise of the independent Negro churches, was the wish of the coloured man himself. Yet, as Professor C. Vann Woodward has stressed, the effort to justify the Jim Crow laws, the most characteristic expression of Southern white offensive-defence against the Negro, "as a consequence of Reconstruction and a necessity of the times is embarrassed by the fact that they did not originate in those times". More than a decade had to pass before the first Jim Crow laws were enacted. Although Negroes were often defrauded and intimidated at the polls, large numbers continued to vote for over twenty years after Reconstruction. And during Reconstruction and for many years after, Southern groups, the heirs of the old Whigs, worked with rather than against the new economic forces from the North, and saw no necessity for discrimination and segregation which often appeared to them as a fetter on the development of the new economy which they envisaged as the salvation of the South. (There is a parallel here in the opposition of the wealthy Oppenheimers in modern South Africa to *apartheid*, which indicates the character of similar Southern forces.) Furthermore, the continuation into the twenty years or so after Reconstruction of some of the paternalism and intimacy between races of the slave days—the familiar "cultural lag" of American sociologists—often gave Southern society an aspect that was the reverse of embittered race relations.

What, then, created the flood of discriminatory laws and anti-Negro bitterness at the turn of the century? The issues are complex and incapable of a brief explanation; but a major element in them was the agrarian depression of the eighties and nineties which swept over the whole of America and was felt most deeply in the South, still acutely impoverished after the Civil War. The economic cleavages between richer and poorer classes of Southern whites were laid bare; and for more affluent, conservative groups the spectre of Populism threatened to break down the monolithic control of the Democratic Party over the South and to redistribute wealth. For a while, a combination between Negroes and less-privileged whites to challenge the conservative ruling groups seemed possible. Both sides bid for the Negro vote, and in the stress and confusion of the times, both of them came to blame their troubles on to the coloured man: the poorer whites not only because the Negro was, in time of depression more than ever, a rival for jobs but also because he seemed to be selling his vote to the highest bidder, and thus appeared to many as a fickle creature who stood in the way of social change in the South; the richer whites feared the Negro because there was the possibility that the very force of the depression might compel the under-privileged amongst whites and blacks to follow their long-term economic interests and combine together permanently against conservative domination of the South. Tensions mounted; and in 1892, the key Populist year, a hundred and sixty-two Negroes were lynched in the South, the greatest number for any year. A situation existed which had many points in common with the rise of Nazism in the 1930's. To ease frustrations and to supply a simple explanation for those who had neither the time, inclination nor training to unravel the details of a highly complex situation, a demand for scapegoats arose. Sensing this, and also partly swamped by it, Southern conservatives abandoned their moderate policy towards the Negro and raised the cry of White Supremacy against him. The poorer whites met them more than half-way. For underprivileged Southern groups, a readier scapegoat was available than the impersonal Gold Standard on which their Northern and Western equivalents relied, a scapegoat on whom they could—and did—put their hands with a vengeance: the Negro. The Populists forsook their coloured allies, blamed on to them the overthrow of Populism, and succumbed to the appeal of White Supremacy. At the same time, problems of acquiring and ruling over eight million coloured people during the era of the Spanish-American War disposed the North and West to be more sympathetic towards the South's own particular "manifest destiny"; and Negro migration from the South into these regions brought them similar problems of plural community. By 1898, the American Supreme Court had got rid of the last constitutional obstacles to segregation and disfranchisement. At a time, then, when white groups were ready to institutionalize the Jim Crow system in the South, the North offered little opposition. Within ten years, by various stratagems, the Negro was deprived of the franchise throughout the South, and the spate of segregation laws was in full flood.

If analyses of this kind demonstrate that the emergence of the characteristic Southern pattern of discrimination against the Negro owes more to the depression of the eighties and nineties than to the twelve formal years of Reconstruction, Reconstruction with a capital "R" played its part. As the Thomas Dixon, Jnr., type of writing shows, Reconstruction as myth was an essential part of the ideology of the growth of the Jim Crow system at the turn of the century, and this was of no small importance in the evocation and organization of emotions against the Negro. Furthermore, the conservative, former Whig elements in the South, for all their moderation towards the Negro before the Populist threat, joined easily in the campaign for White Supremacy in the 1890's because, even when some of them co-operated with Republicans during Reconstruction and had to work closely with Negro nominees, few doubted that the Negro belonged to an inferior race—though this prejudice owed more to the heritage of slavery than to the troubles of Reconstruction. Above all, the impoverishment of the South as a result of the Civil War, and the fact that the amount of economic help which it was given during Reconstruction by the federal government was utterly insufficient in the face of Northern exploitation, meant that the South was unable to build up a resilient economy which would absorb tensions between competing groups, such as whites and Negroes, in time of depression. There was no Marshall Plan for the South after the Civil War, and it remained, with few exceptions, a predominantly agricultural region which, in times of political and economic trouble, was liable to relapse into frontier conditions, with lynch-law and vigilante violence as the arbiter among men.

Much of this frenzied reaction was a response to new conditions that were barely understood. Union had stood before emancipation in the priorities of Lincoln's government; but emancipation had to come before the Union could be saved. The Civil War thus became a revolution in spite of itself. White Southerners, in the midst of this reluctant revolution, were bewildered and dazed; what had happened seemed almost unbelievable. Amidst such confusion, they often resorted to that common explanation of the fundamentally optimistic American when faced with political and economic difficulties: the "conspiracy theory", the concept that nothing but cabalistic interference from outside could overthrow a set of institutions unique in human history. If the North had seen the origins of the Civil War in a fiendish slaveholders' conspiracy, the South beheld its genesis in the intrigues of Republican agitators and dangerous radicals. This concept was extended into the days of Reconstruction. As Professor E. Merton Coulter remarks, "Southerners began to believe that Radicalism . . . was communism or a cult based on the destruction of individual values and the degradation of states." A Politbureau was at hand in the Congressional Joint Committee of Fifteen on Reconstruction which was set up in 1865 to consider the representation in Congress of the former Confederate States, and had reported against it. And a "cult of personality" in reverse was available in the figure of Thaddeus Stevens, leading Radical and inspirer of designs against the white South. If Stevens's death in 1868 necessitated a new scapegoat for the South, and thus made doubly certain that the Negro, in his collective capacity, would be cast for this role, the elaboration of the figure of a malevolent Stevens, with mythical mulatto mistress and unrestrained Negro accomplices, by the Dixon-Griffith tradition is typical of the way in which Reconstruction as myth has been kept alive for the use of later conspiracy theories in which many white Southerners would blame their Negro problems on to interference from outside.

But the North has not lacked its conspiracy theories on race relations. Foremost among these is the attempt to cast the blame for the worsening of relations between black and white in America upon the Ku Klux Klan and similar Southern white intrigues. It is a convenient picture which forgets that the Klan at the time of its greatest expansion, in the 1920's when it boasted five million members, had a larger following outside the South than within; and which passes by such inconvenient episodes as the two days in August, 1908, in Lincoln's home town, Springfield, Illinois, when white mobs, crying "Lincoln freed you—we'll show you where you belong", had burned and destroyed Negro property, lynched two coloured men, and driven hundreds from their homes. Another Northern conspiracy theory with Reconstruction roots is the apparently unfounded belief that the Fourteenth Amendment to the Constitution was drafted in 1866 by the Joint Committee of Fifteen with the aim of protecting corporations, as well as natural persons, against arbitrary State legislation. Conspiratorial complexes, indeed, cross-fertilize themselves. Nowhere, perhaps, is this human tendency to put the blame on someone or something else more apparent than in the sphere of race relations—and this

o

not only in the United States, though here it is reinforced by the conspiracy cult which has flourished in American conditions from the
Jacobin days of Citizen Genêt onwards.

It is an attitude of mind which, in his environment of a predominantly
white culture, has not left the Negro untouched; although, clearly, as the
victim of frequent terror from Klan and gang, he has more genuine
excuse than most for presupposing intrigues. For example, the tendency
of that cast of mind which, by attributing awkward problems to conspiracies makes them seem simpler than, in fact, they are, is illustrated among
Negroes by one particular topic, reinforced by appeal to Reconstruction,
which has been brought forward continually to justify discrimination
against them: the claim that it is necessary to protect the white woman
against the coloured man. The Negro leader, Frederick Douglass, in a
passionate anti-lynching pamphlet of 1894, rejected this charge not only

because it bears upon its face the marks of being a fraud, a makeshift for a
malignant purpose, but because it has sprung upon the country simultaneously, and in manifest co-operation with a declared purpose to degrade the
Negro by judicial decisions, by legislative enactments, by repealing all laws
for the protection of the ballot, by drawing the color line in all railroad cars
and stations and in all other public places in the South, thus to pave the way
for a final consummation which is nothing less than the Negro's entire dis-
enfranchisement as an American citizen.

Though undoubtedly the charge of coloured licentiousness was used quite
deliberately to stir up feeling against the Negro, Douglass in no way
explains the virulence of its effect nor—at least in this context—seems
to appreciate the depth of its roots. This cannot be said of W. J. Cash,
whose study, *The Mind of the South* (New York, 1941)—to which reference must be made for an appreciation of its profundity—offers an explanation of the "Southern rape complex" that seems a better guide than
most to the comprehension of a notoriously complicated question. Briefly,
Cash stresses the necessity of understanding that the Southern white
woman had become identified emotionally with the very notion of the
South even before the Civil War. Any assault on the South, then, would
be felt, in a very real manner, as an assault also on her. What the whites
felt for the Southern woman "more or less continuously, in the conditions
of Reconstruction, was a condition for her as degrading in their view, as
rape itself". Complicated processes of transference occurred. Yet, Cash
claimed, the connection was more than a vague and sentimental symbolism: it was a symbolism with highly material roots. In a notoriously
promiscuous area (another slavery inheritance) property was also at
stake: the white Southerners' concern for the right of their sons in the
legitimate line. Sexual symbolism interfused itself with and increased
the violence of attacks on the Negro, even when the root causes of this
symbolism could be but dimly perceived, if at all. (Some light, perhaps,
may be thrown on this particular identification of sexual elements with a

whole society by a comparison with the central place which the initiation ceremony of clitoridectomy came to occupy amongst the East African Kikuyu during the reconstruction of their own society.) And it should be remembered that the sexual associations of the colour problem have not been altogether absent from the North. The Springfield, Illinois, riot of 1908, for example, began with the claim by the wife of a street car conductor that she had been dragged from her bed and raped by a person whom she identified as a Negro; and one of the two Negroes who were lynched at this time was an eighty-four year old coloured man, who had been married to a white woman for over thirty years. How much of such Northern manifestations is to be attributed to the diffusion of associations from the South, and how much to the curious "Caliban complex"— " . . . most lying slave . . . thou didst seek to violate the honour of my child"—which goes deep into the roots of Western culture is a matter for infinite speculation.

There are other consequences of Reconstruction, with a capital or a small "r", for American Negroes which, in addition to its effects on the Southern Jim Crow system, deserve notice. One is the manner in which Southern poverty and discrimination has helped to push droves of Negroes into parts of the expanding North and West where legal discrimination is less and the opportunity for employment greater than in the South. Here, however, as numerous witnesses pointed out even before the Civil War, there has been no lack of prejudice against Negroes; and this, in situations of urban industrial competition, has been responsible for some of the greatest American race riots. One long-term result, therefore, of Reconstruction has been the creation of special colour problems for some regions north of the Mason-Dixon Line. But, as the Negro historian Professor John Hope Franklin points out, in these Northern battles, unlike their Southern counterparts, the Negro has been able to fight back. Thus, one paradox of the abortive Reconstruction which did so much to push the Negro into these Northern regions of greater, though often limited, opportunity has been to provide him with the means to organize against discrimination wherever it may occur. In this way, in New York in 1909, one of the greatest of Negro organizations was born, the National Association for the Advancement of Colored People, which the Negro has used to carry the fight back into the South itself. Paradoxically, too, American segregation and discrimination against the Negro has forced him to cater for his own internal market, and a basis has thereby been laid for a coloured middle-class which has increased the Negro's economic power to fight segregation, at the same time as it has stirred up further jealousy and prejudice against him from envious whites.

On the whole, although it is true to say that the obliteration of the coloured man's privileges and hopes during Reconstruction and up to the turn of the century crushed much Negro initiative, this can be overstressed; and one of the most interesting studies is the attempt to trace

Negro reactions to Reconstruction, with capital and small "r". If the Negro was deprived of many of the privileges of citizenship, it was impossible to prevent him from trying to increase his self-respect by the study of his past. This, it is true, has not always had fortunate consequences. It has sometimes led to an over-romanticization of the Negro American's African connections, and has encouraged chauvinistic excesses of movements like Marcus Garvey's Universal Negro Improvement Association of the 1920's, with its dreams of Negro colonization in Africa and its tendency, in bitter reaction against white domination, to think in terms of a Negro imperialism. There have been occasions, too, when an uncritical survey of the Negro past has helped to create some Negro support for a special coloured State, a "Black Republic", "Forty-Ninth State" in the United States itself, on the plea that the Negroes in America constitute a nation. Similarly, in the very understandable attempt to increase his self-confidence through the discovery of his own tradition and the demonstration of it to advantage by garnishing it with examples of successful political, economic and artistic activity in which could be traced some Negro contribution, however small or remote it may be, the Negro himself has often been guilty of racialism. This, as has been frequently pointed out, can have the ultimate effect of confirming the Negro's feelings of inferiority.

Another manifestation of an uncritical study of the American Negro past has been the exhibition of a greater degree of unity amongst Negroes than has, in fact, existed. This was clear during Reconstruction, when the distinction between former field hands and house-servants was maintained, particularly by the latter group. There was, too, the difference between Negroes who had been freed or were born free before the Civil War, and those whose emancipation was the result of it. The pre-Civil War free Negro group illustrates two other important divisions among coloured men: a sectional division between those born or resident for long periods in the North, and those who belong to the South; and the colour line amongst Negroes themselves, the distinction between the varying shades of darker and lighter skinned Negroes. To these divisions must be added those economic differentiations which display themselves amongst Negroes as much as other people. On the basis of these divisions has been erected an intricate structure of group rivalries, dislikes and snobbery, which has sometimes gone as far as a total opposition to the Negro by the Negro. A particular manifestation of this is the example of William H. Thomas, a Northern mulatto who went South during Reconstruction and came away disillusioned with his own people: in his book, *The American Negro* (New York, 1901) Thomas wrote that "The negro represents an intrinsically inferior type of humanity, and one whose predominant characteristics evince an appetite for a low order of living." Yet to an outsider, perhaps the most striking thing about the coloured Americans is not the divisions which exist among them—remarkable though these are, in view of the long periods of political, economic and social discrimination to which they have been subjected—but the degree of unity which, in spite of all difficulties, has grown up amongst them.

Another degree of unity that has been examined, often over-optimistically as a consummation devoutly to be wished rather than as an actual fact, particularly during Reconstruction, has been the amount of common ground between the Negro and the less privileged whites. The picture that has frequently been presented of the roots of the American colour problem in the total opposition of poor whites to Negroes during Reconstruction is undoubtedly exaggerated. The Negro historian, Horace Mann Bond, has pointed out that during Reconstruction, "The combination of poor whites and blacks was true throughout the South; it was marked in Alabama." And there are such notable instances of Negro and poor white co-operation during the Populist period as the group of Georgia farmers who remained on guard for two nights to save from lynching a young Negro preacher, H. S. Doyle, who spoke on behalf of Tom Watson's candidacy for Congress in 1892. The Negro delegation that visited Andrew Johnson on February 7, 1866, claimed that Negro feelings against poor whites originated in the slavery days, when masters had divided and ruled, and had used poor whites for their "slave-catchers, slave-drivers and overseers". The overthrow of slavery destroyed the reason for this hostility; give the Negro the vote, and "he will raise up a party among the poor who will rally to him". That this danger was put down by the actions of Southern white conservatives who played on the anti-Negro prejudices of the poor white is apparent. But, whatever may have been the origins of these prejudices on both sides, their longevity and persistence is equally clear. "Rather be a nigger than a poor white man", Negro children had sung before the Civil War. Immediately after it, during the Negro reaction from slavery, "on their industrial holiday", Southern poor whites took advantage of the absence of black competition to secure jobs from which they had previously been excluded by slave competition; and in numerous other ways the circumstances of Reconstruction favoured the poor white. On this, to be sure, Negro and white can agree. The Southern historian, Francis B. Simkins, has stated that "In a very real sense the Civil War freed the common white man to a greater degree than the Negro"; and, as a former South Carolina slave told a W. P. A. investigator, "It was the poor white man who was freed by the War, not the Negro." In similar ways, the small degree of co-operation between white and black industrial workers, both South and North, was short-lived during Reconstruction.

Yet, if some Negro historians and their allies have drawn a rosier picture of Negro-white combination during Reconstruction than really existed, they have shown that some co-operation did occur. In many other ways, too, by their researches and emphases in their writings, they have corrected the traditional white view of Reconstruction; have put the picture of Negro corruption in Southern legislatures into its proper perspective of the national *mores*; have drawn attention to the significant Negro leaders that emerged; have shown the degree of economic enterprise which, in spite of all obstacles, the Negro displayed; and, above all, have proclaimed that the Negro existed, not merely as a group but also as an individual—a fact which white historians have been all too prone to overlook.

It is difficult, however, for anyone to overlook the importance of the Church to the Negro, both during and after Reconstruction. An undue share of attention has been drawn to its more exuberant features: though such lines from the "spirituals" as

> I do believe without a doubt
> That a Christian has the right to shout

and

> If you want to see old Satan run,
> Chase him with a Gospel gun

serve to illustrate that the Negro's church has not been altogether other-worldly but that it has acted as a vehicle for much otherwise frustrated Negro militancy. The independent Negro churches must be classed among the most important results of Reconstruction for the Negro, not only because they have given him institutions which he could genuinely call his own but because out of them have come some of the most important coloured leaders, and through them have developed modes of political reaction, in the broadest sense, to the Jim Crow system. They display, here, similar political functions to independent churches amongst subordinated peoples in many parts of the world. It was certainly not accidental that a coloured Baptist minister led the 1956 Montgomery, Alabama, bus boycott, or that so much of this Negro campaign against segregation was organized in churches. The Negro theologian, Dr Howard Thurman, has written of Christianity in its social genesis that it appears to have been "a technique of survival for a disinherited minority". Looking back—and, perhaps, forward—it seems that these words are not inapplicable for the Church among his own people.

As a minority, the Negro has similar problems to those of other minorities in the United States. Many, indeed, would agree with Frederick Douglass' assertion that the coloured American's predicament is "not a Negro problem, not a race problem but a national problem". Certainly, the Negro American question belongs peculiarly to the United States, as the identification of the coloured man with America has demonstrated, and as the failure of "Back-to-Africa" and "Pan-African" movements amongst the United States Negro has emphasized. The Negro's lack of response to the American Communist Party underlines this. Studying this question, Mr Wilson Record notes that "a striking paradox inheres in the fact that the most convincing demonstration of loyalty to the American system has come from a group which has reaped the least from it". The explanation, of course, lies in the very American-ness of the Negro in the United States.

This has revealed itself in many ways. Martin R. Delany, Negro writer, explorer, Civil War major, and important carpetbagger politician in South Carolina, is often laughed at for the fondness with which he loved to discuss his notable African ancestors. But is not the tracing of ancestors an old American custom? Similarly, jokes are often made about the Negro's cry for "Forty acres and a mule" in the early Reconstruction days. Yet should it not be considered rather as a sensible economic and social demand which reflects the special position that is given to the independent farmer in the American tradition? There has been much comment, too, on the wandering disposition of the Negro in the United States. But, although much of this may rightly be attributed to the freedman's enthusiastic reaction from slavery in the days that followed emancipation and to the desire to find work outside the South, is there not also in it an element of traditional American "Ishmael-ism"? Above all, is not the Negro's demand for complete integration into American society the most typical demand of a United States minority group; and does not the Negro, in his struggle for acceptance, often show many of the characteristics of the "second generation immigrant" when he some-times displays an over-zealous attachment to the norms of American society?

Yet, unless he is a "white Negro", the coloured American, unlike members of most other United States minorities, cannot conveniently secure acceptance by a change of name, length of residence, or a substan-tial income. The colour of his skin keeps him within the bounds of caste. And should he be a "white Negro" and attempt to "pass", he may find himself entangled by the contradictions and circumscriptions of caste such as Mark Twain depicted with biting satire in his study of the light-skinned Negro, *Puddn'head Wilson* (Hartford, 1894). Thus, although he can boast a much older ancestry—the twenty slaves who were brought to Jamestown in 1619—than many American minority groups, it avails the Negro little.

For all its national characteristics, the Negro's predicament remains unique in the American experience: a singularity which the sociologist can term dilemma; but for which, as the words of the Negro poet, Mr Langston Hughes, suggest, the coloured man may often be forced to find a less neutral expression:

> . . . the American heartbreak—
> Rock on which Freedom
> Stumps its toe—
> The great mistake
> That Jamestown
> Made long ago.

What response dare a white man make to this? Perhaps some words, written on the eve of Reconstruction, by Herman Melville in his neglected supplement to a collection of poems, *Battle Pieces and Aspects of the War* (New York, 1866) are pertinent:

Emancipation has ridded the country of the reproach, but not wholly of the calamity. Especially in the present transition period for both races in the South, more or less of trouble may not unreasonably be anticipated; but let us not hereafter be too swift to charge the blame exclusively in any one quarter. With certain evils men must be more or less patient. Our institutions have a potent digestion, and may in time convert and assimilate to good all elements thrown in, however originally alien.

THE AMERICAN MILITARY TRADITION

By Marcus Cunliffe

*

A CURIOUS little book appeared in 1889, with the title of *The Great War Syndicate*. It was the work of the American humorous writer Frank R. Stockton, and it described an imaginary war between Great Britain and the United States which was supposed to have taken place "not far from the close of the present century".

The war is provoked by a Canadian fisheries incident. As in 1812, the American public cries "On to Canada!"; but, as also in 1812, the American government is unprepared for war. In its quandary, the government decides to accept a spectacular offer made by a Syndicate of twenty-three "great capitalists". For a large (and undisclosed) sum the Syndicate proposes "to assume the entire control and expense of the war, and to effect a satisfactory peace within one year". The Syndicate's fee is to vary inversely with the duration of the conflict: the quicker it is over, the larger the profit. On the other hand, the fee is forfeited if the enemy succeeds in landing on the American coast. The government may build up its orthodox forces, but they are not to be used unless the Syndicate's plan fails.

The twenty-three great capitalists set to work. Accustomed to directing vast enterprises, they are businesslike and bold. They consult scientists and engineers, and rapidly devise two new weapons of war. One is a "crab", a monitor-like vessel equipped with a pair of huge underwater claws. The other is a "repeller": a slower craft with special elastic armour mounted in strips, and one big gun, designed to fire a novel projectile known as the "instantaneous motor". These ships—a modest flotilla of them—are manned by merchant seamen and commanded by civilian technicians.

The Syndicate's first operation is against a Canadian port. British warships defending the port find that they cannot penetrate the repeller's armour, even with their heaviest armament. Meanwhile, the crabs render the British ships helpless, ripping out the screws and rudders with their giant claws. Then, taking care not to kill anyone, the repeller demonstrates its "instantaneous motor", which creates a tidal wave when discharged into the harbour, and utterly destroys a couple of forts on land. In each case "the sky above the spot where the motor had descended" is darkened by an immense spherical cloud. Having shown what it can do, the Syndicate's ships (conveniently in touch with head-quarters in New York, by means of a telegraph cable laid for the occasion) announce a blockade of the port. They declare that the port itself will be annihilated if Britain or Canada commit any overt act of war anywhere.

The British refuse to admit defeat; and so the Syndicate is compelled to send a repeller and six crabs to Portsmouth, where—again with no loss of life on either side—most of the British battle-fleet is put out of action. The repeller finally drives its point home, after due warning has been given, by wiping out an abandoned Welsh harbour, where—from a safe distance—thousands of awed observers watch the "motor-bombs . . . tearing up the sea-board, and grinding it to atoms". A peace treaty is immediately signed by Britain and the Syndicate (acting on behalf of the American government). Indeed, they agree to form an Anglo-American Syndicate of War, based on "the use by these two nations, and by no other nations, of the instantaneous motor". "Reduction of military and naval forces, and gradual disarmament," Stockton concludes, "was now the policy of the allied nations . . . [After] the formation of this Syndicate all the nations of the world began to teach English in their schools, and the Spirit of Civilization raised her head with a confident smile."

There are a number of things we might say about this fantasy (only one of many imaginary war novels published in Europe and—less commonly—in America between about 1870 and 1916). Stockton's confidence in the almost supernatural capabilities of the American financier, for example, or his lucky guess at the atomic bomb, or the unconscious irony of his last remarks: these are all interesting in their way. But for our purposes, the significance of *The Great War Syndicate* lies in the following points:

(1) Great Britain is the potential enemy (the *only* potential enemy, we could add, for much of America's history).

(2) Great Britain is also the prime potential ally (the unacknowledged, unwanted, *de facto* half-ally for much of America's history).

(3) Stockton assumes the possibility of swift, humane and decisive victory, at relatively little cost in money and none at all in men, over the strongest power of the age.

(4) The war is won by reliance upon wealth and "know-how": upon equipment rather than manpower, mechanical ingenuity and not formal military prowess.

(5) The victory is civilian, owing nothing to the regular army or navy. Indeed, the army is not once mentioned; and the navy figures merely in one comic episode, when a belligerent captain breaks the rules and takes his ship out of Delaware Bay to attack a British cruiser. Before he can get to grips, however, he is immobilized and towed ignominiously back to port by one of the Syndicate's crabs.

We must beware of attaching too much importance to Stockton's novelette. It is a cheerful minor oddity, hardly akin—in sprightliness at any rate—to the general mass of writing and orating on American military problems. Still, it does embody several common and deep-seated American attitudes. Moreover, it does in some sense represent the beginning of a change in American thought—the change that separates the twentieth from the nineteenth century. Taking Stockton, therefore, as a kind of provisional text, I wish to examine three typical American attitudes expressed in, but by no means confined to, *The Great War Syndicate*: namely, isolationism, anti-militarism and anti-professionalism. I shall then discuss the professionals themselves, and end by considering the "post-Stocktonian" military situation in the United States.

There is no need to dwell at length upon American isolationism. It is, though, worth stressing the elementary notion that isolationism as an emotion derived from isolation as a fact. Until almost the close of the nineteenth century the fact seemed so incontrovertible that it had not developed into an -ism. As late as 1897 the Secretary of the Navy, J. D. Long, speaking more or less for President McKinley, could urge Congress to halt naval expansion in these calm words:

[O]ur remoteness from foreign powers, the genius of our institutions, and the devotion of our people to education, commerce, and industry, rather than to any policy that involves military entanglements, make war to be thought of only as a last resort in defense of our rights, and our military and naval establishments as a police force for the preservation of order and never for aggression.

True, Long's views were emphatically not shared by his Assistant Secretary, Theodore Roosevelt; and within a few months, when America was at war with Spain, Long and McKinley changed their tune. Yet Long was simply saying what Americans had stated as self-evident for a hundred years; the very word "entanglements" harked back to Thomas Jefferson. In terms of *defensive* warfare, isolation still existed. As the French ambassador Jusserand commented, America was geographically the most fortunate of nations: to north and south she had weak neighbours, to east and west nothing but fish. The war of 1846-48 demonstrated that Mexico in the south was no match for the United States. In the north, thinly-populated Canada was a hostage for circumspect behaviour by Britain. While America virtually dispensed with a foreign policy, she thus had no need of a systematic military policy either. Even if no American warships sailed them, the width of the oceans provided the United States with a natural system of defences. This is not to argue that isolationism was altogether wise or feasible; if (in a military sense) America had little to fear from the rest of the world, it did not follow that she should or could have little to do with the rest. But, in looking for the origins of America's military attitudes, we must admit that she has enjoyed more immunity than some of her "preparedness" propagandists have been ready to recognize. Though her immunity to air attack has gone, it would even now be extremely difficult for an enemy to invade America by sea. In 1915, despite the dreadful warnings of imaginary war novels like *America Fallen!*, which tells of a successful German invasion on the eastern seaboard, the United States had some reason to feel snug. Hence, until fairly recent years, the unreality of military plans as far as the bulk of American citizens were concerned. In some ways their inertia and complacence were more sensible than the near-hysteria of *America Fallen!* or, say, Hudson Maxim's *Defenseless America* (another product of the "preparedness" campaign of 1915-16).

American isolationism had something in common with British insularity. So had the American tradition of anti-militarism, which grew out of the fact of isolation and the structure of American society but which also represented a direct inheritance from British experience. Long before the American Revolution, British pamphleteers were insisting that standing armies are fatal to free nations, as instruments of despotism. Barely tolerated in wartime, British regular troops tended to become unpopular as soon as peace was signed. Some argued that they were unnecessary as well as dangerous: their work was best performed by the militia—the old "Constitutional Force"—and by the navy. "A standing army in England, whether in time of Peace or War," said Dean Swift, "is a direct absurdity. For, it is no part of our business to be a warlike nation, otherwise than by our fleets. In foreign wars we have no concern, further than in conjunction with allies, whom we may either assist by sea, or by foreign troops paid with our money." His opinion was widely shared. Hence the 1745 Rebellion found England almost without soldiers to resist the Young Pretender. Hence, in the American Revolution, the use of German mercenaries to augment the inadequate supply of British troops.

Here, then, was the American heritage of anti-militarism: a deep prejudice against standing armies, a milder sentiment with regard to naval forces, and a positive feeling that the "palladium of liberty" must be safeguarded by militiamen. The heritage was reinforced by the events of the American Revolution, and by the distorted memory of what happened during that struggle. Redcoats and Hessians became symbols of inefficient tyranny. Citizen-soldiers, led by the greatest of them all, George Washington, overcame George III's regulars; and the only serious internal threat to the colonial cause appeared to have arisen from plotting among *regular-trained* American officers—Thomas Conway, Horatio Gates, Charles Lee. Like Britain, the United States took care to place its future armed forces under legislative control: Congress imitated Parliament in securing the military purse-strings.

At the period of the Revolution, suspicion of armed forces was only to be expected: there were plenty of historical precedents for military dictatorship, from Sulla to Oliver Cromwell, and the Continental Congress was threatened with more than one mutiny by discontented patriot regiments. The infant nation, neither willing nor obliged to maintain large forces, was—for that matter—not able to afford them. As it was, she established a tiny army and an infinitesimal navy. She passed a militia law in 1792, based on colonial (and therefore British) practice, requiring service—as specified by individual states—of all male white citizens between the ages of 18 and 45. A further militia act of 1808 set the annual appropriation for all states at $200,000. And, in 1802, America instituted a military academy at West Point for the training of army officers.

So the pattern was set, for many years to come. Army and navy remained small—a few thousand men, in peacetime, and a handful of ships. Major Parmenas T. Turnley, speaking of the national mood on the eve of the Civil War, said that dislike of a standing army "has been fostered by every demagogue and stump speaker in the land! . . . In fact, to caution the dear people against the military was the chief stock in trade of nine-tenths of the political mountebanks, whose fields of action were far removed from the large cities, and among constituencies not accustomed to see or mingle with the military of our frontiers." Turnley's comment is accurate enough; and in less extreme form it is true also of more eminent political figures. Through the decades of the nineteenth century, president after president repeated the ancient, ritual formulae, though with gradually altered emphasis. Here is one such typical utterance, which comes from the first inaugural address of Andrew Jackson (March, 1829):

Considering standing armies as dangerous to free governments in time of peace, I shall not seek to enlarge our present establishment, nor disregard that salutary lesson of political experience which teaches that the military should be held as subordinate to the civil power.

Jackson goes on to recommend a moderate increase in the estimates for the navy and for coastal defences. "But," he affirms,

the bulwark of our defence is the national militia, which in the present state of our intelligence and population must render us invincible . . . [A] million of armed freemen, possessed of the means of war, can never be conquered by a foreign foe.

While the burden of his argument is somewhat different, we find Woodrow Wilson paying his respects to this tradition, as late as December 1914, in his second annual address to Congress:

We must depend in every time of national peril, in the future as in the past, not upon a standing army, nor yet upon a reserve army, but upon a citizenry trained and accustomed to arms.

It is hard to believe that Americans, even in Jackson's era, were genuinely alarmed by the prospect of military overlordship. Rather, they objected to a standing army as a federal agency and as a *European* concept.

The regulars were remote from the people, and somehow un-American. In a country where so much remained to be accomplished, the enlisted men were treated as idlers: "Soldier, will you work?" was the taunt in the West. In a country proud of its democratic spirit, the officers bred by West Point were sometimes accused of being a clique of aristocrats— the "kid glove gentry". According to one witness, the West Point cadet of the 1830's was "a wasp-waisted vampyre, . . . a small species of political leech applied to suck out some of the surplus revenue of the plethoric body politic—a thing with nothing to do but to arrange his stiff stock every five minutes, and hold himself straight". The navy was in less disfavour, especially after its remarkable performance in the War of 1812. Nevertheless, the idea of a naval academy was mooted—and rejected—in Congress for over forty years, until in 1845 the Secretary of the Navy, George Bancroft, ignored Congress and with dubious legality created the school that became Annapolis.

Between the War of 1812 and the Civil War anti-militarism was also, more fundamentally, expressed by the American Peace Society and by kindred pacifist movements. Noah Worcester, William Ladd, Elihu Burritt, Charles Sumner and others campaigned vigorously against war and all its trappings. The reign of peace was at hand, they claimed, and America was its rightful kingdom. Ralph Waldo Emerson said that "a company of soldiers is an offensive spectacle". Sumner developed the same opinion, at enormously greater length, in a famous Fourth of July oration at Boston in 1845. Of what use, he demanded (glaring at the uniformed members of the audience), were America's armed forces? Her soldiers were "unproductive consumers of the fruits of the earth" and ought to be abolished. So, likewise, the navy—"a vain and expensive toy"—and the coastal fortifications, in all "the odious mortmain of their everlasting masonry". And so, even, the militia, who (he said) cavorted in the streets like painted savages.

It was a fine diatribe; and certainly there were many Americans who would have agreed with Sumner that the militia as constituted were a most unsatisfactory organization. Apart from the pacifist condemnation of its "legalized homicide", the militia system was criticized on two main grounds, as being inefficient and as being inequitable. As Senator Simmons of Rhode Island observed in 1842: "For fifteen or twenty years, the militia trainings have been mostly a farce, nothing but an exhibition of rags, caps and broomsticks." The broomsticks were borne in place of the muskets that the militia were supposed to furnish; in rural areas, they were alleged even to have drilled with "cornstalks". The rule of universal service meant that far more men were available than were required; and three muster-days a year allowed absurdly little time to put a motley horde through their evolutions. As a military force, the American militia were equivalent not to a standing army but to a standing joke.

Moreover, the militia system was criticized as unjust. Its principle of compulsion was objectionable, not merely to Quakers and others who had conscientious scruples, but perhaps to a majority of the population. True, militia service claimed only three days out of 365, and these were often spent light-heartedly, with a minimum of drill and a maximum of conviviality. But temperance-minded Americans disapproved of the muster day as a "drunken noisy revel"—as one who signed himself "Poor Man's Son" wrote in 1831. And poor men generally, in Jacksonian America, complained of being taken away from their harvest or their bench without recompense, while others—doctors, clergymen, teachers and the like—were exempted from militia duty. If the working man was absent from parade, he was fined several dollars—more than he could comfortably part with; if he did not pay his fine, he was jailed as if he were a common debtor. In view of this widespread opposition, a number of states before the Civil War abolished compulsory militia service; four (New Jersey, Iowa, Michigan and California) abolished imprisonment for non-payment of fines; others (including New York) permitted a small "commutation", of a dollar or less, in lieu of military duty; and throughout the Union, the old militia—as defined by the statute of 1792—continued to decay.

So much for anti-militarism. Yet this is only half the story. The fact is, of course, that the United States has had a stormy history, punctuated with violence and unrest. It was no placid Switzerland, even before the twentieth century's major wars. Whatever their individual grievances against the military, the bulk of Americans were not meek men. They have been far less in sympathy with Charles Sumner than with the Bostonian who once told Sumner that "an Anti-War Society is as little practicable as an Anti-Thunder-and-Lightning Society". The United States was born in warfare; it was again at war with Britain in 1812-14; at war with Mexico in 1846-48; at war with itself in the civil conflict of 1861-65; at war with Spain in 1898; at war with the Central Powers in 1917-18; at war with the Axis in 1941-45; at war—on behalf of the United Nations—in Korea. These were the major episodes, but there were also any number of minor ones: the Seminole operations of 1817-18, the Black Hawk War (1832), the Florida War (1835-41) and other Indian outbreaks, until the last battle with the Sioux at Wounded Knee in 1890. Then there were slave insurrections, or the threat of them; in parts of the South, especially in South Carolina, the "paterollers" or militia patrols were quite active and well-organized. There were the filibustering attempts of the 1850's, from William Walker's Nicaraguan expeditions to George Bickley's Knights of the Golden Circle. Nor should we overlook that northern filibuster, John Brown, studying the history of European campaigns with the scholarly enthusiasm of a West Point instructor as he planned his descent on Harper's Ferry. In the same decade, there were the troubles in Kansas, and the Vigilante movement in San Francisco, when a force of over 2,000 armed and disciplined men was raised without recourse to the state militia. There were the later freebooting attempts against Cuba, and the Pinkerton strike-breaking squads.

Indeed, Americans have shown a remarkable capacity for forming themselves into *ad hoc* military or quasi-military bands. The most important of these were the independent volunteer companies, like the Honorable Artillery Company of Boston or the First Troop, Philadelphia City Cavalry, of which many were in existence before the Revolutionary War. New companies sprang up afterward by the score, some of them short-lived, others still in being. They financed themselves, elected their own officers and chose their own (often gorgeous) uniforms. While many such companies—the Washington Light Infantry of Charleston, for instance—were exclusive social clubs, others catered for special groups. As Colonel Frederick P. Todd has written:

There were entire companies of Frenchmen, of Germans, and of Irishmen to represent the changing tides of immigration, often clothed in foreign uniforms and responding only to commands in a foreign tongue. There were on the other hand the "Native American" units, established to counter-act this ingress of outsiders. There were companies to typify every walk of life and every shade of political opinion. "Silk stocking" regiments marched with bruisers from the Bowery, "Free Men of Colour" drilled in Louisiana, and out along the frontier grizzled pioneers formed battalions of "Riflemen" and "Avengers".

In the 1850's, at the height of the volunteer craze, New York had its Jewish companies; the Chicago Zouaves, with their spectacular costume and drill, were imitated in several other cities; and there were even reports—perhaps apocryphal—of one or two companies of women volunteers. The states which had abolished the old compulsory militia attempted to re-organize on a voluntary basis, so that the independent companies were formed into regiments, and these in turn into brigades and divisions of volunteer militia.

Thus in 1860 the Sixth Regiment, Massachusetts Volunteer Militia, consisted of the following companies:

A, of Lowell (founded in 1855 as the Lawrence Cadets. Dress: blue frocks and pantaloons, with white crossbelts)
B, of Groton (1775, Groton Artillery. Dress: that of regular U.S. infantry—dark blue frocks and light blue trousers)
C, of Lowell (1825, Mechanic Phalanx. Dress: grey, with yellow trimmings)
D, of Lowell (1841, City Guards. Dress: grey, with buff trimmings)
E, of Acton (1851, Davis Guards, named in honour of an Acton minute-man killed in 1775. Dress: U.S. infantry)

F, of Lawrence (1855, Warren Light Guard, named in honour of General Joseph Warren, killed at Bunker Hill. Dress: U.S. infantry)

G, of Worcester (1803, Worcester Light Infantry. Dress: "full dress uniforms of blue")

H, of Lowell (1851, Watson Light Guards. Dress: grey uniforms)

I, of Lawrence (1849, Lawrence Light Infantry. Dress: French infantry—blue frocks, red trousers, kepi).

K, of Boston (1810, Washington Artillery. Dress: grey uniforms).

In the same year, the adjutant-general of New York reported that, instead of the chaos of the old system, his state now had "eight divisions, twenty-six brigades, and sixty-four regiments of bona-fide men, uniformed, armed and equipped, and passably well drilled in the manoeuvres of the field". Their military effectiveness may have been doubtful in some cases, and in the Civil War the volunteer militia were still only liable to service for 90 days. This meant that in war the system had to be scrapped or at least drastically revised. But even so, we still have to reckon with these thousands of companies, spread over every state of the Union (and maintained after the Civil War, to some extent), as evidences of a spirit that was the reverse of anti-militarist.

We must note, too, some other seeming proofs of quasi-military enthusiasm. There was, for instance, the American relish for military titles of the "Kentucky colonel" variety. They were not confined to the South. Rodney Glisan, a regular surgeon, said in his *Journal of Army Life* (1874) that the regular's "hard earned title of captain or major would be eclipsed by every tenth man to be met on the streets of our large cities":

Let any person try the experiment of calling out "halloo, colonel!" in a loud voice in a large crowd, assembled for any purpose in our cities, and he will be surprised at the number of responses.

And there is the American habit of nominating military figures as presidential candidates. Or there is the phenomenon of military schools. Virginia Military Institute and the Citadel at Charleston (founded in 1839 and 1842 respectively) are well-known. Less familiar is the military academy established by Alden Partridge—a former superintendent of West Point—at Norwich, Vermont, in 1820, which moved to Middletown, Connecticut, for a few years. Partridge and his pupils opened similar schools all over the eastern and southern states, and many more "military academies" came into being after the Civil War. School advertisement columns in American magazines usually list a good dozen of such schools nowadays. Or, again, there are the veterans' organizations, beginning after the Civil War with the G.A.R. (Grand Army of the Republic), a powerful and vocal body, followed after the First World War by the no less vocal American Legion. The Second

P

World War likewise produced its crop of ex-servicemen's associations.

It is arguable that these phenomena prove very little of a military nature. Thus the volunteer companies (like the old voluntary fire companies) and the veterans' organizations ministered to the "joiner's" instinct of Americans. In this respect they are akin to the Elks, Lions, Kiwanis, Shriners and other clubs. As for military titles, they have often conferred only a vague, honorary status (like the title of "judge"), with no strict regard for accuracy. And even where merited, as militia-titles, their significance is largely political; so, indeed, was that of the whole militia structure. They were instruments of political patronage and means to political advancement within each state. Muster days provided an opportunity for electioneering, especially since junior officers were invariably chosen by popular vote. Senior appointments were left either to the governor or to ballot among the officers themselves. A militia brigadier or major-general was usually a prominent figure in local politics; and during the Civil War, volunteer generals such as John A. Logan of Illinois were allowed home on leave at election-time to campaign on behalf of the Administration.

As for the choice of military presidents, any man of seemingly heroic stature is apt to be considered as a possible candidate. Few of those actually chosen as presidents have been "real" soldiers; only two—Ulysses S. Grant and Dwight D. Eisenhower—have been graduates of West Point. George Washington was by inclination a Virginia planter; Andrew Jackson, though a warrior, took pains to dissociate himself from the standing army; Zachary Taylor was notoriously unmilitary, and so was Grant. Post-Civil War presidents like James A. Garfield did owe much of their success to their record in that conflict; but with the exception of Grant they were all volunteer officers. When the Democrats nominated a West Point regular, Winfield Scott Hancock, to run against Garfield in 1880, they were careful to include in their party platform a clause favouring the "subordination of the military to the civil power". General Eisenhower was acceptable to the American people because he genuinely seemed to share their idea of civil-military relationships. As he said in 1948, in refusing to consider a nomination at that time:

> It is my conviction that the necessary and wise subordination of the military to the civil power will be best sustained . . . when lifelong professional soldiers, in the absence of some obvious and overriding reasons, abstain from seeking high political office.

And while more "soldierly" soldier-candidates have been put forward, it is noteworthy that—from Winfield Scott to Douglas MacArthur—they have never actually been elected to the presidency.

We could also suggest that military schools offer little proof of a martial spirit in America. Most of Alden Partridge's academies, north and south, closed down after a few years of impecunious effort. The military training which Congress stipulated as a feature of the "land-grant" state colleges was a patchy affair. It has been said, too, that the military boarding schools of more recent date mainly represent an attempt to deal with the problem of the intractable American adolescent—to keep him quiet rather than to fire him with military aspirations.

Moreover, though staunchly patriotic, veterans' organizations have not exactly constituted an army reserve. Nor have their members always been as seasoned as the word "veteran" implies; according to *Time* magazine, the 1957 commander of the American Legion had a military record of "88 days of service at naval training in 1944 terminated by a medical discharge". They have functioned, in part at least, as pension lobbies; and state legislatures as well as Congress have seemed —along with some of the veterans—to feel that an American who is taken for a soldier has *ipso facto* suffered, and deserves special compensation. This is hardly a Spartan military attitude.

It might seem, then, that anti-militarist sentiment has in balance far outweighed military ardour in American history: that this essay might better have been called "The American Anti-Military Tradition". Yet that is too simple a conclusion. There *has* been an unending quarrel between those who dislike and those who admire military pursuits, but the bulk of Americans have never been impressed with the extremists of either camp. In so far as they have taken sides, they have tended perhaps —in the characteristically contradictory fashion of the English-speaking democracies—to agree with some of the contentions of both sides. They have believed in defending America, and have always responded eagerly at the outbreak of a war—although a draft law had to be enacted before the Civil War was over, and conscription has been resorted to again in the twentieth century. They have, in the past, believed in defending their own state or section: witness the readiness of most Southerners to fight for the Confederacy.

This might be expressed differently, so as to say that Americans, historically, have usually preferred particularism to support of federal institutions, the voluntary to the compulsory, the amateur to the professional. As a military tradition this has not been altogether foolish, given as a first premise that America's professional army would be small. Since the regulars were too few to fight large-scale actions, it was logical to have a sizeable and properly administered militia. It was natural, though possibly wrong-headed, for volunteer officers to convince themselves that they and their volunteer units, suitably armed and subsidized, were all the military force that America needed. After all, the United States has won all its wars, except for the stalemates of the War of 1812 and Korea. In the latter case, many Americans think that they were robbed of victory by a pusillanimous Administration; and in the former case, the final triumph at New Orleans (of volunteers over British regulars) is their most vivid memory.

Hence, General Leonard Wood bitterly commented in 1916,

an unwarranted degree of confidence, a confidence which has grown into a belief that we have always been easily successful in war; that, in the language of the Fourth of July orator, we can defeat a world in arms.

America's more thoughtful amateur soldiers have always admitted that volunteers must be well trained to be effective, and that the ordinary militia were often routed in America's early wars. So, in some instances, were volunteer regiments; and even where these fought courageously (as in the Mexican war) their general conduct was sometimes disgraceful. More volunteers were apt to be enrolled than were actually required; paid for at federal expense, they were tempted to regard minor campaigns —especially against the Indians—as opportunities to run wild. Nevertheless, according to tradition they could do no wrong. "Our experience in the war just closed" in Mexico, President James K. Polk asserted in 1848, "fully confirms the opinion that . . . an army may be raised upon a few weeks' notice, and that our citizen soldiers are equal to any troops in the world." It could have been pointed out to him that Zachary Taylor's regulars bore the initial brunt of the war; that it took several months to acclimatize the volunteers to the fighting; and that some of the best volunteer regiments were commanded by former West Point graduates such as Jefferson Davis. Or rather, Polk knew all this but thought it irrelevant.

In consequence, America failed to evolve a satisfactory military system until the twentieth century. It was useless to inveigh against the militia law of 1792, so long as Americans were unwilling to combine regulars and militia (volunteer or otherwise) in one federalized structure. Companies of volunteer militia might wear the same uniform as the regulars: that did not make them regulars, for when a war came they still picked their own officers and were still liable merely for three months' service within the confines of the United States.

Nor could there be an adequate regular army until the twentieth century. Before the Civil War it averaged about 10,000 men, and was not a great deal bigger afterwards. Now and then Congress authorized an additional regiment or two; now and then Congress lopped one or two off. Though pay was reasonably good and enlistments were short (by European standards), it was hard to attract decent citizens into the ranks. The majority were immigrants who had not yet managed to make a civilian livelihood, or men in hiding from their own pasts, or jobless and derelict Americans. Some (the "snowbirds") enlisted to find shelter for the winter, others on the chance of a free trip to the West. Before 1860 the annual desertion rate rose as high as 30%; and for fifty years thereafter it stood at about 10% (in the navy as well as the army). Troops were scattered in frontier detachments, rarely coming together in a complete regiment; in fact, Benjamin F. Butler, who became a major-general during the Civil War, claimed that he was used to manoeuvring with thousands of men at encampments of Massachusetts volunteer militia, while his regular contemporaries only handled a few hundred at a time.

This is not to say that the regular army was inefficient. It acquitted itself very well in the campaigns of the nineteenth century, whether in pitched battles or in Indian skirmishes. Its officers, certainly in comparison with those of Britain, were highly trained; West Point gave them an admirable though somewhat academic education, so that they could always count upon congenial employment in civilian life. Since promotion was drearily slow, many did resign their commissions. When the Civil War broke out, West Pointers secured nearly all the chief commands in the Union and Confederate forces. Yet this was a field-day for the U.S. Military Academy rather than for the regular army. According to the "expansible" army theory developed by John C. Calhoun as Secretary of War in 1820, the regulars were to form a skeleton force in peacetime When war came, the skeleton (6,400 men in Calhoun's day) was to be given flesh by enlarging each company. But it would still be a skinny creation, for he did not envisage more than a threefold increase (to 19,000 men). Nor could his successors—so completely had they accepted the American notion of a miniature regular army. Beyond that, they perforce left matters to the citizen soldiery. In the Civil War, therefore, the regular army filled out its skeleton but remained a quite small portion of the Union's strength, an enclave lost amid a host of volunteer regiments, its officers doomed to stagnation in junior regimental commands when many of them were fit to command volunteer brigades and divisions.

In the eyes of some opponents, the regular army could do nothing right. It was attacked for aloofness and for not being aloof enough. It was derided for its pygmy proportions and challenged as too powerful. John A. Logan, in his *Volunteer Soldier of America* (1887) sums up a great deal of argument along these lines:

> The governments of the Old World owe their continuance to standing armies, raised and maintained by regular pay or by stern compulsion. The United States possesses no standing army in the popular sense of that designation. Its policy and traditions, in fact the very essence of the nation's existence, repudiate any such contrivance . . . From the period of the Declaration of Independence . . . down to the close of the recent Civil War, the volunteer soldiers have constituted the prime military power of the Government. More than that, they must continue in occupancy of that position until the liberties of the people are unfortunately sunk under the iron heel of a standing army.

His language is immoderate, in fact a little ridiculous. There was never a remote danger even that America's standing army would become an "iron heel". It was far too small, and too much on the defensive. The army's officers were drawn from every state in the Union, through the nomination of Congressmen who sent in the names of eligible West Point cadets. Some cadets were wealthy or well-connected, but there are plenty of instances of cadets who were neither. The testimony of Logan and others is, indeed, coloured by personal grievances. Logan himself felt that he should have been promoted to the command of a corps in the Civil War, and instead saw it pass to a West Pointer, Oliver Otis Howard. Alden Partridge, the instigator or author of many onslaughts against the regulars, had been ousted from control of West Point and never forgave that institution.

Nevertheless, Logan and his associates did draw attention to a genuine dilemma. If America were a "unique" experiment, as Logan contended, a radical democracy that had turned its back on the Old World, how could it maintain a standing army? Were not regular forces, even in skeleton guise, European expedients? Did they not embody, with their rigid discipline and their conspicuous gradations of rank and privilege, an aristocratic order of society alien to everything that America stood for? His query had the more relevance in that the American regular army (and navy, though he did not mention it) did retain many of the characteristics of a European army. Armies are by definition hierarchical; they recognize and codify degrees of rank, and must enforce obedience by strict disciplinary rule. But the American regular army, though modified in some respects by American democratic custom, was a more "aristocratic" institution than one might have expected.

Perhaps it unconsciously followed European practice (or even consciously: a number of American officers were sent to Europe to report on military methods there). Perhaps it tended to draw to itself Americans whose instincts were conservative (particularly from the South), and to deepen such instincts, so that entry into West Point or Annapolis became a hereditary custom in some families. Whatever the reasons, an American officer-class did emerge. In the French army of the nineteenth century, great importance was attached to professional training at St. Cyr or Metz, on which West Point was to some extent modelled. In the British army of the same period, the average British officer was very much an amateur; until the latter part of the century, few went through cadet-training at Sandhurst. In the British army, hardly any commissions were awarded from the ranks, except to quartermasters, riding-masters and the like. In the French army, on the other hand, a third or more of commissions were by law given to *officiers de fortune*—enlisted men. The American regular army seemed to mingle the professionalism of the French with the gentleman-officer concept of the British, so that before the Civil War it was almost impossible for an American enlisted man to win a commission. A few direct appointments were made, at presidential discretion; otherwise, the only path to a commission lay through West Point. It is not surprising that Jacksonian America grumbled at this dispensation. As Rodney Glisan said, of the 1850's, "army life is essentially aristocratic . . . There is a sharp line of demarcation drawn between all commissioned and non-commissioned officers. The latter may associate with the . . . private soldiers, but never with the former." Possibly this was inevitable in a regular service: certainly it seemed un-American. After the Civil War it became theoretically easier to win a commission from the ranks, and a number of commissions were granted to volunteers (e.g., to Nelson A. Miles and to Arthur MacArthur—the father of Douglas MacArthur—who both subsequently achieved high rank). But the army had undergone no profound change; it was still, according to *Ladies and Officers of the United States Army,* an account published in 1880, "a little domain of its own, independent and isolated by its peculiar customs and discipline; an aristocracy by selection and the halo of tradition".

This suggests that—at any rate up to the end of the nineteenth century —there have been two distinct sets of American military traditions: one of amateur and anti-professional belligerence, and one of strict and rather lonely professionalism. They had their counterpart in Britain, where there was also a dual structure of regulars and volunteers. In Britain, however, the regulars were much more firmly in the saddle, much closer to the ruling circles in national life. The citizen-soldiery, by contrast, were inferior beings, usually regarded as comical (as we may see by looking through a few old volumes of *Punch*). In America the situation was reversed, and the two traditions were positively inimical.

What of the twentieth century? It has brought astonishing changes: has it completely obliterated the ancient clichés, stigmas and dogmas that governed American military thought in the nineteenth century?

The changes began to occur a little before 1900—indeed, at about the time that Stockton wrote *The Great War Syndicate.* They entailed a transition—often grudging and reluctant—from the idea of isolation to that of involvement in the concerns and dangers of the outside world. More than one American of the earlier era likened his country to China, as a safe, large, apart nation. In our era, Americans place their faith in the nation's technical and industrial potential. We might say in simple terms that the twentieth century has seen a change from a "China" to a "Technocracy" concept of military policy; it is the new marvel of Technocracy that Stockton celebrates. "Poor China," the Secretary of War Elihu Root said in 1903, "today stands helpless, seeing, piece by piece, parts of her territory . . . cut out from her living body . . . China, whose people are industrious, and frugal and enterprising, among the best workmen, the most honest merchants, the most successful business men of the earth . . ."

Root had no intention of following China into ruin. In the 1890's America had started to build up her navy to a size more consonant with her power and pretensions. Since the right "to provide and maintain a navy" was vested in Congress, and not delegated to the states, the task was relatively straightforward. It took longer for Congressmen to convince either themselves or the states that the land forces also required overhaul. But in 1903, through the Dick Act, the militia law of 1792 was at last repealed, and a fresh system introduced under which the militia were divided into a National Guard and a secondary reserve. They were to be organized, equipped and disciplined like the regulars— except that state governors still retained a considerable degree of authority. In the same year, Root established a General Staff, with a Chief of Staff to replace the office of Commanding General of the Army. Naval and Army War Colleges were already in existence. Any one of these steps might have provoked a furious controversy in some previous decade. Now, however, Root was able to act with brisk confidence. He even blandly drew attention "to the provision of the Constitution, in the tenth section of the first article, that 'no state shall, without the consent of Congress, . . . keep troops or ships of war in time of peace'," and congratulated the National Guard on becoming—as a result of the Dick Act —"probably for the first time, unquestionably a constitutional force". And when he laid the corner-stone of the Army War College's new home (in the national capital, where regular troops had once been unwelcome), he took the opportunity to consecrate the building, so to speak, to Emory Upton. Upton was a regular officer who had written a lengthy manuscript to demonstrate that America's military honour had been preserved by the regulars and imperilled by the militia and volunteers. It had been left unpublished at Upton's death in 1881; but Root had it printed as a War Department document, as *The Military Policy of the United States* (1904). It proved to be an earnest, dull compilation that made little impression on the public. Yet at least the army had produced a work to set beside the more readable naval writings of Alfred Thayer Mahan.

Army reformers faced setbacks and disappointments. The National Guard was not actually brought into effective partnership, as a fully federalized militia, until the war emergency of 1917 called forth the requisite legislation. Still, comparatively, these were revolutionary changes. Since then, the United States has moved to the forefront of world military, naval and air strength. The old protests and apathies sound far-off and faint. Some observers feel that America has not only taken a new road, but that it is the road to universal catastrophe. The sociologist C. Wright Mills, in *The Power Elite* (1956), maintains that American policy is controlled by "warlords": namely, by military leaders, in close and equal collusion with the heads of great corporations and an inner cabinet of political chieftains. The historian Arthur A. Ekirch, Jr., shows in *The Civilian and the Military* (1956) that he too fears for the future of what he calls "the American tradition of antimilitarism, peace, and democracy" (i.e., more or less the "China" concept).

My essay is devoted to a discussion of what has been, not to a prophecy of what may be. But if we survey the altered direction of the past half-century, I think we may conclude that it does not constitute an altogether novel, nor ominous, trend. In the nineteenth century the United States enjoyed the luxury of not needing to make up her mind on military as on many other national problems. It was an expensive and wasteful luxury, but she was content with it. Since then she has suffered the discomfort of having to make up her mind belatedly and too rapidly. But her policies are still rather wasteful and expensive, and her utterances still seemingly rather irresponsible. The "Technocracy" concept assumes (though not quite as sweepingly as Stockton did) that it may yet be possible, through capital investment and technical ingenuity, to win quick wars by substituting machines for manpower. Indeed, Congress has been prepared to vote money for a larger air force than was being asked for. It has also been kind to the navy. The army, in direct line of descent from old-style American thinking, has been dismissed as redundant. Proposals to bring in "U.M.T." (universal military training) have been shelved, just as more modest proposals to enforce compulsory militia training have been rejected at frequent intervals all the way through American history. European nations have become accustomed to conscription: America still has only a selective draft. Service in the armed forces is not really more popular among American youths than it was fifty or a hundred years ago. As we might expect, this is more true of the army than of the air force. Among the strip-cartoons that embellish American newspapers, there are at least three—"Terry Lee", "Buz Sawyer" and "Steve Canyon" —whose heroes are air force officers, all handsome and heroic characters. Significantly, there is only one strip-cartoon (so far as I know) that deals with the modern army: "Beetle Bailey", whose "hero" is an enlisted man and whose officers are portrayed as cretinous bores. However, there is no mad rush to join the air force, despite its technological glamour. Adlai Stevenson, the Democratic candidate in the presidential campaign of 1956, even ventured to suggest the repeal of the draft law. Perhaps, as the Republicans alleged, this was merely a vote-catching device. Yet if it was unsound military *policy*, its appeal to American military *tradition* was based on an accurate assessment of public reaction to the splendours and miseries of military life.

Since 1945, America has kept an unprecedentedly large number of men in uniform. But it should be noted that she reduced them at an almost headlong rate just after 1945, and again just before the Korean war. Her prodigious military budget does not appear to be creating a "militarist" nation: at least, not in any common usage of that word. If that process were really under way, there would be various indications. For example, we should see "professional" rituals and habits of thought pervade the armed forces, and gain acceptance in the country as a whole. But the reverse seems to be true, as though the "professional" military tradition were being diluted beyond recognition by the "anti-professional" one. Indeed, the army has been criticized for its soulless indifference to tradition; famous units and formations have been "de-activated" as though they were obsolete factories, or relegated to training routines, to churn out personnel for newer, active units. It seems businesslike and bleak: neither anti-military nor pro-military, but a-military. In fact, much like *The Great War Syndicate*—with the exception that the other side also has an instantaneous motor.

AMERICAN RADICALISM:
JACKSON, BRYAN AND WILSON

By C. P. Hill

*

PRESIDENTIAL elections in the United States are normally conflicts of men rather than of measures, of personalities far more than of programmes. This tends to add to their excitement, but to diminish their reliability as guides to the deeper movements of public opinion. It may be suggested that the three most important elections between the end of the War of 1812 and the entry of the United States into the First World War—apart from the very special case of the first election of Abraham Lincoln in 1860—were the three occasions when something more was at stake than the exchange of one set of men for another: namely, the presidential elections of 1828, 1896, and 1912. Further, it may be observed that the factor which made each of these a conflict of major significance was a spontaneous uprising of public opinion; and that the most important outcome of each was a reinvigorating of American democracy both in outlook and in action. This process on each occasion reflected and gave expression to a national mood of what, largely for want of a better name, may be called "radicalism".

Neither "radical" nor "radicalism" is a word of very precise meaning or usage on either side of the Atlantic; and to give them capital letters merely increases imprecision. British parallels are peculiarly unhelpful here; as one of the most brilliant of all American historians observed, "Knowledge of human nature is the beginning and end of political education, but several years of arduous study in the neighbourhood of Westminster led Henry Adams to think that knowledge of English human nature had little or no value outside of England." Nowhere is this more true than in the study of reform and radicalism in the United States during the nineteenth century. There was in nineteenth-century Britain a "Radical" tradition, continuous, coherent, and clearly-marked. It was incarnate in such men as Cobbett and Hunt, Cobden and Bright, Roebuck and Labouchère, Dilke and Joseph Chamberlain—men for whom "Radical" is the only appropriate political label. This tradition had its recognized place in the national political scene; its functions and its goals —the widening of the franchise, the ballot, the freedom of the press from taxation, cheap or free education and other social reforms—remained of much the same kind throughout the century. The Victorian politician knew a Radical when he saw one; for even though there was no separate Radical party, a Radical was recognizable as a "type". It would be an exaggeration to say that nothing of the sort was true of the United States during the same period, but it would be a pardonable exaggeration. There were plenty of political figures to whom the term "radical" could be applied without making nonsense of the language; and three of these, of whom two became President and the third very nearly did so, are the main subjects of this essay. There were others for whom "Radical" is the only convincing political label; such men as William Leggett and other Jacksonians of the thirties and "Pitchfork" Ben Tillman of South Carolina at the end of the century. But there were not many of this latter kind; and they tended to be local rather than national figures, minor not major politicians. No American Radical of this era enjoys a national historical status, simply as a Radical, comparable with that of John Bright in England. Again, though there are American radical movements by the score, such as the "Barnburning" wing of the New York Democrats in the 1840's or the very widespread Populist movement of the nineties, there is no uninterrupted and coherent Radical tradition at the level of national politics. It is perhaps significant, and it is certainly ironic, that the most celebrated group to whom the word "Radical" is customarily applied is that Republican majority in Congress which was responsible for the legislative pattern of Reconstruction after the Civil War. For this, however strong the idealism and the radicalism of some of its members like Charles Sumner on the great question of the Negro, was on the whole as cynical and ruthless a political faction as can be found in the history of the United States.

It is arguable that the primary reason for the absence of a strong Radical tradition in American national politics is the success of the American Revolution. The United States was a nation born in rebellion; moreover it was, in the eyes of its people (and this is a belief that has haunted American history ever since), a nation of a unique kind, dedicated to human freedom. American democratic society was something new and different in man's experience: all men were born free, but only in the United States did they remain free, and only there, in the fine phrase of Monroe's Message of 1823, had men "enjoyed unexampled felicity". Their freedom was guaranteed by that unique political instrument, the American Constitution. In such conditions, not only was there no place for a revolutionary tradition; there was only limited scope for a genuine radicalism. To be labelled a Radical was to be declared a critic of that sacred thing, the American's birthright. Moreover in practice much of the "unexampled felicity" rested upon the fact that property was from the start of the American democratic experiment very widely distributed in the United States; and in these circumstances, as Tocqueville put it in a famous passage, "not only are the men of democracies not naturally desirous of revolutions, but they are afraid of them". Levellers were not wanted, because all men were equal; Radicals were in general not necessary, because all men were free in what has been called by Louis Hartz "a truly monolithic liberal society". It may be observed also that the parallel absence of any strong conservative tradition with a national appeal was itself a powerful factor in stunting the growth of a Radical tradition. The only genuine rebels in the United States were to be men of the extreme Right.

The lines of development of American history gave practical force to this very unusual heritage. The size of the United States and the rapidity of its expansion, especially after the 1840's; the extraordinary variety of background from which its immigrants came, and the resultant heterogeneity of local political leadership (the student of radicalism will find an interesting contrast between the contributions of the Germans in the Middle West and the Catholic Irish in New York City); the federal system of government and its division of functions, which for so long left so many social issues, the raw stuff of radicalism, to the states—all these things made for fragmentation and discontinuity in reforming movements. So did the absence of any class-based system of government as firmly-rooted as that to be found in Britain before the 1832 Reform Act. Cobbett and his fellows found themselves with an excellent target—it was the one which Sam Adams had attacked fifty years earlier on the other side of the Atlantic; the later American radicals, whose capacity for hatred at least equalled that of Cobbett, had nothing so formidable or concentrated to assail. Nor was the existence of the frontier as wholly favourable to the development of radicalism as might be supposed; its impact here, as in other regions of American life, was somewhat ambivalent. The frontier bred radicals, no doubt, from Andrew Jackson and Abraham Lincoln downwards, and in some ways powerfully encouraged the growth of the radical mind, notably through the very practical stimulus of debt. Yet the frontier, by its very nature, could not easily help to create a coherent and organized radical movement; its small farmers were too individualistic and scattered, too liable to be swept by violent and short-lived enthusiasms, too closely tied to local and personal needs. In so far as it was in any way a means of escape from the economic and social pressures of the towns of the East it probably did at least as much to weaken urban radicalism as to strengthen its rural counterpart. And of course the great question of sectionalism and the Civil War turned the minds of a whole generation of Americans to different issues; men did not divide as "radicals" or "conservatives" on slavery and secession.

There was therefore no American Radical Party; no continuing Radical group in Congress; still less any tradition—and this is perhaps the distinguishing element of British Radicalism over the same period—which its conservative opponents could condemn as being a quarter of the way to revolution and which its supporters could glory in for that very reason. Instead there was something far more widespread even if far more spasmodic in its appearance, and far more effective if it could be organized—namely the profound American belief in the common man, with its accompanying hostility to monopoly and privilege. It was the essence of Jeffersonianism, the source of the American dream; and its periodic resurgence in the nineteenth century is American radicalism. It was in its origins deeply agrarian. The Jacksonian Revolution of the 1830's won most of its backing from small farmers; the local radicalism so common in the Middle West in the post-Civil War years was essentially agrarian; William Jennings Bryan in 1896 was basically and only too obviously an agrarian in outlook; and even Woodrow Wilson as late as the election of 1916 drew much of his support from the agricultural West and South. It was therefore individualist, not socialist; believing in *laisser faire*, suspicious of government control. In economic terms, its greatest need was cheap money and a plentiful currency, and it was invariably ready to condemn the bankers and financiers of the East. But it did not condemn capitalism; indeed one of its permanent objectives was to save capitalism from itself, and one of its constant methods was to deny government support to capitalist enterprises. For agrarianism in nineteenth century America must not be interpreted in terms narrowly agricultural; the small merchant and business man, upon whom rural communities so heavily depended, was himself one of the central figures of the agrarian "myth". The enemies were rather, in Jackson's day, Nicholas Biddle of the United States Bank; and at the end of the century, those whom Bryan, in his speech against the repeal of the Sherman Silver Purchase Act, called "the moneyed interests, aggregated wealth and capital, imperious, arrogant, compassionless".

Here, as the events of 1828 were to show most strongly, was a mighty force. Yet the weakness of this agrarian and entrepreneurial radicalism was to be shown when it came to grips with the problems presented by the growth of American industry in the second half of the nineteenth century. In the simple days of the 1830's Jacksonianism could embrace the wage-earners, could win support from the relatively small trade unions of New York and Philadelphia. But two generations later the problem of economic democracy had assumed a totally different form. It was now predominantly an urban problem, with the trusts as one facet and the slums as another; and its solution, as the Progressives saw, was vital to the survival of political democracy. Was *laisser faire* adequate? And if not how was the nettle of government intervention and control to be grasped? The radical answer to such questions was conservative. Many of the Populists did little more than look back wistfully to the idyll of the 1830's; Bryan had little grasp of the problem, and there is a slightly pathetic ring about the resolution which he put before the Democratic Party Convention at Baltimore in 1912, assuring the American people "that the party of Jefferson and of Jackson is still the champion of popular government and equality before the law". Wilson began his reforms on traditional lines, and not until the end of his first term did he acknowledge by action the need for federal intervention in social problems.

It was out of the West that there came the President with the most obvious claim to be called a radical. This was Andrew Jackson of Tennessee, who was inaugurated in 1829 and served for two terms. Jackson was too strong a personality to represent any movement; and it might even be argued that few American Presidents, except perhaps Woodrow Wilson and both Roosevelts, have been less "typical" of the people responsible for their election. Nevertheless, his background and career, the circumstances of his election, and the uses he made of power help to illustrate the nature and limitations of radicalism in the United States in the 1820's and 1830's.

Born in Carolina in 1767, Andrew Jackson was a child of the backwoods who had known poverty as no earlier President had done; and as a boy he had been beaten across the face with the flat of a sword for refusing to clean the boots of a British officer in the War of Independence. Eventually he had become—in the frontier manner—a lawyer, as well as a celebrated duellist in Nashville, Tennessee, and he had served at Washington both as Congressman and as Senator. But it was as a military hero that he became a presidential candidate; he was much less of a politician than all his predecessors and most of his successors. In the War of 1812 he had won the only notable American victory on land, at New Orleans in 1815, when his force, with a mere handful of casualties, had destroyed two thousand British regulars whose commander threw them in a frontal assault on a prepared position; and he had later been prominent in the curious enterprise of the conquest of Florida from Spain. In the presidential election of 1824 Jackson had been at the head of the popular vote in a four-cornered contest in which no candidate won a clear majority; when the election went to the House of Representatives he was defeated by John Quincy Adams. As a man Jackson would have been distinguished in any community for his bravery, honesty, loyalty, chivalry, and dignity. That he was also simple, prejudiced, and vindictive counted for less than it might have done in a later age; and Jackson was capable of taking advice as well as of making decisions, and he was in fact one of the successful military Presidents.

His personal qualities were to matter much when he took office; in the election of 1828 they were overshadowed by his symbolic value. This election was most significantly a turning point in American history in that it brought to the presidency for the first time one who could be regarded as a man of the people. His six predecessors—the four Virginians Washington, Jefferson, Madison, and Monroe, and the two Adams from Massachusetts—were gentlemen of substance, assured social background, and education, who had come to the presidency as of right. "Old Hickory" had abundant substance; he was in fact a considerable landowner and slaveowner in Tennessee, and in the social conflicts of this frontier state had more often than not shown himself to be on the side of the well-to-do. But his early career as well as his immense sense of duty enabled him to be a tribune of the people, not merely to pose as one. For their part, the people took a greater share in the election of 1828 than in any previous one. The population had grown in the 1820's, the admission of new western states had helped to encourage a widening of the franchise, the nomination of candidates was being taken out of the hands of state legislatures and into those of the people; and over three times as many citizens voted in 1828 as in 1824. It was a "popular" election in other senses, too. There was plenty of mud-slinging and more scurrility than on any previous occasion; the latter was far more the result of the fact that Jackson's opponents regarded the possibility of his victory as a social catastrophe than of the mistaken belief of the Jacksonians that their hero had been defeated in 1824 only by a shady political bargain. Yet even this belief itself is important, for it did more than anything else to promote the political organization of the Jacksonian Revolution. From 1825 onwards the supporters of Jackson had been busy throughout the country creating local support and local party machinery, to ensure that in 1828 his majority should be decisive.

How successful they were was shown in the returns. Jackson got 647,000, his opponent John Quincy Adams 508,000 popular votes; Adams took all New England, New Jersey, Delaware, and Maryland, and Jackson the rest of the country. "The people" looked upon the victory as theirs; as a leading Jacksonian put it, "General Jackson is *their own* president." This was true enough, though in no very precise sense. For Jackson was backed by a strange and short-lived alliance which included not only the small farmers of the West and the growing artisan class of New York and Philadelphia, but also the slaveowners of the South. Little that is fundamentally radical can be found in Jackson's programme in 1828, for Jackson, who was himself a man of action not of ideas, and his advisers took care to have no detailed programme. The General would serve the people; he was understood to be against privilege and against too much government; for the rest, he was a great patriot and a great personality, who stood for change and opportunity. Much the most radical thing about Andrew Jackson in 1828 was his candidature. He appeared at an appropriate moment in the history of American political development, because he became at once the means whereby Jefferson's ideas survived in practical form in American politics and began to be transmitted to the industrial workers of the East. The great Republican Party of Jefferson, having seen the extinction of the Federalists, had in the presidency of Monroe (1817-25) become the only national party in the land. Inevitably and fortunately, this "Era of Good Feelings" could not last, and there was a personal scramble for the succession to Monroe in 1824, while the voices of the sages like John Taylor of Caroline and Nathaniel Macon of North Carolina lamented the decline of orthodox Jeffersonian Republicanism. Jefferson himself died on July 4, 1826, long regarded by many as having forsaken his own creed. At this stage appeared Andrew Jackson, to re-create the party as the Democratic Party—or, more accurately, to serve as the symbol of its re-creation; and to do so on the basis of doctrines which were in all essentials Jeffersonian. They could scarcely be otherwise if they were to appeal to the American people in the 1830's, for the United States was still predominantly a land of small farmers. An agrarian democracy was the ideal because it was to a great extent the reality. Like Jefferson, Jackson believed above all in the small farmer, the independent owner of land; like Jefferson, he preferred a weak government. Yet also like Jefferson he was prepared to use the resources of strong government in action when national necessity seemed to require it; and just as Jefferson had abandoned strict construction and bought Louisiana, so Jackson was to resist the South Carolina doctrine of nullification and thereby ignore states' rights. In all this there was nothing novel; far from being a potential revolutionary, Jackson sought his authority and inspiration along well-trodden paths. The famous scenes of his inauguration day in 1829, when crowds of his supporters invaded the Presidential Mansion and many of them got very drunk, thus transforming the first official function of the new régime into a confused mêlée from which Jackson had to be rescued, were not a foretaste of Jacobinism, as diehards believed; they were merely a piece of natural junketing, a mark of humanity rather than of radicalism or of conservatism.

Against this enthusiastic and rather nebulous background, what did Andrew Jackson achieve? He was sixty-one years old when he took office, ill and emaciated, stricken with grief by the recent death of his wife; many contemporaries believed that he would not live through one term of office. In fact he was triumphantly re-elected in 1832, and lived another eight years after his retirement from Washington in 1837. Contemporaries acclaimed his deeds, and he was in effect able to nominate Martin van Buren as his successor; and later historians, while delivering varied verdicts upon his intelligence and his motives, have on the whole agreed upon his success, observing that like Lincoln and the other great American Presidents he grew to his task during his tenure of office. Something of his achievement rested upon his magnificent bearing and upon the simple dignity which contrasted so sharply with the gloomy anticipations of his opponents and which no later President has equalled; rather more upon his identification of himself with the people, an identification which is itself his greatest claim to be a radical.

Certainly, except upon a single issue, there was little that was extreme in his policy. His first Inaugural Address was a modest and cautious affair. Its most striking paragraph was the statement that "the recent demonstration of public sentiment inscribes on the list of executive duties, in characters too legible to be overlooked, the task of *reform,*

Q

which will require particularly the correction of those abuses that have brought the patronage of the Federal Government into conflict with the freedom of elections, and the counteraction of those causes which have disturbed the rightful course of appointment and have placed or continued power in unfaithful or incompetent hands". From behind this somewhat oblique observation there emerged what has, a little unkindly, become known as the Spoils System. Jackson believed, according to his first Annual Message (1829), that "the duties of all public offices are, or at least admit of being made, so plain and simple that men of intelligence may readily qualify themselves for their performance". It was a belief that was bound to appeal to his supporters, and was therefore also a useful means of party discipline; to outward appearance a radical belief, its immediate result after 1829 was primarily a change of personnel in line with the verdict of an election which had itself been fought to a great extent in personal terms; and in later years it was to contribute at least as much to reaction as to progress. Yet its real importance in the Jacksonian Revolution was the same as that of the attack on the caucus system of nomination and of the development in its place of the national convention, the first example of which met in 1832; it was a practical expression of popular participation in politics, of the new life which Jackson and the Jacksonians brought to American democracy.

Jackson believed in the common man, and thus in that age his policy was basically one of *laisser faire*. Vigorously patriotic in his foreign policy, a loyal champion of national unity, he had yet no wish to increase the power of the Federal Government and still less readiness to lend its support to privileged groups. Hence his opposition to federal backing for programmes of internal improvement. Hence too the attitude of the Jacksonians on the Supreme Court, illustrated by the judgment in the *Charles River Bridge* Case of 1837 delivered by Chief Justice Roger B. Taney, which proclaimed "the object and end of all government" to be "to promote the happiness and prosperity of the community by which it is established" and condemned chartered monopolies which hindered the attainment of that end. And hence above all his prolonged battle with the Bank of the United States, the one issue over which Jackson proceeded to extremes. The second Bank of the United States, a private corporation to which the Federal Government had subscribed one-fifth of the capital and in which the public funds were deposited, had been chartered for twenty years by President Madison in 1816; the question of the renewal of its charter thus became an urgent public issue during Jackson's first term. The Bank served a valuable economic purpose in American society, notably as the country's most powerful safeguard against inflation. But it was widely unpopular, for reasons which contradicted one another. The smaller banks, of the East as well as of the West, were jealous of its power; the large debtor class of the West and South hated its deflationary policies; the working-men and small business men of eastern cities blamed the currency system, which the Bank dominated, for the rising cost of living. It was the wealthiest and most privileged monopoly in the country, and therefore a splendid target for the attacks of the small man; and the greatest of its enemies was Jackson. How far he was moved by his own unhappy earlier experiences with banks, how far by his genuine belief in a hard money policy, how far by his passionate personal reaction to the Bank's intervention in politics ("The Bank, Mr Van Buren, is trying to kill me, *but I will kill it!*"), it is impossible to tell; his opposition was unrelenting, and it was the President who held a wavering party together in the crisis of conflict. In 1832 the Bank got a bill for re-charter through the House of Representatives and the Senate. Jackson vetoed it; fought the election of 1832 on the Bank issue; removed the government funds in 1833; and thus killed the Bank.

As a measure of economic policy Jackson's actions were unwise, and they were politically disastrous to his successor; for the destruction of the Bank of the United States and the transfer of government deposits to numerous state banks stimulated inflation and thus contributed notably to the economic crisis of 1837, which was fatal to Van Buren. Jackson's economic policy reflected the confusion of its supporters, who were a blend of hard-money men and inflationists. But in its deepest sense Jackson's war with the Bank was a social conflict, not merely an economic one, as the ringing tones of his Veto Message make abundantly clear. "In the full enjoyment of the gifts of Heaven and the fruits of superior industry, economy, and virtue, every man is equally entitled to protection by law; but when the laws undertake to add to these natural and just advantages artificial distinctions, to grant titles, gratuities and exclusive privileges, to make the rich richer and the potent more powerful, the humble members of society—the farmers, mechanics, and laborers— who have neither the time nor the means of securing like favors to themselves, have a right to complain of the injustice of their Government . . . If it (Government) would confine itself to equal protection, and, as Heaven does its rains, shower its favors alike on the high and the low, the rich and the poor, it would be an unqualified blessing. In the Act before me there seems to be a wide and unnecessary departure from these just principles." The message—the work of a central group of Jacksonians including Amos Kendall, Andrew Donelson, and Roger B. Taney— contained the heart of Jacksonianism, the simple faith in the basic equality of men and in their equal right to make their own way in the world unhindered by monopoly or special privilege. It was in Jackson's eyes a universal faith, not tied to class—however much support it won from the nascent working-class movement of the towns, however much the policy of the Jackson administration, especially in the second term, veered towards the hard-money views of the town-dwelling radicals of the East. Jackson was no labour radical; he was a capitalist, a land-owner, a slaveowner, a general, a duellist. Yet he was the first effective interpreter of Jeffersonianism to eastern working men in a society which was still predominantly agrarian. His radicalism was a traditional American belief, expressed in action at a time when it appeared that monopoly and privilege were threatening to deprive the common man of his birthright; Andrew Jackson's achievement was thus to give new substance and life to the American dream.

A great gulf separated Jackson and William Jennings Bryan, the defeated hero of the election of 1896. It was not merely or even so much the tragic crisis of the Civil War that differentiated Bryan's America from Jackson's. There were now forty-five states instead of twenty-five, and some 70,000,000 people as against the 12,000,000 when Jackson took office. Railroads had been flung across the continent; the prairies were pouring forth their wheat and corn; gold and iron, copper and silver, coal and oil, the vast resources of the land were being tapped, and the greatest of modern industrial nations was being born. Officially the frontier had ended. Huge cities had arisen out of the wilderness. Millionaires and slums co-existed. It was the America of Rockefeller and Carnegie; a land across which change was moving fast, disturbing and sometimes ominous, the America of Thorstein Veblen, Samuel Gompers, Henry Demarest Lloyd; to the European, Bryce's America, not Tocqueville's. More complex, fundamentally less isolated, the American society was being brought face to face with problems of imperialism and world power at a time when its internal difficulties were being multiplied beyond the imagination of an earlier generation. It was not that American confidence had diminished. The United States was still the land of freedom, still a land different in kind from any other land on earth; no American could really doubt this as the immigrants poured in by the hundred thousand. But how much longer, now that the bright new morning of American life was so visibly over, could this difference be maintained, in the face of corrupt government, trusts, and other evils? And how adequate was the Jacksonian belief in the common man in this new age? To these questions the election of 1896 gave a somewhat inconclusive answer.

Defeated candidates in presidential elections, where they are not forgotten men, have the scales of history weighted against them; and William Jennings Bryan was defeated three times. It is hard to compare men who have been President with men who have not. Yet on his later record it is impossible to believe that Bryan, for all his single-minded enthusiasm and his devotion to causes which he and great numbers of his fellow-countrymen believed good, would have been a successful chief executive. It was not merely that he was narrow and pedestrian in mind; it was more serious that he did not grow in political stature as he aged; and there is a certain rightness about the fact that the great moment of his career, for which history will remember him, came early, when he was only thirty-six, in his nomination by the Democratic Party Convention at Chicago in 1896. Jackson had been a man of action rather than of ideas: Bryan was a man of words who led to defeat the most important organized radical movement in American history. Yet few Americans, apart from the men of the 1860's, have aroused such passion, so much idealism and so much hatred. On the morrow of his defeat, a New York newspaper, while calling him "the wretched, rattle-pated boy" and describing him as a puppet, could claim that he had "less provocation than Benedict Arnold, less intellectual force than Aaron Burr, less manliness and courage than Jefferson Davis". On the other side there was a spirit of revivalism about the campaign which did not by any means come only from Bryan himself, and which found lasting expression in Vachel Lindsay's verses with their lines such as

He brought in tides of wonder, of unprecedented splendour.

The Democratic campaign of 1896 gave unusual sharpness to the strange blend of forces which American politics demands; morality was at least as strong as radicalism, crusading and go-getting and the defence of vested interests rode side by side; and it was perhaps an odd quirk of history that put at their head a conservative demagogue, at once slick and sincere, unimaginative and silver-tongued.

Behind Bryan lay the great force of American agrarianism. Bryan was the Populist candidate for the presidency as well as the nominee of the Democratic Party; and Populism was in a sense the last great challenge of rural America, its last act of defiance before the encroaching industrial civilization. The Populist Party was founded in 1890, when its candidates won four seats in the Senate and fifty in Congress; and in 1892 it nominated James B. Weaver for the presidency. Its platform in that year contained a preamble denouncing inequality based upon the corruption of government ("From the same prolific womb of governmental injustice we breed the two great classes—tramps and millionaires"); its demands included government ownership of railroads, telegraphs, and telephones, the free and unlimited coinage of silver, an increase in the circulating medium, a graduated income tax, and the direct election of Senators. Weaver got over a million votes, mostly in the South, the High Plains and the mountain states; and this total encouraged high hopes that a third major party was arising.

Populism had many roots, and its practical support in the early nineties came from numerous sources, some of them strange ones. Behind it lay a generation of widespread and varied local radicalism, tough, individualistic, and vigorous, notably in the Middle West, which had found expression in movements like the Granges, with their attack on the railroad monopolists, and the Greenbackers, with their cry for an expanded currency (on whose platform Bryan's father once ran for Congress). In general terms it was part of the frontier inheritance, stimulated by the cheap land available under the Homestead Act and from the railroads and other sources. Western Populism reflected the galloping land boom of the seventies and eighties, with its over-rapid settlement of difficult farming areas like western Kansas, its speculation and its crop failures, its load of mortgages, and its inevitable crash, which came in 1887. The discontent and the hatred thus bred turned quickly into political protest, first local then national. The actual beginnings of the party lay in the association of the several Farmers' Alliances of the South and West, themselves more militant than the Granges and with policies immortalized in the slogan of Mary Elizabeth Lease, "raise less corn and more hell". Yet it was from the start protest in terms that harked back to Jacksonianism. There was the same belief in the common man, the same ferocity against monopolists and the privileged (with the railroads joined to the bankers as villains), the same bitter complaint that government was on the side of these groups; and it was taken for granted by many Populists—including for example Weaver himself— that the answer of 1828 was the solution for 1896. Once again it was a deeply conservative radicalism.

Yet Populism was more complex than a movement of western farmers. It attracted a good deal of support in the South; and it has been pointed out that the embattled American farmers on this occasion were mainly those dependent on the great cash crops, cotton and wheat, whose sales were at the mercy of the world market, and that it was an international agrarian crisis, accompanied by falling commodity prices, which was principally responsible for the growth of Populism in the early 1890's. In the mountain states its main support came from those whose livelihood depended on a third commodity the world price of which had declined— silver: and this was to prove an aberration fatal to Bryan. These were the main elements. For the rest, some parts of its programme made a modest appeal to industrial workers in the East—though never enough to challenge the hold of the major parties in the cities. Its attraction, for ill as well as for good, was never merely economic. At its best, Populism was deeply idealist and humanitarian, blending the traditional agrarian myth at its noblest with that sense of the urgency of social reform which was so soon to animate the Progressive movement. At its worst, it was credulous, offering an excellent illustration of the American weakness for discovering imaginary conspiracies, this time by the capitalists of Wall Street; it was racist and jingoist, with anti-Negro, anti-Semitic, and anti-foreign elements prominent in its ranks—and not merely in the South. And the contemporary demand for war with Spain on behalf of Cuba won a good deal of backing from Populist sources.

The greatest victory of Populism came in the summer of 1896, when it in effect captured the Democratic Party Convention; and thereby committed suicide. Events hung upon "free silver". Bryan and the "silver Democrats" had ("with a zeal approaching the zeal which inspired the Crusaders who followed Peter the Hermit") campaigned for control of the party since President Cleveland had in 1893 approved the repeal of the Sherman Silver Purchase Act, with its provision compelling the government to purchase practically the entire output of American silver. For a brief moment currency reform was the central issue of American politics—partly because it was elevated into a moral issue; the prospect of free and unlimited coinage of silver won the hearts of farmers who were convinced that inflation of the currency would solve all their problems. There followed the famous scene at the Democratic Party Convention, when amidst a tumult of emotion Bryan won the nomination with a speech devoted in great part to the silver issue, and ending with the famous peroration "You shall not press down upon the brow of labor this crown of thorns, you shall not crucify mankind upon a cross of gold." The Populists as a whole, despite the opposition of some of the more perceptive reformers in their ranks, like Henry Demarest Lloyd, and after some hesitancy, decided to back Bryan; it would avoid splitting the anti-Republican vote, and it would also mean that the money which the silver-mining interests were spending upon Bryan's cause might help to achieve other Populist reforms. Inevitably, the Populist Party was swallowed up in the ranks of the Democrats.

Free silver was a disaster for its supporters in the election of 1896. This was not so much because it was irrelevant to the larger problems of American society; it was, after all, the central issue of that day. Rather it was because it was at once frightening and inadequate. It frightened the East because it raised the spectre of inflation, and enabled Mark Hanna, who ran the campaign for the Republican candidate William McKinley, to raise a great election fund from business men, and to use the slogan of "the full dinner-pail" and the threat of unemployment to win the votes of industrial workers. And it was inadequate because by itself it could do so little to remedy the ills of many voters, especially in the East. As Hanna said of Bryan, "He's talking Silver all the time, and that's where we've got him." Even so, McKinley's victory was a narrow one: he polled rather under a million more votes than Bryan, whose share of the popular vote was 45%.

For many an American who voted Democrat in 1896, free silver was a symbol: its intrinsic merits as an economic panacea counted little. Unfortunately it was a symbol of the past, of an agrarian America which was passing away. Bryan's radicalism was of an old-fashioned kind, defending equality and continuing to ask that government should not promote privilege. To the more sophisticated problems of an industrial society, his Jacksonian attitude—for in him it was an attitude rather than a philosophy—offered no answer; and this was the verdict of 1896. He took the "Solid South", he took the Rocky Mountain states, he took the western Plains; but he failed in the East, and he failed too in those Mid-Western states whose industry was growing fast and whose farmers did not depend on the great export staples. A great arc of America, from

Minnesota and Iowa eastwards through Illinois, Indiana and Ohio to Pennsylvania, New York and New England, rejected Bryan. When he proclaimed in his "Cross of Gold" speech "What we need is an Andrew Jackson to stand, as Jackson stood, against the encroachments of organized wealth", he was on ground common to western farmer and eastern working-man alike; but when later in the same speech he said "You come to us and tell us that the great cities are in favour of the gold standard; we reply that the great cities rest upon our broad and fertile prairies", he was overstating the role of agrarianism in the United States of the 1890's. The next radical leader would have to match his philosophy to the times, and capture the cities.

On the morrow of the election of 1896 the defeat of Bryan seemed a major disaster to idealism and to radicalism. McKinley, Vachel Lindsay's "respectable McKinley, the man without an angle or a tangle", appeared —partly because of the revivalist and moralistic theme to which Bryan had attuned his campaign—to stand for all the evil things in American life and especially for those associated with great wealth. In fact the failure of Bryan was a setback rather than a catastrophe for radicalism. Various short-term factors, among them the moderation of Hanna and other Republican leaders, prevented McKinley's presidency from being reactionary; and two developments more than offset the defeat of Bryan. The first of these was the rapid spread, during the later nineties and the first decade of the new century, of the Progressive Movement. The work of a very wide range of gifted writers—journalists like Lincoln Steffens, novelists like Theodore Dreiser and Frank Norris, social analysts like Thorstein Veblen, utopianists like Edward Bellamy—and of reformers dedicating themselves to the abolition of specific abuses, it won to its support great numbers of young men, particularly of the professional middle class in the great cities; and thus created the certainty of a powerful climate of reform in the next generation. Its impulse—whether the abuse was trusts, bosses, liquor, or adulterated food—was often a moral one; its criticism was trenchant and its language strong, although its remedies were, with rare exceptions, moderate ones. The second great development was a fortuitous event—the succession of Theodore Roosevelt to the presidency when McKinley was assassinated in 1901. This is not the place for an appraisal of "T. R.", because there was little that was radical about him except his use of the American language; in all his instincts he was a man of the Right, nor were his detailed achievements as a reformer considerable. Nevertheless his tenure of the White House kept alive and vigorous the prospects of social progress by political means in a way that would not have been possible under any other Republican of that day. He was of course shrewd enough to see the growing value of reform at the ballot boxes; he was also sincere enough to want the social evils of the United States not to be too glaring; and he was even more pugnacious than Jackson.

And his final services to radicalism were to quarrel with Taft and to get himself adopted as Progressive candidate for the presidency in 1912, thus opening the way to the victory of Wilson in that year.

The personal and intellectual background of Woodrow Wilson indicated a political evolution in a direction wholly opposite to that which he eventually followed; in this his experience was like that of Gladstone, whom he much resembled as a politician both in strength and weakness. He was born in 1856, the son of the Presbyterian minister of Staunton, Virginia; the family moved shortly to Georgia, and Wilson lived out his boyhood under the shadow of the Civil War and Reconstruction. As a child of the defeated South, he inherited traditionalism and a distrust of liberalism as well as of corrupt Republican politicians; from the Calvinism of his home there came perhaps, as well as a lifelong sense of duty, a certain intolerance that led him to resent criticism and ultimately to base his judgments on what Robert Lansing called "a matter of conviction formed without weighing evidence and without going through the process of rational deduction". English literature and history left their mark on his mind primarily by strengthening its bias in favour of tradition; Wilson was an Anglophile and it is customary for Englishmen to think of him and of his career in terms of British liberalism, but this is a comparison which is only justified if one remembers that he shared some of the liberal prejudices as well as the liberal virtues. No great figure of the twentieth century, for example, has believed more violently and more narrowly in the middle class; he disapproved strongly of the Populists; he was against the labour unions. A university teacher at Princeton, he was open to the charge so often levelled against academics, namely that he habitually thought in terms of abstractions rather than of human beings; and there is evidence that in his public life he was more often guilty of this than most academics.

From this unpromising background there ultimately emerged a radicalism which in its chosen field was almost as intense as Gladstone's and even more autocratic, though nothing like so various in its ends. There were in fact some elements in Wilson's southern inheritance which pointed to liberalism; the most interesting of these was his devotion to free trade. Moreover it was difficult for an able and ambitious young man in the Democratic Party in the nineties not to be a reformer; and Wilson was very able and very ambitious. He had in him that elusive mixture of high moral purpose and power to respond to change without which no politician can attain real distinction in a modern democratic state. And so, though for long he went no further than *laisser faire* liberalism and was deeply distrustful of much of the Progressive Movement, he underwent a slow process of conversion, swinging gradually to the left as he climbed the ladder of political success. The reforming President of Princeton University fell because he challenged the established clubs in the name of a greater democracy—and became instead, by grace of the local boss, the reforming Governor of New Jersey, where he ruled without reference to the boss. His successes as a moderate reformer in New Jersey—which included school reform, workmen's compensation, and electoral reform—made him eminently available as a Democratic presidential candidate at a time when the more forward-looking elements in the party were in control. At the Baltimore Convention of 1912, Bryan—still, despite his three defeats and his obvious weaknesses, the mightiest figure on the radical side in the party—came out in favour of Wilson: but his assistance counted for little. It was the support of the machine politicians that eventually carried Wilson's candidature—a phenomenon which was in itself a notable tribute to the state of the nation in 1912.

The presidential election of 1912 was in effect a contest between rival versions of reform politics. Two years earlier the mid-term elections had made it plain that the progressive elements in the Republican ranks, especially in the West, were no longer satisfied with the leadership of President Taft, and they returned to the leadership of Theodore Roosevelt. The Republican Convention split; the conservatives stood by Taft and renominated him, while the progressives walked out and formed a new party which in revivalist mood nominated "T. R.". There followed a strange contest in which from the start Taft had no real chance, and in which Wilson, not Roosevelt, was the middle-of-the-road man. Roosevelt campaigned for a programme which he called "The New Nationalism" and which seems to have been based largely on a single book, Herbert Croly's *Promise of American Life*. It was an adventurous and important programme—and was one day to become Wilson's. "The New Nationalism" was a bold reversal of American tradition: for it asked that the people of the United States should abandon their hostility to a powerful central government. They should acknowledge that great industrial groups had come to stay—and put them firmly under federal regulation. At the same time the Federal Government should be called on to undertake a wide range of social reforms, such as the prohibition of child labour, social insurance, workmen's compensation, and a minimum wage for women workers. "T. R." had put himself at the head of the progressive forces; yet he was as much and as little the Radical as Disraeli had been in 1867, and his reward was the same as Disraeli's. Wilson for his part fell back on the tried recipe of American radicalism, a policy of *laisser faire* in which the role of the Federal Government would be strictly limited to the removal of all barriers to free competition—a policy to which he gave the name "The New Freedom". The statement of this policy owed much to the great liberal lawyer Louis D. Brandeis. Economic well-being must be founded upon competition—but free competition, not the "illicit competition" embodied in the trusts. Far from government taking additional powers to regulate the trusts, what was needed was the complete separation of government from business; only thereby could business—particularly the business of the small man—be set free from monopoly and privilege. Laws must be passed which would reopen the way to free competition. This was old-fashioned; it was also obscure (Wilson once said "I am for big business, and I am against the trusts"); but it pointed the way to that freedom of economic action which was at the heart of Jeffersonianism and of traditional American radicalism. To Wilson this meant political freedom too. He condemned Roosevelt's social proposals as unwanted paternalism, and his economic policy an leading to slavery.

The result of this election was both illuminating and ambiguous. In the popular vote Wilson polled over 6 millions, Roosevelt over 4 millions, Taft nearly 3,500,000; it was thus a clear triumph for progressive ideas—even Eugene Debs, the Socialist candidate, got nearly 900,000. Yet Wilson was a minority President, with only some 42% of the total vote; in fact fewer Americans voted for Wilson in 1912 than for Bryan on each of the three occasions (1896, 1900, and 1908) when he had been the Democratic candidate, and his proportion of the popular vote was lower than that of any winning candidate since John Quincy Adams in 1824—with the solitary exception of Lincoln in 1860. He had won basically because of the Republican split, and secondly because not enough voters of a progressive turn of mind trusted Roosevelt. What was not clear was which particular version of progressivism the American people wished to see in action. In fact they were to get both—first "The New Freedom" and then "The New Nationalism", under the compulsive pressures of environment and another election. In this process a further interpretation of radicalism was to emerge which would point the way to Franklin D. Roosevelt and the "New Deal".

For most of Wilson's first term, the most striking features of his policy were his steadfast devotion to *laisser faire* liberalism in economic matters, and his opposition to progressivism in social ones. Like a good traditional southern Democrat, he carried a notable downward reduction of the tariff by the Underwood Act. Like a good Jacksonian, he took banking and currency in hand, setting up—in defiance of bankers' opinions—the Federal Reserve System, described by Arthur S. Link as "the greatest single piece of constructive legislation of the Wilson era". And like a good twentieth-century reformer, he set out to tackle the great problem of the trusts on the lines of "The New Freedom", by the introduction of the Clayton bills condemning certain trade practices as unfair and banning interlocking directorates. These were all measures well within the bounds of the existing economic order; their beneficiaries were intended to be, and no doubt largely were, the traditional small men of American society. There was no suggestion of legislation designed to enable the Federal Government to assist the great and growing multitude of wage-earners—the major social need of the first half of the twentieth century. And the record of the first three years of Wilson's first term suggests that Wilson himself wanted to go no further. It is understandable that an administration as subject to southern pressures as Wilson's (the first Democratic presidency for sixteen years) should be at first illiberal on the colour question, and—until halted by public protest—extend segregation in government departments, and allow the down-grading of Negroes in government offices in the southern states. But on a whole range of other issues Wilson showed himself at best reluctant to make social reform government policy; and this was an attitude more serious than ever before, for no previous administration had so firmly set out to organise a legislative programme and steer it through Congress, and no previous President had enjoyed such authority over Congress. Thus he declined to lend government support to a programme of farm credits, to a federal child-labour law, to women's suffrage; and he showed something of his old antipathy to labour unions on the complex problem of their relationship to anti-trust laws. In a public letter of November 1914 he went so far as to give the impression that "The New Freedom" had achieved its purpose, and that the days of reform were over.

Not until 1916 did another step forward, and this a vital change in government policy, come; significantly, it was an election year, and it seems clear that Brandeis and other progressives in the Democratic Party were responsible for driving Wilson on. A second programme of legislation—or, more properly, the social legislation complementary to the economic measures already enacted—followed. Farm credits, workmen's compensation, a federal child-labour law went through Congress in 1916; Wilson came out on the side of labour in a railroad strike, and approved the Adamson Act establishing an eight-hour day; the administration set up a tariff commission, and yielded to an old demand for anti-dumping laws. Such measures belonged more to "The New Nationalism" than to "The New Freedom", and they, rather than the earlier economic steps, were the beginnings of the new radicalism of the twentieth century, a radicalism whose emphasis was social and whose method was more government intervention, not less. Meanwhile they helped Wilson to win the election of 1916; there is no doubt that, in conjunction with the peace issue, they brought him enough progressive support to enable him to scrape home in a very close-run contest. Yet there was a traditional flavour about the way the American people voted in 1916. For it was very largely the old radical alliance of West and South that backed Wilson; the Republican candidate Charles Evans Hughes carried nearly all the East, despite the considerable amount of trade union support that went to his opponent.

The narrow verdict of 1916 was to be the last national victory of radicalism until the great depression of the 1930's swept Franklin Roosevelt into power in circumstances that made a radical policy inevitable. Like the events of Andrew Jackson's day, the developments of Wilson's presidency demonstrate that radicalism in the American tradition cannot be understood if it is looked on merely as the continuing political activity of a "ginger" group; but that it is rather the periodic upsurge of democracy, a necessary release of spirit in the body politic, a national rather than a class or a party phenomenon. There is no American radical "type"; American radicalism may select as its leader a slave-owning duellist, an opponent of evolution, a college principal—or an aristocrat from up-state New York. It reflects a political spectrum from which the extremer colours are excluded; and it functions within a political framework where the room to manoeuvre is less than that of Britain, or of the democracies of western Europe. In theory, all Americans are born radicals: in practice, the evidence of the years 1814 to 1917 suggests that a surprisingly large number of them are radicals—at irregular intervals. In such circumstances, it is scarcely surprising that American radicalism has been traditional and conservative; finding its inspiration in the grass roots and its economic justification in private property; ceaselessly opposing monopoly and privilege—and government as the supreme example and source of monopoly and privilege. "We have made up our minds to square every process of our national life again with the standards we so proudly set up at our beginning and have always carried in our hearts. Our work is a work of restoration." Wilson's words in his First Inaugural Address fitly summarize its aim, its spirit, and its methods.

AMERICA, HALF BROTHER OF THE WORLD

By Alan Conway

★

FEW present day immigrants and travellers who arrive in the United States by way of New York fail to look across the water to where the vividly green Statue of Liberty lifts her lamp beside the golden door. The sightless eyes are seemingly averted from the inscription on the base by Emma Lazarus, and the huddled masses, the homeless wretched refuse of the world's teeming shores are no longer so welcome as once they were. Since the 1920's the drawbridge has been raised, the portcullis lowered and none but the selected few may enter through the postern guarded by immigration officials; the concept of "fortress America" has thereby been extended to the question of uncontrolled immigration. The damming up of the flow of people from the old world to the new marks the virtual end of three centuries of immigration, and the quietness on the western front is in startling contrast to the hurly-burly of the previous century when between 30 and 40 millions of immigrants from every country in Europe and from parts of Asia flooded into the United States, creating a new America by their efforts and a host of new problems by their presence. Once immigration ceased, the "melting pot" was able to attempt the task of assimilating those races from Southern and Eastern Europe most alien to the accepted concept of the standard American.

Franklin Roosevelt, a direct descendant of the early Dutch patroons, is reported to have had the temerity to address the Daughters of the American Revolution as "fellow immigrants"; he was thereby assailing the concept of some older stocks that "immigrant" was something of a dirty word and also underlining the fact, deliberately ignored by many, that all Americans, with the exception of the Indians, were either immigrants or the descendants of immigrants, the heirs of those who fled from oppression or of those who aspired to the new world El Dorado or an American utopia. Immigration spread over three centuries had been responsible for the building of the United States from the bed rock of the wilderness to the modernity of the city skyscraper. The major question for the student of immigration is, what were the factors that induced millions of Europeans to move from one side of the Atlantic to the other?

Of these factors four predominate, personal, religious, political and economic. The first of these, the personal, is largely intangible in that every emigrant had his or her own reason for emigrating; ambition, fear, despair and disillusionment being but a few of the emotions involved in departure. Emigrant letters, the closest contact which the historian has with the emigrants, reveal all these in full measure—and in some cases the failure of the new country to fulfil ambitions or to dispel despair and disillusionment. Most of these letters show, however, that their writers were more than satisfied, by the very sincerity with which they urged their relatives and friends to join them in America and to share their good fortune. Typical of such sentiments is the following extract from a letter written by two Welsh brothers to their parents, from Racine, Wisconsin Territory, late in 1846:

We like this new country very much and we are keeping in excellent health, living like gentlemen with some new and strange delicacy every day. This is a good country for young lads if they are keen to work, especially for tailors, shoemakers, carpenters and farmers . . . It would be better for you by far together with our relatives and friends and anyone else who wants to get on in the world to come to America.

The religious factors in emigration tend to loom larger, with the Puritans occupying the centre of the canvas and partially obscuring the movements of Catholics, Jews and others who in their own lands found themselves subject to pains and penalties for their beliefs and who hoped that in the new world lay an earthly Kingdom of Heaven where conformity with the state religion was not the *sine qua non* of existence. The strength of the religious exodus was spent, however, as the countries of Europe became more tolerant of religious nonconformity. The one exception was the Jew, seemingly destined until the establishment of Israel to be the eternal wanderer, an object of suspicion because of the international nature of Judaism in a world of increasingly self-conscious nation states. The United States, although not free from anti-semitism itself, has undoubtedly been one of the greatest beneficiaries of the expulsion of talented Jews from Europe.

The political factors, which early entwined themselves with the religious ones, have been more constant historically, whether the refugees fled from the Stuarts, from the Cromwellians, from the upheavals of 1848, from the racist purity of the Nazi régime or from the monolithic orthodoxy of Communism. Many political refugees saw themselves not as permanent emigrants from the countries of their birth but only as temporary exiles until such time as the situation at home should change and enable them to return, but for many such change did not take place and temporary exile became permanent residence, to the benefit and sometimes to the dismay of the United States.

Historical research has revealed that it was the economic forces behind emigration which had the greatest effect for the greatest length of time upon the greatest number of immigrants. It was not only the economic motives of individuals seeking better wages or a higher standard of living; it was also the overall effect, unrealized at the time by the emigrants themselves or by the economists, of the trade cycle, of slumps and booms and of their interaction on both sides of the Atlantic, exerting their pressures upon the emigrants and demonstrating the unity of the Atlantic community.

The original settlements in North America, with the exception of Plymouth Plantation, Pennsylvania, and Maryland, were primarily economic in intent. Indeed, had America produced the same type of wealth as did the lands belonging to Spain it is probable that trading posts rather than settlements *per se* would have been favoured: but it was found that the wealth of the country must come from the land itself, from crops and pelts rather than from precious metals. This economic emphasis continued for the next three centuries: it was at no time exclusive but, as the industrialization of the United States and the European countries progressed in the nineteenth and twentieth centuries, it became of necessity even more marked.

Before 1815 the colonies, and then the states, remained predominantly British in composition and orientation despite the large numbers of Dutch, French, Germans and Scandinavians who migrated to them. By the end of the War of Independence the population of the country was in the region of three and a half million whites and half a million slaves; how much of this total was the result of natural increase and how much the result of immigration is difficult to determine with any precision. The success of the colonists in breaking away from Great Britain captured the imagination of Europeans and boosted the reputation of the United States as a political and religious asylum. Such was the interest aroused in America amongst potential settlers that Franklin in Paris found himself deluged with requests for information about the country and with schemes for the emigration *en masse* of whole communities. To meet this demand for information he had a pamphlet printed (in English, French and subsequently German) entitled *Information to Those who Would Remove to America*. In this he pointed out that America was a land of hard work and not what the English called "Lubberland" and the French "Pays de Cocagne". Franklin can be claimed therefore as an early, though very cautionary, emigrant agent. Hardly had the immigrant traffic between Europe and America restarted after the War of Independence than Europe entered upon the long struggle with France and Napoleon, and the war at sea and the blockade drastically reduced the opportunities for large-scale emigration. This situation was not improved by the deterioration in the relations between Great Britain and the United States which by way of the British blockade and the American Embargo and Non-Intercourse acts disrupted shipping and culminated in the War of 1812. It was thus 1815 before emigration could again begin, and the numbers arriving in the immediate post-war years were not such as to cause any uneasiness that America would be unable to cope with the new arrivals.

Post-1815 statistical information, although much more plentiful than before that date, is far from satisfactory and it is not until comparatively recent years that real reliance can be placed upon the figures. Particularly is this so at times of heavy immigration when the numbers entering the ports of the United States were such that it was quite beyond the ability of a few officials to check carefully names, nationalities, occupations and so on. Indeed there is one example on record of the same immigration figures being returned for two different quarters and the numbers being incorporated without question into the Federal statistics. Nevertheless, from the figures available, a clear if not decimally precise picture is obtainable. Emigration from Europe to the United States between 1815 and the 1920's is far from being simply a steady rise in numbers culminating in a peak just before immigration restriction went into practice. Instead the statistics reveal that, although there was an overall increase, the period was marked by peaks and troughs of entry occasioned by the political and, more important, by the economic situations in the United States and in the countries of origin. In this respect, one of the most valuable of recent works on the subject is that of Brinley Thomas, *Migration and Economic Growth,* which shows quite convincingly that, although the minor motives for emigration cannot be dismissed lightly, by far the greatest factor in emigration was the transfer across the Atlantic not only of population but of the labour and capital that went with it, which strongly affected the economic situations in all the countries concerned. Before the Civil War, about five million immigrants entered the United States, mostly between 1847 and 1857 when both the Irish and the Germans were prominent. Between 1860 and 1930 over thirty million immigrants came into the country; the peaks occurred between 1880 and 1890 and between 1900 and 1920 and were occasioned by the numbers coming from Southern and Eastern Europe, although until the end of the century the older emigrating nations continued to send substantial contingents. Outbreaks of war have tended to restrict immigration but the flow has never wholly ceased. It may be worth noting that between 1932 and 1935 a not inconsiderable reverse movement took place from America to Europe, the excess of departing emigrant aliens over immigrants being not far short of 140,000. Whether this reversal is of any real significance is open to question; it does not necessarily stem from the same causes which brought many back from the United States in the nineteenth century disillusioned and disappointed.

Though the overall economic influence upon emigration must not be forgotten, the statistics, the graphs and the diagrams are but part of the story; the human elements of fear, ambition, hope and endurance provide depth and substance to the greatest movement of population in modern history. The mere titles of three well known books have the flavour of an epic—Carl Wittke's *We who built America, the Saga of the Immigrant,* Oscar Handlin's *The Uprooted* and Theodore Blegen's *The Land Lies*

R

Open. The most immediate question that requires an answer is why did the United States attract the bulk of European emigrants. It is impossible to draw a line between the attraction of the United States and the repellent force in the European countries, for they were interlocking and interacting. The more difficult and depressed the conditions at home the more attractive seemed the opportunities in America. Apart from those individuals who emigrated for the sheer love of change and adventure, the majority of emigrants were by nature conservative. It was not easy to pull up long established roots, to cut oneself off from relations and friends, to give up one's own land (however meagre its extent) for any number of possible acres in a foreign country across three thousand miles of ocean, often with little capital to cushion the first days of adjustment to strange conditions. Particularly was this the case with emigrants from rural areas many of whom could never have seen any larger body of water than the nearest lake or tarn. But all over Europe the pressure of population upon the land was being felt as the result of a higher birth rate and a lower death rate. Holdings in land were found to be less and less adequate to maintain larger families and the need arose for some members of these families to migrate either to urban industrial areas or overseas. This process can be seen in Britain more forcibly than in Europe, where industrialization was slower to get into its stride, with the result that the pressure upon the land received less relief from internal migration. In Britain this relief was in itself impermanent; industrial slumps meant lower wages and, more often than not, dismissals, an inability to return to the land and the possibility of semi-starvation until recovery took place. The urban worker could thus find himself in a more precarious position than his rural counterpart, whose proximity to the land could at least make starvation a more remote possibility, with the tragic exception of Ireland and those countries too dependent upon the potato. For some, the answer to these economic problems was political agitation for industrial and agrarian reform; for others it was emigration. Yet the cost of passage to America could be the equivalent of six weeks' wages for one person so that the man with a large family found himself in a difficult position. As the would-be emigrant accepted as inevitable the good and the bad times, so too he recognized the necessity for emigrating at the end of the good times or alternatively of putting sufficient aside to secure passage when depression set in, although many families were not above the "moonlight flit" with tradesmen left holding promises to pay instead of hard cash.

In good times and bad, the letters of those who had already taken the plunge arrived from America overflowing with encouragement, advice and warnings. In many villages they virtually became public property, their contents being debated in communal readings. The advantages of America, such as freedom of religion, no conscription, cheap land in abundance, high wages, no hereditary overlords, every man free to seize the equal opportunities for all, and freedom from onerous taxation were weighed against the difficulties of the crossing, the strange customs of the new land, the high cost of living, the survival of the fittest, the loneliness of those who lived on the edge of civilization, the rigours of the climate and the danger from the Indians. The optimism and enthusiasm for America of those who had been successful was countered by the nostalgia for the familiar scenes in the old country of those who had failed. More powerful even than letters was the visual proof of prosperity contained in passage money or tickets to the United States from father, husband, brother or relative, while a personal return by a former emigrant could influence a whole district. A striking example is the impact which Mormon missionaries had upon emigration from Great Britain, Germany and the Scandinavian countries, especially between 1845 and 1875, which raises the interesting question whether the Mormon faith or the personal contacts with former emigrants had the stronger influence upon those whom they took to America.

Throughout the nineteenth century, to satisfy the demand for information about the United States, a spate of emigrant guide books was produced and eagerly perused, the advantages of Illinois balanced against those of California or those of Texas against both. Many of the guides were completely unreliable especially when sponsored by those with personal interests in the development of particular states, but on the whole they proved valuable in familiarizing Europeans with the mechanics of transporting themselves to America. The tradition was also established and continued to the present day, by which every traveller in America, even though his stay was brief and his journeyings limited, committed his experiences to print together with advice and warnings. It is not surprising therefore, that the United States was probably better known to Europeans than much of their own countries and certainly better known than the rest of Europe. Lest the personal letter and the traveller's guide cum emigrant's handbook prove insufficient, the state governments themselves entered into the market for settlers and after the Civil War the railroads spread their web of agencies throughout Europe in search of emigrants who would make of their land holdings the big bonanza. Much of the information purveyed was false or misleading but none the less effective for its purpose, and the railroads could justly claim that they were colonizing agents in their own right.

The proponents of emigration who maintained that the draining off of surplus labour would increase the wages and strengthen the bargaining powers of those left behind did not have the field to themselves. Their opponents, conscious of the industrial and military value of manpower in the nation state, could argue with some conviction that the export of people to the United States was the export of a valuable commodity which enriched a country rapidly challenging the industrial supremacy of Europe. Particularly was this so with the opponents of emigration in

Great Britain who found it difficult to understand why so many emigrants preferred to go to the United States rather than to Australia, New Zealand or Canada where emigration would be a transfer rather than a loss of strength. The advantages of Empire settlement were widely advertised by the British government, by the colonial agencies and by private bodies; subsidized passages were offered and imperial preference advocates were not lacking to point to those who returned empty-handed from the United States. Whilst the "Empire first" advocates met with some success, the main stream continued to flow to the United States. Apart from the psychological attraction of America, this was primarily due to the fact that the distance across the Atlantic was much shorter than than to Australia and New Zealand, where land and agricultural conditions were not so attractive as in America and where the peculiar skills of an industrialising society were not so sought after and did not have the same cash value as in the United States. The distance drawback of Australia and New Zealand did not apply to Canada; but once in Canada there was always a strong movement southwards into the United States. It is worth noting here that this was not a one-way traffic and although the statistics of much emigration to the United States lie embalmed in the figures of Canadian emigration, the reverse is also true on account of the quite considerable mingling of the Canadian and American peoples. It is not, however, until the beginning of the twentieth century that emigration from Great Britain to the Dominions exceeded that to the United States, a fact which may well reflect the belief that the day was gone when America was ideally suited for the absorption of British emigrants. The advantages of Crown protection were of little moment to the European nations and although some Europeans were attracted to other parts of the world, as for example the Germans who went to Brazil, the United States remained the greatest magnet for European settlers. The same applied to the Irish who viewed the prospect of continued subordination to Westminster with little enthusiasm, particularly those who had suffered eviction at the hands of English landlords. They left Britain with a strong sense of injustice and formed in the United States an "Ireland of retribution" where the bitter fruit of anti-British feeling was nurtured in several of the states of the Union.

Above and beyond all other reasons for the predominance of the United States as an immigrant country was the close commercial bond linking her to Europe and especially to Great Britain, particularly in the early days of emigration when the emigrant was so much paying ballast and before the emigrant trade became a business in itself. Commerce spanned the world but the volume of traffic between America and Europe together with the shorter run meant that there were more vessels available with a faster turn round than to other parts of the world. Although Hamburg, Bremen and Le Havre were no mean ports, the giant of the transatlantic trade was Liverpool, with shipping links to all the major ports of the United States.

Before the application of steam to ocean shipping, which cut both time and cost of transportation, the sailing ship with its erratic times of departure and lengthy duration of voyage had to suffice, and the early emigrants found themselves called upon to endure the hardships of a nineteenth-century "middle passage", not chained together as the Negro slaves had been but oftentimes at the mercy of unscrupulous captains who could charge high prices for food, water and medicine should the voyage prove longer than anticipated or should illness strike down the emigrant. The latter was wedded closely to the established lines of commerce, whether he bedded down among the slates exported from North Wales or made his way from Germany to Le Havre to pick up the cotton boats returning to America with the finished goods of Europe or waited on the quays at Bremen for the tobacco boats. But as the century progressed the number of emigrants descending upon the ports of departure was such as to justify their being considered as a cargo in themselves, and at times of heavy pressure it was a constant temptation to owners and captains alike to squeeze the quart of emigrants into the pint pot of their ships. Regulation by fines and inspection on the part of both European and American governments lessened this practice somewhat but the profits to be made from the trade induced many ships to take the chance of heaving to off an Irish port and taking aboard excess numbers to find what room they could. Many owners and captains were caught out but the high returns from the emigrant traffic made this peculiar form of smuggling well worth the risk. To the advantage of the emigrant, high profits also brought keen competition, and the cost of passage was slashed to as little as £3 10s. or £4 to the United States and sometimes as low as £2 10s. to Canada.

With the development of the traffic came the rise of a new occupation, that of the "runner" who early began to plague the great ports. At a price, he was prepared to find the emigrant and his family temporary accommodation at the port, excellent passage to America if not already booked, provisions for the voyage together with equipment like tin mugs, pots and pans, and tickets inland from the American port of arrival. These prototypes of the confidence man worked by arrangement with lodging-house keepers and provision merchants to the mutual benefit of all except the emigrant. Despite the warnings contained in emigrant manuals and letters from America, many an emigrant found the attentions of the "runner" much too pressing to be refused, especially should the difficulty of a foreign language be encountered, for this could turn bewilderment into panic. More often than not the emigrant was swindled over his accommodation, his provisions were bought at excessively high prices and his passage ticket might be found to be worthless. On arrival in America, the steamboat or railroad tickets that had been carefully guarded during the voyage might also be found to be spurious or valid only for a distance far short of that desired. Many of the reputable emigration agencies tried to overcome the unsavoury reputation created by their shady brethren by establishing sub-agents in emigrating localities who would sell passenger tickets for specific vessels with a good name and sometimes with a guarantee of a rebate in cash for every day beyond the published date of sailing that the vessel was held up. Boarding-house keepers emphasized the national character of their establishments and the advantages which could be gained by staying with a person of one's own race and language, foremost among which was the personal supervision of embarkation.

The spheres over which the operations of the great ports extended were considerable. Liverpool drew upon the feeder lines of coastal shipping to bring emigrants from Ireland and the coastal regions of Great Britain, upon the railways to bring emigrants from all over the country, and upon the Hamburg-Hull route to tap the German market. Le Havre likewise drew upon Germans from Alsace, and Bremen and Hamburg reached deeper into the heart of Europe. The attempt in 1854 of a certain M. Vanderest to raise Dunkerque to the same status as Le Havre, likewise based on the importation of cotton and the export of emigrants, failed in face of the tight grip which the larger ports kept upon the trade routes.

Once aboard ship the difficulties of the emigrants really began, in a situation completely different from anything they had previously experienced. The great majority, who could only afford to travel in the steerage, found themselves with hundreds of others in search of the best place to sleep below decks. Nothing better than racks might be provided, with little headroom between each and the most room available, when lying down, to the emigrant with the broadest shoulders. Dark and ill-smelling from the lime, burnt pitch or vinegar of primitive disinfection and with the crudest of sanitary facilities, the steerage deck was far from ideal for a lengthy voyage. Privacy was non-existent except on the better run vessels where the problem of the segregation of the sexes was solved by keeping the single women forward and the single men aft, separated by married emigrants with their families. Despite such precautions immorality was prevalent aboard emigrant ships, single women receiving unwanted attentions from fellow emigrants and the crew. Communal kitchens were set up on deck which acted as focal points for gossip and often for arguments and fights. When the weather deteriorated some captains simply battened down the hatches leaving the immigrants to endure as best they could the miseries of sea-sickness, foul air, semi-darkness and the fears of drowning. Others of a more humane nature allowed the immigrants on deck in relays providing that the handling of the ship was not hampered. In addition to the hazards of the journey, fire was a constant danger and should this be avoided conditions were such as to provide excellent opportunities for the outbreak of ship fever. The various nationalities aboard tended to form exclusive groups, regarding the strange habits and customs of their fellow passengers with suspicion if not hostility. During fine weather the edge of race consciousness was blunted, but under the stress of bad weather and food and water shortages personal and racial animosities would flare up into savage brawls. To a limited degree each ship carried in embryo the racial pattern which was to reproduce itself in a hundred cities and towns of the United States. In fairness to those who brought the great bulk of the emigrants safe, if weak and unhealthy, to land, it must be said that the life was hard for the crews and that harsh discipline was essential with such difficult cargo if the ship was to reach port. Much space is devoted in emigrant letters to complaints about conditions aboard ship and the conduct of the captains and crews. The better ships were therefore at pains to publish in the press of the various countries testimonials as to courtesy and good treatment signed by satisfied passengers, with the names of ministers given prominence. Humanitarians on both sides of the Atlantic brought pressure to bear on their governments for the better regulation of the emigrant trade with the result that legislation was passed stipulating the ratio of passengers to tonnage, the amount of food and water which should be issued to the passengers daily and the carrying of a surgeon on all vessels above a certain tonnage. These regulations did secure some improvement in the trade but breaches of them continued, and the real improvements owed much more to the shorter duration of the voyage by steamship than to government attempts at supervision.

The arrival in America, whether at New York, Philadelphia, Boston, New Orleans or the smaller ports, undoubtedly brought relief from the monotony of the ocean passage; but for some it brought swift disillusionment. The fortunate ones were met by relatives or friends who could help the non-English-speaking immigrants over the initial difficulties; for those who were not so well blessed there were the American counterparts of the European "runners" eager to fix up accommodation and transportation into the interior provided that the immigrant had a little money left from the voyage. The wary made their way to recommended lodging houses run by people of their own nationality and made haste to leave the seaports for their final destination before their funds were exhausted. The friendless and those without money to attract the "runners" found what accommodation they could and hoped to secure employment of some sort which would tide them over until such time as they had saved sufficient to resume their journey. For the sick and the completely destitute, charitable organizations and national societies, run and supported by established Germans, Irish, English, Scots and the rest, provided food and clothing and if possible passage money inland. At the times when labour of any kind was in demand, the assistance provided by these societies was not unduly strained, but any glut on the labour market could swiftly exhaust their resources. They did much good work on a racial basis and afford evidence of the strength of national consciousness in America.

Those immigrants who landed at Southern ports gained a major advantage in the cheapness of transportation for themselves and their belongings into the interior by river steamboats which would take them 1500 miles and more up the Mississippi for about three dollars. To counterbalance this advantage, it was found by those unable to proceed immediately upstream that employment in a Negro-dominated economy was not often of the best. Under slavery the jobs open to white immigrants were dangerous and unhealthy, the Southern employer preferring to gain a week's unclaimed wages rather than to lose a valuable slave should a fatal accident occur. To this must be added the dangers of yellow fever and cholera, all too prevalent in the Southern states before the Civil War, when "Bronze John" took a heavy toll of unacclimatized immigrants living in poor conditions. This is not to suggest that immigrants shunned the Southern states; Ella Lonn's *Foreigners in the Confederacy* reveals strong contingents of foreign born fighting for the South. Yet the majority of immigrants favoured the free economy of the North especially when cheap railroad transportation offset the advantages formerly held by the steamboats.

The immigrants who had had their passages inland paid for or who had sufficient capital left to pay their own, made their way westwards by river, canal, railroad and stage, not to the frontier itself, but to those regions behind the frontier which needed settlers to consolidate the gains made by the pioneer farmers. Their traditional skills and methods ill fitted them for the life of the true frontiersman, which remained essentially the province of the native-born American, but on the penultimate frontier they were able to serve an apprenticeship in American ways by working for others until such time as capital and experience were sufficient to warrant them taking up land for themselves. The natural tendency of the newly arrived immigrant was to go, if possible, to those regions where his countrymen preserved, if but temporarily, the customs and language of the old country, where his stumbling efforts to speak English would be overlooked, where refuge could be taken in native tongue or dialect and where he could draw upon racial credit to get established. Outstanding examples of this concentration of racial groups are those of the Scandinavians in Minnesota and the Dakotas and of the Germans in Wisconsin and Missouri. Attempts to found small national states within the states foundered on the Federal Government's refusal to set aside specific areas for the creation of racial *imperia in imperio* and upon the inability of the settlers themselves to remain apart from the general development about them. No race could be an island to itself as was instanced by the failure of the Giessener Gesellschaft of 1833 in the

Mississippi Valley, of the Adelsverein between 1843 and 1847 in Texas and of the Welsh in Tennessee in 1857. The misuse and disuse of the national languages marked the first breaches in racial self sufficiency. National dress was unsuitable and not easily replaceable in America and although the foreign language presses continued to print books and newspapers it was a losing struggle against Americanization. At all times the hot-iron of standardization was smoothing out the racial wrinkles, but slowly and by no means completely. Emigrants from the British Isles with the exception of the Irish found little need and had no burning desire violently to assert their national origins. Chameleon-like they blended into the American racial landscape, and closer investigation was necessary to distinguish them from native-born Americans because the language presented no difficulty and the openings for their talents were much more diverse, so that they rarely congregated in national communities or at set levels of society or occupation.

The pattern of immigration contributed to—but was influenced more by—the natural development of the United States. While the country remained predominantly agricultural and before agriculture reached the dimensions of an industry in its own right, the opportunities for the immigrants from the rural areas of Europe were quite considerable provided that they were prepared to adapt themselves to different conditions. But at the same time the growing towns and cities of the United States were attracting much skilled and unskilled labour from the industrial centres of Europe. Cotton operatives, miners, potters, iron moulders and the like were making for similar centres in the United States and as R. T. Berthoff has shown quite conclusively in his book, *British Immigrants in Industrial America*, immigration tended to follow closely along craft lines. The artisan had an advantage not only over unskilled labour but also over the agricultural immigrant, however skilled the latter might be. The agricultural skills of Europe had to be adapted to American conditions and even an independent farmer still needed both time and capital before a cash crop could be secured. In comparison, the craftsman in industry found his particular skills and knowledge in demand, his capital provided by his technical knowledge, and the cash for his work in his pay packet at the end of the first week of employment. The contribution which the skilled workman made to the development of the United States as an industrial power is too well known to need reiteration and several European governments, particularly that of Great Britain, were well aware of this contribution and attempted in vain to prevent the emigration of their skilled craftsmen.

The main objection to the thesis of emigration along occupational lines is the example of the Irish in the earlier period. This essentially agrarian emigration made no attempt comparable to those of the Germans and the Scandinavians to take up agriculture, and congregated instead in the large cities like Boston, New York and Philadelphia. This reveals one added factor which must be taken into consideration; in addition to the effect which the prevailing economic situation in the United States had upon the immigrant, the economic situation of the individual emigrant before departure could have a strong predetermining influence on his settlement in the United States. Obviously those emigrants who left Europe with little or no capital were unable to move far into the agrarian regions, except possibly to the poorer parts of New England, which were declining in face of the competition from the Mississippi Valley; this was especially true since no previous substantial settlements of their country-men had been established there capable of easing the way for the new arrivals. Lacking in addition any marketable industrial skills and with brawn and muscle their major assets, the Irish in general found themselves forced into the ranks of the unskilled in the cities closest to their point of disembarkation. The main recourse for those who did make their way westwards was to wield pick and shovel on canals and railroads as members of construction gangs, and incidentally to enjoy the privilege of multiple voting en route. The majority, however, found employment in building the expanding cities, digging the drainage systems and—seemingly—making the police forces their especial preserve, all of these occupations serving to keep them within reach of their fellow Irishmen and their political leaders.

The last quarter of the nineteenth century in America was marked by a retreat from the land to the cities under the spur of agricultural depression and discontent, and also by the arrival of the "new immigration" from Southern and Eastern Europe on ships from Naples, Genoa, Palermo, Hamburg and Bremen. Many emigrants came from as far afield as the Volga and Asia Minor and cities like Cracow, Vienna, Prague and Bukharest became major collecting centres. It was a poorer, more un-skilled immigration than that of the older stocks, largely illiterate and thus not averse to heavy manual labour, which was needed to erect the concrete monuments to the progress of the United States. To counter-balance the disadvantages of lack of skill, mechanization and mass pro-duction had been instituted, replacing the craftsman's cunning of hand and eye with the automatic efficiency of the machine so that with a few weeks' training, unskilled or semi-skilled labour could turn out more, and not greatly inferior, products than skilled labour had previously been able to do after a long apprenticeship. This resulted in a movement of the skilled craftsman downwards into the ranks of the technically ignorant but mechanically capable, there to bewail the prostitution of his skill; or upwards to more responsible managerial positions, there to supervise the work of Hungarians, Poles, Italians and other new immigrant groups who were swiftly replacing the rank and file of the older stocks.

In order to meet the demand for housing from the new citizens, there grew up in the big cities the tenement type of dwelling. The first steps had been taken by the conversion of the large houses in the older parts of the cities, from which the more prosperous had moved out; they were turned into multiple dwellings by cheap partitioning. When these proved insufficient to deal with the numbers needing houses the true jerry-built tenement was erected. Sanitation was of the most primitive with a single outside privy serving many families. Cold and dank in winter and stifling hot in summer, they were potential funeral pyres at all seasons of the year. Before the so-called closing of the frontier in 1890, the West had provided a psychological if not an actual safety valve for the city dweller, but henceforward there was slight chance of escape from reality. Yet so long as it was possible for a very small minority to realize the classic story of "rags to riches", disillusionment was tempered by hope. Many of the immigrants of the later period were handicapped in their struggle to emerge from the lowest stratum of society, but their children were given the opportunity to realize some of the ambitions and hopes of the parents.

To improve somewhat the conditions of the immigrants, charitable organizations and social reformers once again came strongly to the forefront, the founding of the Hull House settlement in Chicago by Jane Addams being but one of many such enterprises in the large cities. It was the local political boss, however, an American *deus ex machina*, who probably did the most in a positive way for the immigrant, but only in return for his vote. He could secure jobs for the party faithful when employment was scarce, intervene for them in time of trouble with the police and see to it that at Christmas time they did not go cold or hungry. There thus evolved in the United States a form of fourteenth-century bastard feudalism, the local boss becoming the patron and paymaster of all those in his racial bailiwick, offering retainers to those prepared to give allegiance and championing the causes of those who were prepared, in return, to fight his political battles. This is not to suggest that the immigrants were more politically amoral than native Americans in like situations but that racial solidarity by the city block begat political solidarity. Immigrant groups might well have voted for one party or the other irrespective of local favours on the ground that one party at the national level had more to offer in its platform than the other, but if this could be combined with real and present benefits then so much the better. The earlier immigration, particularly that portion which made its way independently into rural areas, tended to be conservative and gave considerable support to the Republican party; but the later immigration found its destinies tied up more closely with the Democratic machines such as Tammany Hall and its counterparts in other large cities, a tradition which lasted, by Lubell's analysis, until 1948.

Poverty, bad housing conditions and rootlessness contributed considerably to the increase in crime, vice and lawlessness in American cities, which unfortunately became associated with immigrant groups. To this must be added the suspicion that the voting power of the new immigrants was being used to subvert the American political system. Every writer seemed to have his own particular racial *bête noire*: soap-box philosophers and ivory tower historians alike tended to develop their own interpretations of Darwinian biology in search of a sound basis for ethnic superiority. Yet xenophobia and ultra-Americanism was no hot-house plant of late nineteenth- or early twentieth-century America. One can see traces of it in the Alien Act of 1798 despite the fact that this piece of legislation was primarily a political manoeuvre. The Know-Nothing movement of the 1850's, although revealing flatulence rather than chronic racial indigestion of the body politic, emphasized a fundamental antipathy to the immigrant. The nineteenth century is studded with complaints from solid citizens about immigrants, sometimes on the ground that they placed a heavy burden upon the charity of individuals and the funds of the cities, sometimes on the ground that epidemics were brought in by them or bred in their sections of the city, sometimes in the belief that there was a conspiracy afoot to Catholicize America and sometimes from the fear that too many racial strains would mongrelize if not totally emasculate the American people. These protests increased in volume during the second half of the century although most of the states were in favour of the encouragement of immigration and maintained their own agents abroad for this purpose. The attempts of the seaboard states like New York, Pennsylvania and Massachusetts—which contended that they supported the immigrant dregs while other states took the cream—to impose a head tax on immigrants were ruled unconstitutional as interfering with the Federal Government's prerogative of the regulation of commerce. It was the growing strength of organized labour which was to have, however, a decisive influence in instilling fresh life into demands for a reappraisal of immigration policy. Much play was made with the assertion that the European nations were making use of the United States as a dumping ground for their paupers and criminals, but the focal point of working-class opposition was the use of European contract labour. This was but a part of the larger problem of immigrant labour which occupied such a vital position in the struggle against big business. One of the strongest weapons in the hands of the employers was the knowledge that, if faced with a strike, there was always a large pool of immigrants upon which they could draw, cheap labour which kept down the wages of native American workers. If the supplies of labour from Europe could be restricted, the position of American workmen would automatically improve with the decline in competition for employment. It was significant, however, that the initial attack came from a flank when in 1882 Congress passed an act which would exclude, for a period of ten years, any additions to the Chinese labourers who had flocked into California, first in response to the gold discoveries of 1848 and then in response to the demand for labour on the construction of the Central Pacific railroad. This move not only underlined the fear of competition from coolie labour but also the realization that the Chinese were obstinately determined to remain Chinese, square pegs resistant to the whittling process of assimilation. Their exclusion was made permanent in 1902 and was extended to the Japanese in 1907 by Roosevelt's "gentleman's agreement" with the Japanese government for the non-encouragement of their emigrant labourers. California moved into the arena with discriminatory legislation against Japanese owning real estate; but it was not until the Immigration Act of 1924 that oriental immigration came virtually to an end, with Japan and China being allocated a mere 100 places each under the quota system.

Having taken the first steps towards a new immigration policy, the United States had to decide more precisely whether to be simply selective, harshly restrictive or wholly exclusive in its approach. Beginning in 1882, a series of acts elaborated a policy of selection by an increase in the head tax on immigrants and the turning away of convicts, idiots, paupers, polygamists, prostitutes, anarchists, alcoholics and all those with inferiority complexes. This final basis for exclusion, despite its amusing aspect, was probably of considerable use when an immigrant proved to be generally undesirable but came under no specific bar. This selective policy, which may possibly have improved the general standard of immigration, did little to halt the mass flow of immigrants into the country and the legislators were forced to take up fresh positions behind their second bastion, that of restriction, which in alliance with selection would ensure that none but the best, and even those in smaller numbers, would be allowed to enter. The instrument chosen to weed out more immigrants was the literacy test, which was an ingenious device in that it affected most seriously the greater number of illiterates entering from Southern and Eastern Europe without providing grounds for international ill feeling such as happened with the Japanese. It could be truly pointed out that the test applied equally to all races and if any country felt that its nationals were being discriminated against on this score, the remedy was in the hands of the home government which could ensure that its people attained a higher standard of literacy before emigrating to the United States. Cleveland, Taft and Wilson (twice) vetoed such legislation but it was finally passed over the presidential veto in 1917. By its terms every immigrant over the age of sixteen had to be able to read a passage in English or some other language or dialect in order to gain admission. When it was discovered that still too many immigrants were entering the country it was an easy step to move on to strict exclusion by the so-called quota system. The Immigration Act of 1921 reduced to little more than 350,000 the total number of admissions in any one year; the more drastic act of 1924, basing its figures on two per cent of total nationality numbers resident in the United States in 1890, reduced admissions once again and slanted them more firmly towards immigrants from Northern and Western Europe; and finally by the National Origins

Act of 1929 the annual intake was stabilized at 150,000, with 1920 national origins as the basis of assessment. This secured for immigrants from Northern and Western Europe roughly four-fifths of all places available, the full number of which are rarely if ever taken up, whilst, if permissible, the places for Southern and Eastern Europeans would be mortgaged for several generations to come. The ultimate refinement was the McCarran Act of 1952 which further meshed the immigrant grills within an international political context.

The crucial years of the twentieth century for the immigrant were also the legislative expression of America's disappointment that the First World War had not brought into being some degree of international co-operation in Europe. The cherished tradition of non-entanglement in the affairs of Europe seemed to have been jettisoned to no avail. As a result many Americans sought for a "return to normalcy" and demanded the erection of immigration barriers lest the hordes assembling in war ravaged Europe should bring with them its problems to reproduce and multiply on American soil. In the attempt to retire once more within the safety of isolationism from the rest of the world, the need was felt for the strength of an American nation rather than that of a polyglot mixture of races with close emotional and political ties to Europe. The development of nationalism in the United States thus left little room for racial nonconformity and the quickest way to achieve this desired result was to stanch the flow of unassimilable aliens.

The end of the open door policy for immigrants brought to the surface a reality which many had for long suspected, namely the fact that the famous "melting pot" was proving far less efficient under heavy pressure than had been assumed. Before the Civil War and even until the 1880's a fair amount of success had been achieved. The main barriers to assimilation had been the tendency of many groups to cling together, whether in rural or urban areas but particularly in the latter, as the means whereby the strangeness of the customs and habits of the new world could be tempered by the retention of some of those of the old. This was to a degree a two-way process in that whilst much of the European was sloughed off in the face of ways of living already established in America, a deep impression was made upon those ways by the incorporation into the general mixture of newer immigrant words, ideas and culture. This prepared the way somewhat for the arrival of those immigrants furthest removed from the norm, but not sufficiently for the period from 1890 to 1920 to show any major advance towards uniformity. The operation of the "melting pot" was hampered by the number of new immigrants every year; and the halt that was called made assimilation a possibility in the next thirty years. This has given time for the native-born of immigrant stock to assert their influence. It has always been a notable phenomenon that the first generation of native-born Americans is more violently American than either the immigrant parents or their own children. As they grew up in the American environment there was a serious weakening in the biblical injunction to honour father and mother, because their parents in speech and habits were unconventional, their attempts to speak English stumbling and often ludicrous, and their ways those of the much despised old world. The revolt of this generation was thus violent yet pathetic. Their parents were of Europe, they themselves were neither European fish nor American fowl. Later generations, often removed from the racial conglomerations of the large cities, belonged much more fully to America.

Much attention has been given to the tragedy of the hyphenated German-American particularly in those years when Germany was the major enemy of the Allied powers. Suspicion was rank that their loyalty was not complete and that, despite all that the "melting pot" had been able to do, they remained more German than American. This suspected failure was not, however, limited to the Germans; had Poland or Italy or Ireland or England been in a similar position there can be little doubt but that the racial idiosyncrasies of each would have been subjected to the spotlight of public attention and the conclusion reached that the half-and-half American was a phenomenon not limited to the Americans of German descent. The hyphenation of racial groups is therefore the distance that has separated the "melting pot" from its goal of complete success. Since the 1920's the process has moved much more quickly but that it is by no means finished is amply demonstrated by the continued grouping together of nationalities in the large cities into Italian sections, Greek sections, Hungarian sections, Polish sections and so on, although in fairness it must be admitted that such grouping has declined, largely through inter-marriage and increased mobility in search of better-paid employment. A second point which substantiates the thesis of the shortcomings of the "melting pot" is that when the State Department is called upon for decisions in international matters, it cannot ignore the internal political implications of the anti-English sentiment of the Irish, the anti-German feeling of the Poles, the anti-Arab feeling of the Jewish people of all nationalities, or the peculiar racial antipathies of any major group. Moreover the importance of race is never neglected by the professional politicians and the result can be seen in many cases by the inclusion of Italians, Irish, Germans, Negroes or members of other dominant races in lists of candidates for office.

The history of the "melting pot" emerges, therefore, as one in which the racial composition of the United States has been constantly in flux. The movement away from the quasi-English model established by the earlier settlers had been considerable and the influx of Germans, Scandinavians and Irish in the first half of the nineteenth century put little strain upon the powers of the "melting pot" because substantial injections of their particular cultures had already been received; but with the arrival in droves of non-Nordic stocks the process of assimilation slowed down perceptibly and serious misgivings were felt by older stocks that it might come to a complete standstill if some respite could not be secured from the mounting number of immigrants. These fears eventually found expression in restriction, which could restore the balance between northern and southern Europeans and usher in the really dynamic period of the process during the last thirty years. Without restriction such a development would not have been possible; but it is tempting to speculate what riches the United States may have sacrificed for this achievement. It is even possible that the United States has sheathed its strongest weapon in its struggle with international Communism by preventing participation in the American system by those would-be immigrants from Europe who are most susceptible to Communist influence on account of their economic condition.

The debt which the United States owes to the immigrant is beyond computation. Apart from the contributions which have been made to the fine arts, to literature, to science, to medicine and to American culture generally, there remain those made in the currency of hard, unremitting toil in factory, mine, mill and steelworks, on the farms and in the cities, on the roads, canals and railroads which made the West accessible to the millions who consolidated the work of the pioneers and which made possible the nation's physical unity; in the unglamorous but essential work of an army of clerks, accountants, cobblers and seamstresses: the tinker, the tailor and the atom-bomb maker have all shared in the creation of a new civilization and penetrated into every aspect of the nation's life, or, as it has been put more succinctly by Philip James Bailey,

> America, thou half-brother of the world;
> With something good and bad of every land.

THE RISE OF AMERICAN LABOUR

By Henry Pelling

*

THE history of labour movements, in America and elsewhere, has all too often been at the mercy of dogmatic thinkers seeking to produce a universal theory suitable to their political preconceptions. For the Marxists it seems that a labour movement is never "mature" unless it has developed a full political and economic "class consciousness"; and the failure of the American workers to follow this pattern is ascribed to retarded development, with the implication that sooner or later they will catch up with the "more advanced" elements in Europe. Such interpretations have naturally produced strong reactions among American observers, and some of these, particularly the Wisconsin School of labour historians, have gone far in the opposite direction. Thus Professor Selig Perlman, writing his *Theory of the Labor Movement* in the nineteen-twenties, turned Lenin upside down by suggesting that the maturity of a labour movement came only with its emancipation from the political philosophies of the intellectuals, and its development of its own "home-grown" ideas based on working rules and "job consciousness" rather than "class consciousness".

For present purposes, a different and less theoretical approach may be suggested, based more upon the peculiar features of historical change in the United States than upon any universal characteristics of the behaviour of working men. Two main forces, it may be held, have shaped the environment of the American worker: on the one hand, the almost bound-less opportunities for economic advancement in a land full of resources, where the demand for labour was always greater than the supply; and on the other hand, the influx of immigrants from diverse cultural back-grounds in the Old World, often reducing but never eliminating the differential scarcity of American labour, and at the same time adding a heterogeneity of social outlook which erected fresh barriers of a non-economic character to the development of "class consciousness".

The high cost of labour in the United States has always vividly impressed itself on visitors from abroad. Mrs Trollope, living in the new West of the eighteen-twenties, was hard put to it to secure adequate domestic help, and described the social pretensions of the "lower classes" of American society with immense disdain. Tocqueville, generalizing from similar observations, regarded the scarcity of labour as an inevitable concomitant of democracy: "The high wages which they [*sc.* the workers] have already obtained make them every day less dependent on their masters; and as they grow more independent, they have greater facilities for obtaining a further increase of wages." Richard Cobden, visiting the Middle West just before the Civil War, found that "man instead of being a drug in the market is at a premium", and regarded this as "the chief claim of the valley of the Mississippi". Even in the growing industrial centres of New England and Pennsylvania, which were already attracting many immigrants from overseas, wages remained comparatively much higher than in Europe, although conditions of work may have been no better. And this was in spite of the virtually complete absence of effective pressure from trade unions. The Jacksonian period had seen the accomplishment of a social revolution—a revolution which gave the workers votes and enabled them to secure a high degree of equality of opportunity for their children through the system of public education. These advantages, together with the economic mobility afforded by the rapid development of new territories and new industries, account for the absence of any marked tendency to class solidarity among the American workers. In the words of Norman Ware, the historian of the two decades of labour history before the Civil War: "The labor movement in America finished the period 1840-60 as it had begun— practically in nothingness." And yet labour had a status in America incomparably higher than in Europe: and Lincoln was just about to tell Congress that "Labour is the superior of Capital, and deserves much the higher consideration".

It was this scarcity of labour, too, which laid the foundation for the future continuous progress of American industry, by obliging manufacturers to take every opportunity of installing new types of labour-saving machinery. As early as 1854 official British observers attending the New York Industrial Exhibition stressed the importance of the high price of labour, combined with the good education of the workers, in leading to the swift technical advance of American industry. Half a century later the British trade unionists visiting America on the Mosely Commission were amazed to find how favourably disposed towards new machinery both management and workers were: "Here lies the distinctive feature of American industry", said one of them, "the hankering after the latest machinery and best methods of working, which pervades American industrialism." After yet another half century the same type of remark was being made by members of the Anglo-American productivity teams.

Thus American industry acquired a dynamic which it never lost. This was of vital importance to the national economy, for the process of geographical expansion could not go on for ever, and the impetus that it gave was bound to end sooner or later. Frederick Jackson Turner, the greatest of American historians, feared that the closing of the frontier in the eighteen-nineties might end the great period of progress for his country: but he paid too little attention to the growing predominance of industry. In this sense, as Selig Perlman pointed out, "the opportunity of the West . . . never ceased"; the frontier continues to exist, although it is measured by the rise of productivity in manufacturing rather than by the westwards movement of the pioneer farmers.

But this is not to say that the continuity of American expansion could be taken for granted at all times: perhaps least of all at the time when Turner was writing, in the last quarter of the nineteenth century, a period of social discontent and revolt, of urban and rural distress, and, as Turner suggested, of an apparent slackening in "the expansive character of American life". For a time the flood of migrants from European lands seemed to have raised the supply of labour above the demand, so that unemployment and destitution appeared on a large scale, and gave some justification to Henry George's argument that the rich were getting richer and the poor poorer, thus bringing American society closer to the European pattern. (Significantly, it was Andrew Carnegie, the industrialist, who was foremost in the attempt to refute George's argument on this point.) At the same time, the character of immigration changed sharply, and now came to consist predominantly of unskilled workers from Eastern Europe and the Mediterranean, who on grounds of racial origin, religion and social background were less easily assimilable to the American pattern of life. From this time forward, the American labour force was to be even more lacking in social solidarity, for the native workers and earlier immigrants looked with little favour on the workers of the "new immigration", who supplied the bulk of the labour for the hard, dirty, unskilled and unremunerative jobs of the new mass production industries like steel and meatpacking.

These critical years of the later nineteenth century were decisive for the future pattern of the American labour movement. Two rival national bodies emerged, the Knights of Labor and the American Federation of Labor, based upon contrasting methods of organization. The Order of the Knights of Labor, which came into existence in 1869 as a secret society of a masonic character, evolved into a national union of workers of all trades, abandoning most of its secrecy, if not its elaborate ritual. Under the leadership of "Grand Master Workman" Terence V. Powderly, a Pennsylvania man of Catholic Irish extraction, it sought to comprehend and to organize in "Mixed Assemblies" workers of all skills and trades. Powderly was a strong believer in the arbitration of disputes, and nearly always opposed strike action, preferring some form of boycott if the exertion of pressure upon employers became necessary. In spite of this somewhat impractical leadership, the Knights expanded rapidly in the early eighteen-eighties to a maximum of some 700,000 members in 1887. Thereafter, however, the Order rapidly lost members, and it became clear that the attempt to unite workers by some general loyalty other than that of their particular skills and crafts was bound to fail in the American environment. The only permanently successful elements of the Knights were, in fact, craft unions such as the Window Glass Workers which, in defiance of consistency, had been incorporated in their entirety into the Order by special dispensation. By the late eighteen-eighties the American Federation of Labour, a federation of national craft unions under the Presidency of the cigarmaker Samuel Gompers, had replaced the Knights as the principal American labour organization.

Gompers, himself an immigrant from England but of Dutch-Jewish origin, has often been personally blamed for the shortcomings of trade unionism in the United States—for its conservatism and lack of flexibility, for its reluctance to form a political party of labour, and above all for its failure to "organize the unorganized", especially in the growing mass-production industries. Such criticism ignores the whole social environment of the American labour movement. In reality there was no alternative to Gompers's opportunism—except the disintegration of the Federation. Gompers realized that the only stable base for a labour movement was to be found in the collective agreement of the larger craft internationals. These were really "national" unions, assuming the more grandiose title for the sake of recruitment in Canada. Gompers was obliged to recognize the independent status of each of these bodies inside his Federation. Himself a man of broad human sympathies, he found it necessary to subordinate much of his idealism to the paramount aim of maintaining an orderly and as far as possible comprehensive association of the principal unions in the difficult conditions of his time. Thus, for example, while personally opposed to racial discrimination, he soon discovered in the case of the Railroad Brotherhoods that it was futile to try to force unions to omit discriminatory clauses from their constitutions. The only result of his efforts in this direction—at a time when racial discrimination in America was actually on the increase—was to cause several of the Brotherhoods to stay in independent isolation outside the Federation: a state of affairs which has persisted to the present day.

Gompers was, above all, the master of the possible, the Fabius Cunctator of American labour. As he pointed out during the Federation's great political debates of the eighteen-nineties, the decisive argument against attempting to form a political party of labour on the national scale was, quite simply, that local experiments in political intervention indicated clearly the unwillingness of union members to obey the bidding of their officials at the polls. The discipline of class which operates all too strongly in European society was rarely an important factor in American political motivation; and it was already difficult enough for Gompers to keep the bulk of the unions in some sort of association even in the purely economic sphere. Under his patient hand the Federation slowly achieved recognition and status in American society—a "labour aristocracy" admittedly, as its Marxist critics were especially fond of pointing out, but still a force which challenged the tenets of *laisser faire* capitalism and sought ultimately to comprehend the whole of American labour in its ranks. There were setbacks, such as the sorry defeat of the steel strike of 1901, which virtually ended unionism in that industry for a generation; there were prolonged legal struggles over boycotts and injunctions; occasionally, and especially in the untamed West, there were sudden outbursts of violence between employer and worker, which gave the impression of a bitter class warfare. But there was also a growing recognition among political and industrial leaders that the Federation at least had come to stay, and that it was better to negotiate with it than to try to fight it down. Gompers worked with the great industrialist Senator Mark Hanna in an organization called the National Civic Federation, with the object of finding ways and means of reconciling labour and capital; and the prestige of the Federation reached a high point in the First World War, when President Wilson's administration took the view that its co-operation was essential for the success of the industrial war effort.

The gains of membership made by the unions during the war were not subsequently retained: but by this time Gompers himself was growing old, and he could not effectively cope with the new problems of the post-war situation, with its climate of almost frantic individualism. He died in 1924: and it was not his fault that after his death the principal unions composing the Federation rejected strong leadership, adopted an attitude of rigid conservatism, and consequently failed to take advantage of the fresh opportunities for extending the frontiers of organization in the early years of the New Deal.

The best justification for Gompers's policy during the forty years of his leadership is provided by the repeated failure of attempts made during the period to organize the unorganized workers on some other basis than that of the Federation. It was inevitable, of course, that the social dichotomy of the workers on ethnic lines should lead to "dual unionism" —that is, to rival unions competing in the same fields of recruitment. Thus, the Amalgamated Clothing Workers emerged under the leadership of Jews of the "new immigration" as a rival to the older and more conservative United Garment Workers. But the bulk of the workers of the "new immigration", being largely unskilled and unused to American ways, had great difficulty in organizing unions for their own special needs: some of them sought a solution in more political forms of association. Thus the Industrial Workers of the World, which was formed in 1905, was an attempt to shape labour organization on industrial rather than craft lines, and on loyalty to class rather than on "job consciousness". But the "Wobblies", as they were called, never presented any serious challenge to the A.F.L.: they included only one important union, the Western Federation of Miners, whose tradition of bitter struggle against the Western mineowners gave them a unique degree of militancy.

Although the I.W.W. became involved in a series of highly publicised strikes, such as that at Lawrence, Massachusetts, in 1912, where it provided a leadership for a large community of immigrant textile workers, it was totally unable to secure any degree of continuous support. Today, it may be that the I.W.W. is best remembered by the folksongs of Joe Hill, which, expressing as they do the tough independence of the hobo, seem to fit squarely into the tradition of American popular poetry. Yet the I.W.W. made a genuine attempt to solve a real problem of American society—the problem of the exploitation of the unskilled immigrant. But in this task it failed: and it was in the nature of the American environment and of the character of the immigrants themselves that failure was inevitable. In the face of the mobility of the American economy and the heterogeneity of the immigrants, no all-embracing economic or political creed—no gospel of industrial unionism or Socialism—could acquire effective strength. The One Big Union could never come to be, for there was no one big American working class. Before the immigrants were assimilated, they thought of themselves as members of particular European ethnic groups as well as workers; after the process of assimilation had begun, they thought of themselves as capable of moving beyond the working class environment. This fact is perhaps most vividly illustrated by the experience of the American Socialist movement at the beginning of the First World War. The rapid growth of trusts in the last decades of the nineteenth century had given a certain plausibility to the Marxist theory of the concentration of capital; but the adherents of the Socialist Party of America were predominantly those who felt the call of European loyalties above all else. Consequently, when the European nations fell out with each other in 1914, the Socialist Party of America collapsed into fragments which were never to be put together again.

The "new immigration" was eventually halted by the First World War and by the restrictive Quota Acts of 1921, 1924 and 1929. Although the history of trade unionism in the succeeding years largely remains to be written, the hypothesis may be offered that the outstanding developments of the period since 1920—the creation of the C.I.O. in 1935 and its absorption into the A.F.L. twenty years later—can largely be explained as stages in the Americanization of the "new immigration". By the creation of the C.I.O., the immigrants attained a degree of economic status, and even of social status, with the assistance of a friendly legislative climate at Washington. And by its merger with the A.F.L. the growing assimilation of themselves and their families with the rest of the American labour force has been recognised.

In 1930 the total membership of American unions amounted to only about $3\frac{1}{2}$ million, and they were rivalled by "company unions" run by paternalistic employers, which accounted for almost as many workers as the whole of the A.F.L. In the A.F.L. itself, the absence of support in the greatest industries of the country is indicated by the fact that the fourth largest union in 1932 was the American Federation of Musicians; the ninth largest was the Brotherhood of Painters, Decorators and Paperhangers. Automobile manufacture, iron and steel, chemicals, and meatpacking were among the great industries virtually without independent organization, although charters pre-empting these fields had been secured from the Federation by various member unions. It was not merely the craft exclusiveness of the A.F.L. unions that hindered the spreading of the union gospel: it was also the belief, held rightly or wrongly by large sections of the workers in these industries—Jews, Italians, Poles, Negroes—that they were being discriminated against by their fellow-workers of native or Western European origin. In some cases, this feeling of discrimination was linked with bitter memories of the recent past, when Negroes or "new immigrants" had been brought in by employers as strike-breakers, and had aroused the animosity of the more established groups, to the extent of provoking racial or ethnic riots, for instance in Chicago at the end of the First World War. According to the Inter-Church Commission of Inquiry into the 1919 Steel Strike:

It is evident that the great numbers of Negroes who flowed into the Chicago and Pittsburg plants were conscious of strike-breaking. For this attitude, the steel strikers rightly blamed American organized labor. In the past the majority of A.F.L. unions have been white unions only. Their constitutions often so provide. Through many an experience Negroes came to believe that the only way they could break into an unionized industry was through strike-breaking.

Similar conditions prevailed in the Chicago stockyards, where the employers organised a "company union", the American Unity Labor Union, for Negro workers only. It is against this background of mutual conflict and suspicion among the workers that the foundation of the C.I.O. as a separate organization must be seen: indeed, it is largely true that the organization of the mass-production industries had to be effected independently of the A.F.L. in order to succeed. John L. Lewis's blow to the jaw of William L. Hutcheson, leader of the influential and highly conservative United Brotherhood of Carpenters and Joiners, at the 1935 A.F.L. Convention, was thus a symbolic gesture of great propagandist value.

Indeed, as the C.I.O. emerged in the later years of the New Deal and during the Second World War, it became clear that its leadership as well as its rank and file was very different from that of the A.F.L. It was considerably younger, much more radical in political and economic attitude—many in fact were Communists—and also, as C. Wright Mills has shown, it was much more fully representative of the "new immigration" to which the bulk of the union membership belonged. Thus the C.I.O., coming into existence when it did, fulfilled the historic function of providing a focus for the economic aspirations of a wide section of the "underprivileged". But to say this is also to indicate the limits of the

C.I.O.'s possibilities. It could never replace the A.F.L., which in fact continued to exist and to grow. Some radicals had supposed that the C.I.O., with its industrial basis, would replace the A.F.L. altogether; but this was to ignore the fact that social as well as economic issues had been responsible for the C.I.O.'s emergence, and that social as well as economic factors accounted for the existence of the A.F.L.

In the upshot, after the two organizations had lived and worked side by side for twenty years, the A.F.L. had twice as many members as the C.I.O., and a merger was even more a necessity for the younger body than it was for the older. With the steady assimilation of the families of the "new immigration", and the absence of any successors to them in comparable numbers, the historic function of the C.I.O. was after twenty years already fulfilled. Its more radical political philosophy had withered away in the Cold War, and its organisation now threatened to disintegrate. The leaders of both A.F.L. and C.I.O. realized that there was something to be gained by a unification of their forces for mutual support against dissident groups.

The consolidated labour organization, A.F.L.-C.I.O., whatever its initial stresses and strains, is a power far beyond the dreams of Samuel Gompers at his most exuberant. Its membership of over sixteen millions represents a more than fivefold increase on the total of twenty-five years ago. Its unions' treasuries are full as never before; their welfare funds are booming; their headquarters buildings, huge monuments of shining steel and glass, burgeon upon the avenues of the nation's capital like the embassies of great and prosperous foreign powers. Yet there are serious weaknesses behind the fine façade of modern American unionism: weaknesses that have their origins deep in the country's social history. Many American employers have yet to make up their minds that unionism is here to stay: the tradition of individualism, of the "American Plan" and company paternalism, dies hard. The workers themselves, sharing this tradition, resent the intrusion of the union official into politics, and still refuse to follow the dictates of their industrial representatives at election time. Consequently, the unions have proved unable to safeguard the privileged position that they obtained under the Wagner Act and the New Deal. The Taft-Hartley Act, bitterly opposed by all union officers, has found its way to the statute book and stayed there virtually unchanged; and only in a few special areas such as the State of Michigan, where the automobile workers are concentrated, can it be said that organized labour as such wields effective political power. The prospect of an independent political party of labour in America is even further off today than it was when Gompers dismissed it in the eighteen-nineties.

Even more serious for the unions, because even more directly linked with their industrial strength, is the fact that the recruitment of new members now hardly makes up for the wastage, and consequently that large areas of the country, where unionism has traditionally been at a disadvantage, but where industrialism is now rapidly taking place, are virtually without unionism. This applies particularly in the South, where racial tensions continue to dominate social life. Lucy Randolph Mason, one of the most active labour organizers in the South in the days of the New Deal, has described graphically the difficulties of recruiting workers into unions with the Ku Klux Klan hovering in the background. The problem is hardly easier today, especially since the emergence of the White Citizens Councils. Nor is the weakness confined to the South: although large metropolitan areas are well unionized, small towns generally have proved resistant. Certain industries, too, are hardly unionized at all. Whereas in manufacturing, transportation, construction and mining over half the workers are in unions, in wholesale and retail employment, government service, catering, and finance the figure is well below one-fifth. In chemicals and petroleum less than a third of the workers are organized, and the textile unions are facing special difficulties as their industry gradually migrates to the South in search of cheaper labour.

Even where unionism is strong, its aims often seem uncertain, and its leaders at cross-purposes with each other. While some of the unions, such as the International Typographical Union, have fine records of internal democracy, others, and especially the Teamsters, and the unions of longshoremen and of building workers have repeatedly been plagued by corruption, racketeering, and collusion with the employers. Although no labour movement can hope to be entirely free from individual self-seeking, a higher degree of class solidarity among the American workers might well have kept a higher proportion of their union officers to the path of virtue. The absence of any animating principle other than that of the interest of the small group of members of a particular union can lead easily to cynicism and apathy both among the rank and file and among the officials.

Yet the American labour movement also has great and peculiar advantages, arising out of its special evolution. Its large industrial unions, being recent in origin, correspond to the pattern of the most progressive parts of manufacturing industry much more effectively than do the unions of Great Britain. One single union, for instance, the United Automobile Workers, can effectively conduct all negotiations with the American motor manufacturers, while in Britain a dozen or more separate societies are seriously involved in the industry. This tendency has been encouraged by the provisions of the Wagner Act, whereby elections are conducted by an independent National Labor Relations Board in order to select a single bargaining agent for each firm's body of workers. At the same time, partly owing to geographical circumstances, bargaining tends to be decentralized and consequently much more a matter between the individual employer and his workers than it is in Britain, where national agreements are common. Though strikes are considerably more frequent, they tend to be short official stoppages coming at the end of a contract period, and therefore to some extent predictable and less damaging to the national economy.

The attitude of the American unionist towards the problems of increasing productivity deserves special consideration. The comparative absence of class solidarity has always enabled him to see the standpoint of management more readily than does his European counterpart. The fact that labour itself has so continuously been the scarce factor in production has not only encouraged managements to seek for labour-saving devices; it has also encouraged in the mind of the worker himself an attitude of mind which is not unfavourable to technical innovation. This is not to say that there has been no hostility to change in American industry: indeed, the early pioneers of scientific management, such as Frederick Winslow Taylor, encountered bitter opposition from the American Federation. But this was because the early pioneers, in their enthusiasm for the expansion of production, had ignored the human factor in management problems; and it was not long before reconciliation was effected between the two sides of American industry on this question. As Milton J. Nadworny has put it in his instructive work on *Scientific Management and the Unions, 1900-1932,* "The history of Scientific Management's relations with the unions may be divided roughly into two major periods: the hostility before 1920 and the collaboration during the twenties." Since those days, many of the American unions have come to employ their own experts in management problems, and have been known in some cases to force technological improvement upon employers in industry.

Accidents happen in industrial history as in any other sphere of life, and personality is always important in shaping the development of institutions. But, by and large, a nation is likely to get the type of labour movement that is dictated by long-term factors in its social and economic evolution. The critic, and especially the critic from abroad, who seeks to redirect the entire philosophy of American labour is indeed wasting his breath. For good or ill, unless the entire conditions of American society undergo drastic change, the labour movement of the United States is likely to remain politically conservative, though economically progressive, whereas European labour tends to be economically conservative and (within limits) politically progressive. While the British miner and his family are cared for by the National Health Service, which was introduced into Parliament by a miner who had become a minister in a Labour Government, the American miner and his family can turn to the lavishly equipped hospitals built out of the welfare funds extorted by John L. Lewis's tough negotiations with the employers.

Yet American labour has by no means abdicated from the political sphere. Its task is rather that of conserving what the workers of other countries, often proceeding by a more theoretical process of reasoning and by more direct political activity, may regard as their aspiration: the welfare provisions of the New Deal, the full employment of the succeeding years, and the degree of equality of opportunity which has been part of American life for over a century. If the American working man in recent years has been politically apathetic, it is because these gains have never been seriously threatened. The interest of sixteen million organized workers and their families in the maintenance of a particular way of life is likely to prove an effective guarantee of its survival, whether they have a political party of their own or not.

INDUSTRIAL AMERICA

By J. Potter

★

"GOD has predestinated," wrote Herman Melville in 1850 in an oft-quoted passage, "mankind expects, great things from our race; and great things we feel in our souls. The rest of the nations must soon be in our rear. We are the pioneers of the world; the advance guard, sent on through the wilderness of untried things, to break a new path in the New World that is ours. In our youth is our strength; in our inexperience, our wisdom." Melville's prophetic words aptly summarize both the reality and the promise of American life in the middle of the nineteenth century.

Economically, the ties with the outside world were still strong. The people of the United States of America were until 1850 still outward looking. America imported very much the same kinds of goods as in 1789, with manufactures predominating. She produced no manufactures which the rest of the world wanted to buy and her only important exports were unworked products of the soil, with raw cotton by far the leading article. Indeed, although textile manufacturing was the most advanced American industry, three-quarters of the raw cotton crop was exported. The American balance of trade was still unfavourable; between 1811 and 1870, annual imports exceeded annual exports in all but thirteen years. Above all, the economy relied upon foreign aid to assist its development and looked to the outside world for credit to make internal investment possible. At mid-century, then, the potential of the American economy was still quite undeveloped. Agriculture was the predominant activity of the majority of the population and such industry as existed was for the most part conducted on a small scale and for local markets.

It is true, however, that many portents for the future were already to be seen in 1850. American railroad mileage was almost double the British; stupendous engineering feats had been accomplished in the building of the Cumberland road, and the Erie and Pennsylvania canals, and at least three schools of engineering were in existence; New York city was well on its way to commercial dominance; in manufacturing, Eli Whitney's principle of interchangeable parts was being widely adopted; future business methods were being foreshadowed in New England by a group known as the Boston Associates; the idea that machinery might lead to the economic use of the limited supplies of capital and labour was rapidly gaining ground and the love of gadgetry had taken hold; the first large wave of immigration was already beating against the shores; gold had just been discovered in California. Yet these were no more than portents. To apply a metaphor used recently by an American economist, the economy was still on the runway; its wheels were on the ground and the throttles were not even fully open; the speed of progress was not yet sufficient to sustain the machine in independent flight.

American industry depended for its development in the nineteenth century almost entirely on internal demand, foreign markets being of little significance for American manufactures until the very end of that period. Similarly, American industry derived almost the whole of its raw materials from within the national boundaries. The growth of industry in the U.S.A. thus caused American eyes to turn away from the outside world inward to the American continent. And, after the beginning of settlement in California, to look inward was to look across the land at other Americans.

The years between 1850 and 1870 saw a number of important events which gave great significance and strength to the portents already noted. First, the fifties, a decade of rapid economic advance in the U.S.A., saw a more than threefold increase in railroad mileage, from 9,000 to over 31,000 miles of completed track by 1860, and the creation of through traffic for virtually the entire region east of the Mississippi. Chicago was reached in 1852—a significant landmark—and by 1860 the Old North-West alone had more miles of railroad in operation than the whole of the British Isles.

Secondly, the early 1850's were marked by a considerable increase in immigration. Between 1847 and 1854 over $2\frac{1}{2}$ million immigrants, about half of them Irish, entered the U.S.A., a figure which represented a higher rate of immigration in relation to the existing American population than occurred at any other period. These immigrants helped to provide both the labour and the markets for the economic developments of the 1850's and the subsequent decades. The Census of 1860 showed that, out of a total population of $31\frac{1}{2}$ million, there were over 4 million foreign-born, or one in thirteen, a proportion which remained remarkably steady in every Census until 1920.

Thirdly, the Civil War of 1861-65 limited the importation of many types of manufacture while the requirements of war gave a tremendous impetus to the process of industrialisation. The victory of the North meant that the Southern States became the economic colonies of New England instead of Old England. Further, the war helped to lay the foundations of the great American fortunes. Until the middle of the nineteenth century wealth and incomes in the U.S.A. were distributed among the population relatively evenly. There were perhaps four Americans in the late 1840's with fortunes of two million dollars; to build the Baltimore and Ohio railroad alone cost fifteen million, the New

York Central about thirty million, the Erie about twenty-five million. An increase in the inequalities of wealth and incomes generally results in a higher rate of saving and an increase in the availability of investable funds. The proportion of the American national income devoted to investment rose in each decade until the end of the nineteenth century; the peak was reached in the decade 1889-98, when over 16 per cent of national income went to capital formation. With the gradual equalization of incomes in the twentieth century, this percentage again declined.

Two other significant events were direct consequences of the Civil War. The federal government's need for revenue during the war caused customs duties to be increased progressively until by 1864 the average rate of duty was 47 per cent. The raising of the tariff was, however, more than merely an expedient of war; it was a principle of Northern policy. Lincoln had used the promise of a tariff to gain the votes of certain of the more industrial states, especially Pennsylvania and New Jersey. The rates of 1864 were so high that it could no longer be pretended that tariffs existed to raise revenue; the rates of duty were clearly protective, even prohibitive. The imposition of the tariff of 1864, more than any other single act, announced the severance of the ancient commercial links with the old world and amounted to a declaration that the U.S.A. could and would live by her own exertions. America was able to maintain huge tariff walls, and yet continue her industrial expansion, above all because of the expansion of the domestic markets. Unlike Britain, she had nothing to fear from retaliation since she had no important foreign markets to lose.

The last factor in the transformation of the American scene was the completion in 1869 of the first trans-continental railroad, making the internal markets truly national in scope. Even more important than the immediate economic consequences of the first trans-continental was its symbolism. Optimism and buoyancy had never been lacking in American economic life. The challenge of the west was such that the conquest of space brought its own satisfaction; the act of reaching a place was as important as what was done on arrival. As one seemingly impossible physical barrier after another was broken down by human skill and ingenuity, the belief in human infallibility grew; no obstacles existed or could exist which could not be overcome in course of time. "The difficult can be done immediately; the impossible will take a little longer", became the slogan of American progress. The nation's success story thrived on success and the trans-continental railroad could be regarded as the greatest engineering achievement of all time. What Drake and the Elizabethan sea-dogs did for English superiority complexes, Congress, engineers, and Chinese and Irish labourers did for the American faith in the inevitability of material progress when they planned and completed the first railroad across the continent.

By 1870, then, America's economic relations with the outside world had changed. Events in the U.S.A. were beginning to determine, instead of being determined by, events outside. Immigrants increasingly came to America because of the positive magnetism of prosperity there instead of the negative repulsion of hard times in their own country. From 1870 onwards, America's dependence on the rest of the world lessened. It is true that European capital continued to enter the U.S.A. long after 1870, attracted there by the high expectations of profit which America seemed to offer. Nevertheless, America's visible balance of trade was unfavourable only in seven years during the rest of the nineteenth century, as the new railroads brought the fruitfulness of the western lands to the ports and the new steamships carried cheap food to Western Europe, and as American mineral resources were exploited and drawn upon by foreign as well as American industries. By 1900 manufactures were becoming increasingly prominent among American exports and in the twentieth century her balance of trade has never once been unfavourable.

The transformation of the American economy between 1850 and the present day defies the eloquence even of Texan superlatives. Statistics are of little more avail than words, since no more than the roughest estimates can be made of most of the data one would wish to compare. The measurement of economic phenomena is a hazardous undertaking especially when comparisons are to be made between different time-periods or between different countries. Even the best statistics indicate quantities only and say nothing about quality, either of the goods concerned or of life itself.

The broad facts, however, seem to be indisputable. By the end of the Second World War, the American economy, with one-fifteenth of the world's labour force, working shorter hours than were to be found in many other countries, produced over one-third of all the world's goods and one half of all its manufactured goods. Industrial workers in the U.S.A. had on an average the assistance of 8 h.p. of mechanical power compared with $2\frac{1}{2}$ h.p. in Europe. The average income per head of population in the U.S.A. approximately doubled from 1860 to 1930, while hours of work were in some cases halved; by 1952 it stood at $1,823 per person compared with $751 in the United Kingdom and $684 in France. The American economy in 1952 produced twice as much coal and coke as any other single country outside the U.S.S.R. (for which statistics are not available), four times as much iron, five times as much steel; its production of electricity amounted to 46 per cent of the total production in all other countries; it produced more than half the world's petroleum and over four-fifths of its motor spirit. In 1954 the number of private motor-cars in use in the U.S.A. was 29·8 per hundred of population compared with 17·6 in Canada, 7·4 in Sweden and 6·1 in the U.K.

Between 1850 and the present, therefore, the gulf is wide and American economic progress in that century almost certainly surpasses that of any other nation in the history of mankind. A recent calculation has estimated that the American real national product per head of population increased

NATIONAL INCOME OF THE U.S.A.

Date	Total Private Production	Income realized by				Columns 2-5 as percentage of Column 1			
		Agri-culture	Manu-facturing	Transport and Com-munications	Trade	Agri-culture	Manu-facturing	Transport and Com-munications	Trade
	mill. $	mill. $	mill. $	mill. $	mill. $	%	%	%	%
	1	2	3	4	5	6	7	8	9
1849	2,326	737	291	398	196	31·4	12·5	17·1	8·4
1859	4,098	1,264	495	694	494	30·8	12·0	16·9	12·0
1869	6,288	1,517	1,000	718	1,039	24·0	16·0	11·4	16·3
1879	6,617	1,371	960	896	1,166	20·7	14·6	13·6	17·6
1889	9,578	1,517	2,022	1,154	1,803	15·8	21·1	12·0	18·8
1899	13,836	2,933	2,714	1,528	2,578	21·2	19·7	11·1	18·7
1910	25,569	5,563	5,447	2,853	4,496	21·7	21·3	11·1	17·6
1920	60,995	10,569	16,811	7,474	10,048	17·3	27·6	12·2	16·5
1930	61,968	6,761	15,958	7,012	10,628	10·9	25·7	11·3	17·1
1937	54,959	6,757	16,629	5,934	8,414	12·3	30·2	10·8	15·3

Columns 1-5 from U.S. Department of Commerce, *Historical Statistics of the United States, 1789-1945*, p. 14.

between 1860 and 1950 at an average rate of 2·2 per cent per year; the comparable figures for Germany, Sweden and Denmark are all 1·4, for the United Kingdom 1·2 and for France 0·9. The American lead is more marked still if aggregate figures are considered and no account is taken of population changes.

American industrial progress was not maintained at a uniform pace and was certainly not achieved without distress. Indeed the years which in retrospect appear to have seen the most rapid advance were often those in which the lamentations were the loudest. But over-riding the fluctuations, one finds the gradual emergence into a predominating position of the manufacturing sector of the economy. Already by 1890, manufacturing was making a larger contribution to total national income than any other type of economic activity. In that year 15 per cent of the total labour force was engaged in manufacturing, but produced over 20 per cent of the national income, while the 44 per cent of the labour force still engaged in agriculture produced only 16 per cent of the national income. The physical output of industry has continued in most years of the twentieth century to grow faster than the total national income.

The period from the late 1890's to the outbreak of the First World War saw fundamental changes in the structure of American industry. In the decade 1899-1908, the net national product increased by rather more than 25 per cent over the preceding decade, compared with an increase of 15 per cent in 1889-1898 over 1879-1888. After 1899-1908, a clear retardation in the rate of growth is observable. In the first decade of the twentieth century, the total output of manufacturing, fuel production and metal mining all more than doubled, while the capital and horse-power per worker in manufacturing both increased by more than half. In that decade the American business civilization of the twentieth century came into being, characterized by the giant corporations and mass production; heavy industries became the symbols of American achievement and the motor-car industry began its prodigious career. Industry, and the towns in which industries were concentrated, came to present the nation's major social problems.

It is commonplace to say that, as man increases his knowledge and his command over his environment, he needs to devote fewer and fewer resources to the production of the necessaries of life and is able to devote more and more resources to providing himself with conveniences, comforts, and luxuries. This truism summarizes in a phrase the main trends of American economic history in the past century. When the U.S.A. became a nation, over 90 per cent of the working population was employed in agriculture; by 1850, this proportion had been reduced to just over 60 per cent, by 1870 to just over 50 per cent; in 1954 it was about 13 per cent. The absolute numbers employed in agriculture increased throughout the nineteenth century to a peak of $11\frac{1}{2}$ millions in 1910, but this rate

T

of increase was always slower than that of the total population. After 1910 the numbers gaining their livelihood from agriculture declined absolutely as well as relatively, to 8½ millions in 1954.

Since American agriculture produced all the main food necessities for the American population, imported food amounting to a mere 5 per cent of domestic production, it is clear that the continually increasing total population has been fed by an ever diminishing proportion of the nation's labour force. This was made possible by the greater output per person employed in agriculture. Increased agricultural productivity may indeed be regarded as the *sine qua non* of American industrialisation. Expanding industrial output has usually coincided with falling agricultural prices. The process of industrialisation, of course, in turn assisted the increase of agricultural productivity by providing more and better machinery for the farmer. Writing sixty years ago, D. A. Wells in *Recent Economic Changes* drew attention to the value of a single mechanical innovation, the corn-husker. The six states of Illinois, Indiana, Missouri, Iowa, Ohio and Kansas produced, towards the end of the nineteenth century, more than one half of the total American corn (maize) crop. The census of 1880 showed that just over 2 million persons were engaged in agriculture in those states. If this number of agricultural workers had been obliged to shell the entire corn crop of those states by the methods of shelling used in the 1830's, i.e. by scraping the ears against the sharp edge of a frying pan or shovel, they would have needed to work, in Wells' estimate, for one hundred and ten days in every year at the single task of shelling corn.

It may even be noted in passing that in certain periods, especially 1873-95 and 1920-40, the pace of industrialisation has not been rapid enough to keep up with the rate of increase of agricultural output. Too many resources continued to be devoted to the production of foodstuffs and the rate of transfer to other activities was too slow. The result was that agricultural production overshot the demand for its produce. In consequence, farm prices, and with them farmers' incomes, fell and farming became depressed. In the periods of agricultural depression, the rate of industrial expansion has not been rapid enough to provide an adequate market for the expanding output of farm commodities which the opening up of new lands or the introduction of new methods permitted.

The same processes may be viewed from the side of consumption instead of production. Because Americans have been able to buy the food they needed at prices which over the whole period fell relative to their total incomes, they have had more and more left over with which to buy their conveniences, comforts and luxuries. In 1870 the American people spent about one-third of their current incomes on farm products; already by 1890 this proportion had fallen to one-fifth. The ever-increasing efficiency of American agriculture released productive resources and purchasing power from the provision of food and the freed resources and incomes were diverted to other purposes. How was the process of re-allocation accomplished? To what did the labour formerly needed to produce food turn? How did people spend the money they no longer needed to buy necessities? The answer to these questions is basically the same.

One might be tempted to answer that the relative decline in numbers employed in agriculture from 60 per cent of the total in 1850 to below 20 per cent since 1940 would be offset by a commensurate increase in the numbers engaged in manufacturing. But this is not what happened. The massive increase in American industrial output has not been accompanied by a comparable increase in the relative numbers employed in industry. The proportion of the population engaged in industrial pursuits—manufacturing, handicrafts, building, etc.—in 1850 was roughly the same as the proportion engaged in agricultural pursuits in 1940, i.e. about 17 per cent. Yet, whereas in 1850 almost two-thirds of the labour force was in agriculture, it was not until 1920 that manufacturing became the biggest employer of labour; and at no time has the industrial sector of the working population exceeded one-third of the total working force. The table overleaf shows the structure of the working force in each Census year in the U.S.A., and inserts some comparable figures for the U.K.

These figures are simply explained if we look at the developments from the point of view of consumption instead of production. When people find that they have an increasing proportion of their incomes left in their purses after buying their food, they do not spend all this increase in buying goods. Prominent among the conveniences, comforts and luxuries they demand are such items as more travel and entertainment, improved education, better shopping facilities, more doctors, dentists, lawyers, policemen, civil servants, psychiatrists, and so forth. As the size of industrial operations increased, so did the need for office workers of all sorts. Much more spectacular, therefore, than the increase in the industrial sector of the working population has been the increase in the numbers in tertiary occupations. In 1850, the numbers employed in providing all the different types of services were about the same as the numbers employed in all types of industry, just below a million and a half or about 17 per cent of the employed population. In 1940, tertiary occupations gave employment to almost 23 million, or about 47 per cent of the total. Between 1910 and 1940, clerical workers of all sorts increased faster than any other group, by 135 per cent; next came the professions by 107 per cent; semi-skilled (largely industrial) workers not quite doubled; farm labourers declined by almost 50 per cent. By 1940, about one in five Americans was employed in agriculture and one in three in industry, but every second person in employment was in some form of transport, in trade, professional or personal service, or government. The increase in the number of clerical workers is reflected

STRUCTURE OF LABOUR FORCE

Date	Total gainfully employed (mills)	U.S.A. Percentage of gainfully employed in					U.K. Percentage of gainfully employed in		
		Agriculture	Manufacturing and hand trades	Construction	Transport trade and Finance	Other Services	Agriculture, Forestry, Fishing	Mining, manufacturing, building	All trades, and services
1850	7·7	63·6	16·9*		5·2	11·6	22	47	31
1860	10·5	59·0	18·1*		7·6	12·4			
1870	12·9	53·5	16·3	5·4	10·9	13·2			
1880	17·4	48·8	18·3	5·2	12·9	11·3			
1890	23·3	43·8	15·4	6·0	15·4	14·0			
1900	29·0	37·9	21·1	5·5	16·8	13·3			
1910	37·4	30·5	22·2	6·1	19·4	16·2	8	46	46
1920	42·4	25·2	25·7	5·2	21·5	15·4			
1930	48·8	21·5	22·1	6·1	27·2	19·0	6	44	50
1940	52·1	17·3	20·9	6·7	25·0	22·0			

* Manufacturing, hand trades and construction. (American figures calculated from *Historical Statistics*, p. 64.)

in an increase in female employment in the twentieth century. The labour force in 1940 was estimated to consist of 39 million principal income earners (representing the total number of families in the country) and 15·2 million secondary income earners; about half the families in the country had more than one income earner at some time in the course of every year. One important social aspect of these figures is the decline in the number of self-employed persons from well over half the total number in 1850, to one-third in 1870 and, by 1940, to less than one-fifth, reflecting of course, among other things, the decline of the yeoman farmer.

An associated process is observable in the type of goods to which productive resources and consumers' incomes are allocated. As manufacturing efficiency improves and fewer resources are required to produce the most necessary manufactures, more resources are released for manufactures supplying conveniences, comfort and luxury. At the time of the Civil War about half the output of durable household goods consisted of furniture and this was still true in 1900; by 1929 the proportion was down to below 15 per cent. In 1900 the motor car industry, the radio industry, the aircraft industry, the electrical industries, the motion picture industry, many of the chemical industries, either did not exist or were not yet out of swaddling clothes. The durable goods which are now to be found in so many American homes began to make a wide appearance, not only in the U.S.A., of course, in the 1920's: electric and gas cooking ranges, washing-machines and refrigerators, radios and private cars. Since 1940 the American gross national product has increased at an average rate of about 5 per cent per year, but the rate of increase in the production of such goods as television sets and air-conditioning units has been many times greater. The total national bill for repairs to household equipment has increased in each year since 1940 by some 15 per cent.

Marked changes have also occurred in the twentieth century in the types of food consumed. Since about 1910 the consumption per head of potatoes has fallen by half, of cereal products by one-quarter, while the consumption per head of dairy products has increased by almost one-half, of fruit and vegetables by one-third. In the last ten years, on the other hand, the proportion of income spent on food has remained more or less constant. Housewives have taken advantage of the greater availability of "labour-saving" foods, frozen fruit and vegetables, canned juices, "instant" puddings and beverages, in which the food processing industries have added considerably to the value, economic if not nutritional, of the crude agricultural product.

American railroads dispersed the population across the entire continent but they also enabled population to be concentrated in towns. As in Britain, industrialisation in the U.S.A. was accompanied by urbanisation and its all too familiar social problems. The total urban population increased from $3\frac{1}{2}$ millions (or 15 per cent of the total) in 1850, to 30 millions (or 40 per cent of the total) in 1900 and 89 millions (or 59 per cent of the total) in 1950. It is important, however, to point out that the American census defines as urban any place with a population of 2,500 or over; a place, in other words, of the size of Cheddar, Somerset, or Broadway, Worcestershire. The 1951 Census showed that in England and Wales over 39 million people lived in 887 towns of over 3,000 inhabitants, representing 89·9 per cent of the total population. The concentration of population in towns is obviously very much more intense in Britain than in the U.S.A.; four out of ten people in the U.S.A., compared with only one out of ten in England and Wales, live in places with fewer than 3,000 inhabitants. British figures also show a somewhat greater concentration of population in the major conurbations. In England and Wales in 1951, 16 million people (36·8 per cent of total population) lived in 5 conurbations of over 1 million inhabitants; in the U.S.A. in 1950, 44·5 million people (29·5 per cent of total population) lived in the 14 conurbations with over 1 million inhabitants. None of these figures, of course, gives any indication of the area covered by the towns in question or the distance away from the next town. Two features of the British, and especially the English, scene, are absent from the American; on the one hand the village, and on the other the agglomerations of medium-sized towns such as are found in Lancashire and the West Riding of Yorkshire. The American town of every size is, even in the most densely populated states, much more of an isolated unit than the British, a fact of political and social, as well as economic, significance. Town loyalty and inter-town rivalry, the Boosterism of the Babbits, may be synthetic emotions but are not without some influence on human behaviour.

The growing industrial towns, depending for their existence on transport, attracted the newly arrived immigrants. It is not very surprising, therefore, to find that periods of great activity in transport building were also periods marked by rapid town growth, by frantic efforts to build houses and provide other urban amenities, and by a large influx of immigrants. As transport facilities improved, towns and industries developed, attracting to them the immigrant worker. After a few years of expansion of this sort, a period of quiescence and consolidation followed. It is not proposed in this account to attempt to analyse these ebbs and flows of activity any more closely, but merely to draw attention to their existence. The 1880's and 1900's in particular were decades in which all the factors mentioned were active. The social problems of the first years of the twentieth century, the decade of the Muckrakers, with new industrial techniques being introduced, with mushroom towns springing up and police, housing and sanitation lagging far behind the expansion of their populations, and with immigrants willing and eager to accept much lower wages than native workers—these social problems, and the reaction to them of "do-gooders" of all creeds, were reminiscent of the "Condition of England question" of the 1830's. Writers bewailed the "curse of bigness" and the "shame of the cities". Industrialist and banker alike were regarded as enemies of the people; so much so that one obituary notice of 1913 read: "We verily believe that J. Pierpoint Morgan has done more harm in the world than any man who ever lived in it . . . "

From the foregoing survey of some of the main aspects of American industrial growth in the past century, we may be led to ask two questions. How and why did the total of goods and services produced by the American economy increase at a rate surpassing that of any other country in any other period of history? Secondly, how have the proceeds of this ever-increasing output been distributed among the different sectors of the economy, the different geographical regions and the different social classes? To provide even the most tentative answers to these broad questions involves complexities which extend far beyond the range of either the historian or the economist. To answer the first question it is not enough to analyse, both quantitatively and qualitatively, the supply of the factors of production, the familiar trio of land, labour and capital, with the added catalyst of enterprise. The political scientist, the anthropologist and the sociologist must also be consulted. What, for example, were the effects on American economic life of the early achievement of manhood suffrage and of the federal system itself? How great has been the influence of the early development of universal education, and the emphasis at the higher levels on theology and engineering? Where lie the roots of American "materialism"? What were the effects of the great variations in climate experienced within the boundaries of the U.S.A.? What of the frontier, the immigrant?

The second question involves consideration of politico-economic dissatisfaction in all its manifestations. It asks the eternal problem of the economic philosopher: how are the proceeds of economic activity to be allocated to the different producers? What constitutes a "fair" allocation and how does the actual allocation differ from it? Since every person had his own view as to what was "fair" and since these views rarely corresponded with actuality, rumblings of discontent are heard throughout the whole period. And not merely of workers against bosses; merchants, railroad owners, farmers in New England, planters in the South, cattle-raisers and wheat-growers in the West, financiers, and industrial wage earners, all sought to achieve a distribution of the proceeds favourable to themselves. "Charge what the traffic will bear", cried the railroaders; "Free coinage of silver", cried the Western farmer; "More, more, more, now", cried the trade unionist; "Limit the rigours of free competition", cried the less successful businessman; "Abolish monopoly", cried all and sundry. Intellectuals by and large did not associate themselves with any single element. There was, for example, nothing in the

U.S.A. corresponding to the Fabian Society in England. At no time in nineteenth-century America was the industrial wage-earner the exemplar of social virtues.

American manufacturers are enterprising and inventive; they adapt labour-saving machinery to every branch of productive industry. Their workshops and factories are recruited from the industrial centres of Great Britain and the European continent, and the genius, skill and experience of those peoples largely contribute to develop and build up American industries.

So began a letter-writer to *The Times* in January, 1879. At about the same time a *Report upon the Commercial Relations of the United States* for the year 1878 was being compiled and included in it were certain comments emanating from the U.S. Consulate in Bradford, Yorkshire.

The channel of commerce is changing . . . and instead of changing with the stream, English manufacturers continue to sit upon the bank of the old water-course and argue from plausible but unprofitable scientific and commercial premises that it had no right to alter.

Enterprise, inventiveness, the introduction of machinery, skill and industry and adaptability to changing circumstances are represented by these writers as the mainsprings of American progress. Both extracts are dated before 1880, before the vast coal-fields of West Virginia were opened up, when steam had only just become the main source of power in American industries; when Carnegie had scarcely begun the development of the Pittsburgh iron and steel industry; when mass production and scientific management still lay largely in the future. American industry already had tariff protection. Why, with the spurs of external competition blunted, did it not fall asleep and lapse into inefficiency?

It is obvious that the absence of external competition did not eliminate internal competition. The fact that virtually all markets were domestic did not remove the need for adaptability. An important reason for this was the constant westward movement of the population, the constant westward displacement of the nation's economic centre of gravity. American industry did not stay rooted to the places in which it was first established but moved with the frontier. Capital as well as labour was highly mobile. Distances were so great that it was often found to be cheaper to set up new centres of production nearer to the markets than to face the high costs of distribution from existing factories. Sometimes the newer centres of production were able to achieve greater efficiency than the older centres and the latter declined; tariff protection could not be provided between state and state. As early as 1850 the Jeremiahs were predicting the day, not far distant, when cotton manufacturing in the South would bring ruin to the textile towns of New and Old England alike and when grass would grow in the streets of Lowell and Lawrence, Manchester and Bolton. The readiness to dig up established roots and to plant afresh was a marked characteristic of American industry and affords a significant contrast with many other countries. Dependence on internal rather than external demand did mean, however, that the markets which American producers supplied were highly homogeneous. They did not send their goods to innumerable different foreign markets and were free from the resultant need to diversify their products.

Much has been written about the influence of the frontier on American life. No one would pretend that the existence to the west of unsettled land would in itself promote economic development. Other countries, especially Russia and Australia, have had vast areas of unsettled land at their frontier but have developed economically at a very much slower rate than did the U.S.A. in the nineteenth century. Equally, no inhabitant of Western Europe is likely to be convinced by any argument which seeks to show that American economic development would have followed a similar pattern to the actual one if the western frontier had remained stationary at the boundary of the Proclamation of 1763 or even at the actual boundaries of 1865. The line of the frontier did more than induce young men to follow Horace Greeley's advice and "Go west". It is inconceivable that a territorially confined America would have attracted either European capital or European labour on the scale on which both entered the U.S.A. in the second half of the nineteenth century. What attracted both was the prospect which frontier conditions seemed to offer of higher returns than were obtainable at home.

Frontier conditions, then, created an optimistic environment favourable to profit-seeking and profit-making. Even for the small farmer of the Plains, profit-making was essential to independent existence and survival. The frontier farmer often enough regarded even his land as a means not to a regular income but to a windfall gain since he hoped to re-sell it at a profit after five years or so of cultivation. Labour, whether one's own or a fellow-creature's, was regarded fundamentally as a means to profit, an attitude which continued long after the frontier environment had become a thing of the past.

The effects of the frontier were reinforced by the influx of immigrants. The immigrant provided a potential market as well as a cheap labour force. American "materialism" was compounded of two elements: the profit-making potential of the West and the quest of economic betterment on the part of the immigrant. Immigrants came in order to improve their physical lot. Their aim on arrival was to improve their material standard of living and to increase their possessions. All ties and allegiances were left behind and acquisitiveness was an essential condition of security. Yet it was a relatively short step from acquisitiveness for security to acquisitiveness for social emulation since possessions were in such conditions the mark of success. The immigrant's feeling that he was isolated and one of a minority merely added to his desire for possessions. Single-minded devotion to the improvement of material conditions was strengthened by social *mores* which determined one's position in society not by parentage, by accent, or by schooling, but above all by income. American life thus came to be largely freed from the dictates of caste, religion or social status and to be dominated by economic motivations.

These many factors taken together gave to American industry a sense of urgency, drive and willingness to take risks which is often lacking in other parts of the world. In the words of Lewis Mumford, "Puritan fanatics like Goodyear brought to the vulcanization of rubber the same intense passion that Thoreau brought to Nature."

Against this general background, then, American manufacturing industries developed along the now familiar lines: mass-production and scientific management; large-scale units of production; intense competition; and constant attention to the expansion of markets through improvements in distribution.

The economic advantages of mass-production are generally agreed. The working efficiencies which follow from the integration of processes are of the greatest importance, but other advantages also accrue in bulk purchases of raw materials, in research, in advertising. One of the most important features of the spread of mass-production in American industry has certainly been the increase in the amount of capital equipment and power which the worker has had at his disposal. Of the total resources devoted to capital formation, agriculture has always taken a considerable share, but the proportion absorbed by industry increased continually from 1880 to the early 1920's. Output per man-hour increased from an index figure of 100 in the decade 1891-1900 to 196·4 by 1921-30 and 281·3 by 1941-50. On the other hand, the constant search for technical improvement has resulted in great economies in the use of capital. Dr Daniel Creamer has shown that the amount of capital per unit of *output* as a whole reached its peak in 1919 and has since then declined. Although some industries show exceptions, the general trend since 1920 has been that, while the amount of capital per worker and output per man-hour have both continued to increase, the capital-output ratio has declined. These trends reflect, among other things, the greater scarcity and therefore higher price of labour during part of that period and the replacement of labour by capital; but at the same time a very marked improvement in the efficiency with which a given amount of capital was used. The prosperity of the 1920's and the years since 1940 as well as the depression of the 1930's provided incentives to make the best use of available capital.

The development of mass production methods would have been impossible without the simultaneous improvements made in methods of industrial management. As the size of firms increased, industrial bureaucracy expanded to menacing proportions and the optimum size of firms from a technological point of view has constantly tended to exceed the managerial optimum. The names of those who tried to counterbalance this tendency, such pioneers in scientific management as Frederick Winslow Taylor, and Frank and Lillian Gilbreth, deserve to be as well known as those of the Carnegies, Morgans and Edisons, the businessmen, financiers and inventors.

Why has industrial mass-production been more widely introduced in the U.S.A. than elsewhere? Undoubtedly, the mere size of the American market has been of the greatest importance. Yet, obviously, the size of the population alone explains nothing; we do not have to explore the pages of history very far to find examples in which population increases have been accompanied by deteriorating standards of life, as Malthus predicted. The questions to be asked are, what factors in America have made businessmen and workers willing to use mass-production methods, what have been the peculiarities of the American market? A Swiss observer, W. E. Rappard, in *The Secret of American Prosperity* has recently suggested that the absolute size of the American population is less important than what he calls the "social depth" of demand, which, in turn, he attributes to the egalitarian basis of American society. This large national market has, he suggests, thus become "the paradise of the standardized product". The process has been furthered in the twentieth century by the deliberate policy of industrial leaders of limiting the variety of goods on the market, simplifying the processes by mechanization of production and increasing the total quantity produced. One may deplore the social consequences of this economic egalitarianism, the outward manifestations of *Admass*, but one can scarcely deny that without it mass production, the cheapening of products and the raising of material standards, is impossible. The willingness on the part of consumers to accept standardized products is an element just as essential to high productivity as the willingness of producers to accept conveyer belt systems of production.

The characteristics of the American market exerted an important influence on the process of industrial development. Sociologists have written of the frontiersman as the materialist *par excellence*. Like the earliest colonial settlers, his problem was first to come to terms with and then to establish mastery over his physical surroundings. Per Hansa, Rölvaag's hero, and Old Jules, Marie Santos's father, were occupied in a grim struggle for survival, a life without refinements, luxuries or abstract ideologies, if not without romanticism. Their entire pre-occupation was with the material needs of themselves and their families. The frontiersman may have been the individualist he is shown to be in the western novelettes, but his wants were simple and standardized. It is no accident that mass production methods were introduced from an early date in the production of the type of goods the westerner, whether frontiersman or farmer, required: barbed wire, rifles and revolvers, farm machinery, sewing machines.

The potential market afforded by the rapidly growing population was immense but means had to be found of allowing demand to make itself felt. It had to be made possible for people to buy the goods produced through a lowering of their prices and through attention to the great problems of distribution. Remote frontier farmers in particular suffered the disadvantage that the prices they received for the goods they had to sell were generally low in comparison with the prices they had to pay for the goods they wanted to buy. Manufacturers saw the need to produce goods cheaply if they were to expand their markets—their rural markets in particular—while retailers began to devise means of bringing those goods to the very doorsteps of potential customers at prices the latter could pay. In 1872, Aaron Montgomery Ward, a 29-year-old travelling salesman of St. Louis, put all his savings into a business which he set up in a livery stable in Chicago. He bought goods in bulk from manufacturers and sold them to farmers by mail at low cash prices, promising to accept the goods back without charge if the customer was not satisfied with their quality. His original single-sheet catalogue had expanded to eight sheets by 1876, and by 1888 his annual sales were of one million dollars. In 1879 Frank Winfield Woolworth opened his first 5 cent store in Utica, New York. This failed within the year but his second venture at Lancaster, Pennsylvania, put him on the road which, just over thirty years later, brought the first example of sky-scraper Gothic to Manhattan Island, the 57-storey Woolworth building, opened in 1912. In 1886 Richard W. Sears, a railroad employee in Minnesota, began to sell watches by mail. Within a few years he had joined forces with A. C. Roebuck and by the turn of the century the Sears Roebuck catalogue entered into the remotest household, providing students of later generations with one of their most instructive social documents. The Mail Order house and the chain store had become established American institutions. About the same time, on the west coast, car salesmen began to allow purchase by instalments. Similar attention has continued to be paid to distribution and marketing in the twentieth century and in certain industries efficiency of distribution has been as marked a characteristic as efficiency of production. Latterly, the so-called Super-market has spread through the length and breadth of the country, transforming social habits as well as introducing a new element in economic life.

Inevitably, the development of mass-production methods involved an increase in the size of industrial units. The concentration of industrial activity into the hands of fewer and larger enterprises began even before the Civil War; the pace quickened around the turn of the century and there have been no significant departures from the trend in subsequent decades. By 1935, in round figures, one-half the total labour force was employed by about 3 per cent of all firms. Nevertheless the number of small firms remains surprisingly large. In 1914, 87·4 per cent of all firms in the U.S.A. employed fewer than 50 workers and in 1939 that percentage had only fallen to 83·1.

The study of industrial concentration forms a bridge between the two broad questions asked at the beginning of this section. It concerns both productivity and the allocation of proceeds. Industrial concentration has arisen from two entirely different motives: on the one hand, firms have extended the scale of their operations in order to improve the efficiency of their production; on the other, firms have absorbed, or united with, their rivals in order to destroy competition in their branch of production and so to eliminate, for the time being at least, the necessity of improving their efficiency. The effect of the second type of consolidation was, when successful, to put the firm in a monopoly position and enable it to increase considerably its own share of the total proceeds of economic activity.

The process of industrial concentration met with violent opposition, arising firstly from the fear of size itself and secondly from the belief that when a customer had only one source of supply for a commodity he wished to buy he was at the mercy of the supplier who was able to charge a "monopoly price". At first, especially in the first decade of the twentieth century, the two fears were assumed to be coterminous. Size meant monopoly and monopoly meant exploitation. Yet, historically, monopoly in the U.S.A. was by no means a function of the size of the productive unit. Geographical remoteness often meant that the small townsman could only buy from the local supplier while the size of the local market was too small to support more than one supplier. Local monopolies, though less spectacular, were often just as harmful to the consumer as national monopolies. To that extent, the development of national markets by giant firms put an end to the local monopolies of the nineteenth century. Did they merely result, however, in the substitution of national for local monopolies?

Large-scale operations do not necessarily imply monopolization any more than it is necessary for a monopoly to be large-scale. The word "monopoly" itself may be used either as an economist's definition or as an epithet of opprobrium. Even in the economist's usage, no word is more difficult to define and no phenomenon more difficult to measure. One might demonstrate, according to differing definitions of what constitutes monopoly, that American industry is (or, at any given time, was) completely controlled by monopolies, or, conversely, that the possibilities of monopolization in such an economy as the American are slight. When an institution, or set of institutions, has been so consistently and for so long deplored and legislated against, when it has been attacked before Congressional committees, in popular periodicals and novels, by scholars, preachers and poets, it is just as difficult to discover how much of this hostility has been justified as it is to avoid reacting too far in the opposite direction.

To large sections of the American population in the nineteenth century, to New York merchants as well as farmers producing a staple crop, to unorganized workers as well as professional men, the concept of monopoly was absolute. Anything to which the label could be attached was by definition evil and aroused an American's instinctive fears of concentration of power, absentee ownership, coercion of the individual by distant and uncontrolled forces, the destruction of competitive opportunity, as well as sometimes more pressing fears based on immediate self-interest. For similar causes the colonists had rebelled in the eighteenth century and Andrew Jackson had led the attack on the Second Bank of the U.S.A. Yet intermixed with this very real fear of monopoly was an element of envy and sometimes undisguised admiration for the individual who could make so much of his liberty and his opportunities as to create a huge dominating business out of nothing. Despite the public outcries against business concentration, the social climate was on the whole not antagonistic towards the building up of economic empires. Unfortunate though it may have been for those individuals who felt themselves to be the victims, the growth of large businesses was the logical, and perhaps not wholly undesirable, outcome of the Horatio Alger tradition, that the way was open to the humblest to climb to the top of the highest tree.

If one judges from the space devoted to the subject in economic and political writings, the concentration of industry and the dangers of monopoly have been a, if not *the*, major problem of American economic life in the past five decades. Gradually it has been accepted that size of itself need not be evil, but may even bring certain advantages. Nevertheless, monopolization and monopoly power continue to be attacked and the decline of competition deplored with unanimous agreement. In the first period of consolidation between 1896-1904 many combinations secured control over very high percentages of the output of particular commodities, seldom less than 50 per cent, often 90 or over. While pure monopoly was seldom achieved, monopoly power was often unquestionably the main objective. Many attempts were made in the first decade of the twentieth century, to "bust the trusts" and break up the giants, but, although legal dissolutions were obtained, the dominant firms were usually able to retain their hold over their markets. In general, although there are exceptions, the trend since the end of the First World War has been that the share of an industry's production controlled by the dominant firm has declined as other firms have risen to challenge its position. Since the early days of the large corporation in the still relatively restricted economic life of 1898-1911, the ability of any corporation to monopolize a particular corner of the market has gradually diminished although the trend towards large-scale operations has continued. Oligopoly—the dominance of markets by a few firms—has thus come to replace near-monopoly in some industries and emerged in others to replace the former situation of competition.

It is not easy to assess either the main developments of recent decades or the present situation. The large firms have certainly grown larger but so have the smaller ones and it is possible that the latter have in fact somewhat increased their relative share of markets. But the general picture of oligopoly is accurate enough and oligopolistic restrictions may be as damaging to the interests of consumers as those imposed by a pure monopolist; perhaps even more insidious, since a façade of apparent competition can be maintained. But if this picture is accurate, how has it been possible for the economy to continue to generate a higher production per capita of goods and services than any other economy?

Numerous economists have attempted to answer this question in the past few years. One attractive solution to the dilemma has been to draw a parallel with American constitutional arrangements and suggest a doctrine of countervailing power. It is argued that the growth of giant distributing firms has gone a considerable way towards modifying the power of the giant producing firms and that the ultimate beneficiary from the struggle between the two is the consumer. Other writers have asserted that oligopoly positions have become increasingly difficult to maintain because of the increased possibilities of substitution. Technical progress makes possible the development of new raw materials and the diversion of old materials to new uses. Despite the existing structure of industry, expenditure on industrial research in the U.S.A. was nine times as large in 1939 as in 1920 and over the whole period of concentration of the past 70 years, technicians such as physicists, chemists, engineers and metallurgists have increased in number over 10 times as fast as the total gainfully employed. To estimate the validity of either argument takes one back to the basic difficulties of definition and measurement mentioned earlier; even if it be conceded that these arguments contain important elements of truth, they do not destroy the possibility that enough is still left to constitute a formidable core of oligopoly power, strong enough at least in certain sectors to prevent increases in the efficiency of production and to withstand the reduction of prices.

There are other factors in the situation which may not be without importance. The first is the professionalization of management. Competition between one firm and another has to some extent been replaced by competition for promotion within a single firm. The result is that the long-term planning of industrial leaders has come to be dictated by the professional scientist's interest in his work as well as by market considerations. Many large concerns have gone far towards decentralizing decision-making. A corporation may consist of tens of factories in every state of the union and, within the broad strategies laid down centrally, the factory manager may be left a surprising amount of autonomy. Even where the price of a commodity is fixed centrally, the factory manager is on his mettle to increase his own sales at the fixed price and he seeks to do this by improving the quality of the goods produced or the services offered the consumer.

A vast improvement has occurred, moreover, in the collection of information for the assistance of potential buyers. Consumer advice services exist in the U.S.A. on a scale unknown in Western Europe and are a powerful safeguard against complacency on the part of any producer.

The foregoing arguments have been concerned almost solely with aggregates and averages. The figures given conceal very considerable variations between industry and industry, region and region, worker and worker, and the picture is far from static over the period covered by this survey. The absence of inter-state tariffs and the mobility of American industry have been reflected in the loss of position by the states industrialised earliest and in the advance of others. The industrial output of the South Atlantic states, for instance, was in 1899 only one-quarter of that of the New England states and about 7 per cent of the national total. In 1947 the South Atlantic states surpassed New England in industrial output ($6·9 billion compared with $6·8 billion), producing about 10 per cent of the national total. Meanwhile the contribution to total industrial output of the Middle Atlantic states fell from 38 per cent in 1899 to 28 per cent in 1947 and that of the East North Central states increased from 26 per cent to 32 per cent. Most spectacular of all, perhaps, has been the industrial advance of the Pacific states, and above all of California, in the past fifteen years.

The degree of industrialisation and urbanisation, the occupational structure of the labour force and the *per capita* real incomes received in consequence show very considerable deviation in the different states from the average figures given earlier. The significance of the mass market as a prime condition of American economic prosperity is perhaps best illustrated when one looks at that region of the U.S.A. which has benefited the least from the economic advance of the past 100 years, the Southern states. The absence there of many of the general characteristics found elsewhere in the country had economic as well as social consequences. So long as coloured people were regarded as a source of cheap labour, that region remained backward. Already in the 1930's a few southern writers began to appreciate that economic progress in the South depended upon the creation and stimulation of purchasing power in the South and slowly certain businessmen have come to see in the non-white population of the South a potential market as well as a source of labour.

The fluctuations in the real incomes of the different occupational groups have been severe and to examine them in detail is beyond the scope of this essay. Generalizations about the wages of industrial workers would conceal great differences between skilled and unskilled as well, again, as between region and region. The growth and effects of Trade Unions are the subject of a separate essay in this book. Let it suffice here to quote the words of an American writer on trade unionism, C. E. Lindblom, who writes in his book *Unions and Capitalism*, "By contrast with the impoverished European, the American worker lives in abundance and security." With these words, coming from an author who is in strong sympathy with the cause of the trade unionist, few workers in American industry would disagree.

A further question of great significance concerns the role of government in influencing the distribution of economic rewards in the U.S.A. over the past century. To what extent was the allocation of resources and rewards left to the free decisions of price or to what extent were the market forces subjected to governmental intervention? The existence of a tariff in itself involved some degree of governmental direction of resources, causing certain types of goods to be produced instead of certain others. The problem is complicated by the existence of the numerous layers of government in American life. During the first half of the nineteenth century, local or state intervention had been accepted as both necessary and desirable in most parts of the U.S.A., especially in those where there was little or no private capital. There can be little doubt that this condition continued in many spheres after the Civil War. The important question was whether, as local markets expanded into national ones and as the size of economic operations grew, the federal government would and, under the Constitution could, play a similar role to that played earlier by the states. The real question for those who sought intervention was not so much whether intervention would take place—the duty of the government to intervene was not seriously questioned—but at what level of government and to whose advantage intervention would occur. If government was to intervene in the problem of monopoly, for example, should action be taken on the basis of injury suffered by a competitor or of injury suffered by a consumer? Economic conflicts often worked themselves out as struggles for control of government at all the different levels so that its power could be used to private advantage. Whether such governmental intervention as occurred was ever successful in achieving the precise effects intended is yet a further question which must in this essay remain unanswered.

The theoretical distrust of government remained strongly entrenched, throughout most or all of the period covered by this survey, in large sections of the population, always with the special pleading that one's own condition was deserving of assistance. Many of the positive needs for government to be found elsewhere were lacking in the U.S.A. Defence expenditure was negligible for a great part of the period and armed forces could be kept to a minimum. There was no legacy from past wars of a burdensome national debt. This meant not only that almost the entire productive capacity of the nation could be devoted to peaceful purposes, but also that taxation, in the nineteenth century a government's main weapon of intervention, could be largely confined to customs duties. And finally, the very size of the territory to be administered itself inhibited the growth of detailed centralized government. Governmental bureaucracy grew up, like industrial bureaucracy, with the telephone and typewriter and with a change in the status of women. The vast expansion of the activities of the federal government in the past twenty years has had great economic significance, not least in improving the central government's ability to exercise influence over the fluctuations of economic fortunes and check recessions before they are able to deteriorate into general depressions.

This chapter would be incomplete without some mention of the word, despised by economists and philologists alike, automation, a word which for the first time found its way into the *Encyclopaedia Britannica*'s Book of the Year in 1956. Machines were developed in the Second World War for purposes of gun-fire control which reacted without human interference to impulses they received. Since the war machines to control other machines have been introduced in certain branches of American industry. Such machines, with faculties of "memory" and even "thought", have been recognized as containing tremendous potentialities for good and ill. The American reaction to their introduction has been characteristic. They have been cautiously welcomed and no time has been lost in turning scientific invention into industrial innovation. At the same time the social problems involved have been seriously considered. An American mathematician, Norbert Wiener, has coined the word "cybernetics" and written of *The Human Use of Human Beings*.

Yet the problems raised by automation are different in severity rather than in kind from the problems raised by other forms of economic innovation. The human problems created by displacement and redundancy are the same whether the worker is replaced by a machine or whether, say, synthetic fibres come to be preferred to cotton cloth and raw cotton producers find that mills no longer want to buy what they produce. The tentative American approach to the "problem" of automation has been to seek means of smoothing the inevitable short-run frictions in order to achieve the expected long-run benefits. The "wilderness of untried things" still offers its challenge and most Americans still believe that "God has predestinated" and "mankind expects, great things" from their race and nation.

AMERICAN FOREIGN POLICY AND WORLD POWER: 1871-1956

By Max Beloff

*

THE year 1871 is often chosen as a starting-point for the study of modern international relations because the creation of the German Empire appeared to have consolidated the supremacy of the Great Powers of Europe both in Europe and overseas. By the middle of the following century, however, this situation was a thing of the past. World politics were dominated by the rivalry of two Powers, one of which, the Soviet Union, represented the Russian component of the earlier European constellation, while the other, the United States, was not in 1871 regarded as a great Power at all. In this way, Tocqueville's genial prophecy of the 1830's was justified in the event. But this is not all. By the 1950's it was also clear that the struggle between the Soviet Union and the United States would turn largely on the paths to be taken by the peoples of Asia. By 1871 both Russia and the United States were established on the Pacific littoral, and the purchase of Alaska in 1867 had put an end to any Russian hopes of a permanent footing on its further side. But the involvement of either of them in Asian affairs was still very largely limited to matters of commerce. It was only the 1890's—the decade that saw both the completion of the trans-Siberian railway and the establishment of the United States in the Philippines—that produced the real confrontation of Russian and American power in the Far East.

The history of American foreign relations in the period under consideration when taken in its long-term aspect has thus one principal theme, the emergence of the United States as a world Power, and one secondary one, its increased participation in Asian affairs in an era which saw both the apex of "White" imperialism and its decline and fall. But for the European student of this process both are likely to be overshadowed by the importance of the successive phases of American intervention in Europe; its participation in the two wars fought to prevent the domination of Europe by Germany and its action in the wake of the latter to limit the westward expansion of Soviet Communism. A European historian will probably stress aspects of the subject which an American might neglect. This is not to say, however, that Americans themselves would agree in their presentation or interpretations of it. On the contrary, one of the principal features of the story is that every step has been accompanied by a prolonged and often bitter debate over the policies to be adopted, and that these discussions have naturally tended to take the form of historical inquiries. Whereas then it is probably true to say that the United States has its own version of "Whig" historiography, in the sense that each generation sooner or later accepts as desirable, or at least inevitable, domestic changes brought about by its predecessor, and re-writes its history so as to justify them in terms of a general theory of "Americanism", and while the "unreconstructed" Southerners are per-haps the only important exception to this general principle where the internal history of the United States or its pre-1871 expansion are concerned, this broad area of agreement ceases as soon as one comes to the development of United States foreign policy since the 1890's. And one must therefore begin any attempt at an assessment of it with a frank acknowledgment that it must necessarily be a highly subjective one; for the European, too, is almost bound to take sides in this great debate, and is almost certain—Communists and "neutralists" apart—to be unfair to those who have struggled against the tide and who have tried, or still may be trying, to keep the United States in that happy position of peaceful isolation which is still an important part of the "American dream".

Such sympathies should not, however, mean alignment with one or other of the two rival American political parties. It is a mistake to equate Republicanism with either isolationism or nationalism, as though this held good at all times, and even more erroneous to regard the Demo-cratic Party as necessarily embodying a tendency towards greater inter-national co-operation. Both errors are understandable. The involvement of the United States in both World Wars took place under Democratic Presidents; it was one of them who unsuccessfully tried to get the United States into the League of Nations for whose existence he was largely responsible, and the other who successfully brought about the creation of the United Nations Organization, with the United States playing a principal role within it. Again it was his successor, President Truman, who was responsible for the series of commitments ranging from the Marshall Plan and the North Atlantic Treaty to the intervention in Korea by which the United States assumed, on behalf of the United Nations, the major share of the free world's resistance to Soviet Com-munism. But against this must be set the fact that the Democratic Party at times appealed especially to elements in the population which, either because of their remoteness from Europe, or because of ancestral memories connecting them all too closely with it, objected to any kind of American participation in European affairs, or alternatively to the parti-cular kind that the current situation appeared to demand—notably support for Great Britain. Woodrow Wilson came into office dedicated to a programme which—outside the American continent at least—was one of almost total isolation; and with a belligerent pacifist in W. J.

Bryan as his Secretary of State. And Populism out of which Bryan emerged was a movement at once deeply isolationist, fervently jingoistic and bitterly anti-British since the London money-market was held responsible for maintaining the gold standard. Franklin Roosevelt, it is true, was active in politics under Wilson's aegis at a time when the pendulum had swung far in the other direction. But there is no reason to suppose that he did not share by now the revulsion against American participation in international affairs which was part of the disillusion brought about by the aftermath of the First World War. The "New Deal" of his early period in power drew inspiration from precisely those circles of earnest reformers with a Populist or progressivist background whose instincts were thoroughly isolationist; and after some hesitation, the recovery policies adopted were essentially autarkic in their approach. The Franklin Roosevelt of the first administration was by no means the internationalist that he later became. Nor was the internationalism of even the later Roosevelt or of Truman entirely unqualified.

The continental expansionism of the mid-nineteenth century of which the Democratic Party was the vehicle had by no means affected the party's adherence to the anti-colonialist doctrines of the Revolution. Once the United States had reached its continental boundaries, the Democratic creed objected to further expansion which would mean the establishment of permanent domination over other peoples. From this advantageous moral position it was possible to criticize the actions of other Powers who had taken a different view and assumed imperial burdens. As a result of the Spanish-American war at first supported by the Populists, the United States, under Republican leadership, assumed similar burdens of its own, and in subsequent years added to them something like an informal suzerainty in parts of Latin America. Of this embryonic empire it was the intention of the Democratic Party to be the liquidators; and wherever straightforward strategic considerations did not counsel the contrary, its Presidents acted accordingly. The independence of the Philippines, the "good neighbour" policy in Latin America, and the granting of full self-government to Porto Rico were all Democratic achievements. This meant that Roosevelt and Truman were free to use American power to insist that other Powers followed the American example, even where the circumstances were quite different and the common cause by no means self-evidently served. It is clear that the errors in Roosevelt's attitude towards the Soviet Union, and in his handling of French susceptibilities, as well as his never entirely removed suspicions of Churchill arose from his fundamental anti-colonialism. The same doctrinaire attitude was responsible for post-war American policy in regard particularly to South-East Asia and the Middle East, although there was by then a greater awareness of the realities of Soviet policy. It was not clear that Truman's great political realism ever extended to grasping the fact that there were vast areas in the world to which the simple assumptions of the American democratic faith did not apply.

The belief that the Republican party is by nature the more isolationist of the two is one which it was natural to hold in the Harding-Coolidge era of withdrawal from European affairs; but it cannot be maintained without qualification if a longer perspective is taken. From the Civil War until 1885 the Republicans, who were in power throughout, combined isolationism where European affairs were concerned with annexationist sentiments towards Canada, and with a forward policy in Latin America, and to a lesser extent in the Pacific. In Latin America the main objective was to break the mid-century agreement with Great Britain under which an ultimate isthmian canal was to be a joint enterprise. This object was finally achieved, again by a Republican administration, when the Clayton-Bulwer treaty of 1850 was superseded by the Hay-Pauncefote treaty of 1901. This made possible the actions through which Panama seceded from Colombia, and the subsequent construction and operation of the Canal as a wholly United States affair in a zone under a perpetual lease. The first post-Civil War Democratic administration, President Grover Cleveland's, marked something of a reaction against imperialism, and his Secretary of State Thomas Bayard has been described as the first American statesman to understand that Canada had to be dealt with as an autonomous nation; yet it was not until some time in the following century that this was fully realized by the majority of his compatriots and hopes of its eventual annexation abandoned. Indeed, American clashes with Canada, notably over the Alaskan boundary arbitration in 1903, did much to hamper the growth of better relations between the United States and Great Britain. It was not until the emergence of the Nazi threat and the Ogdensburg Agreement for joint defence, in 1940, that we get the contemporary notion developed, that Canada is a natural link between the two halves of the "English-speaking" world.

The return of the Republicans to office in 1889 saw a return to imperialism with the attempted annexation of Hawaii as the climax of the movement; the Democrats coming back into power with Cleveland in 1893 repudiated this action, but this by no means implied a general retreat. For it was under Cleveland that the American claim to invoke the Monroe Doctrine as giving the United States a positive right to interfere in any issue in the Western hemisphere in which a non-European Power was involved, brought her closest to a conflict with Britain in the crisis over the boundary between Venezuela and British Guiana.

It was during the McKinley-Roosevelt period of Republican domination that followed the defeat of Bryan's bid for the Presidency in 1896, that the Republican Party went furthest in the direction of an American imperialism with the Pacific as the main scene of its operations and with naval power as its principal instrument; and it was under President Taft that the link between governmental policy and U.S. business enterprise both in Latin America and the Far East gave rise to the term "dollar diplomacy". It was the "expansionists of 1898"—such men as Senator Lodge, later Woodrow Wilson's major antagonist in the question of the League of Nations, the naval historian A. T. Mahan, McKinley's and Roosevelt's Secretary of State, John Hay, and Theodore Roosevelt himself—who first voiced on the American scene the leading ideas of late nineteenth-century imperialism: the obsolescence of small States, the duty of the white man to spread the benefits of "civilization", the demand that one's own nation should not fall out of the race. The striking development of American industry which is the main theme of American history in the post-Civil War decades had now reached the point at which foreign markets began to seem necessary and at which, therefore, important business classes hitherto hostile to expansionism began to jump on the imperialist bandwagon. Both in Europe and in such spheres of imperialist rivalry as China, the era of free trade appeared to be coming to an end. America had to get its foot in at the door before it was too late. (In agriculture, significantly, the development was in the opposite direction. The agricultural depression out of which Populism grew arose from European conditions; the recovery from it was due to the growth of the urban market at home. Henceforward American farmers could afford to ignore the economic health of Europe and to provide a principal source of support for isolationism.)

The apparent enthusiasm with which the country welcomed the war with Spain and the territorial acquisitions which followed it, could not conceal the misgivings that were widely felt. It is significant that these were only partially concerned with the general effect upon the United States' relations with other countries that was likely to be produced by abandoning the principle of hemispheric self-limitation. Some did indeed foresee that the Philippines would ineluctably involve the United States in all the intricacies of Far Eastern policies. It would not be stretching the point too far to say that the shadow of the beleaguered garrison of Bataan in 1942 hung over the debates of 1899. But more typical were the arguments adduced to prove that the acquisition of overseas territory was something hostile to the very genius of American institutions, that the Constitution itself had not envisaged the incorporation of any non-contiguous territory not inhabited predominantly by the white race, and not therefore easily capable of participating in the full rights and benefits of statehood. Hawaii remains a perpetually unsuccessful candidate for statehood; though as in the case of Alaska this may be for party reasons. An Empire involved the possession of permanent military forces and the whole apparatus of conscription which weighed down the European nations with its ever-rising demands for men and money. And again, the debate carries us forward across the decades. Although the Civil War itself had been in many respects the first mass-conflict of the industrial age to be fought anywhere in the world, it had not produced any permanent militarization of American society or thought. The Army had

been allowed to relapse into the small professional force with wars
against the Indians as its principal justification—these it must be remembered did not end until the 1880's—that it had been since the Revolution.
The brief Cuba campaign had shown up its weaknesses in organization
for any more complex operation. It was only after this, during the tenure
of the post of Secretary of War by Elihu Root, that we get the foundations
of the modern American general staff system and army organization. In
peacetime, the American people remained wedded to the idea of a voluntary army. In both world wars, however, the United States succeeded
more rapidly than either its friends or its enemies thought possible, in
raising vast military forces under the principle of universal service, and
in placing behind them the full resources of the great American industrial
machine. It was after the Second World War when the need of "containing" Soviet communism brought a halt to the rush towards total de-
mobilization that the unpleasant likelihood of a permanent commitment
towards maintaining large military forces was generally perceived. Even
then it was not possible for the administration to get a permanent scheme
of universal military training accepted by a nation still looking back
nostalgically to the relative isolation of the pre-atomic age. The wartime
"draft" became the foundation of "cold war" defence. But with the new
weapons of mass-destruction, and with the consequent possibility of
sudden decisions being needed for the sake of national survival itself, the
whole military apparatus and particularly that of the air-force became
for the first time a dominant feature of the American scene—the inescapable penalty of world power.

In 1898-9, all this was in the future. The only seriously professional
service was the navy which began to assume its modern shape in the
1890's. In Britain the need for a powerful navy to protect the commerce
of an island totally dependent upon it, was axiomatic among the old
governing classes and the obvious threat from Germany enabled them to
pass the doctrine on to their successors. In the United States where
maritime commerce itself could be viewed as a luxury—and in a sense it
remained one to the very end of our period—it was possible in 1898-9
to argue that a strong navy was unnecessary and merely provocative.
The expansion of American trade had proceeded without such protection
and could go on doing so. Here the opponents of imperialism were least
successful with their pleas; a more fruitful career awaited a final argument,
namely that if America held herself aloof from armed conflicts and refused
to give hostages to fortune in the shape of overseas possessions or bases,
she would both gain the moral prestige of neutrality and be in a position
to make her influence felt at the point when the combatant nations would
all find themselves exhausted.

The anti-imperialist movement in so far as it was a political one was,
as we have seen, largely an affair of the Democrats. But the instincts to
which they appealed were national not party. And this can be seen in

the severe restrictions that the Republican administrations accepted as far as their own action was concerned; Cuba, for instance, was not retained. Despite the appreciation of the sympathy towards the United States shown by Britain in the Spanish War, the prospects of an Anglo-American entente or alliance entertained by men like Joseph Chamberlain were quite illusory. The idea of the English-speaking countries policing the world in concert ran up against the deep-rooted American anti-colonialism, and it was only the cautious attitude of the administration that prevented the strong pro-Boer sentiments expressed by Congress from resulting in action disadvantageous to the British position. In fact, with the growth of the American navy and with the increasing pre-occupations of Britain nearer home, the long period in which the Royal Navy had been the effective guarantee of the Monroe Doctrine now came to an end; the withdrawal of British naval strength from the Caribbean was the signal that this was indeed a fact. But the American public mind was very little exercised about its implications.

In the Far East the inability of the United States to take on permanent military and political commitments limited the effectiveness of its policies. The claim that John Hay's "open door" notes, insisting upon an equality of advantages for all nations in China, had an important effect upon developments there has been shown to be baseless. The United States had to accept the continued disintegration of China into "spheres of influence", and failed to make good its persistent belief that economic penetration could be divorced from political responsibilities. Under Wilson, the American attempt to extend its footing was called off. It was not capital but sentiment that Americans chiefly invested in China; the remission of the U.S. share of the Boxer Rising indemnity for educational purposes was the best symbol of the country's attitude, and Christian missionaries its main exponents. It was because this was so that the passing of China under Communist rule in 1945–9 was so great a blow to American self-esteem; American gifts had been flung back in America's face, and high-minded missionaries jostled shady financiers in the "China Lobby" of post-World War II Washington.

The theory about the advantages of neutrality that found expression in anti-imperialist propaganda at the turn of the century was the source of much of the thinking about foreign policy of both Wilson and Franklin Roosevelt. Wilson's hesitations about taking up the German challenge at sea—and in spite of all "revisionism" it was the submarine campaign that eventually brought America into the war—were bound up with his belief in the contribution that an America that stayed neutral might make to an enduring peace. The serious friction with Britain in the period before America's entry arose indeed from an insistence on neutral "rights" in a time of war at sea that went straight back to the American attitude under the very different circumstances of the French Revolutionary and Napoleonic wars. But it was envenomed by the American feeling that neutrality was a virtuous and constructive attitude, just as on the other side, British ire was roused by the claim that Britain's seizures of conditional contraband were morally on a par with the sinking of unarmed merchantmen, and by the equanimity with which many Americans seemed to view her life and death struggle against the brutal violators of Belgium. Even when Wilson overcame his scruples and brought his country into the war, he persisted in regarding the American role as something separate from that of those "associated" (not "allied") Powers who had borne the brunt of the fighting. America was out for loftier objectives; and significantly enough, although once in the war her use of sea-power was no less all-embracing than Britain's, as indeed the North's conduct during the Civil War might have led one to expect, the "freedom of the seas" figured prominently among her own "war-aims". It is true that subsequent historians have tended to under-rate the speed with which Wilson educated himself in the realities of international politics, once the need was inescapable. The malicious and foolish caricature that Maynard Keynes succeeded in producing of him, with deplorable consequences both in Europe and in the United States, is no more accurate than the charge of being a dupe of communism or worse levelled by Senator McCarthy and his friends against Truman, Dean Acheson, George Marshall and the memory of Franklin Roosevelt. On the contrary, one's admiration for the extent to which Wilson discerned the main issues in the torn Europe of 1919, and understood the necessity of securing a settlement which would range more interests behind it than against it, must increase as the records of the Peace Conference are studied. There is something to be said for a trained mind—even a trained academic mind.

Wilson had abandoned neutrality for the United States in favour of neutrality for no-one; but this idea and the League of Nations that embodied it were rejected by American public opinion, still possessed by illusions that the President had outgrown, and deluged with propaganda that he had not the political skill to counteract. Franklin Roosevelt—in no sense the equal of Wilson intellectually—would at least not make that mistake. But as a result of his success in avoiding it, he could not help but be carried along with the flood of national sentiment in the 1930's that was engaged in resurrecting the discarded notion of neutrality, and in turning it into the keystone of national policy. It is true that Roosevelt had misgivings about the form taken by the neutrality legislation of the 1930's, and in particular in its elimination of any executive discretion in discriminating, however mildly, between an aggressor and his victim. He became aware sooner than many Americans that the actions of Japan and the European dictators might reach the point at which the United States would not secure its own safety simply by refusing to exercise its rights as a maritime nation—the core of the neutrality legislation. It can be argued that his hesitations about suggesting any more positive action after the hostile public reaction to the "Quarantine" speech of October 1937 arose simply out of a refusal to go one step beyond what the people would accept. But this is not the whole story. He also seems to have envisaged a role for constructive neutrality—a policy that seemed the more persuasive in the greater importance now of the United States in the world economy. In his suggestion for a conference at Washington made to Neville Chamberlain in January 1938, Roosevelt made the customary distinction between economic problems to whose solution the United States was willing to contribute, and those territorial and political problems of Europe which were not her concern. Given the nature of Hitler's and Mussolini's objectives this distinction was of course quite unreal, and a positive neutrality based upon it, almost meaningless. Between September 1939 and Pearl Harbour the issues were quite different from those that Wilson had faced between 1914 and 1917. It was only in retrospect that people now argued that the United States had perceived the threat to itself of the German drive for domination on the earlier occasion, and that America had really gone to war in 1917 in order to preserve a world balance of power. But it was true that it was the case this time that the United States could be in no doubt where its interests lay, and that its neutrality as regards Germany was only technical. The hope that armed intervention could still be avoided was not however abandoned for a long time; and the steps by which the United States was caught up in the struggle did not follow each other in any regular rhythm; at times the administration was behind rather than in front of some of its unofficial pacemakers.

What is more to the point in the present context is that even when its cause became almost wholly identified with that of Britain and her allies, the United States felt that it occupied a ground apart, that it was "neutral" still in the sense that its aims, unlike those of its associates, were wholly disinterested, and that its power should be used not only to defeat the common enemy but to secure a settlement on its own terms. The American interpretation of the "Atlantic Charter" reflected both the anti-colonialism already referred to, and the insistence upon non-discrimination in trading and financial policies which was Cordell Hull's particular contribution to the later and more "liberal" period of the "New Deal", and which was especially directed against the British system of imperial preference. The doctrine of non-discrimination was of course popular with important American economic interests, and played a considerable role in the shaping of the international economic institutions of the post-war world, as well as in the Anglo-American diplomacy of that period, with the Americans hoping that both imperial preference and the sterling-area might disappear for good. Again, in its "Vichy" policy and in its subsequent refusal to accept, until the last possible moment, General de Gaulle's claim to speak for France, the United States government was moved not only by the President's personal prejudices against the French leader, but by the view that its role could somehow be that of an arbiter seeking to provide an impartial framework within which the French could be summoned to work out solutions of their national divisions.

The full story of inter-allied diplomacy in the Second World War cannot of course be understood solely in the light of this conception of a separate American mission, whether in Europe, or in the Far East, where the U.S. Navy in particular, after the disgrace of Pearl Harbour, was determined to see that its role in the defeat of Japan was the cardinal one, and did not welcome the notion of an important contribution by British forces, where the pressure to concentrate on land in support of Chiang Kai-shek cut across the British preference for campaigns aimed against the Japanese control of British and Dutch colonial territories, and where as far as peace-making was concerned, the U.S. Navy was determined to secure the bases it needed, irrespective of general notions about self-determination or trusteeship. Indeed as these differences over the conduct of the war in the Japanese theatre show quite clearly there is not much reality in the idea that the dominant American characteristic in wartime is to concentrate on purely military issues and leave politics to look after themselves. Where the United States had political aims of its own it took good care of them in strategic planning. What happened in Europe was that the United States with few direct post-war interests was suspicious that Britain which was more concerned would give these too much weight in deciding upon the course of military operations. It is now fairly clear that much of this suspicion was misplaced, that in the major planning decisions of 1943, the British were as keen as the Americans that complete priority should be given to the landings in northern France. It was over the secondary aspects of the invasion in 1944, and in particular over the question of whether the Italian front and the possibilities it offered of exploitation towards the Balkans and the Danube valley should be denuded in favour of the landings in southern France that the main clash came, and was unfortunately settled in favour of the American point of view.

The reason for the Americans' insistence upon this course was partly their military doctrine of concentration upon the enemy's most vital front with all available forces—a doctrine which memories of the horrors of the trench warfare of 1914-18 made highly suspect to the British; partly the strong American preference for keeping to plans once made, and their suspicions of improvisation (all of which may be natural to a country which approaches war with an outlook derived from the large-scale industry upon which its war-making ultimately depends); and partly, certainly, the fact that Roosevelt's suspicions of the Russians took so much longer to awaken than Churchill's. The same combination of motives helps to explain—alongside more technical and even personal considerations—the American refusal to accept Montgomery's plan for putting everything into a left-hook movement after the liberation of most of France, and Eisenhower's insistence upon an advance on a broad front. The refusal to take advantage of the rapidity of the final German collapse to alter the arrangements already made with the Russians even to the extent of waiting so that the latter could liberate Prague, and the failure to make certain of an adequate connection with a Berlin left islanded in the Soviet zone of occupation, can both be traced perhaps to the operation of similar factors. Where there was no real doctrine about the political future other than that expressed in vague aspirations for democratic self-determination, the simplest thing to do was to plead the priority of military considerations in wartime, and to claim that this made for a more efficient conduct of operations than was possible under the British system, where, so it was believed, the contact between the statesmen and the generals was unnecessarily intimate. But Britain and Europe benefited enormously from the purely "strategic" decision to tackle Hitler first.

A similar danger of over-simplification arises in the case of another interpretation of American foreign policy during the whole of the period now under consideration which stresses as the source of its failures a tendency to visualize its issues too much in terms of an abstract morality, to regard pronouncements in this field, whether specific like Hay's "open door" notes or more general like some of Wilson's "Fourteen Points"—some were specific enough—or the Atlantic Charter, as though they had some kind of validity irrespective of the strength the country was prepared to put behind them. It stresses too the use of "non-recognition" as a weapon against régimes the U.S. disapproves of and appeals to "peoples" over the heads of governments. It regards it as having come to a climax in the Republicans' slogan "liberation" (of Eastern Europe) in the election of 1952. The argument arises from a consideration of the fact that the Americans of the generations in which their country's rise to world power took place inherited from their predecessors not only a utopian vision of the world in which a peaceful isolation from international problems was compatible with perpetual growth, but also a set of institutions which made it particularly hard for a more realistic policy to be followed. All democracies suffer from some disadvantages when it comes to the matter of making sacrifices for an objective that appears remote from their daily concerns, though they have the compensating advantage of being far tougher when they have to face the ultimate test of strength. The United States by dividing the powers of the Executive from those of the legislature and by making rivalry between them an almost inescapable part of the political scene gives a peculiar twist to this congenital weakness. The jealousy with which the Senate regards the treaty-power makes it peculiarly hard for an American administration to use treaties for the furtherance of its national policies—as John Hay for instance, bitterly complained—and has tended to drive it into various subterfuges—"executive agreements", for instance—to avoid a direct clash. Where the treaty-power might be used to curtail the country's future autonomy in foreign relations, whether by the innocuous arbitration treaties of President Taft or by Wilson's proposed adherence to the League, the Senate will be more on its guard than ever. The massive support for the ratification of the United Nations Charter and the North Atlantic Treaty might seem to have marked the passing of this attitude; but that this was not true was shown by the later expression of fears that the President's authority as Commander-in-Chief to move more troops to Europe at will might be a derogation of Congress' ultimate power over peace and war—a power which Roosevelt's handling of the Japanese negotiations in 1941, which inevitably led to a breach, might be said to have called into question anyhow. The support for the proposed "Bricker amendment" which would place still further limitations upon the Executive's power in foreign negotiations and upon the domestic effectiveness of treaties was another testimony to this abiding tension. In the post-World War II decade the importance of aid programmes and consequently of the financial powers of the House of Representatives made it necessary for the outlook of this body to be taken into account as well. And since the House is for obvious reasons even more sensitive to the public temper than the Senate the area of democratic control has been enlarged accordingly.

The result of this state of affairs, according to American critics, has been the constant necessity of making a direct appeal to the people whenever the Executive needs support for its policies. Since the mass of the people cannot be expected to follow the highly technical arguments that foreign policy often involves, the only choice is to appeal to their fears, or to their moral feelings. In peace time they can only be induced to act by being told that there are devils afoot—and this explains some of the internal excesses of the "cold war": in war time they must be encouraged to accept the view that they are fighting not for some laudable though limited end but in a veritable crusade, to save the world for democracy, to end all wars, or to destroy fascism. Once they accept this view, so it is argued, the whole thing goes into reverse; it is now the people who make the running and insist upon an all-out victory, upon "unconditional surrender" and the other impediments to a cool appraisal of the always shifting and complex issues of wartime and post-war diplomacy. This would explain for instance, the large measure of popular support received by General MacArthur when he complained of having been forced by the President to keep to a limited war in Korea instead of carrying it over into a direct attack on the Chinese sources of North Korean strength.

While one can understand the background of such thinking and sympathize with many of the points made, the non-American is likely to conclude that too much can be made of all this, that the idea of international relations as being something altogether concerned with the adjustment of material differences of which experts are the best if not the only judges, is as unrealistic as the popular feeling that if only one more troublemaker could be got out of the way—the Kaiser, Hitler, Stalin or Mao Tse-tung—a permanent peace could be established, and the United States permitted at last to withdraw from responsibilities for which she never asked.

It is perhaps significant of the weakness in the position of those intellectuals who criticize the over-moralistic attitudes of their American compatriots, that they do not seem to give much credit to the American President of the period, who, more than any other, did try to get the nation to take a more realistic view. It is not easy, admittedly, to be an apologist for Theodore Roosevelt; his curiously ill-adjusted personality, his capacity for self-dramatization, to put it no worse, which grew with the years, his lack of veracity where his own past actions were concerned —the "ultimatum" to the Kaiser he claimed to have sent in regard to the blockade of Venezuela in 1902, for instance—his streak of sheer childishness, are as much against him as the fact that the boy-scout system of values he affected is as out-dated in modern intellectual circles as the creed of Rudyard Kipling. Nevertheless, Theodore Roosevelt—like his friend the historian Henry Adams—did at least see that whatever world history might be, it was unlikely that it was something that could be reversed by a simple act of will. The emergence of new great States in competition with each other, the current challenge of Germany, the future challenge of Russia, the certainty that Asia would not be quiescent for ever and the likelihood that Japan, the first of its nations to awaken, at bottom lumped "Russians, English, Americans, Germans, all of us simply as white devils inferior to themselves not only in what they regarded as the essentials of civilization but in courage and forethought"— all these he did perceive as primary elements in the world-picture that American statesmanship had to have in mind, it if were to make sense of its foreign policies, now and in the years to come. It is not surprising that at a time when such considerations were remote from the minds of most of his fellow-countrymen, and when the speed of change was so rapid and the alignments between the Great Powers so uncertain, Roosevelt's attempt to translate his feelings about power-relationships into concrete action were often rather amateur. Yet he was right in believing that, in spite of the original hostility felt in America towards Russia at the time of the Russo-Japanese war, it was not in fact desirable in the general interest that Russia should be forced into total collapse. Indeed the mediatory role of the United States in bringing about the Peace of Portsmouth represents perhaps the most successful example of the policy of "constructive neutrality". Again, though he certainly over-rated the significance of the American role in the Algeciras conference, he did at least grasp the fact that what was at stake was not simply a dispute about which groups of investors were going to do well out of Morocco, but whether Germany was to be allowed to crash her way unhindered into the unchallenged hegemony of the European continent. Again, he grasped the fact that the policy of excluding from the United States Asiatic immigrants in any significant numbers—a policy of which he approved—was bound to produce resentment in Asian countries, and that the maximum effort ought to be made to bring the restriction about with the smallest blow to the *amour-propre* of the peoples concerned, and to avoid submitting their nationals to petty indignities. Instead of that, the Japanese in California were insulted and provoked, as the Chinese had been before them, by the very people who demanded advantages in Asiatic markets, and who were indifferent to naval defence. Finally, Theodore Roosevelt condemned in language which the modern "realists" could hardly better, the persistent American tendency to make representations on behalf of the oppressed in countries whose policies they were not in a position to affect, and in whose affairs they did not in fact intend to intervene. His comparison of certain aspects of American behaviour to that indulged in by the England of Palmerston and Russell was apt enough. The slogan "speak softly and carry a big stick" has been mocked at by the sophisticated; but it is certainly a better maxim for statesmen than the reverse.

The particular aspect of moralistic behaviour involved in the criticism of the internal policies of foreign Powers is connected, where the United States is concerned, with another aspect of the link in these years between its internal history and its foreign relations. How far, one may ask, was American foreign policy affected by the presence on the national scene of groups whose attitudes were affected by their European origins? (The Asians were too few to count politically and the Africans showed no desire to renew the ties with their continent of origin, just as Communist propaganda failed to get them to accept the idea of themselves as a separate nationality to be treated along the lines of the Soviet "nationalities" policy. One could almost argue that the least "hyphenated" Americans have been coloured Americans.) The period, it must be recalled, was one of rapid change in the composition of the population itself. In the immediately post-Civil War period the domination of the Anglo-Saxon element was being challenged by the children of the Germans, Scandinavians and Irish who had formed the bulk of the non-English immigrants in the immediately pre-Civil War period. This immigration continued, but in the 1890's and 1900's was overwhelmed by the "new immigration" from southern and eastern Europe. For a variety of reasons this new movement was looked at askance by representatives of the older stocks, and the combination of racial and religious prejudice with straight protectionism on the part of labour produced the immigration restrictions of the 1920's, and the introduction of the "quota" system which roughly stabilized the existing make-up of the population, and left the "melting-pot", tempered by differential birthrates and some religious and social inhibitions against inter-marriage, to do the rest. The importance in foreign policy of the minority groups depended upon a combination of several factors: the extent to which the groups themselves possessed a unity of sentiment—and this declined with successive generations and the rise of previously depressed groups to a higher social status; the extent to which particular policies seemed to affect the interests or sentiments of a particular group; and finally the extent to which the geographical distribution of such groups made their views politically effective.

A special problem is presented by the "Anglo-Saxons" themselves whose role at the seats of power and influence in government and business and academic life was always greater than their numerical weight would warrant. It has been argued that they provided a pressure-group none the less powerful for being unseen in favour of policies designed to uphold the cause of Britain. A British historian may be excused from making a judgment on this point; he is too likely to regard Britain's cause as self-evidently just and as needing no special support. Where the remainder are concerned, the general principles stated are not difficult to illustrate. The Irish were persistent throughout in their hostility to any form of rapprochement with Britain; in the pre-1914 period the Jews were active in their propaganda against Tsarist Russia, and achieved some success when the United States refused in 1911 to renew its long-standing commercial treaty with that country. During the 1914-18 war the Germans and Irish were strongest against United States involvement, while the Poles, Czechs, Slovaks and others did their best to secure American support for their respective national claims in Europe. In the inter-war years the process of assimilation made rapid progress, and it is arguable whether the particular strength of isolationism in the mid-West was due to the importance of German (and Scandinavian) elements in its population or to its geographic remoteness from Europe. The hopes that the Nazis had pinned upon the German-Americans as sympathizers with their cause hardly bore fruit, although the German-American "Bund" caused some alarm for a time. In the event, German-Americans proved much less important as a pressure-group than they had a generation earlier. The possible sympathies of Italian-Americans for Mussolini were at no time an important factor. Indeed the outstanding example of sectional pressure in the 1930's was that presented by Catholic support for Franco against Republican Spain. This undoubtedly played a part in the American attitude towards "non-intervention".

In the post-war decade it is hard to discern how far minority groups were responsible for the sharpening attitude towards the Soviet Union which was oppressing so many of their homelands, because their hostility towards communism was so widely shared by Americans who had no special connections with eastern Europe. The U.S. had recognized the Soviet régime a decade later than the other Great Powers—in 1933. A

x

new feature was the attempt to reverse the familiar process and use
minority groups to forward American national aims, as in the enlistment
of Italian-Americans to try to influence their relatives and friends in Italy
to vote anti-Communist. The attention of the outside world was particularly directed towards the part played by the Jewish minority with its
heavy voting concentration in New York, in determining American
policy towards the Palestine problem. It is probable that their influence
was vastly exaggerated, particularly in Britain. In the first place, Ernest
Bevin's heavy-handedness and apparent indifference to the fate of the
pitiful survivors of European Jewry was genuinely condemned on
humanitarian grounds by many non-Jewish Americans. Secondly, as the
United States itself became involved in Middle Eastern politics the same
instinct to seek solutions by placating Arab nationalism made itself as
obvious in the State Department as it was in the Foreign Office. And
once American national or economic interests were, or seemed to be,
concerned, the "Jewish vote" appeared almost powerless to affect policy
towards Israel. For it must not be overlooked, in dealing with this whole
question of minority influences upon foreign affairs, that the major purpose of all immigrant groups so far, has been to Americanize themselves;
and in the last resort they are unlikely to let sentiment run away with
them to an extent that might jeopardize their right to be regarded as
one-hundred-per-cent Americans. The criticism of American policy in
the Palestine dispute can hardly be based upon Truman's pressure on the
mandatory régime to admit more immigrants, or upon his recognition of
the State of Israel immediately it was proclaimed. What one can say is
that it provides another example of the American refusal to accept the
fact that actions of this kind are a commitment to more than verbal support
of the situations so reached. And here, as we have seen, we touch upon a
much wider aspect of the adaptation of the United States to its role of
World Power.

In examining how far it achieved this adaptation in the period under
review three aspects of the problem deserve attention. That just mentioned—the willingness to support policies by appropriate means—is, as
we have seen, a recurring one. A second is institutional, and has been
alluded to; though one would have to add to the problems presented by
the relations between the President and Congress, several others within
the executive sphere itself. One result of the long reign of isolationism
has been the difficulty in persuading Congress to provide properly for
the foreign service. This was to some extent overcome and a good
professional service built up largely after the First World War. The
publication of the diplomatic documents for the 1930's has showed that
the United States was better served in Europe by its diplomats than
Britain. But the China débâcle and the ensuing witch-hunt revived all
Congress' old suspicions of professional diplomacy and dealt a severe
blow to the morale of the foreign service and to its prospects of satisfactory

recruitment. This is a serious problem. Most important of all there is the need to work out clear principles for the governing of civil-military relations in a country whose ideology denies that these are a problem of government at all. Somehow the Pentagon must be brought within the Constitution; some aspects of the Truman-MacArthur controversy suggest that this has not yet been done; what would have happened if Truman had not had the unanimous and powerful backing of his chiefs of staff? Finally there is the question whether a country that has so suddenly become one of two World Powers can accept the fact that even in such a situation it requires allies and has to learn to understand them.

The idea of a particularly close partnership with Britain, cherished by Churchill, did not survive into the post-war period. The parting of the ways was signalized by the American refusal to continue co-operation in the field of atomic research, thus forcing both countries into the costly search for self-sufficiency in the ultimate weapons of destruction. It is notable also that the U.S. strategic air force—the means for the delivery of the atom and hydrogen bombs—remained wholly under American control, and was not subjected to the N.A.T.O. machinery.

On the whole United States policies in Europe since 1947 have clearly been to the advantage of the Free World. But the fact that the United States is not universally beloved does not spring only from the traditional unpopularity of benefactors. It is genuinely felt that its policy has at times been unnecessarily unmindful of European feelings; its pressure for German re-armament in 1950 caused by a misinterpretation in Washington of the significance of the Korean affair set back the cause of European unity without, in the event, providing any German divisions until the circumstances that had produced the demand for them had completely altered. The attempt to bludgeon France into the European Defence Community was a further example of an unwillingness to believe that honest men may hold different views even on vital matters. Americans, it is argued, tend altogether too readily to judge other countries and statesmen wholly by the extent to which they seem ready to conform to the immediate policies of the United States—hence the favour shown to Western Germany and Dr Adenauer. As against the Marshall Plan and N.A.T.O., these things should not bulk too large, but they provide some of the question marks against the popular and attractive notion that the real future of the United States as a world power lies within some wider community of free nations.

It is indeed remarkable enough that such a possibility can be seriously discussed at all. The wartime thinking of President Roosevelt and his circle ran on quite different lines; it was hostile to any form of regional organization (other than the Pan-American Union which, like the Monroe Doctrine in the League Covenant, was bound to have a special dispensation), and in favour of a single world organization. The United Nations Organization is an American conception to a greater extent than was

Wilson's League, many of whose roots lay in Europe. At first the only spheres that seemed to be excluded from it were those involving America's security against her former enemies; the quadripartite occupation of Germany which would have been tripartite but for Churchill's vigorous defence of French rights, and Japan where General MacArthur devoted the years of his satrapy to planting the seeds of American democracy on a rather stony soil. Later, when the Soviet interpretation of the veto—natural enough when the United States could command so many votes—made the original conception of U.N.O. obsolete, United States' policies were still devoted to trying to make use of it where possible, if necessary by extending the powers of the General Assembly at the expense of the Security Council. The U.S. opposition to seating Communist China is significant here. It was only with the development of "neutralism" in Asia, and the consequent likelihood that the temper of the United Nations would not harmonize too easily with the American outlook that action outside its framework became more acceptable in both the political and the economic field. But it remained true even then, that the universalist appeal of the United Nations was an important obstacle to a renewed burst of disillusion with an unsatisfactory world, accompanied perhaps by a new bout of the isolationism which can never be far below the surface of a people brought up to respect the American dream.

At this point, history ends and speculation begins. But there is one more historical lesson that deserves recall and that not the least important. As one looks over the enormous distance traversed by the United States from the almost complete isolation of the 1870's to the almost total involvement of the 1950's, one is bound to ask oneself whether one cannot make altogether too much of the whole question of popular attitudes, national or sectional, and of the policies of individual statesmen. So much of what happened seems to have been the inevitable outcome of vast unplanned changes in American society itself and in the outer world. Before the First World War the United States, though already a Great Power in virtue of her industrial and naval strength, was still on the periphery of international politics. She emerged from it as the dominant industrial and naval power and as a major creditor; domestic decisions like the imposition of immigration quotas, and the decision to devalue the dollar, domestic events like the Wall Street "crash" of 1929 had their immediate repercussions everywhere in the world. It is true that the United States could, and did, in her actual policies refuse to accept the seeming logic of her new position. Her tariff policy remained that of an underdeveloped debtor-country and did not make the same transition to free trade as Britain had done at a comparable moment in her own history, though the importance of the tariff factor has been over-rated; the ill-effects of her commercial policies were magnified by her application of non-political and hence invalid principles to the highly political questions of reparations and war-debts. New York seemingly performed the function of the world's financial capital less efficiently than London had done. But errors in policy could not alter the facts nor destroy the real relations of power. In the same way the consequences to her of the unchallenged rise of the dictators were ineluctable whatever her politicians might say or do.

The Second World War still further altered the economic relationship between the United States and most of the rest of the world, and posed new questions of how best America's great economic power could be used to contribute to the general welfare, and to prevent the further spread of Soviet communism in which most Americans saw the antithesis of all they believed in. Here also there were uncertainties. It was easier for Congressmen and the public to appreciate the need for military assistance for those tied to the United States by military pacts like S.E.A.T.O., than for economic aid to countries like India which expressed disapproval of many United States policies, and arrogantly claimed to be the exponents of a more correct and morally superior outlook on world affairs. The United States, having stepped in the course of a single generation across the gulf that separates the modern welfare state from the "rugged individualism" dear to an earlier America, had now to face a world in which there was a demand for a greater equality not only within communities but also between them. At the same time it was forced into calculating the relationships of power—itself an unfamiliar exercise—in terms of capacities for mutual destruction never before at the disposal of a State. It is not surprising if the men seemed dwarfed by the magnitude of events.

AMERICAN LIBERALISM TODAY

By D. W. Brogan

*

WE have been long accustomed to the ambiguity of the terms "Democrat" and "Republican" in American political nomenclature. We know that all Republicans, or nearly all, profess to be democrats, that all Democrats profess to be republicans (although some, in the South, would hedge on being "democrats"). The ambiguous word "liberal" suffers from the same fate. All Americans in public life, or nearly all, are "liberals". The word has been used by such different academic figures as Nicholas Murray Butler and Morris Cohen, by such different political figures as Herbert Hoover and Franklin D. Roosevelt. It has not much more meaning than "Christian" and is used as generously.

But "Liberal" with an upper case initial is a different matter. It indicates, if not a party or a body of doctrine, at any rate a point of view. The "Liberal" whom I shall discuss is an optimist; he may believe in original sin (as does Dr Reinhold Niebuhr), but he thinks that society can change, should change, and that the state is a chosen instrument of that change, an indispensable tool of progress. There are, it is true, die-hard defenders of the old economic order like Mr Henry Hazlitt for whom liberal, upper case, lower case, means a believer in the free market, the gold standard, *laisser faire, laisser passer*. And certainly Mr Hazlitt can point with pride to the views of such eminent liberals of the past as Thomas Jefferson who had such a deep, engrained scepticism of the state, to Andrew Jackson who had such a devotion to hard money, to Grover Cleveland who took so narrow a view of the functions of the federal government, such firm action in defence of the established economic and social order. The modern American Liberal may be a heretic, a wolf in sheep's clothing, an equivalent of a modernist or Anglo-Catholic cleric "accepting" the Thirty-Nine Articles in ways that would have astonished Matthew Parker, but in popular speech, the modern American "Liberal" sees in the state more than a mere traffic cop of the economic order, more than a mere protector of "the Rights of Man and the Citizen". He is a defender of the theory and practice of "the general welfare state", to borrow a useful term from R. M. MacIver. For him American society is still afflicted by grave evils, by crippling inequality, by indifference to social values, by a complacent acceptance of business rule, by an indifference to the great forces that are moving and shaking the world. He doubts that the American "classless" society has really arrived, that Big Business has totally reformed, that the managerial revolution is totally beneficent. He takes a more kindly view of the American Federation of Labor than of the American Association of Manufacturers. He is not a "Socialist", but he sees in the Tennessee Valley Authority, in low-cost federal housing, in some federal aid for the poor faced with the high cost of health, not "creeping socialism", but a partial fulfilment of the American promise. This attitude is not confined to the American Liberal party, or even to the Democratic party. It is strongly represented in the ranks of the "Eisenhower Republicans". It has its most recent prophet in Mr Arthur Larson. On housing questions, its favourite statesman was, or ought to have been, the late Robert Taft. But all in all, the problem of the American Liberal is his relationship with the existing non-doctrinal party system and that, in turn, means in most cases, with that old political holding company, the Democratic party.

It would be wrong to confine the discussion to the internal quarrels and squabbles of the Democratic party, as wrong as to make the "Americans for Democratic Action", the ADA of ostentatiously frightened right-wing propaganda, monopolists of the word "liberal". The problem of the Liberal or liberal is not confined within the bounds of organized politics or of the United States, but his political problem in America comes first.

The American Liberal today is confronted first of all by the memory of something that did not happen, that is the embodiment of the "New Deal" as a spirit, as an attitude, if not as a precise programme in an identifiable national political party. To some historians of the hopeful days of 1933-6, Franklin D. Roosevelt missed, in those years, the chance of remaking the American party system, creating a true, national, "Liberal" party that would have forced the creation of an openly conservative Republican party and, above all, freed the Democrats from the "body of this death", the alliance with the great city machines of the North, with the unreconstructed "Bourbon" Democratic politicians of the South. Because Roosevelt failed to take an opportunity when he was "all-powerful", the Liberal, today, is torn in two, torn between his realization of the fact that the only way effectively to check the rule of the new business-political alliance, which he is convinced the Republican party is and must be, is to support the Democratic party, and his angry resentment that this means supporting elements in the Democratic party far to the Right of many Republicans and far more potent for mischief than are their Republican brethren, at any rate for the moment.

If F.D.R. had taken the plunge, how much simpler the moral and political problem would now be! True, the particular dead weight on the Liberal conscience that was most resented under F.D.R. no longer weighs so heavily. The New Jersey Democrat no longer has to swallow his leader's alliance with Frank Hague, the unsavoury "Boss" of Jersey City.

Governor Robert Meyner is another type of politician. Mr Carmine de Sapio is a more respectable and effective Tammany leader than any the Hall produced in the past. Mr David Lawrence, the Mayor of Pittsburgh, is not a boss of the old school, although he is a ruler. Only in Chicago, and in Cook County, is the old moral and aesthetic dilemma deeply felt—and there are plenty of Liberals ready to put, gingerly, some faith in Mayor Daley. But no such comparative peace of mind can be got from Liberal contemplation of Messrs Eastland and Talmadge. And even Southern Liberals, otherwise in good standing, like Senator Fulbright of Arkansas, are bound to rally to the "white" cause, to the distress of northern admirers, or to keep silent when their state is at the centre of the storm as in the case of Alabama's two Liberal senators, Messrs Hill and Sparkman.

If the American Liberal is clear-sighted, he will reflect—and does reflect—that the job that F.D.R. failed to attempt to do, was not simple or easy, however necessary. For central to F.D.R.'s problem in 1933—and to the dilemma of the American Liberal in 1956—is the ineluctable fact of the American political system, that every attempt to rationalize, on doctrinal lines, the American national party system, has failed since the newly christened Republicans destroyed the other opposition parties between 1854 and 1860. The fate of the Populists, the three parties that have called themselves "Progressive", the Liberal party, the American Labor party, the Farmer-Labor party, the Non-Partisan League has been the same. They have fizzled out or have been absorbed in one or other of the great parties to which they contributed some ideas, some person-alities, but whose fundamental character they did not, could not change. It is difficult for an outsider, especially an historian, not to be impressed by this fact and not to speculate on whether it is the *given* character of the American party system that accounts for so much of the Liberal's frustration. For that frustration is real and seems likely to be per-manent. The American Liberal is forced to work inside a party system that not only does not give him a party he can totally love, but does not give him or has not recently given him a party that he can totally hate. He cannot, in the context of the American party system, ever find that emotionally satisfying identification which the British Labour intellectual zealot can find, if not in thinking about the "Party", at least in thinking (and talking) about the "movement". Sometimes, the American Liberal suffers "the pangs of disprized love", when he sees party leaders care-fully dodging his embraces as harmful to party prospects. More com-monly, he is all dressed up and has nowhere to go. He turns up, rather sulkily, at the Democratic party conventions, national and state, but he sees the dancing partner the historical situation has given him, not with the loving and uncritical eye of the satisfied zealot, but with eye of the man who has drawn something less than perfection on a "blind date".

Why is he reduced to this unromantic situation, to a *mariage de convenance*—at best? In the first place, for general doctrinal reasons that will be discussed later. He cannot see, in the other side or in his own, two opposing groups with profoundly different views of the good life and its possibilities of attainment in American society. The British Labour party can give a home to many who are deeply convinced of two comforting articles of faith, that they are morally and intellectually right, that the other side is morally wrong. (Its intellectual errors are merely the more or less conscious result of its refusal to face its moral duty. No good man or woman can be a Conservative.) American Liberals are not immune from this innocent self-admiration; what they lack is a party mirror to admire themselves in. Since the American Liberal does not propose a root and branch reform of American life, he cannot know the moral exultation that animated the early Republicans when theirs was "the party of moral ideas", such as animates the preachers and their flocks inside the big tent of "the Labour movement".

But there are material, institutional reasons for the discomfiture of the American Liberal. First of all, he is as much handicapped by the electoral system of the states as the English Liberal is by our electoral laws. The rulers of the two "national" parties do all they decently can (and their notion of decency is elastic) to make the life of third parties impossible. Like our own front-benches in face of Television, they resent and prevent the rise of any competition. The lesson has been painfully learned; until the state election laws are altered, third parties may find it hard to get born and will find it impossible to live. *If* you could persuade electors that reform of these restrictive laws was the first thing necessary, you might not be wasting your time in working for a rational party system, but since you can't, you are.

Then the American Liberal has to face the fact that the United States is very large, very diversified, that the price of having any national parties at all is an absence of pharisaical rigidity and purity. The issues that "burn up" New York may have no resonance or a different resonance in North Dakota. Indeed the "Liberal" in North Dakota and the "Liberal" in New York may be not only different but opposed. Here, the urban Liberal is beginning to rethink—and rewrite—American political history in a disconcerting way. He is faced with a problem that can be illustrated by a name. The ideologue of the Wisconsin Progressives was Charles McCarthy, the preacher of "the Wisconsin idea". Wisconsin was the ideal state of the Liberals of the twenties. The Robert La Follettes (Junior and Senior) were the ideal senators. In the dark days of Harding and Coolidge (and of Democratic candidates like John W. Davis of West Virginia and Wall Street), there, in the unseduced breasts of the American farmer, lay the last, best hope of the Republic. Today, the McCarthy whose name recalls Wisconsin, is not Charles but Joseph. The name La Follette is no longer revered in Liberal circles. The Nebraska of George Norris seems lost in an irrecoverable past. The embattled farmer of Minnesota infuriates the "eggheads" (and all Liberals are eggheads) by preferring Senator Kefauver to Mr Adlai Stevenson. In short, the natural, necessary and desirable alliance between the "farmers" and "Liberalism", between farmers and workers, is seen, today, in a much less cheerful light. The townsman is harder and harder to win to sympathetic tears by stories of the farmer's plight. And the Liberal, if he does not despair of the farmer, puts his hopes rather on his increasingly important role as a part-time industrial worker (as in Michigan), than in the moral and political virtues that, so Jefferson thought, only the farmer could be relied on to display. The Farmer, as much as the South, is a headache to the Liberal today.

Nor is the role of Labour quite satisfactory. The Liberal is a politician. He believes in state action, in a national minimum. But the powerful unions have largely contracted out of the state system. Of course, they want all they can get from the state. They want kindly police interpretation of "picketing", for instance. They want kindly disposed judges as "capital" wanted and wants kindly disposed judges. They want to dovetail their welfare schemes into the state social services. But, basically, the great unions, automobiles, steelworkers, miners think they can do better for themselves than a more egalitarian state system of social services can do for them. Their leaders are "the new men of power", not the interesting and worthy spokesmen of the downtrodden, to be kindly helped by the middle-class intellectual, that they were thought of as being a generation ago. The Liberal does think of himself largely as a consumer, of politics as the refuge of the unorganized. He is baffled and often irritated by these new behemoths over whose birth he presided, as he thought, so benevolently. He is irritated, whether he knows it or not, when he wants to repaint his apartment and discovers what it will cost if done by union labour. There may be no reason why a carpenter or housepainter should not be paid more than a high school teacher or even a university professor (I know of none), but the egghead Liberal doesn't like it all the same—even if he is ashamed of himself for feeling that way. Some of the resentment at the dog-in-the-manger policies of the American Medical Association, the condemnation of its methods as being those of a trade union, not of a profession, reveal the unconscious stereotype that the Liberal uses when he thinks of "typical" trade union practice. So unions, like the Automobile Workers, may protest that it is grossly unjust to compare them to the American Medical Association. (I think that they are right.) Others may point out that the nefarious Carpenters are just the union in which Republicanism is strongest. Others may point to the resolution with which the leadership of the united A.F.L.-C.I.O. has refused to be taken in by the alleged repentance and reform of the Longshoremen. But all in all, the Labour movement, if not such a disappointment as the farmers or as the national political parties, is no more like the dream world of the sponsors of such panaceas or nostrums as the Plumb plan for union control of the railways, than the contemporary British trade union movement is like the dream world of Professor Cole's youth.

It is not only that the facts of political and social life disconcert the American Liberal. He is constantly tempted to deals that are individually justified, but which may add up to something less than a totally admirable political practice. The American Liberal, unlike the British Liberal, is always subject to the temptation to *get things done* and open to the opportunities that the American political system offers him to get things done. For the very fissiparous character of the party system which prevents the creation of an effective, national "Liberal" party offers plenty of opportunity for Liberal action *inside* the existing system. It is not only that in alliance with the unions, a Liberal group can take over a state as has happened in Michigan and in Minnesota—and may be on the way to happening in Pennsylvania. Not all of the oddities of the American political system work for them that wreak evil. We all know that, thanks to the "seniority rule", chairmanships in congressional committees go to the veterans of long service, and this means that, in both parties, seniority tends to be in the hands of the most reactionary elements since the safest Democratic and Republican seats are those where doctrinal novelties are least appreciated. The sad case of Senator Eastland of Mississippi, chairman of the Judiciary Committee and passionate defender of "white supremacy", is the most famous but far from being the only one of these examples of the dilemma of the Liberal who, by working for a "Democratic" Congress, ensures power to Mr Eastland. But there are two modifications to be noted. A Southern Democrat, firm, indeed rabid on the question of "white supremacy", may, as was Representative Rankin of Mississippi, be "sound", "very sound" (from the Liberal point of view) on public power, as the late Senator Taft was "sound", "very sound", on public housing. Then the working of the seniority rule can carry into power good "Liberals" from northern industrial states. True, they tend to come from the regions long dominated by machines, like New York and Chicago. But a realistic Liberal is tempted to study the *Congressional Directory*, as a soldier does the *Army List* or the young academic the *University Calendar*, to speculate, hopefully, on what age and death may do to bring better things. The dissipation of authority in Congress, the comparative meaninglessness of party lines, these make limited success worth having, even if that success is achieved by accepting, philosophically, "the contagion of the world's slow stain". The *New Republic*, in the twenties, could be purer than the *New Republic* in the fifties, because, in the twenties, what the *New Republic* stood for was a pattern laid up in a heaven, not to be attained in this world. Once you begin to think that you can affect *action*, you cease to be able to be content to announce that you are not like the publicans and sinners. You must deal, not denounce. The alternative is to be totally ineffectual, preaching mere doctrine to a congregation that, in secular as in lay matters, has always preferred works to words. It is not only the temptations of power that force compromise on the active American Liberal; it is not the vulgar appeal of the "Bitch Goddess Success" that diverts him from the narrow path. It is the temptation to get down off his high mule (a sterile animal) and help the wayfarer fallen by the wayside. There are, of course, plenty of priests and Pharisees in the American Liberal movement but the role of the Good Samaritan is much preferred.

But, it will be asked, does not this adjustment to the existing American political system mean an abandonment of the duty of the Liberal to give testimony to the wickedness and emptiness of modern capitalism? How can an academic economist like Senator Paul Douglas of Illinois consent to deal with people like Mayor Daley of Chicago? Why is there no serious spokesmen of the "Left" point of view in Congress? Why, in short, is there no Labour party?

This is a wide question and some of the answers are irrelevant to the subject I am trying to treat. One answer has already been given; any new party starts with two strikes on it; with serious legal as well as psychological handicaps, one reinforcing another, to make starting a new party something to frighten all but the boldest. But are there no bold spirits, ready to sow that others may reap, to act the Keir Hardie if not the Gaitskell?

There are or were plenty; some of them did make a splash in national politics. But they do so no longer and that for two reasons. It is not only that much that the old radicals, the old Socialists preached has been enacted. It is not that no conceivable administration in Washington, or even in the most benighted state capitals, would dream of going back to Coolidge or even to Hoover. The social service state, the general welfare state is here to stay. But the old Socialist panacea preached by Debs, by Norman Thomas, hankered after by a good many Democrats and some Republicans, has lost its appeal. The Plumb plan, to which allusion has been made, would find few supporters today simply because the railways are seen as a sick and possibly dying part of the economy, and for them to be taken over by the state or by the unions would be simply to introduce a new element of waste, pressure and confusion into an already bad situation. A solution like that offered by nationalization in Britain does not seem a solution in America, where the well-known perfection of the British Civil Service, loyal collaboration of the unions, competence in planning and sound direction in the economic high command are not available. They have to put up with that they have got, railroaders like Mr Robert Young and Mr Patrick McGuinness. If they have equivalents of Sir Brian Robertson, they do not want to waste them on railways. The examples could be multiplied. Nationalization as a panacea cuts no ice in America where admiration for the competence of the American businessman is at least as widespread as our confidence in the managers sitting in the Coal Board, the Transport Commission, or the like. Without having had a groundnuts scheme, the American suspected that political economists, advertising men, well-meaning elevators of the heathen were not the best people to be entrusted with a difficult, possibly impossible "crash" operation, that perhaps they were not the people to be entrusted with any serious economic operation and that if state action, the direction of the economy by politicians was the "Socialist" answer, he did not want Socialism. Business is too serious to be left to politicians. But, and it is an important "but", it is also too important to be left exclusively to businessmen. "What is good for General Motors is good for the United States." Mr Charlie Wilson of General Motors and now of the Department of Defence was both misquoted and misunderstood but other businessmen felt as he was reputed to have said. It would be difficult to think of any praise of "free enterprise" too silly, for example, to be put into the mouth of Mr Sinclair Weeks, President Eisenhower's Secretary of Commerce. To be brief and so unjust, the American Liberal has not enough belief in the state to want it to run the economy or in the businessman to want him to run it uncontrolled. He does not believe (and nothing that has happened in Britain has shaken his unbelief) that the modern, "liberal" democratic state has found a way to combine liberty and economic efficiency under a direct state control of the major sectors of the economy. If told that liberty has not suffered in Britain, he will usually (not always) agree; but that is not what he thinks suffers first.

This means, in turn, that the *entrepreneur*, the businessman, whose greed can excite torpid delegates at a Labour party conference, is admitted to be worthy of his hire, even in cases where he hires himself. The American Liberal will be cut off from the simple-minded admirer of the American system of free enterprise, not because he is indignant in the manner of the modern Veblen, Professor Wright Mills, at the rake-off the manager gets. He will accept, in business as in politics, a good deal less than apostolic devotion to the common good unsweetened by special reward. He *will*, however, wonder whether the managers do not overpay themselves. They are seldom owners and even if they are not robbing say the shareholders of the great Telephone monopoly, perhaps they are overcharging the customers. He will not, that is to say, be silenced by the claim of the contemporary American business man to be really a public servant to whom the mere cash is of no moment, the opportunity for service and achievement all. The businessman, even the businessman out of the Harvard Business School, will bear watching. And the state and politics are the only watchtowers not under the control of the watched. He is sceptical (possibly too sceptical) of the press, of radio, of T.V., of the "mass media". The United States needs politics and politicians to keep an eye on the men who make the wheels go round.

And (though he may be less candid in expressing this view), politicians are needed to keep an eye on the rulers of the great unions when they get together with their opposite numbers in Big Business. In this if in nothing else, the American Liberal is a good disciple of Adam Smith. People in trade get together to cheat the consumer; his main, ineffectual, but solitary weapon is the despised politician.

What is the function of the state in the direction of the economy? If "full employment" is less of a mere fetish in America than in Britain, the fact remains that the Eisenhower administration like the Truman administration, like any possible administration, is committed to the doctrine that the government must prevent a depression; that avoidance of the Valley of Despair of 1929-33 is the first civil duty of the Government of the United States. Where the Liberal who is not an Eisenhower Republican (as some are) will differ from the run of the mill politician, is in being ready to see signs of bad times sooner than the booster spirit is likely to permit and to see the roots of the trouble in the sorrows of the weak rather than in the grievances of the strong. This is no doubt a matter of sentiment but it is not only a matter of sentiment. The perilously lofty credit structure of the United States may need readjustment and the Liberal believes that, in this process, care should be taken for the little man, even at the expense of the big and middling man. His Liberal bias will be reflected in tax policy, in credit policy, in his readiness to use directly created purchasing power (e.g. by the subsidizing of low cost housing). The Liberal, if only because he remembers the euphoria of 1929 and is ready, perhaps too ready, to see in the present boom a return to those dangerous days, is adverse to giving business all it wants and still more opposed to making the small man bear the brunt of the necessary readjustments. Budget balancing will be offset against social costs. It is possible that sentiment plays a dangerously large role here and that the Liberal wants the government to prevent what may be a necessary "shake-out". At any rate, here, it seems to me, is a genuine social bias, openly admitted and one that is not dominant in the high command of the Republican party, even under President Eisenhower.

But there is another non-economic bias that is, I think, openly admitted —the bias against the growth of such great industrial combinations as General Motors. Here the Liberal may be a believer in "trust-busting", or a believer in the real economic efficiency of the great trusts, or a believer that it is a fundamentally wasteful method of production. But whether this is the basis of belief or not, all Liberals, in the sense that I have given to the word, are afraid of such giants as General Motors, even if they believe (with the late Joseph Schumpeter) that the economies of mass production are so great that they more than compensate for the waste and rigidity of economic "giantism". If it be true that by using its reserve power, General Motors could knock out all competitors except Ford and, possibly after an interval, even Ford, the Liberal is hostile to such an agglomeration of power in the hands of any one corporation (differing from the old-fashioned Socialist who often welcomed the process of concentration). Even at a cost of lessened economic "efficiency", the Liberal objects to such a parody of the free enterprise system as a motor monopoly, run by its managers and not even by its stockholders, would be. Whether the danger be real or not is a matter of opinion, but it is probably safe to say that the emergence of such a monster would convert (or re-convert in a few cases) many non-Socialists to the merits of nationalization. The state exists, among other reasons, to keep business flexible, to promote opportunity, to limit, if you like, the natural end of "free enterprise" which is often monopoly.

But there is an ambiguity in the word "state" that the American Liberal has to deal with. Traditionally, the Democratic party was the party of states rights. In the early years of this century, when so many Liberal traditions were made, some states (like Wisconsin) had a more or less deserved reputation as laboratories of social experiment. That hope for the state (and the city) is faint if not dead among Liberals today. There are two reasons for that. One is that the American economy is more and more integrated, American social life more and more alike, the American population more and more mobile. To most social problems, in this more and more unified nation, there must be a national answer. Many states are too poor to provide the necessary social services; others are incompetent or unwilling. Only the Federal Government can effectively promote the "General Welfare". These are what may be called functional arguments. In the world of General Motors and the Automobile Workers Union, only the United States can cope.

But there is another reason for the abandonment of states rights by the Liberals. He (as a politician) is much weaker in state than in national politics. He may be a force behind electing a governor, but how seldom do the candidates he supports carry a legislature! Partly this is due to the gross and grotesque over-representation of the rural areas; serious in Congress, it is a scandal in many states and almost a provocation to revolution in some others. By and large, the states are ruled by farmers and, by and large, the Liberal no longer trusts the farmer. He is not always unconscious of the dangers of too much federal activity; of remote control; of the possibilities of ingenious and well adapted state action to deal with local problems. But he does not believe that most states (perhaps any states) have the tax resources, the professional expertise, the political institutions to make it safe to leave much of the job of succouring the weak solely to them. He cannot see, in the modern American state, the viable, effective *polis* that Republican intellectuals like Mr Arthur Larson see in it.

And he is inclined to see (the American Liberal has a generous view of mankind in the mass, a low view of it in detail) in the campaign for giving power back to the states, a scheme for giving it back to the "interests". The oil companies wanted the states to have the tidelands oil because they could make a better deal (for themselves) with the state governments than with the federal government. Federal control is more open, effective, efficient, long-sighted and responsive to public opinion than is state control, in all but a tiny handful of states. To take power from the Union to give it to the states, is to make sure that it will be lost *en route*. Again, the American businessman will bear watching—and only the federal Argus is up to the job.

It is a little more difficult to decide whether or not the "Liberals" are marked off by preoccupation with the less favoured, the "underprivileged" as the revealing American phrase puts it. (In a real democracy *everybody* would presumably be privileged.) Gone are the days when Grover Cleveland vetoed aid to hard-hit Texas farmers. Gone are the days when Mr Hoover threw the burden of relief on local agencies. Even the New Deal was timid in its assumption of federal responsibility for distress, compared with the Eisenhower administration. It may be that federal aid to education foundered in the last Congress on that Administration's indifference, but certainly southern hostility to a federal intervention in the field of education that *might* lead to legislative interference in racial questions, combined with rural northern suspicion of "waste" and eastern suspicion that the great taxpaying states were to be milked, killed federal subventions for schools. But it would be hard to claim for the Liberals a monopoly of concern for the plight of the schools. It would be safer to claim for them a greater readiness to spend federal money on subsidized housing, for the Liberal today (unlike his nominal ancestors) does not believe that the market can be trusted to supply all social needs. Good housing makes good citizens (or limits the manufacture of bad citizens) and good housing often cannot be paid for by those who need it most, notably the Negroes.

Here the Liberal conscience is most deeply touched and his political behaviour seems (to the unfriendly outsider) most schizophrenic. The representative Liberal is a Democrat, or an ally of the Democrats, but in the ranks of "the Democracy" are most of the most violent enemies of the integration of the Negro into the American community. This is no doubt accidental; it arises from the localization of the most acute form of the colour problem in the region where the Democratic party is traditionally strongest. The necessity of holding the national party together makes for strange bedfellows and strange deals—as the section of the Democratic platform of 1956 dealing with "integration" in the schools proves. It is perhaps on this question that the Democratic Liberal is most vulnerable to the attacks of the Republican Liberal or the "Independent". He is tempted to put to the southern Democrats the dilemma of following the party line or of getting out. If the Democrats lose again, especially if they lose northern states because of a defection of the Negro vote and do not regain all the states lost in the South in 1956, notably Texas, the Liberals will be under a temptation to "punish" the South and to liberate their consciences at the same time, the more so since a party thus purified might offer more chances for local action and office in the North than the present unideaéd party offers to the egghead. The Liberal may not in fact do much about the race problem in the North and he may decide that he can do nothing useful in the South, but such impotence makes him feel bad.

He feels bad, too, about the state of civil liberties. True, he has here an easy target. Senator McCarthy is a Republican. He was accepted as an ally by the Eisenhower administration until he attacked Republicans. But Representative Walter, enemy of the Reds (and of dangerous immigrants) is, like the late Senator McCarran, a Democrat. Some of the abuses of "security" regulations, now rightly deplored, were begun under President Truman as Mr Dean Acheson has candidly admitted. but there is more to the uneasiness of the Liberal than that. He cannot but remember (though he tries to forget it naturally enough, often enough), that most Liberals or, at any rate, too many of them, fell for a great deal of open and covert Communist propaganda in the thirties. There were false "fronts" which the foolish Liberals joined in large numbers. Even if we leave the doubtful cases out and extend the category of doubtful until it includes Alger Hiss, there are enough undisputed cases of secret Communist penetration of the federal government and of some "neutral" Communist political and intellectual organizations to make the Liberal conscience uneasy. How this came about has been admirably explained by Mr Granville Hicks, by Mr Murray Kempton and by others. But, Liberals *were* taken for a ride, *were* victims, in disconcertingly large numbers, of the great Communist invention, the deliberate and mendacious exploitation of private trust and friendship for secret ends, the breach of the most honourable conventions of public service, the exaltation of a doubtful end to cover the basest means. It would probably have been better for the Liberals to have admitted all this and explained why and how they were duped; not all the reasons were discreditable in all cases. One common reason enough was the refusal of the young, faced with the doctrinal emptiness of the major parties, to accept this fact of American political life. True, the degree of deception was no greater and lasted for a shorter time than in England. But Americans hate being "played for suckers", so that they must either deny the fact or resent their deception. So an astonishing amount of time and moral energy is spent in debating the lies, follies, crimes and credulities of the thirties. The *déception d'amour* that ensued is still bitter.

Then the history of Left movements in America is not like that of such movements in Britain. There is no equivalent here of the I.W.W., the "Wobblies"; no equivalent to such famous trials and convictions as those of Sacco and Vanzetti and the McNamara brothers (who confessed). Social war, bordering on civil war, is not in the far past in states like

Washington and Arizona. (Oklahoma, at the time of the play, was a stronghold of militant radicalism and even of Socialism.) The founders of the American Communist party really believed in the coming, in the near future, of a "Workers and Peasants Republic". True, they were mostly foreigners with their heads and their hearts in Moscow, Warsaw, Berlin, Riga rather than New York or Detroit, but they were in America.

Just as one reason for the superficial character of the impact of Marxism was that the most zealous Marxists thought, wrote, agitated in Russian, German, or Yiddish rather than English, a consequence of this alienation was that genuine revolutionary belief (and readiness for action) were far more common in America than in England. Mr Henry Wallace and his closest supporters may have represented the old agrarian tradition, been the heirs of the La Follettes, but the places where they got mass support, above all Manhattan Island, were full of radicals with a more exotic and more dangerous tradition. The campaign of the "Progressives" in 1948 proved that. These were very different Progressives from those who had followed Theodore Roosevelt in 1912, the elder La Follette in 1924, Franklin D. Roosevelt in 1936.

But it was and is very hard for the old-fashioned American Liberal to admit that. Without quite falling into the trap of "no enemies on the Left", he has been unwilling to admit some painful truths of the modern world. For him, the death of F.D.R. prevented sensible dealing with the other "old pro", Stalin. But for intrigues by mere politicians, Mr Wallace would have succeeded in 1945 and without Mr Truman there would have been no Truman doctrine. In part, this infatuation is simply a sample of the very human reluctance of men and women to admit how far they have gone wrong. The loved one must be, must have been worthy of the love poured out on her. Human bondage can be illustrated from politics as well as from amorous infatuation. But there is more to the dilemma of the American Liberal who finds himself (like Mr Wallace and like some of Mr Wallace's followers) supporting Mr Eisenhower. It is not only that the President knows "how to deal with the Russians". It is that fate has cast the Democratic party in a role profoundly distasteful to the Liberal who joined it as a means to ends not shared by the mass of the party. The Democratic party has been forced to fight three wars in this century (it is one of its handicaps today). It has been forced to spend money on armaments, to impose conscription, to make entangling alliances, continually to recall its adherents to certain painful truths about the modern world. The Republican party would have had to do the same, but the Republican party was not only not in office; it was better fitted by its history to deal with hard, unsympathetic facts like power, armies, diplomacy. Only the southern Democrats were emotionally prepared for this harsh world—and they were and are a stumbling block to the Liberals. It is often forgotten how isolationist the New Deal was in its first years. It took Hitler to convert it to a more realistic view of the world and for New Dealers like Mr Wallace (who was and is a representative figure) this conversion to reality was for that occasion only. Of course, there is much that is unedifying in Russia but if the Russians behave oddly it is because the United States, led by a machine politician, Mr Truman, drove them to it by menaces! To a Liberal of this school, President Eisenhower is the lesser of two evils.

For the Democratic party, unlucky in having to make war, in having to leave the making of "peace" in Korea and Indo-China to the Republicans, are unlucky in that some of their most important criticisms of the Eisenhower Administration, its handling of defence problems, of foreign policy, its fondness for verbal solutions, its postponements of the evil day of unpopular decisions, criticisms that are plausible if not just, are criticisms that the traditional "Liberal" does not want to hear. In this posture of attack, the old-fashioned Liberal is deeply uncomfortable. The optimism that he brings to domestic, he also brings to foreign affairs. A "realistic", tough, unidealogical foreign policy is the last thing he wants or understands. Where these two severed wings of the Liberals come together is on the question of "imperialism". Here sentimentality, a plausible guess as to the way the world is going, a Wilsonian desire to demonstrate American moral superiority, all combine to make the Liberal think of the problems of the post-imperial age in terms of comforting slogans; slogans about racial equality, about economic aid not military alliances, about friendship with peoples rightly struggling to be free, all the quiver of optimistic arrows that the Liberals in all countries shoot into the air, without taking too much interest if they fall, they know not where. Doubts about the viability of some of the new states, doubts about the beneficent effects of nationalism (a nearly unmitigated curse in Europe, it is a nearly unmitigated blessing in Asia and Africa) are non-Liberal. And some of the frustrations the American Liberal feels, faced, say, with the realities of political and social life in Mississippi, can be compensated for by good will on a world scale. This may lead to inconsistencies, to uncritical support both for Arab nationalism and for Israel, but there is a higher synthesis of good will in which men dwell together in peace, in Jerusalem if not in Texarkana. Faced with the drab necessities of American politics, the representatives of the men and women of good will take the whole world for their parish. Even when they settle for a good deal less in domestic politics than their heart's desire (faced with southern intransigence, some of them will settle for next to nothing), they are ready to expiate the sins of the Americans by repenting those of the British and the French.

Liberals, even American Liberals, are human, inconsistent, ready to tackle the impossible rather than the difficult. But they are also that section of the American body politic which has, over the past generation, most affected the American idea of what is socially and politically desirable and attainable. And their greatest monument is not a unified and probably impotent "Liberal party"; it is not even the Democratic party's slow evolution to being a party with, at any rate, a "Labor" basis and bias, if no Socialist doctrine, that is their greatest achievement. It is the present Republican party, not even the party Mr Eisenhower is trying to create, but the party that, at San Francisco in 1956, cheered Mr Hoover to the rafters, but turned innocently away from the lesson he, a voice from the Republican past, tried to read them.

BOOKS FOR FURTHER READING

THE brief lists which follow are in no sense intended to serve as full biblio-graphies. They merely contain the titles of a number of selected works which the authors of the several essays feel may be useful to British readers who are anxious to extend their study of American history along the lines considered in this book.

THE MAKING OF THE CONSTITUTION

Charles A. Beard: *An Economic Interpretation of the Constitution of the United States*. (New York, 1913)

Robert E. Brown: *Charles Beard and the Constitution*. (Princeton, 1956)

Max Farrand: *The Framing of the Constitution of the United States*. (New Haven, 1913)

Alexander Hamilton, James Madison, and John Jay: *The Federalist*. (Numerous editions)

Homer C. Hockett: *The Constitutional History of the United States*. Vol. I. (New York, 1939)

Merrill Jensen: *The New Nation*. (New York, 1950)

A. C. McLaughlin: *A Constitutional History of the United States*. (New York, 1935)

A. Nevins: *The American States during and after the Revolution*. (New York, 1924)

Arthur T. Prescott: *The Framing of the Constitution*. (Baton Rouge, 1941)

Conyers Read, ed.: *The Constitution Reconsidered*. (New York, 1938)

R. L. Schuyler: *The Constitution of the United States*. (New York, 1923)

J. Allen Smith: *The Spirit of American Government*. (New York, 1907)

C. B. Swisher: *American Constitutional Development*. (Boston, 1943)

DIVIDED SOVEREIGNTY

J. T. Carpenter: *The South as a Conscious Minority*. (New York, 1930)

E. S. Corwin: *John Marshall and the Constitution: a chronicle of the Supreme Court*. (New Haven, 1919)

W. A. Dunning: *Essays on the Civil War and Reconstruction*. (New York, 1897)

Max Farrand: *The Framing of the Constitution of the United States*. (New Haven, 1913)

C. G. Haines: *The American Doctrine of Judicial Supremacy*. (2nd ed. revd. and enld.) (Los Angeles, 1932)

A. C. McLaughlin: "The background of American federalism", in that author's *Britain and America*. (London, 1919)

L. Mayers: *The American Legal System*. (London and New York, 1955)

A. O. Spain: *The Political Theory of John C. Calhoun*. (New York, 1951)

Woodrow Wilson: "The states and the federal government". *North Am.
Rev.*, clxxxvii (1908), 684-701. Reprinted in R. S. Baker and W. E.
Dodds, eds.: *The Public Papers of Woodrow Wilson.* 6 vols. (London
and New York, 1925-7). *College and State . . . (1875-1913).* 2 vols.
(1925), ii, 32-53

THE IDEAS AND INFLUENCE OF
ALEXANDER HAMILTON

The most recent of many editions of *The Federalist* is ed. Max Beloff (Oxford,
1948). Selections from Hamilton's public papers are found in most
collections of documents; of those most readily available, *Speeches and
Documents in American History*, ed. R. Birley (Oxford, 1944), Vol. I,
gives abridged versions of the First *Report on Public Credit* and of the
Report on Manufactures, and *Documents of American History*, ed. H. S.
Commager (New York and London, 1948), gives the opinion of
Hamilton on the constitutionality of the Bank.

W. E. Binkley: *American Political Parties: Their Natural History.* (New
York, 1943)
C. G. Bowers: *Jefferson and Hamilton.* (Boston and London, 1925)
Irving Brant: *James Madison: Father of the Constitution.* (Indianapolis, 1950)
W. S. Culbertson: *Alexander Hamilton: An Essay.* (New Haven, 1911)
Manning J. Dauer: *The Adams Federalists.* (Baltimore, 1953)
A. H. Kelly and W. A. Harbison: *The American Constitution.* (New York,
1948)
N. Schachner: *Alexander Hamilton.* (New York, 1946)
L. D. White: *The Federalists.* (New York, 1948)

THOMAS JEFFERSON AND THE JEFFERSONIAN IDEA

J. Truslow Adams: *Jeffersonian Principles and Hamiltonian Principles*: extracts
from the writings of Thomas Jefferson and Alexander Hamilton.
(Boston, 1932)
Charles A. Beard: *The Economic Origins of Jeffersonian Democracy.* (New
York, 1915)
Carl Becker: *The Declaration of Independence*: a study in the history of
political ideas. (New York, 1922)
Max Beloff: *Thomas Jefferson and American Democracy.* (London, 1948)
Daniel Boorstin: *The Lost World of Thomas Jefferson.* (New York, 1948)
Julian P. Boyd, ed.: *The Papers of Thomas Jefferson.* (In progress: twelve
vols. to date.) (Princeton, 1950)
Gilbert Chinard: *Thomas Jefferson, Apostle of Americanism.* (Boston, 1929)
J. H. Hazelton: *The Declaration of Independence, its history.* (New York,
1906)
Bernard Mayo: *Jefferson Himself.* (Boston, 1942)
V. L. Parrington: *Main Currents in American Thought.* Vol. I: *The Colonial
Mind.* (New York, 1927)
F. C. Rosenberger: *Jefferson Reader: a treasury of writings about Thomas
Jefferson.* (New York, 1953)
C. M. Wiltse: *The Jeffersonian Tradition in American Democracy.* (Chapel
Hill, 1935)

AMERICAN POLITICAL PARTIES

W. E. Binkley: *American Political Parties: Their Natural History.* (New York, 1943)
D. W. Brogan: *The American Political System.* (London, 1947)
D. W. Brogan: *Introduction to American Politics.* (London, 1954)
H. F. Gosnell: *Boss Platt and his New York Machine.* (Chicago, 1924)
H. F. Gosnell: *Machine Politics, Chicago Model.* (Chicago, 1937)
W. B. Graves: *American State Government.* (Boston, 1941)
V. O. Key: *Politics, Parties, and Pressure Groups.* (New York, 1948)
V. O. Key: *Southern Politics.* (New York, 1949)
Samuel Lubell: *The Future of American Politics.* (London, 1952)
C. E. Merriam and H. F. Gosnell: *The American Party System.* (New York, 1950)
C. E. Merriam and L. Overacker: *Primary Elections.* (Chicago, 1928)
Harold Zink: *City Bosses in the United States.* (Durham, N.C., 1930)

COMMERCIAL AMERICA

R. G. Albion: *The Rise of New York Port, 1815-60.* (New York, 1939)
L. E. Atherton: *The Southern Country Store, 1800-1860.* (Baton Rouge, 1949)
Louis Hartz: *Economic Policy and Democratic Thought: Pennsylvania, 1776-1860.* (Cambridge, Mass., 1948)
R. W. Hidy: *The House of Baring in Anglo-American Trade and Finance.* (Cambridge, Mass., 1949)
A. B. Hulbert: *Paths of Inland Commerce.* (New Haven, 1920)
L. C. Hunter: *Steamboats on the Western Rivers.* (Cambridge, Mass., 1949)
W. J. Lane: *Commodore Vanderbilt.* (New York, 1942)
S. E. Morison: *A Maritime History of Massachusetts, 1783-1860.* (Boston, 1921)
K. W. Porter: *John Jacob Astor, Business Man.* (Cambridge, Mass., 1931)
W. B. Smith: *Economic Aspects of the Second Bank of the United States.* (Cambridge, Mass., 1953)
W. B. Smith and A. H. Cole: *Fluctuations in American Business, 1790-1860.* (Cambridge, Mass., 1935)
Caroline Ware: *The Early New England Cotton Manufacture.* (New York, 1931)

MANIFEST DESTINY

T. A. Bailey: *A Diplomatic History of the American People.* (New York, 5th edition, 1955; rev. ed. in preparation)
S. F. Bemis: *A Diplomatic History of the United States.* (New York, 4th ed. 1955)
S. F. Bemis: *John Quincy Adams and the Foundations of American Foreign Policy.* (New York, 1950)
S. F. Bemis: *John Quincy Adams and the Union.* (New York, 1955)

A. L. Burt: *The United States, Great Britain and British North America.* (New Haven, 1940)
A. Nevins, ed.: *James K. Polk: The Diary of a President, 1845 to 1849.* (London and New York, 1929)
Dexter Perkins: *The Monroe Doctrine, 1823-26.* (Cambridge, Mass., 1923)
Dexter Perkins: *The Monroe Doctrine, 1826-67.* (Baltimore, 1933)
Dexter Perkins: *A History of the Monroe Doctrine.* (Boston, new ed., 1955)
J. W. Pratt: *A History of United States Foreign Policy.* (New York, 1955)
R. W. Van Alstyne: *American Diplomacy in Action—A Series of Case Studies.* (Stanford and Oxford, 1944)
A. K. Weinberg: *Manifest Destiny.* (Baltimore, 1935)

F. J. TURNER AND THE FRONTIER IN AMERICAN HISTORY

Carl Becker: "Frederick Jackson Turner" in *American Masters of Social Science*, Howard W. Odum, ed. (New York, 1927)
R. A. Billington: *Westward Expansion, A History of the American Frontier.* (New York, 1949)
L. P. Kellogg, ed.: *The Early Writings of Frederick Jackson Turner.* (Madison, 1938)
J. G. Leyburn: *Frontier Folkways.* (New Haven, 1935)
F. L. Paxson: *History of the American Frontier.* (Boston, 1924)
R. E. Riegel: *America Moves West.* (New York, 1947)
E. Semple: *American History and its Geographic Conditions.* (Boston, 1903)
G. R. Taylor, ed.: *The Turner Thesis Concerning the Role of the Frontier in American History.* (Boston, 1949)
F. J. Turner: *The Frontier in American History.* (New York, [1950])
F. J. Turner: *The Significance of Sections in American History.* Intro. by Max Farrand. (New York, 1950)
W. P. Webb: *The Great Plains.* (Boston, 1931)
W. P. Webb: *The Great Frontier.* (London, 1953)

SECTIONALISM AND THE CIVIL WAR

Henry Adams: *The Formative Years: A History of the United States during the Administrations of Jefferson and Madison.* Edited and abridged by Herbert Agar. (London, 1948)
Avery O. Craven: *The Growth of Southern Nationalism, 1848-1861.* (Baton Rouge, 1953)
Merle Curti: *The Roots of American Loyalty.* (New York, 1946)
Merrill Jensen, ed.: *Regionalism in America.* (Madison, 1951)
A. Nevins: *The Ordeal of the Union.* 2 vols. (New York, 1947)
A. Nevins: *The Emergence of Lincoln.* 2 vols. (New York, 1950)
V. L. Parrington: *Main Currents in American Thought.* (New York, 1927)
D. M. Potter and T. G. Manning: *Nationalism and Sectionalism in America, 1775-1877: Select Problems in Historical Interpretation.* (New York, 1949)
J. G. Randall: *The Civil War and Reconstruction.* (Boston, 1937)

R. R. Russel: *Economic Aspects of Southern Sectionalism, 1840-1861*. (Urbana, Ill., 1924)

C. S. Sydnor: *The Development of Southern Sectionalism, 1819-1848*. (Baton Rouge, 1948)

F. J. Turner: *The Significance of Sections in American History*. (New York, 1932)

RECONSTRUCTION AND THE COLOUR PROBLEM

Herbert Aptheker: *A Documentary History of the Negro People in the United States*. (New York, 1951)

S. A. Brown, A. P. Davis and Ulysses Lee, ed.: *The Negro Caravan: Writings by American Negroes*. (New York, 1941)

E. Merton Coulter: *The South during Reconstruction, 1865-1877*. (Baton Rouge, 1947)

J. H. Franklin: *From Slavery to Freedom: A History of American Negroes*. (New York, 1947)

R. W. Logan: *The Negro in American Life and Thought: The Nadir, 1877-1901*. (New York, 1954)

Gunnar Myrdal: *An American Dilemma: The Negro Problem and Modern Democracy*. (New York, 1944)

Ira De A. Reid, ed.: *Racial Desegregation and Integration*. (Philadelphia: The Annals of the American Academy of Political and Social Science, Volume 304, 1956)

Arnold M. Rose: *The Negro's Morale: Group Identification and Protest*. (Minneapolis, 1949)

F. B. Simkins: *A History of the South*. (New York, 1953)

F. B. Simkins and R. H. Woody: *South Carolina during Reconstruction*. (Chapel Hill, 1932)

C. Vann Woodward: *Reunion and Reaction: The Compromise of 1877 and the End of Reconstruction*. (Boston, 1951)

C. Vann Woodward: *The Strange Career of Jim Crow*. (New York, 1955)

THE AMERICAN MILITARY TRADITION

C. Joseph Bernardo and Eugene H. Bacon: *American Military Policy: its development since 1775*. (Harrisburg, Pa., 1955)

E. C. Boynton: *History of West Point*. (New York, 1863)

Sidney Forman: *West Point*. (New York, 1950)

J. H. Franklin: *The Militant South, 1800-1861*. (Cambridge, Mass., 1956)

W. A. Ganoe: *The History of the United States Army*. (New York, 1942)

Frederic L. Huidekoper: *The Military Unpreparedness of the United States*. (New York, 1915)

Jerome G. Kerwin, ed.: *Civil-Military Relationships in American Life*. (Chicago, 1948)

Dudley Knox: *A History of the United States Navy*. (New York, 1948)

John McA. Palmer: *America in Arms*. (New Haven, 1941)

Louis Smith: *American Democracy and Military Power*. (Chicago, 1951)

Oliver L. Spaulding: *The United States Army in War and Peace*. (New York, 1937)

Harold and Margaret Sprout: *The Rise of American Naval Power, 1776-1918*. (Princeton, 1946)

AMERICAN RADICALISM:
JACKSON, BRYAN, AND WILSON

H. U. Faulkner: *The Quest for Social Justice, 1898-1914.* (New York, 1931)
Paxton Hibben and C. H. Grattan: *The Peerless Leader.* (New York, 1929)
J. D. Hicks: *The Populist Revolt.* (Minneapolis, 1931)
Richard Hofstadter: *The Age of Reform.* (New York, 1955)
A. S. Link: *Woodrow Wilson and the Progressive Era.* (New York and London, 1954)
A. T. Mason: *Brandeis: A Free Man's Life.* (New York, 1946)
R. B. Nye: *Midwestern Progressive Politics.* (East Lansing, Michigan, 1951)
A. M. Schlesinger, Jr.: *The Age of Jackson.* (Boston, 1945)
F. A. Shannon: *The Farmer's Last Frontier.* (New York, 1945)
C. B. Swisher: *Roger B. Taney.* (New York, 1935)
F. J. Turner: *The United States, 1830-1850.* (New York, 1935)

AMERICA, HALF-BROTHER OF THE WORLD

Edith Abbott: *Historical Aspects of the Immigration Problem.* (Chicago, 1926)
W. F. Adams: *Ireland and Irish Emigration to the New World from 1815 to the Famine.* (New Haven, 1932)
R. T. Berthoff: *British Immigrants in Industrial America.* (Cambridge, Mass., 1953)
T. C. Blegen: *Norwegian Migration to America.* (Northfield, Minn., 1931)
R. Ernst: *Immigrant Life in New York City, 1825-1863.* (New York, 1949)
A. B. Faust: *The German Element in the United States.* (New York, 1937)
O. Handlin: *Boston's Immigrants, 1790-1865.* (Cambridge, Mass., 1941)
M. L. Hansen: *The Atlantic Migration, 1607-1860.* (Cambridge, Mass., 1940)
M. L. Hansen: *The Immigrant in American History.* (Cambridge, Mass., 1941)
John A. Hawgood: *The Tragedy of German-America.* (New York, 1940)
Brinley Thomas: *Migration and Economic Growth.* (Cambridge, 1954)
C. Wittke: *We Who Built America.* (New York, 1939)

THE RISE OF AMERICAN LABOUR

J. R. Commons and associates: *History of Labor in the United States.* 4 vols. (New York, 1918-35)
Lewis L. Lorwin: *The American Federation of Labor.* (Washington, D.C., 1933)
Milton J. Nadworny: *Scientific Management and the Unions, 1900-1932.* (Cambridge, Mass., 1955)
Selig Perlman: *A Theory of the Labor Movement.* (New York, 1928)
Philip Taft: *The Structure and Government of Labor Unions.* (Cambridge, Mass., 1954)
Lloyd Ulman: *The Rise of the National Trade Union.* (Cambridge, Mass., 1955)
Norman J. Ware: *The Industrial Worker, 1840-1860.* (New York, 1924)

Norman J. Ware: *The Labor Movement in the United States, 1860-95.* (New York, 1929)

INDUSTRIAL AMERICA

F. L. Allen: *The Big Change, 1900-50.* (New York, 1952)
Spurgeon Bell: *Productivity, Wages and National Income.* (Washington, D.C., 1940)
T. C. Cochran and W. Miller: *The Age of Enterprise: a social history of Industrial America.* (New York, 1942)
Daniel B. Creamer: *Capital and Output Trends in Manufacturing Industries, 1880-1948.* (New York, 1954)
Joseph Dorfman: *The Economic Mind in American Civilisation.* Vol. III, 1865-1918. (New York, 1949)
J. K. Galbraith: *American Capitalism.* (Boston, 1952)
Louis M. Hacker: *The Shaping of the American Tradition.* Vol. II, 1860-1944. (New York, 1947)
J. R. Hicks and A. G. Hart: *The Social Framework of the American Economy.* (New York, 1945)
Richard Hofstadter: *The Age of Reform.* (New York, 1955)
W. E. Rappard: *The Secret of American Prosperity.* (New York, 1955)
Ross M. Robertson: *History of the American Economy.* (New York, 1955)
L. Rostas: *Comparative Productivity in British and American Industry.* (Cambridge, 1948)
Brinley Thomas: *Migration and Economic Growth.* (Cambridge, 1954)
U.S. Department of Commerce: *Historical Statistics of the United States, 1789-1945.* (Washington, D.C., 1952)

AMERICAN FOREIGN POLICY AND WORLD POWER:
1871-1956

H. C. Allen: *Great Britain and the United States.* (London, 1954)
T. A. Bailey: *A Diplomatic History of the American People.* (New York, 5th ed., 1955)
Max Beloff: *Foreign Policy and the Democratic Process.* (Baltimore, 1955, and London, 1956)
S. F. Bemis: *A Diplomatic History of the United States.* (New York, 4th ed., 1955)
F. R. Dulles: *America's Rise to World Power, 1898-1954.* (New York and London, 1955)
E. F. Goldman: *The Crucial Decade: America, 1945-1955.* (New York, 1956)
G. F. Kennan: *American Diplomacy, 1900-1950.* (Chicago, 1952)
W. L. Langer and S. E. Gleason: *The Challenge to Isolation, 1917-1940.* (New York and London, 1952)
W. L. Langer and S. E. Gleason: *The Undeclared War, 1940-1941.* (New York and London, 1953)
A. Nevins: *The United States in a Chaotic World, 1918-1933.* (New Haven, 1950)
A. Nevins: *The New Deal and World Affairs, 1933-1945.* (New Haven, 1950)
R. E. Osgood: *Ideals and Self-Interest in America's Foreign Relations.* (Chicago, 1953)

AMERICAN LIBERALISM TODAY

Dean Acheson: *An American Vista*. (London, 1956)
Charles A. Beard and George H. E. Smith: *The Old Deal and the New*. (New York, 1940)
Arthur A. Ekirch: *The Decline of American Liberalism*. (New York, 1955)
Leslie A. Fiedler: *An End to Innocence*. (Boston, 1955)
Richard Hofstadter: *The Age of Reform*. (New York, 1955)
Albert L. Guérard: *Testament of a Liberal*. (Cambridge, Mass., 1956)
Leo Gurko: *Crisis of the American Mind*. (London, 1956)
Granville Hicks: *Where We Came Out*. (New York, 1954)
Archibald MacLeish: *A Time to Speak*. (Boston, 1941)
A. M. Schlesinger, Jr.: *The Vital Center*. (Boston, 1949)
Harold E. Stearns: *Liberalism in America*. (New York, 1919)
Norman M. Thomas: *The Choice Before Us*. (New York, 1934)

INDEX

z

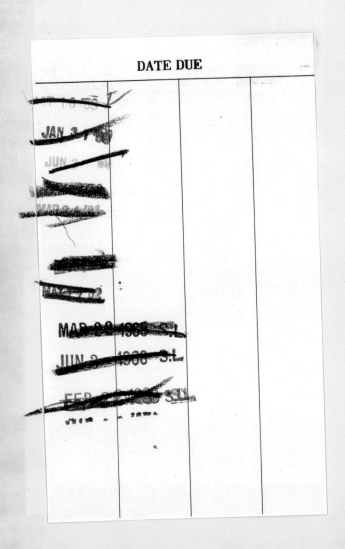